IMMORTAL
WORDS

'Reading is to the mind what exercise is to the body'

Tatler, 18 March 1710

SIR RICHARD STEELE
1672–1729

IMMORTAL WORDS

---— ☙ —---

HISTORY'S MOST MEMORABLE QUOTATIONS AND THE STORIES BEHIND THEM

---— ☙ —---

TERRY BREVERTON

Quercus

INTRODUCTION

Over the last four and a half millennia, humankind has been inspired to humility, compassion, fortitude, bravery, and above all progress by the spoken and written word. The intention of this book is to give a sense of the power of words to move us, by the inclusion of some of the remarkable quotations that have passed down over the centuries. The absolute power of language across nations to make us feel courage, compassion, sadness – all the emotions – is probably the greatest achievement of humanity.

The quotations in this book have been included for the emotion that they convey – for their remarkable power to inspire us or equally to make us reflect upon man's inhumanity to man. The language that makes up the book's content comes from statesmen, monarchs, poets, reformers, scientists, novelists and warriors. It has been gathered from monuments, gravestones, speeches, encomiums, broadcasts, books and pamphlets – in fact, from most of the evolving forms of communication over the years. Sometimes quotations may disclose an ignoble personality – perhaps Stalin or Goering – but in all cases their language has achieved an everlasting effect. They are included because, in the words of George Santayana (1863–1952): *'Those who cannot remember the past are condemned to repeat it.'*

Some authors have not been included owing to space limitations, and for any notable omissions, I apologize unreservedly. There could be over 100,000 entries if all the worthy representations had been incorporated. On the other hand, some personalities such as William Shakespeare, Franklin D. Roosevelt and Winston Churchill have multiple entries. The genius of Shakespeare, as the foremost literary personality in the history of the English language, forces his prose and poetry into this work. Roosevelt, equally, shines through history, with his remarkable leadership of the world's greatest nation during the Depression and World War II. And Churchill's literary rhetoric inspired a nation upon its knees to defy the evils of Fascism in one of the very, very few 'just' wars in recorded history. When President Kennedy conferred honorary US citizenship upon Churchill in 1963, he alluded to the power of his speeches: *'He mobilized the English language and sent it into battle.'*

We can change history, by the spoken and written word, by not electing demagogues or extremists. We can help other countries in distressing circumstances by pressurizing our politicians. We can stop the abuses of billionaires and multinationals. For humankind, language is our greatest – perhaps our only – weapon against injustice, iniquity and war. Perhaps the greatest anti-war slogan of all time came anonymously during World War II: '*A bayonet is a weapon with a worker at each end.*' Informed language is not only educative, but it is also our greatest force against greed and materialism, the twin axes of anti-humanitarianism. We can see that human good constantly overcomes human evil – we may re-invent a phrase originating with the Greeks, but we still have the same concerns, the same aspirations and hopefully the same sense of wonder as they did. All this is communicated by the universal medium of language.

This book has been organized chronologically – to rank quotations in order of their importance in history, or of the brilliance of their author, would be impossible. I have tried to place each quotation in order of when it was written or spoken. If this is impossible, the date of the author's death is used. Thus we have the author and their birth and death dates; a headline quotation and sometimes an extension of that quotation, with, where possible, the date on which the quotation was made. Each entry is accompanied by contextual information giving the circumstances in which it was said or written and a brief biography of the author. Sometimes the quotation speaks for itself and there is a shorter explanation, but collectively the entries have been picked from all the stages of history to reveal the absolute power of language to change our feelings or to make us think. The book is leavened by a few humorous quotations to balance those on the darker side of man's nature, and I hope that the selection is both thought-provoking and inspirational.

Terry Breverton

'Thou shalt have no other gods before me'

'Thou shalt have no other gods before me.

Thou shalt not take the name of the Lord thy God in vain.

Thou shalt not make unto thee any graven image, or any likeness of anything that is in heaven above, or that is in the earth beneath, or that is in the water under the earth.

Thou shalt not bow down thyself to them, nor serve them. Remember the Sabbath day, to keep it holy.

Honour thy father and thy mother: that thy days may be long.

Thou shalt not kill.

Thou shalt not commit adultery.

Thou shalt not steal.

Thou shalt not bear false witness against thy neighbour.

Thou shalt not covet thy neighbour's house, thou shalt not covet thy neighbour's wife, nor his manservant, nor his maidservant, nor his ox, nor his ass, nor anything that is thy neighbour's.'

The Ten Commandments (or Decalogue) were given to Moses by God, on one or two tablets of stone on Mount Sinai, and recorded in Exodus 20. Moses had led the Hebrew slaves out of Egypt after the Ten Plagues, through the Red Sea. He then received the Ten Commandments during their 40 years of wandering in the desert. The Protestant, Catholic and Hebrew versions are slightly different. This version is from Exodus 20, but the tablet was broken and another version is given in Exodus 34.

'Give a man a fish and you feed him for a day.
Teach him how to fish and you feed him for a lifetime.'

Lao-tzu (Old Master) was born between 600 and 300 BCE, and is thought to have written the *Tao-te-ching* (*Tao* – the way of all life; *te* – the fit use of life by men; *ching* – classic or text). His wisdom attracted many followers, and his philosophy was that men should lead a life full of serenity, goodness and respect. We can gain respect by being able to fish rather than accepting fish as charity. Our own instinct and conscience should be followed to achieve these goals. We are constantly affected by outside forces, but must look for 'simplicity' to find truth and true freedom: '*Be content with what you have; rejoice in the way things are. When you realize there is nothing lacking, the whole world belongs to you.*' By understanding the laws of nature we will develop intuition and build personal power, and that power can then be used to live a life of love, without force.

It is said that Lao-tzu, when he grew old, was saddened by the evils of mankind, so he left civilization and headed into the desert on the back of a water buffalo. However, when he reached a gate in the Great Wall to leave China forever, the gatekeeper encouraged him to stay and record his beliefs for the future. His 81 sayings form the *Tao-te-ching*, one of the most translated texts after the Bible. Every management textbook should carry his dictum – '*A leader is best when people barely know he exists; when his work is done, his aim fulfilled, they will say: we did it ourselves*'. Another of Lao-tzu's sayings, adopted by Mao Tse Tung, was: '*A journey of a thousand miles must begin with a single step*'.

AESOP
c.620–c.560 BCE

'Familiarity breeds contempt'

'When first the Fox saw the Lion he was terribly frightened, and ran away and hid himself in the wood. The next time, however, the Fox came near the King of Beasts he stopped at a safe distance, and watched him pass by. The third time they came near one another the Fox went straight up to the Lion and passed the time of day with him, asking him how his family were, and when he should have the pleasure of seeing him again; then turning his tail, he parted from the Lion without much ceremony... Familiarity breeds contempt.'

Moral from 'The Fox and the Lion', *Aesop's Fables*

Aesop lived for some time at the court of King Croesus of Lydia in Sardis, modern Turkey. His name is derived from the Greek Aethiop (Ethiopia) and Aesop's marble statue at Rome's Villa Albani is that of a black man. The 'fables' are short stories which illustrate a particular moral and teach a lesson to children. However, it seems the fables were originally used to make disguised social and political criticisms, rather than being children's stories, and many have since been found on Egyptian papyri dated up to 1,000 years before Aesop's era.

The characters of his tales are usually animals which act and talk just like people, but retain their animal traits. A moral is added at the bottom of each of Aesop's fables, e.g. *'Appearances often are deceiving'* from 'The Wolf in Sheep's Clothing'; *'Slow and steady wins the race'* from 'The Hare and the Tortoise'; *'One man's meat is another man's poison'* from 'The Ass and the Grasshopper'; *'Things are not always what they seem'* from 'The Bee-Keeper and the Bees'; and *'Never trust a flatterer'* from 'The Fox and the Crow'. Other stories tell us about the boy crying wolf, never to count our chickens before they are hatched, not to trust a man who blows hot and cold in the same breath, about sour grapes and that the gods help those who help themselves. In 'The Wolf in Sheep's Clothing' we read *'The lamb that belonged to the sheep whose skin the wolf was wearing began to follow the wolf in the sheep's clothing.'*

Mark Twain would later famously recycle the line *'Familiarity breeds contempt'*, adding *'– and children'*.

THALES
c.635/620-c.546/543 BCE

'The most difficult thing in life is to Know Thyself'

Diogenes Laertius, *Lives and Opinions of Eminent Philosophers*

The history of Western philosophy begins at the same time as historical records start being passed down to us. Thales of Miletus was later included in the Seven Sages of Greece, a list of outstanding politicians and philosophers, along with Solon the Lawgiver, Periander and others. He travelled to Egypt to study geometry, deduced new theorems and became famous for predicting the eclipse of 585 BCE. Thales thought that water was the origin of all matter. In early Greece, there was no differentiation between philosophy and the natural sciences, so Thales was also a scientist and mathematician. Thales is the first person we know of to practise deductive reasoning, deriving statements from observation by means of logic.

According to Aristotle, Thales was the founder of the school of natural philosophy, and his questioning of the movement of heavenly bodies was the beginning of Greek astronomy. None of his writings survives, but he was so esteemed by succeeding thinkers such as Aristotle, Heraclitus, Democritus, Pythagoras, Euclid and Anaxagoras that in matters of investigation they were advised to consult Thales' thoughts first. Thales had said '*Nothing is more active than thought, for it travels over the universe, and nothing is stronger than necessity for all must submit to it*'. He is also attributed with being the first to write of the immortality of the soul: '*All things are full of God... Hope is the only good that is common to all men; those who have nothing else possess hope still.*' He also informs us that '*The past is certain, the future obscure*' and '*A multitude of words is no proof of a prudent mind*'.

The quotation '*Know Thyself*' is inscribed on the temple of Apollo at Delphi, in Greece.

GENERAL SUN TZU
c.500 BCE

'All warfare is based on deception'

'All warfare is based on deception. Hence, when we are able to attack, we must seem unable; when using our forces, we must appear inactive; when we are near, we must make the enemy believe we are far away; when far away, we must make him believe we are near.'

The Art of War

Traditionally, Sun Tzu was a general of the King of Wu (*c*.544–496 BCE) but some historians place him in the Warring States Period (403–221 BCE). His importance lies in his collection of 13 essays, each devoted to one aspect of warfare. Knowledge of Sun Tzu reached Europe in 1782 in the form of a synopsis by a French Jesuit priest. The fundamental principles are that *'All warfare is based on deception'* and *'The supreme art of war is to subdue the enemy without fighting'*. In the light of post-war conflicts in Vietnam, across Africa, Afghanistan and Iraq, Sun Tzu foretold *'There is no instance of a nation benefitting from prolonged warfare.'* His teachings rapidly spread across Asia, and have affected the thinking of military strategists and politicians (such as Mao Tse-Tung) across the world. *The Art of War* has also been applied to business, sports, diplomacy and personal lives in management textbooks.

Sun Tzu was the first to recognize the importance of 'positioning' in strategy, and tells us that planning does not work properly in a competitive environment, because competing plans create unexpected situations. In the film *Wall Street* (1987), Michael Douglas, playing Gordon Gekko, says *'I don't throw darts at a board. I bet on sure things. Read Sun Tzu, The Art of War. Every battle is won before it is ever fought.'* Charlie Sheen, playing Bud, reads the work and later paraphrases the text: *'All warfare is based on deception. If your enemy is superior, evade him. If angry, irritate him. If equally matched, fight and if not: split and re-evaluate.'*

PYTHAGORAS
582–500 BCE

'Declining from the public ways, walk in unfrequented paths'

The Golden Verses of Pythagoras and Other Pythagorean Fragments,
selected and arranged by Florence M. Firth (1904)

The above quotation is typical of the methodology of Pythagoras, one of the greatest thinkers, philosophers, mathematicians and mystics of all time. Born in Samos, he moved to Croton to escape the dictator Polycratus. He was a committed vegetarian, writing: '*As long as man continues to be the ruthless destroyer of lower living beings he will never know health or peace. For as long as men massacre animals, they will kill each other.*' He also believed in the immortality of the soul, and that we pass from one body to another forever. Perhaps because he believed in the transmigration of the soul, he tells us: '*Reason is immortal, all else mortal*' and '*The most momentous thing in human life is the art of winning the soul to good or evil*'.

Most of us remember the Pythagorean theorem about right-angled triangles: $a^2+b^2=c^2$, but it was known in India about 800 BCE. It seems that Pythagoras proved it and popularized it in the Western world. He founded a society of disciples where, unusually for the times, women had equal rights with men. Pythagoras told his followers: '*Most men and women, by birth or nature, lack the means to advance in wealth and power, but all have the ability to advance in knowledge.*' He studied the connection of music with mathematics, and saw numbers in everything – '*Numbers rule the universe*'. '*There is geometry in the humming of the strings, there is music in the spacing of the spheres.*' For Pythagoras, mathematics purified the soul along with music, and the two were interconnected.

PHEIDIPPIDES
c.530–490 BCE

'We have won!'

According to Herodotus, Pheidippides was a herald who ran from Athens to Sparta, about 150 miles (245 km), to ask the Spartans to join Athens in the fight against the invading Persian army, who had landed near Marathon. He arrived in Sparta the following day, but the Spartans were celebrating a religious festival, the Carneia, and could not take any action before the full moon. Though there is no record to support it, legend has him running from Marathon to Athens, telling the Athenians of victory before collapsing and dying, saying either '*Victory!*' or '*We have won!*'.

For the revival of the Olympic Games, Baron Pierre de Courbertin decided that the final event should include a 'marathon run', from Marathon to Athens, in the spirit of the great Pheidippides, with the winner being awarded a silver cup. The original Olympic Games, said to have begun in 776 BCE, had no such race, but it seems that the baron had been influenced by the popular poem, 'Pheidippides' (1879), by Robert Browning.

The revival was held in 1896 in Greece and the last event was a 24.85-mile (40-km) run from Marathon Bridge to the Olympic stadium in Athens. The Greeks had not yet won a medal, and of the 25 runners assembled on Marathon Bridge, only nine men finished, eight of them Greeks. Spiridon Louis, a Greek postal worker, won this first modern marathon with a time of 2 hours, 58 minutes and 50 seconds. At the 1908 Olympic Games in London, the marathon distance was changed to 26.2 miles (42 km) to cover the ground from Windsor Castle to White City Stadium, with the 2.2 miles (2 km) added on so the race could finish in front of the royal family's viewing box.

BUDDHA
c.563–c.483 BCE

'Doubt everything. Find your own light.'

These were the last words of Buddha, in the Theravada tradition. The title Buddha means 'Enlightened One' or 'Awakened One'. In Buddhism, the Buddha refers to Siddhattha Gautama, born in Lumbini in modern Nepal. According to most traditions, he lived many lives before coming to our present world era. Born a prince, at the age of 13 he was escorted out of the palace. Buddha came across the 'four sights': an old crippled man, a diseased man, a decaying corpse and finally an ascetic. Gautama realized that age, disease, death and pain were inescapable, and that the poor would always outnumber the rich. However, even if one was wealthy, everyone shared age, disease, death and pain. Neither money nor peace can relieve people from fear and anxiety, or lead them to ultimate happiness.

Departing from the palace and wearing rags, Gautama studied meditation, becoming an ascetic in his search for enlightenment. He found that the true liberation from worry could be attained only by reaching a state of absolute tranquillity and enlightenment. Buddhism has evolved into three major schools of teaching, and its peaceful and forgiving tenets have influenced later religions. After 45 years of teaching, the Buddha passed into Parinirvana, the state of Nirvana attained at death. In his last sermon, he encouraged his disciples to diligently *'doubt everything'* and seek the truth, not holding on to that which is impermanent.

CONFUCIUS
551–479 BCE

'A man should practise what he preaches, but a man should also preach what he practises'

The Analects of Confucius 479–221 BCE

This is the 'golden rule' of the teachings of Confucius. He was a thinker, political figure, educator and founder of the Ru School of Chinese thought. His teachings, preserved in the *Lun Yu* or *Analects*, are the foundations of following Chinese philosophy upon the 'ideal man' – how he should live his life and interact with others, and what are the ideal forms of society and government. Confucius' influence in Chinese history has been compared with that of Socrates in the West. Confucius deplored the internecine warfare of his day and the subsequent lack of moral standards. He believed that the only remedy was to convert people to the principles of the sages of antiquity, and lectured to his pupils on the ancient classics.

The *Analects* were compiled by his disciples and are the best source of information about his life and teachings, which developed into the system of philosophy known as Confucianism. Whether Confucianism is a religion or a system of ethics is a matter of debate, but there are six million followers worldwide. Some of its sayings are:

> *'We don't know yet about life, how can we know about death?'*

> *'By three methods we may learn wisdom: First, by reflection, which is noblest; second, by imitation, which is easiest; and third by experience, which is the bitterest'*

> *'Choose a job you love, and you will never have to work a day in your life'*

> *'Everything has beauty, but not everyone sees it'*

> *'I hear, I know. I see, I remember. I do, I understand'*

$c.535-c.475$ BCE

'Nothing endures but change'

Diogenes Laertius, *Lives and Opinions of Eminent Philosophers*

Laertius' *Lives and Opinions of Eminent Philosophers* is thought to have been written around the third century BCE, and comprised a large number of earlier works from various Greek philosophers from Thales to Epicurus.

Heraclitus, who was born in Ephesus in Ionia, was a misanthrope who shunned his fellow Greeks and became a hermit in the mountains. He broke away from the Milesian philosophers, who focused on the material beginnings of the world, to study the internal rhythm of nature, which moves and regulates all things. He accepted only one primordial source, *Pyr* (fire), the essence of the *Logos*, which creates an infinite and uncorrupted world, one without a beginning or end. '*This universe, which is the same for all, has not been made by any god or man, but it always has been, is, and will be an ever-living fire, kindling itself by regular measures and going out by regular measures.*'

There is an eternal river of nature, constantly renewing itself: '*Everything flows, nothing stands still*' – in fact, 'change' is the only constant. A harmony of opposites occurs, shaping the world and sustaining nature: '*Opposition brings concord. Out of discord comes the fairest harmony.*' 'Good' and 'bad' are essentially different sides of the same thing. '*To God all things are beautiful and good and just, but men have supposed some things to be unjust, others just.*' Heraclitus also wrote:

> '*You could not step twice into the same river; for other waters are ever flowing on to you*'

> '*The road up and the road down is one and the same*'

> '*It is in changing that things find purpose*'

> '*Much learning does not teach understanding*'

Dying of dropsy (oedema, excess water retention), Heraclitus returned from the mountains to Ephesus and attempted to sweat it out in a cows' byre, but he died aged 60.

'Go tell the Spartans, thou who passest by, That here, obedient to their laws, we lie'

Epigram used as epitaph for the Spartan dead at Thermopylae

Xerxes, the son of Darius I, led a force of perhaps 100,000 Persians across the Dardanelles over a bridge of boats to begin the Second Persian War. His army progressed through Thrace and Macedonia and into Thessaly. The Olympic Games were in progress, and a small army was sent to Thermopylae Pass to hold the advance, guarding the entrance to Boeotia and Attica. In 480 BCE, after three days of fighting, the Greek traitor Ephialtes showed the Persians a flanking route through another pass. The defending Phocians were forced to withdraw to save their own city. To give the main army of 5,000 Greek Hoplites time to withdraw before the whole army was surrounded, King Leonidas I of Sparta remained at the pass with 300 of his bodyguards and 700 Thespians to fight a rear-guard action. Leonidas had been asked to surrender his arms, but had famously replied '*Come and get them*'.

All the Greek defenders were killed, but they delayed the Persians long enough to allow the Greek army to reform at the Isthmus of Corinth and win at Plataea, and for the Athenian navy to win the Battle of Salamis, effectively ending the invasion. One of the departing Hoplites reported: '*Such was the number of the Persians, that when they shot their arrows the sun was darkened by their multitude.*' A Spartan shouted to all in earshot, '*Our friend brings us good news. If the Persians darken the sun with their arrows, we will be able to fight in the shade.*'

Though none of his complete poems survives, it is clear from the many epigrams attributed to him that Simonides was a prolific and accomplished elegist, who focused particularly on the Persian Wars.

AESCHYLUS
525–456 BCE

'God loves to help him who strives to help himself'

Fragment of Plays no. 223 in Stobaeus, *Anthology iii. 29. 31*

Known as the 'Father of Tragedy', Aeschylus was born in the Attican town of Eleusis, near Athens. As a child he was told in a dream by the god Dionysus to write tragedies, and began writing as Greek theatre was in its first stages of evolution. Plays were little more than a poet with a chorus and dancers, but he introduced the second actor, and involved the chorus in the play's action. For example, in *Agamemnon* the chorus becomes the 'Furies' to pursue Orestes. In *Agamemnon* we read: '*Death is better, a milder fate than tyranny*' and '*It is in the character of very few men to honour without envy a friend who has prospered*'.

Aeschylus directed many of his own works. Only seven plays survive, one of which, *The Persians*, tells the story of the Battle of Salamis, where Aeschylus fought. His *Prometheus Bound* and *Seven Against Thebes* are also performed today. His trilogy, *The Oresteia*, dealt with the curse on the House of Orestes. Aeschylus was charged with revealing the 'Eleusinian Mysteries', secret rites, but was not convicted. In legend, he died when an eagle dropped a tortoise on his bald head, mistaking it for a rock. He also gave us the quotes: '*Time brings all things to pass*' and '*In war, truth is the first casualty*'.

The larger play from which this fragment is taken is unknown to modern scholars; this quote survives in the *Anthologion* by Johannes Stobaeus, his anthology of short Greek poetry and prose excerpts originally compiled for the tutelage of his son, Septimius.

PINDAR
518–438 BCE

'A dream of a shadow is our mortal being'
Pythian Odes 8, line 95, 446 BCE

'Creatures of a day! What is a man?
What is he not? A dream of a shadow
Is our mortal being. But when there comes to men
A gleam of splendour given of Heaven,
Then rests on them a light of glory
And blesséd are their days.'

From Cynoscephalae in Boeotia, Pindar is renowned as the greatest of the 'nine lyric poets' of Ancient Greece. Of his massive output of over 50 years of writing, the only works to have survived complete are a series of odes written to celebrate the victors in various athletic games. Forty-five victory odes remain, grouped into four books based on the various games – the Olympian, Pythian, Isthmian and Nemean. The oldest remaining ode dates from the Pythian Games of 498 BCE, celebrating a Thessalian victory in the double-stadium race, and his last ode was for a wrestler in the same games in 446 BCE.

In the Medean Wars of 490 and 480 BCE, it seems that he had connections with Xerxes' Persians when Thebes was occupied, but his reputation was undamaged throughout the Greek world. In fact, Pindar's house in Thebes was spared by Alexander the Great as Pindar had composed verse for his ancestor, Alexander I of Macedon. Pindar travelled far, to work for patrons in Syracuse, Aegina, Delphi and Athens. He also wrote choral works and hymns for religious festivals. In his *Nemean Odes*, he writes, '*To tell the whole truth with clear face unveiled; Often is man's best wisdom to be silent*' and '*For words live longer down the years than deeds*'. Fragment 110 of his writings is: '*War is sweet to those who have no experience of it, but the experienced man trembles exceedingly at heart on its approach.*'

EMPEDOCLES
490–430 BCE

'The nature of God is a circle of which the centre is everywhere and the circumference is nowhere'

Empedocles: The Extant Fragments

Born in the Greek colony at Acragas (Agrigentum) in Sicily, Empedocles was a philosopher, physician and poet, who followed the ideas of Pythagoras. He was the first philosopher to give us the four primordial elements of earth, air, fire and water. Heraclitus had said that fire was the origin of everything, to Pythagoras it was water, and for Anaximenses the primordial element had been air. A committed vegetarian, Empedocles was the last Greek philosopher to write in verse, but only fragments remain.

Empedocles was remarkably ahead of his time, stating that the moon shines by reflected light and that solar eclipses are caused by the interposition of the moon. He was the forerunner of Einstein, stating that light takes time to travel, but so little time that we cannot observe it. He also discovered centrifugal force, whirling a cup of water around on a piece of string. In addition, he conceived a theory of evolution which included the idea of 'the survival of the fittest'. He thought that in prehistoric times strange creatures had populated the world, of which only certain forms had survived. He wrote that motion and change actually exist, and that at the same time reality is fundamentally changeless: '*And in addition to them [elements] nothing comes into being or ceases.*' Like Anaxagoras (see opposite), he thus believed that matter was immutable, always in existence. There is a legend that his desire to be godlike led to him ending his life by leaping into the crater of Mount Etna.

'Everything has a natural explanation. The moon is not a god, but a great rock, and the sun a hot rock.'

Fragment of a book on philosophy, preserved by Simplicius of Cilicia, 6 CE

This Ionian philosopher maintained that the sun was not a golden chariot steered across the sky by a distant god, but instead a fiery mass of metal or stone. Similarly, he said the moon was a cold mass of stone, and merely reflected the sun's rays. This led to charges of impiety under Cleon's rule, and he was sentenced to death in Athens. To escape punishment, Anaxagoras was forced to leave Athens forever, spending the rest of his life in exile. He wrote '*It is not I who have lost the Athenians, but the Athenians who have lost me.*' He also believed that in the physical world, everything contains a portion of everything else. He concluded that in order for the food an animal eats to turn into bone, hair, flesh, etc., it must already contain all of those constituents within it.

Anaxagoras noted: '*The Greeks are wrong to recognize coming into being and perishing; for nothing comes into being nor perishes, but is rather compounded or dissolved from things that are. So they would be right to call coming into being composition and perishing dissolution.*' Today we know that every atom in existence has always existed, verifying Anaxagoras' claims. He said the only exception to this rule was the mind. The mind was not made up of other constituents, as it is '*something infinite and self-controlling, and that is has been mixed with no thing, but is alone itself by itself*'.

Also an astronomer, Anaxagoras believed that the world was created through the rotary motion of a spiral, where initially all mass was united in the centre, then flung out by centrifugal force to create celestial bodies, elements and substances. Galaxies could not be observed at this time as the Greeks did not possess telescopes, so some hypothesize that his thoughts derive from a previously unknown civilization. (Telescopes are believed to have been invented in the Netherlands in the early 17th century.)

HERODOTUS
c.485–c.425 BCE

'The most hateful torment for men is to have knowledge of everything but power over nothing'

The Histories, Book 9, Section 16, c.425 BCE

The only reliable source we have on Herodotus is his *The Histories*. The *Histories* is the story of the rise of the Persian Empire and its wars with Greece, and the battles of Marathon, Thermopylae and Salamis are described. Herodotus gives us the historical record of events that happened when he was a child. He questioned his elders about the events in both Persian Wars to get the details he wanted for his story, and realized that despite his great knowledge, he was powerless to alter the events of the day. In its prologue, we find he was born in Halicarnassus – today's Bodrum in Turkey. Nearby is the island of Samos, which is prominent in *The Histories*, so he may have lived there and in Athens, which also features strongly. His prologue begins, '*Herodotus of Halicarnassus hereby publishes the results of his inquiries, hoping to do two things: to preserve the memory of the past by putting on record the astonishing achievements both of the Greek and the non-Greek peoples; and more particularly, to show how the two races came into conflict.*'

Herodotus was the world's first historian – the 'Father of History', describing the expansion of the Achaemenid Empire under Cyrus the Great, Darius the Great and Xerxes' attacks on Greece at Salamis and Plataea. It seems that he was a hoplite, a heavily armed infantryman, like other Greeks of his class and age, which explains his confused accounts of battles – he was a soldier, not a general. He also seems to have travelled to Babylon, Sicily, the Crimea and Egypt, but we know nothing of his life except that his character – in his periods of optimism and pessimism – is on display throughout the text. His perspective was that '*No one is stupid enough to prefer war to peace; in peace sons bury their fathers and in war fathers bury their sons. However, I suppose the gods must have wanted this to happen.*'

PROTAGORAS
c.490/481–420 BCE

'Man is the measure of all things: of things which are, that they are so, and of things which are not, that they are not'

Fragment 1, passed down without context

Protagoras did not believe the gods made a difference to life, only man. A famous agnostic, he wrote: '*Concerning the gods, I have no means of knowing whether they exist or not or of what sort they may be, because of the obscurity of the subject, and the brevity of human life.*' This pre-Socratic philosopher was born in Thrace, and Plato credits him with inventing the role of '*a teacher of virtue*', becoming a professional 'sophist'. Sophism was a series of techniques to acquire wisdom, taught by teachers of philosophy, rhetoric and debate, which were vital to Greek public life.

Protagoras instructed: '*Let us hold our discussion together in our own persons, making trial of the truth and of ourselves.*' He was eternally fascinated by the correct usage of words in the correct context. He knew that the less appealing argument could hide the best answer, which is why it was constantly necessary to strengthen the weakest argument, and thereby develop consensual truth – '*There are two sides to every question*'. Protagoras also told us: '*No intelligent man believes that anybody ever willingly errs or willingly does base and evil deeds; they are well aware that all who do base and evil things do them unwillingly.*'

EURIPIDES
480–406 BCE

'Events will take their course, it is no good of being angry at them; he is happiest who wisely turns them to the best account'

Bellerophon, Fragment 298

Born near Athens, the great dramatist Euripides had little recognition in his day, because of his criticism of superstitions and government hypocrisy. It seems that his ongoing difficulties with authorities led him to the above quotation, channelling his anger into fiercely satirical literature. Writing at the same time as Aeschylus and Sophocles, he was influenced by Anaxagoras, and his free-thinking humanitarianism can be seen in all his plays. Remarkably, Euripides was a pacifist in times of the wars against Sparta, and he spent a great deal of his life living as a hermit in a cave on the island of Salamis. His characters explored personal issues, and his plays such as *Hippolytus* and *The Bacchae* were psychological dramas. Still performed today, *Medea* is the story of the terrible jealousy of a middle-aged woman who has lost her husband's interest.

Euripides portrayed Athenian heroes such as Menelaus and Agamemnon as anti-heroic, so became unpopular with the citizens of Athens. *Trojan Women* deals with slaughter and the desecration of shrines in Troy, but was based on the Athenian destruction of Melos in 416 BCE. *Hecuba* likewise details the cruelty of Greek warriors who sacrifice the Trojan queen's daughter. Euripides' closest friends were banished or killed for being liberals, and after a trial he had to leave Athens. Later, he was accidentally torn to pieces by the hounds of King Archelaus of Macedonia. An innovator in drama, some of his other lines are:

'*Love is all we have, the only way that each can help the other*'
'*Leave no stone unturned*'
'*He was a wise man who originated the idea of God*'
'*Happiness is brief. It will not stay. God batters at its sails*'
'*Time will explain it all*'

SOPHOCLES
495–406 BCE

'One word frees us of all the weight and pain of life: That word is love'

Oedipus at Colonus

Born just outside Athens, Sophocles became one of the great playwrights of the 'golden age of Greek theatre'. The son of a wealthy merchant, he enjoyed all the comforts of the prosperous Greek Empire, serving as a treasury director, priest and public administrator. Ending his studies aged 28, he took first prize in a festival for new plays, and wrote at least another 120 in his lifetime. An excellent actor, he also performed in many of his own plays.

Oedipus at Colonus was written shortly before Sophocles' death in 406 BCE, and was preceded in the 'Theban Plays' sequence by *Oedipus Rex* and succeeded by *Antigone*. It is set in the village of Colonus outside Athens, where the blinded Oedipus has come with his daughters Antigone and Ismene. Through love, piety and hardship, Oedipus achieves redemption after a lifetime of being stripped of dignity and wandering in a wilderness of suffering. Oedipus begins to 'see' again with the eye of his soul, recognizing his faults and realizing the importance of love and right living with the help of his daughters. In his last hours, Oedipus is accepted and absolved by Zeus.

Sophocles also innovated in the form of his plays, and was the first dramatist to add a third actor. Of his seven surviving plays, *Oedipus Rex* is probably the finest, and has been called a 'perfectly structured play'. In it he writes: *'The greatest griefs are those we cause ourselves'* and *'Time eases all things'*. In *Antigone*, we read, *'Nobody likes the man who brings bad news'*, *'Reason is God's crowning gift to man'* and *'Wisdom outweighs any wealth'*. *Electra* has the lines: *'The end excuses any evil'* and *'It made our hair stand up in panic fear'*, while *'Stranger in a strange country'* comes from *Oedipus at Colonus*. Sophocles excelled in writing about social drama, spending more time on characterization and motives than most of his contemporaries. His death marked the end of the great age of Greek tragedy, coming shortly after the deaths of Aeschylus and Euripides.

THUCYDIDES
c.460/455–c.400/395 BCE

'The strength of an Army lies in strict discipline and undeviating obedience to its officers'

The History of the Peloponnesian War, Book 2, c.404 BCE

Thucydides' detailed study of the 25-year struggle between Athens and Sparta became the model for every succeeding historian. The growth of the Athenian Empire caused fear in other Greek states, especially Corinth, whose trade interests were threatened by Athens' control of the ports in the Aegean. The Peloponnesian War (431–404 BCE) ended when Athens was defeated. Thucydides realized the critical importance of this war in the history of mankind – '*I have written my work, not as an essay which is to win the applause of the moment, but as a possession for all time*'. In 424 BCE he had been elected an Athenian general, but failed to prevent the loss of an important city to the Spartans, so was exiled from Athens. He spent the rest of the war gathering evidence, and talking with participants in the various actions. He wrote: '*The bravest are surely those who have the clearest vision of what is before them, glory and danger alike, and yet notwithstanding, go out to meet it.*'

A few decades earlier, the historian Herodotus had recorded almost everything he had heard, whether he believed it or not. However, Thucydides gathered all the available evidence, sifted it, verified it and made his narrative as factual as possible. He begins by explaining his rationale for believing that this is the greatest war of all, more important than the Trojan or Persian Wars. He shows us that human nature alone, not the fates or the gods, is responsible for historical events, and informs us that his history will not be as entertaining as others, but will be instead a rational analysis. He says that if we understand the past, it will allow us to understand the causes and progress of future wars, and hopefully prevent them or ameliorate their effects: '*Wars spring from unseen and generally insignificant causes, the first outbreak being often but an explosion of anger.*'

'The life which is unexamined is not worth living'

The Apology of Socrates, Plato

With the example of his own life, his use of critical reasoning and his commitment to truth, the Athenian Socrates set the standard for subsequent Western philosophers. He left no writings, so we are reliant upon the words of contemporaries such as Xenophon, Plato and Aristophanes.

Socrates served as a soldier during the Peloponnesian War, and later retired from political life to work as a stonemason and to raise his children. When his father left him some money, he used his time to innovate the practice of philosophical dialogue, now known as Socratic dialogue. For the rest of his life, Socrates devoted himself to discussions with the young citizens of Athens, constantly questioning their confidence in the truth of popular opinions. An Athenian jury found him guilty of corrupting the youth and interfering with the religion of the city, and sentenced him to death. Refusing to try and escape from prison, he drank hemlock and died in the company of his friends and disciples, telling them: '*I was really too honest a man to be a politician and live.*'

He was an early feminist, declaring: '*Once made equal to man, woman becomes his superior*', but he was also unsure of the value of marriage: '*As to marriage or celibacy, let a man take which course he will, he will be sure to repent... By all means marry. If you get a good wife, you'll be happy. If you get a bad one, you'll become a philosopher and that is a good thing for any man.*' One of his sayings most relevant to today's consumer society is: '*Worthless people live only to eat and drink; people of worth eat and drink only to live.*'

ARISTOPHANES
c.448–380 BCE

'Make hay while the sun shines'

'When the soldier returns from the wars, even though he has white hair, he very soon finds a young wife. But a woman has only one summer; if she does not make hay while the sun shines, no one will afterwards have anything to say to her, and she spends her days consulting oracles that never send her a husband.'

Lysistrata

Aristophanes' eleven surviving plays are all that remain of the time of classical Attic comedy, when he had at least five major contemporaries, but he was recognized as the greatest comic writer of his day. His works were written during the Peloponnesian War that so demoralized Euripides, and therefore are always touched with elements of grief.

Lysistrata is a pacifist play following Athens' great losses at Syracuse, where Athenian women decide to deny sex to their men until there is peace with Sparta. *The Acharnians* was an anti-war comedy about a farmer from Attica, the rural area surrounding Athens, who wished to make a private peace with Sparta, satirizing Euripides the pacifist. His next play, *The Knights*, was a disguised satire on the demagogue Cleon, who had replaced the great Pericles as the leader of Athens: '*Under every stone lurks a politician*'. In *The Clouds*, Socrates was Aristophanes' target: '*The old are in a second childhood*'. *The Wasps* was another attack upon Cleon and the failing state of Athenian power, and his next two plays, *Women at the Festival of Demeter* and *The Frogs*, were two more attacks on the tragic poet Euripides.

'As to diseases, make a habit of two things — to help, or at least, to do no harm'

Epidemics, Book I, Ch. 2

Born on the Greek island of Kos, Hippocrates is known as the 'Father of Medicine' and regarded as the greatest physician of his time. He founded a medical school on Kos and travelled across Greece, preaching his ideas. The 'oath' of medical ethics he developed for physicians, the Hippocratic Oath, is still sometimes taken by doctors today as they begin their medical practice. Hippocrates based his practice on observations and on the study of the human body, holding the belief that all illnesses had a rational explanation. The belief during his time was that illnesses were caused by evil spirits and the gods. He explained: *'Men think epilepsy divine, merely because they do not understand it. But if they called everything divine which they do not understand, why, there would be no end of divine things.'*

The above quote usually appears these days as the aphorism *'Whenever a doctor cannot do good, he must be kept from doing harm.'* Hippocrates seems to have been the first to believe that the body must be treated as a whole and not as a series of parts. He wrote: *'Cure sometimes, treat often, comfort always'*, and he accurately ascribed symptoms, being the first physician to describe the symptoms of pneumonia. He believed in the natural healing process of rest, a good diet, fresh air and cleanliness, noting that some individuals were better able to cope with disease and illness than others. He was also the first physician to hold the belief that thoughts, ideas and feelings come from the brain and not the heart, as others of his time believed. Also attributed to Hippocrates is *'Walking is man's best medicine'* and *'Persons who are naturally very fat are apt to die earlier than those who are slender'*.

'Whenever I go into a house, I will go to help the sick'

'I swear by Apollo the healer, by Aesculapius, by Health, by Panacaea and all the powers of healing, and call to witness all the gods and goddesses that I may keep this Oath and Promise to the best of my ability and judgement.

I will pay the same respect to my master in the Science as to my parents and share my life with him and pay all my debts to him. I will regard his sons as my brothers and teach them the Science, if they desire to learn it, without fee or contract. I will hand on precepts, lectures and all other learning to my sons, to those of my master and to those pupils duly apprenticed and sworn, and to none other.

I will use my power to help the sick to the best of my ability and judgment; I will abstain from harming or wronging any man by it.

I will not give a fatal draught to anyone if I am asked, nor will I suggest any such thing. Neither will I give a woman means to procure an abortion.

I will be chaste and religious in my life and in my practice.

I will not cut, even for the stone, but I will leave such procedures to the practitioners of that craft.

Whenever I go into a house, I will go to help the sick and never with the intention of doing harm or injury. I will not abuse my position to indulge in sexual contacts with the bodies of women or of men, whether they be freemen or slaves.

Whatever I see or hear, professionally or privately, which ought not to be divulged, I will keep secret and tell no one.

If, therefore, I observe this Oath and do not violate it, may I prosper both in my life and in my profession, earning good repute among all men for my time. If I transgress and forswear this oath, may my lot be otherwise.'

The Hippocratic Oath

XENOPHON

431–c.355 BCE

'Thalassa! Thalassa!'
(The sea! The sea!)

Anabasis Kyrou

Xenophon was an Athenian author, historian and mercenary who led the epic retreat of 'The 10,000' from Mesopotamia to the Black Sea coast. His best-known work *Anabasis Kyrou* (*The Persian Expedition*) is the true story of Greek mercenaries who fought their way back from Babylon to the Black Sea. Xenophon had joined an expedition of Cyrus the Younger, who intended to oust his brother King Artaxerxes II of Persia, into Asia Minor, but Cyrus was killed in the battle of Cunaxa. The Greeks were left leaderless, over 1,000 miles from home. Xenophon was elected a general, and led the continuing fight to retreat through the 'barbarian' world. Less than 6,000 mercenaries survived, and Xenophon's *Anabasis* describes military virtues, discipline, leadership and courage. A famous part of the *Anabasis* is his description of the Greeks shouting, '*Thalassa! Thalassa!*' at the top of a great sand dune, when they at last saw the Black Sea. '*Thereupon they began running, rear-guard and all, and the baggage animals and horses came galloping up. But when they had reached the summit, then indeed they fell to embracing one another – generals and officers and all – and the tears trickled down their cheeks.*'

Xenophon gives us the qualities required for leadership: '*The true test of a leader is whether his followers will adhere to his cause from their own volition, enduring the most arduous hardships without being forced to do so, and remaining steadfast in the moments of greatest peril… There is small risk a general will be regarded with contempt by those he leads, if, whatever he may have to preach, he shows himself best able to perform.*' Unlike many modern leaders, Xenophon knew how to motivate his men: '*The sweetest of all sounds is praise.*'

PLATO
427–347 BCE

'No evil can happen to a good man, either in life or after death'

*Apology c.*399–395 BCE

The *Apology* **is Plato's** account of Socrates' speech, when he defended himself against charges of being a man *'who corrupted the young, did not believe in the gods, and created new deities'*. Socrates displayed no fear of his accusers, despite the fact that he knew he would be condemned to death.

After Socrates' death Plato travelled to Egypt and Italy, studied with students of Pythagoras and eventually returned to Athens. He set up his own school of philosophy at the Academy, using the Socratic Method to progress through mathematical learning to achieve abstract philosophical truth. Plato's *Dialogues* ask (in the circumstances of Socrates' punishment) whether the citizen is ever justified in refusing to obey the state, whether virtue can be taught and they develop arguments demonstrating the immortality of the human soul. His masterpiece is *The Republic*, discussing the nature of justice and planning a beneficent state ruled by philosophers. Some of his aphorisms and sayings are as follows:

'Never discourage anyone... who continually makes progress, no matter how slow'

'All men are by nature equal, made all of the same earth by one Workman; and however we deceive ourselves, as dear unto God is the poor peasant as the mighty prince'

'And what, Socrates, is the food of the soul? Surely, I said, knowledge is the food of the soul'

'The greatest wealth is to live content with little'

'It is right to give every man his due'

'He was a wise man who invented beer'

'Necessity... the mother of invention'

'As empty vessels make the loudest sound, so they that have the least wit are the greatest babblers'

DIOGENES OF SINOPE, 'THE CYNIC'
c.412–323 BCE

'I am a citizen of the world'

Diogenes Laertius, *Lives and Opinions of Eminent Philosophers*

Diogenes gave this response when asked his nationality, calling himself a 'cosmopolites', and thus has been credited with the first use of the word 'cosmopolitan'. He actually came from the ancient city of Sinope on the Black Sea, Galatia (modern Turkey). Diogenes is the best known of the school of philosophy known as the cynics. He was an ascetic, who, according to the later Diogenes Laertius, *'lighted a candle in the daytime, and went round saying "I am looking for an honest man"'*. By this means he claimed to expose the vanity and selfishness of man.

The school of the cynics was founded by Antisthenes (444–370 BCE), a pupil of Socrates, and its followers were indifferent to ease, wealth and the enjoyments of life. Diogenes, on coming to Athens from Sinope, was a rake and a spendthrift, but fell under the example of Antisthenes. He *'became at once an austere ascetic, his clothing of the coarsest, his food the plainest, and his bed the bare ground. At length he found himself a permanent residence in a barrel.'*

In the first century CE, Plutarch related in *Parallel Lives* that the young Alexander the Great (356–323 BCE) met Diogenes, then a very old man, in Corinth. Being solicitous of the ancient philosopher, Alexander asked what he could do for him. Diogenes replied, *'Stand a little less between me and the sun.'* Alexander told his aides, as he took his leave, *'If I were not Alexander, I would be Diogenes.'*

DEMOSTHENES
384–322 BCE

'The man who runs away may fight again'

From *Collected Works of Erasmus: Adages*

In 338 BCE, **Demosthenes** was at the great Battle of Chaeronea, when Phillip II's Macedonians defeated the Athenians and 3,000 Athenians died. Demosthenes fled from the defeat, and to critics who called him a coward, Demosthenes always answered, *'The man who runs away may fight again'*, from which we have today's: *'He who fights and runs away will live to fight another day.'*

Demosthenes is considered the greatest of all Ancient Greek orators, and his works provide an insight into the life and culture of Athens during his time. As a boy, Demosthenes suffered from a speech impediment and he worked at a series of self-designed exercises to overcome it, hence a legend that he talked with a mouthful of rocks to improve his diction, while he shouted over the roar of the waves. He became a speechwriter to make his living, and when asked the three most important aspects of his oratory, answered, 'Action, Action, Action.'

Before anyone else, he saw that Phillip and then his son Alexander the Great intended to rule Greece, and he urged all the Greek states to make a combined defence: *'Close alliances with despots are never safe for free states'*; *'Every dictator is an enemy of freedom, an opponent of law'*. Demosthenes was exiled when Alexander the Great ruled Greece, but was recalled after Alexander died. He attempted again to rally the people against Macedonia, but was unsuccessful and took poison rather than face capture and punishment. He also gave us the phrase: *'The facts speak for themselves.'*

ARCHIMEDES
c.287–212/211 BCE

'EUREKA! EUREKA!'
(I have found it! I have found it!)

The greatest scientist of antiquity, Archimedes was born in Syracuse, then an independent Greek state. His father was the astronomer Phidias, and Archimedes probably studied in Alexandria. He was an expert in hydrostatics and mechanics. As well as being regarded as the 'Father of Mathematical Physics', his contributions to geometry, which revolutionized the subject, led to him being called the 'Father of Integral Calculus', his methods anticipating integral calculus 2,000 years before Newton and Leibniz. Archimedes is now recognized as one of the three greatest mathematicians of all time, alongside Newton and Gauss. He was also a practical inventor who developed a wide variety of machines, including compound pulley systems and the Archimedean water screw pump. Archimedes said: *'Give me a lever long enough and a fulcrum on which to place it, and I shall move the world.'*

When Syracuse was sacked by the Romans, he was killed by a Roman soldier who did not know who he was. The Romans had wanted to take him alive for his knowledge after the long siege, having suffered attacks from his war machines. Many of his writings survive. His *'Eureka!'* moment occurred when he noticed his body displacing water in his bath. In *'On Floating Bodies'*, his fifth proposition was that *'Any solid lighter than a fluid will, if placed in the fluid, be so far immersed that the weight of the solid will be equal to the weight of the fluid displaced'*.

'Nothing from nothing ever yet was born '
(Nothing can be created out of nothing)

De Rerum Natura

Lucretius stands out as the only Roman philosopher worthy of the name, but he had huge difficulties in translating the language of Greek concepts into Latin. All we really know about him is in his 200-page poem, *De Rerum Natura (On the Nature of Things)*. An Epicurean scientist, Lucretius scorned the multiple gods of his day (*'so much wrong could religion induce'*), believing that things are actually what they seem to be as perceived by our senses. He watched matter dividing, subdividing and rejoining, and decided that matter must be made of tiny building blocks, of atoms forming and reforming. His ideas were utterly opposite to Aristotle's continuous elements of fire, earth, water and air, which prevailed in the West for another 1,700 years.

Lucretius' work survived only because he was a superb poet. He literally reshaped the Latin language to create poetry, e.g. when he describes the movement of atoms in solids and gases:

> 'Globed from the atoms falling slow or swift
> I see the suns, I see the systems live
> Their forms; and even the systems and the suns
> Shall go back slowly to the eternal drift.'

In *De Rerum Natura* we find modern ideas on heat transfer, gravity, laws of conservation of matter and energy, molecular attachments, biological mutation and the survival of the fittest: *'Some races increase, others are reduced, and in a short while the generations of living creatures are changed and like runners relay the torch of life.'*

GAIUS IULIUS CAESAR
100–44 BCE

'Veni, vidi, vici'
(I came, I saw, I conquered)

Julius Caesar was the main power behind the transformation of the Roman Republic into the Roman Empire, conquering Gaul to push Rome's borders to the Atlantic Ocean. In 55 BCE he had landed in Britain but left soon after without leaving a garrison. He finally defeated Vercingetorix in 52 BCE and informed the Roman Senate with the message *'Gaul is subdued'*. In 49 BCE he led his legions across the River Rubicon, beginning his victorious Civil War with Pompey. He was supposed to keep his army in Gaul, so *'crossing the Rubicon'* was an irrevocable step, of which Caesar stated *'The die is cast'*. He then pushed out into Asia Minor, winning at Zela in Central Turkey in 47 BCE, sending the message *'Veni, vidi, vici'* to Rome. The emphasis on 'I' in *'I came, I saw, I conquered'* was a warning of Caesar's personal might and the totality of his victory to the powerful patrician Senate back in Republican Rome.

De Bello Gallico (*Caesar's Gallic Wars*) describes his victories and his expedition to Britain, and his *The Civil War* describes the campaign against Pompey. In legend, Caesar's wife Calpurnia foresaw Caesar's assassination at the Senate in a dream. She pleaded with him not to go, but he responded, *'We have not to fear anything, except fear itself'* – this echoed the words of his contemporary Pubilius Syrus.

PUBLILIUS SYRUS
*fl.*46 BCE

'*Judex damnatur ubi nocens absolvitur*'
(The judge is condemned when the guilty is acquitted)

Maxim 407, *Sententiae*

An Assyrian, Publilius was taken as a slave from what is now northern Iraq to Italy, and because of his intelligence and wit was freed and educated by his master. He wrote mimes, in which he performed, being successful in Italian provinces and at Julius Caesar's games in 46 BCE. In a contest a year later he defeated all other mime writers, including the veteran Decimus Laberius, with his improvisation, and Caesar gave the prize. His *Sententiae*, a series of around 700 maxims in verse, remain. They were probably abstracted by contemporary scholars from his mimes some time in the first century BCE. Maxim I was '*As men, we are all equal in the presence of death*' and there are many, many aphorisms that we use today because of Publilius; for instance:

'*Many receive advice, few profit by it*'

'*To do two things at once is to do neither*'

'*While we stop to think, we often miss our opportunity*'

'*There are some remedies worse than the disease*'

'*Anyone can hold the helm when the sea is calm*'

'*Practice is the best of all instructors*'

'*Never find your delight in another's misfortune*'

'*It is a bad plan that admits of no modification*'

'*The fear of death is more to be dreaded than death itself*'

'*It is only the ignorant who despise education*'

'*Every day should be passed as if it were to be our last*'

'*No one knows what he can do till he tries*'

'*Everything is worth what its purchaser will pay for it*'

'*A rolling stone gathers no moss*'

'Et tu, Brute?'
(You too, Brutus?)

Shakespeare *Julius Caesar*

Julius Caesar was murdered by a group of senators, led by Marcus Junius Brutus (85–42 BCE), who had been a close friend. These words come to us from Shakespeare's play, *Julius Caesar*, in which Caesar begins to resist the attack, but resigns himself to death when he sees Brutus. In the play, Caesar had been warned to *'beware the Ides of March'*, and on that day, 15 March, he was assassinated by a group who believed that he was over-powerful.

Shakespeare copied the Roman historian Suetonius (*c.*69/75–*c.*130/135 CE), who reported that Caesar's last words were in Greek, '*Kai su, teknon? (You too, my child?)*'. Caesar entered the Senate, and all senators stood to show respect, but some moved behind his chair and others approached as if to greet him. One pulled his robe to show the beginning of the attack, then the circle of senators tightened around Caesar, stabbing him. When Caesar saw Brutus among them, he stopped resisting and pulled his robe over his face. Brutus stabbed him in the groin, and Caesar was found to have been stabbed 23 times. Such was the frenzy of the attack, started by Casca, that some of the conspirators were themselves wounded.

Caesar had previously spared Brutus' life when Brutus fought for Pompey in the Civil War. Brutus was allowed to leave Rome after Caesar's assassination, but the Emperor Octavian (Augustus) declared the group of senators to be murderers, and Brutus committed suicide after the second Battle of Philippi.

HORACE
65–8 BCE

'Nil desperandum'
(Never despair)

Odes, Book I, No. 7, *c*.23 BCE

Quintus Horatius Flaccus was a lyric poet, satirist and literary critic, generally considered to be one of the greatest poets of all time. The son of a freed slave, Horace studied in Rome and at the Athens Academy where he met Cicero, but his studies were interrupted by civil war after the murder of Julius Caesar. In Greece, he joined the army of Brutus and Cassius and was a military tribune in the defeat at Philippi to the forces of Octavian (Augustus) and Mark Antony. His family's properties were confiscated. In 39 BCE, after Emperor Augustus' amnesty, Horace went to Rome, where he became a secretary in the Roman treasury. Virgil introduced him to a rich artist's patron named Maecenas who gave him a villa and farm in the Sabine Hills.

The quote is echoed in another entry in the *Odes*: '*In adversity, remember to keep an even mind*'. Horace had been exiled, lost his properties, but regained wealth himself. '*Never despair*' comes from the mouth of Teucer (the half-brother of Ajax), who fought in the Trojan War. Because of Ajax' suicide, Teucer was forced to emigrate, and his departing words to his sorrowing companions were:

> 'Never despair, if Teucer leads, of Teucer's omens!
> Unerring Apollo surely promised,
> In the uncertain future, a second Salamis
> On a fresh soil. O you brave heroes, you
> Who suffered worse with me often,
> Drown your cares with wine:
> Tomorrow we'll sail the wide seas again.'

Horace became the most respected poet during the Augustan age and his most famous work is his *Odes*, four books of short lyrics. He was favoured by Augustus to write a poem, the 'Carmen Saeculare' for the Secular Games of 17 BCE. From Horace's works we have the terms: '*purple patch*', '*the golden mean*', '*moderation in everything*' and the well-known war epitaph '*dulce et decorum est pro patria mori*' ('*sweet and fitting it is to die for one's country*').

HORACE
65–8 BCE

'Carpe diem'
(Seize the day)

Odes, Book I, No. 11, *c.*23 BCE

Horace suffered many vicissitudes – being exiled and losing his inheritance – before being accepted by the new Emperor of Rome, Augustus. His motto, 'Carpe diem', endures to this day as a maxim that reminds people to live in the present, enjoying what they have whilst they have it. Living in uncertain times, he never knew what tomorrow would bring.

Suetonius tells us that Horace was short and fat, liked lascivious pictures and spent most of his time in retirement on his farm. When Horace died, he left his estate to Augustus, in gratitude for his pardon. In his *Epistles*, Horace asks us to '*seek for truth in the groves of Academe*', and in *Satires*, '*In Rome you long for the country; in the country – oh inconstant! – you praise the distant city to the stars*'. When in exile he longed to be in Rome, but when in Rome longed to be on his farm in the Sabine Hills. In Book III of *Odes* can be found a lesson that still resonates today – that every generation is thought of as inferior by its predecessors:

> 'What do the ravages of time not injure?
> Our fathers' age was worse than our grandfathers'.
> We their sons are more worthless than they:
> So in our turn we shall give the world
> Our children yet more corrupt.'

Horace's greatest lesson is that we should enjoy life while we have it, as expressed in the following two quotes. '*Think to yourself that every day is your last; the hour to which you do not look forward will come as a welcome surprise.*' '*He will through life be master of himself and a happy man who from day to day can have said, "I have lived: tomorrow the Father may fill the sky with black clouds or with cloudless sunshine."*'

PUBLIUS VERGILIUS MARO (VIRGIL)
70–19 BCE

'Do not trust the horse, Trojans. Whatever it is, I fear the Greeks even when they bring gifts.'

Aeneid, Book II, *c*.29–19 BCE

Publius Vergilius Maro is the greatest Roman poet, and has influenced Western literature for two millennia. He is better known by the Anglicized form of his name, Virgil or Vergila. He was an 'Alexandrian', the name given to a group of poets who sought inspiration in the writings of third-century Greek poets. After the battle of Philippi in 42 BCE his property was confiscated, but seems to have been restored at the command of Augustus. From 42 to 37 BCE Virgil composed the pastoral poems known as *Eclogues* and then the *Georgics*, a townsman's view of farming and the country. In the *Eclogues* we read, '*There's a snake hidden in the grass*', and in the *Georgics*, '*meanwhile it is flying, irretrievable time is flying*'.

Augustus asked Virgil to write of the glory of Rome under his rule, so for the rest of his life Virgil worked on the *Aeneid*, the national epic tale of Rome's history. It begins with the story of Aeneas, the fabled Trojan hero who escaped the fall of Troy and founded Rome – '*I sing of arms and the man who first from the shores of Troy came destined an exile to Italy...*' The Sybils prophesized to Aeneas: '*I see wars, horrible wars, and the Tiber foaming with much blood*'. Also in the *Aeneid* we see the phrases '*Fortune favours the bold*', '*Fear gave wings to his feet*' and '*Night came down, and enfolded the earth in her dusky wings*'.

The Trojan Horse is one of classical literature's most enduring stories. Greek warriors, including Odysseus, hid inside the huge wooden horse, which was presented as an offering to Athena by a deserter from the Greek army. The Trojan priest Laocon's words of warning would prove prescient, as the Greeks crept out of the horse at night to attack Troy from within.

PUBLIUS OVIDIUS NASO (OVID)
43 BCE–c.18 CE

'Time the devourer of everything'

The Metamorphoses, 8 SCE

In Rome's 'Golden Age', Ovid wrote witty love poetry. In Rome, he began reading his works and by 13 BCE had become the city's most successful poet. For two decades he was feted, until Augustus suddenly exiled him, then aged 50. The circumstances are still unclear. Ovid spent his last decade writing elegiac poetry, pining for Rome, in Tomis (modern Costanza, in Romania).

Ovid was married three times by the age of 30, and his five-book collection, *The Amores*, reflects his attitudes towards love. He wrote about adultery, made illegal by Augustus, and his poem *'Ars Amatoria'* (*The Art of Love*), focused on seduction – it was probably the cause of his banishment: *'Rough seduction delights them. The boldness of near rape is a compliment.'* In his book of poems *Tristia*, written in exile, Ovid apologized for his immoral reputation: *'My life is respectable, my Muse is full of jesting. A book is not evidence of one's soul.'*

Of all his poetry, his masterpiece was the 15 books known as the *The Metamorphoses* (8 CE), which in the Middle Ages rivalled the Bible in popularity. His influence on Western art and literature is immense, *The Metamorphoses* being our best classical source of 250 Greco-Roman myths such as that of Daedalus and Icarus. Galinsky wrote *'The poem is the most comprehensive, creative mythological work that has come down to us from antiquity'*. Ovid was a major inspiration for Dante, Chaucer, Shakespeare, Spenser, Milton and others.

ᶜRerum gestarum divi Augusti, quibus orbem terrarum imperio populi Romani subiecit, et impensarum quas in rem publicam populumque Romanum fecit.ᵓ

(List of the actions done by divine Augustus, by which the whole world was put under the rule of the Roman people, and of the (personal) expenses he incurred in favour of the Roman Republic and people.)

This is the opening statement of the most important historical inscription of the ancient world, carved in Latin and Greek on the white marble temple known as Monumentum Ancyranum in Ankara, Turkey. In 14 CE, Augustus dictated a summary of his achievements, which was cast in two bronze columns for his mausoleum in Rome, the text also being sent to the provinces to spread the message throughout the whole empire. The bronze columns in Rome are lost. There are 35 short paragraphs in the inscription, mainly dealing with military expeditions, and Augustus often pointed out the peace ensuing from his strategic conquests.

Augustus was formerly known as Gaius Julius Octavius, or Octavian, when he took part in the power struggle following the assassination of Julius Caesar in 44 BCE. He found that he had been adopted by Caesar in Caesar's will, and used this fact to get backing from the people of Rome. When Mark Antony and Cleopatra died, Augustus took control of Egypt and Parthia and consolidated expansion on the Rhine. In 23 BCE he was honoured as 'Augustus', and in 2 BCE the Senate made him *pater patriae* (the father of the country). Augustus achieved a huge expansion of the Roman Empire.

'It is worthwhile for those persons who despise all things human in comparison with riches, and who suppose that there is no room either for exalted honour, or for virtue, except where riches abound in great profusion, to listen to the following...'

Ab Urbe Condita (A History of Rome), iii. 26–29

This is the beginning of Livy's account of Lucius Quinctius Cincinnatus (519–c.430 BCE), who was regarded as one of the heroes of early Rome, being a role model of virtue and simplicity. After serving as a consul in 460 BCE, he retired to his smallholding of about four acres.

In 457 BCE, the Aequians trapped the consul Minucius Esquilinus and the Roman army in the Alban Hills. Five cavalrymen escaped to warn Rome, and there was panic in the Senate. They authorized the other consul to nominate a dictator to save Rome and he nominated Cincinnatus, now 61 years old. Some senators found Cincinnatus ploughing and told him they hoped '*It might turn out well for him and his country*'. He went to the Forum, then called the people and asked everyone of military age to assemble in the Field of Mars.

Cincinnatus led the infantry and Tarquitius the cavalry, and the surprised Aequians were cut to pieces. Cincinnatus allowed the remaining enemy to pass under the yoke, submitting to Rome, and freed them. Next, Cincinnatus disbanded his army, resigned and returned to his small farm. He had served 16 days of the six months in power granted by the Senate. In 439, the 80-year-old was again asked to come out of retirement to put down a rebellion of plebeians, which he did before again retiring. He was known to be an inspiration to George Washington.

'Blessed are the meek: for they shall inherit the earth.'

'And seeing the multitudes, he went up into a mountain: and when he was set, his disciples came unto him: And he opened his mouth, and taught them, saying:

Blessed are the poor in spirit: for theirs is the kingdom of heaven.

Blessed are they that mourn: for they shall be comforted.

Blessed are the meek: for they shall inherit the earth.

Blessed are they which do hunger and thirst after righteousness: for they shall be filled.

Blessed are the merciful: for they shall obtain mercy.

Blessed are the pure in heart: for they shall see God.

Blessed are the peacemakers: for they shall be called the children of God.

Blessed are they which are persecuted for righteousness' sake: for theirs is the kingdom of heaven.

Blessed are ye, when men shall revile you, and persecute you, and shall say all manner of evil against you falsely, for my sake.'

Sermon on the Mount, Matthew 5.3

These verses are the beatitudes (blessings) of Jesus' Sermon on the Mount (*c.*30 CE) and the later verses also contain the Lord's Prayer and pacifist injunctions. Many Christians believe that the passage demonstrates that Christ was the true interpreter of the Law of Moses, and that it is a commentary on the Ten Commandments.

SENECA, THE YOUNGER
4–65 CE

'It is quality rather than quantity that matters'

Epistles 45, Line 1

Lucius Annaeus Seneca studied philosophy in Rome where he was influenced by the teachings of the Stoics, whose doctrine he would develop. In 49 CE he was elected as a magistrate and appointed as a tutor of Nero, the adopted child of the Emperor Claudius. When Claudius died in 54 CE, Nero was elected Emperor. Seneca was known for his honesty and moderation, which influenced the first five years of the Emperor Nero's rule. However, from 62 CE Seneca seemed to lose all his control over Nero. The fortune that Seneca had accumulated aroused Nero's jealousy, and the Emperor unsuccessfully tried to poison him.

Seneca sensibly retired from public life, and dedicated all his time to writing and studying philosophy, but many of his scientific works and discourses have been lost. In 65 CE he was involved in a failed conspiracy to murder Nero, and committed suicide. Seneca's remaining dialogues and moral treatises are more humane than dogmatic, reflecting his humility. Among his most celebrated works are his *Moral Essays*, 124 letters addressed to a friend called Lucilius, providing advice and wisdom on stoicism. He also wrote nine tragedies in verse, all adaptations of ancient Greek legends, the first four being based on the work of Euripides. Seneca is among the most brilliant of the Stoic philosophers, empiricists who believed in virtue being the sole good. Some of his other sayings passed down to the present day are:

> *'Modesty forbids what the law does not'*
>
> *'All art is imitation of nature'*
>
> *'The greatest remedy for anger is delay'*
>
> *'There is no great genius without some touch of madness'*

PETRONIUS
d.66 CE

'One good turn deserves another'

Satyricon, Sec. 45

Satyricon, a fragmentary manuscript of fiction in prose and verse, was written by Petronius Arbiter, Petronius the Judge, and is considered one of the early examples of the novel form.

Petronius served as proconsul of Bithynia and then became acting consul, or first magistrate, of Rome. A favourite of Emperor Nero, he was called the 'judge of elegance', but his position made him enemies. The commander of Nero's guard, Tigellinus, accused Petronius of treason. Arrested at Cumae in 66 CE, Petronius did not wait for the sentence, but committed suicide. He made an incision in his wrists, bandaged them up and conversed with friends, giving presents to some of his slaves but having others flogged. He disclosed Nero's excesses, naming the Emperor's male and female companions in debauchery, and sent his account to Nero before passing away.

The *Satyricon* is a realistic picture of the decadence and social manners of Rome under Nero. Petronius also wrote:

'*Not worth his salt*'

'*Education is a treasure*'

'*What the gods want happens soon*'

'*What power has law where only money rules?*'

'*You see a louse on someone else, but not a tick on yourself*'

Many sources attribute the following modern quote to his authorship: '*I was to learn later in life that we tend to meet any new situation by reorganizing; and a wonderful method it can be for creating the illusion of progress while producing confusion, inefficiency and demoralization.*'

Federico Fellini made the Oscar-nominated film *Satyricon* in 1969, loosely based on Petronius' writings and set in Nero's Rome.

'In these matters the only certainty is that nothing is certain'

Historia Naturalis 77CE

Gaius Plinius Secundus was a military man, encyclopedist and natural philosopher who wrote *Historia Naturalis*. Born at Como, he became a cavalry commander, but under Nero stayed out of trouble, away from Rome, until Vespasian's succession in 69 CE. Pliny then returned to Rome and eventually became a procurator and admiral.

Of all his writings, only the *Historia Naturalis* remains extant. Divided into 37 chapters, it was completed in 77 CE, and Pliny called it the study of '*the nature of things, that is, life*'. There are sections on cosmology, astronomy, geography, medicine, zoology, botany, agriculture and even descriptions of Druid rituals. By recording the Latin synonyms of Greek plant names, he made most of the plants mentioned in earlier Greek writings identifiable.

With the decline of the ancient world and the loss of the Greek texts on which Pliny had depended, his *Historia Naturalis* became a substitute for a general education, one of the most influential books ever written in Latin. In the Middle Ages many of the larger monastic libraries possessed copies, which ensured Pliny's place in European literature. He died while undertaking a rescue mission to Pompeii during the eruption of Vesuvius. Pliny also wrote:

'The best plan is to profit by the folly of others'

'From the end spring new beginnings'

'Home is where the heart is'

'There is always something new out of Africa'

'Dear me, I believe I am becoming a god'

Quoted in Gaius Suetonius Tranquillus, *c.69–c.122* CE,
The Lives of the Caesars, c.121 CE

The founder of the line of Flavian emperors of Rome, Vespasian stabilized the empire after Nero's excesses. He commanded the second legion in the invasion of Britain in 43 CE, and became a consul, then Governor of Africa. Trusted by Nero, he suppressed the Jewish Revolt of 66–70 CE. Following Nero's death in 68 CE, he secured the approval of the Senate in 70 CE, after his forces took Rome in 69 CE. In 70 CE, his son Titus took Jerusalem and destroyed the Temple, and the spoils were used to finance the building of the Coliseum. Under Vespasian, Rome settled down after the Civil Wars, and his son Titus succeeded him.

Vespasian set an example by living a simple life, leading to Tacitus observing that he was the first man to improve after becoming Emperor. Titus complained about a tax on public lavatories, but Vespasian told him *'Money has no smell'*. In 79 CE, Vespasian died of an intestinal inflammation which led to excessive diarrhoea. Suetonius recorded his last words as *'Væ, puto deus fio'* (*Dear me, I believe I am becoming a god*). Vespasian had come from a relatively humble background, and thus mocked the Roman tendency to turn dead emperors into gods. However, he was indeed deified. He had brought Rome through bitter civil war and left the empire stronger than ever, but by declaring, *'My sons will succeed me, or no one will'* tried to establish hereditary rule.

PLINY THE YOUNGER
63–c.113 CE

'Augustus, the child of fortune, lived to perfect what Julius [Caesar] had only designed'

Letters

Gaius Caecilius Secundus changed his name to Gaius Plinius Caecilius Secundus (Pliny the Younger) upon inheriting the full estate of his uncle Pliny the Elder in 79 CE. (He had been adopted by his uncle when orphaned.)

Pliny the Younger was a lawyer, administrator, author and a natural philosopher of Ancient Rome, in which he served as a tribune, prefect, consul and ambassador. Pliny's letters are preserved in ten books, the first nine containing 247 personal letters, and the tenth being his official correspondence with Trajan from Bithynia. The above quotation means that Augustus completed Julius Caesar's efforts in building the Roman Empire and solidifying power in a person rather than in the Senate.

Pliny the Younger was with his uncle on the mission to Pompeii, and describes the events there during the eruption and his uncle's death. His collection of letters offers insights into public and private life and is the best source available for the political and social history of Rome at its height of power. Pliny the Younger was sent by Emperor Trajan in 110 CE to investigate corruption in Bithynia, where he died. Other quotes from Pliny the Younger are:

'An object in possession seldom retains the same charm that it had in pursuit'

'Joking set aside'

'That indolent but agreeable condition of doing nothing'

'And as in men's bodies, so in government, that disease is most serious which proceeds from the head'

'The happier the time, the quicker it passes'

'He has no fault except that he has no fault'

'They make it a wilderness and call it peace'

Speaking of the destruction of war in the *Agricola*

Tacitus is known for his remaining fragments of the history of the Roman Empire: the *Annals* (covering 14–68 CE) and the *Histories* (69–96 CE). He is also the author of the *Agricola*, a biography of his father-in-law, and the *Germania*. Tacitus ranks highly among men of letters of all ages, and lived through the reigns of the emperors Nero, Galba, Otho, Vitellius, Vespasian, Titus, Domitian, Nerva and Trajan. He was concerned with the concentration of power into the hands of emperors, displaying a particular hatred for Tiberius (reigned 14–37 CE), and his writings are filled with tales of corruption and tyranny. Tacitus survived several reigns of terror, becoming a senator, then a consul in 97 CE, and in 112 CE becoming Governor of Western Anatolia. Pliny the Younger was a friend who greatly admired him. Tacitus called Petronius *'the arbiter of taste and elegance'* at court and tells us:

'Rumour is not always wrong'

'The more corrupt the state, the more numerous the laws'

'The gods are on the side of the stronger'

'It is part of human nature to hate the man you have hurt'

In the *Annals* we read: *'The originator of this name, Christ, was sentenced to torture by Procurator Pontius Pilate, during the reign of Tiberius, but although checked for a moment, the deadly cult erupted again, not just in Judaea, the source of its evil, but even in Rome, where all the sins and scandals of the world gather and are glorified.'*

PLUTARCH
c.46–c.120 CE

'I am writing biography, not history'

'I am writing biography, not history, and the truth is that the
most brilliant exploits often tell us nothing of the virtues or
vices of the men who performed them, while on the other hand
a chance remark or a joke may reveal far more of a man's
character than the mere feat of winning battles in which
thousands fall, or of marshalling great armies, or laying siege
to cities.'

Parallel Lives: Alexander

Plutarch was a Greek of Chaeroneia, the senior priest
of Apollo at Delphi and wrote the famous *Parallel Lives*. These
are character studies of famous Greeks and Romans in pairs,
from Theseus to Plutarch's own era. There were in all some
50 *Lives*, of which 14 are lost. His *Roman Apophthegms* is
dedicated to the Emperor Trajan, who died in 117 CE. Nothing
else is known of the greatest of all biographers, but it has been
said that if we could save but one book in the world, the most
valuable to preserve would be his unique record of antiquity.

His ethical writings, *Moralia* (*Customs and Mores*), are a brilliant description of
the manners and thought of his day. It is Plutarch who first tells us '*He is a fool
who lets slip a bird in the hand for a bird in the bush*' and '*Ill news goes quick and far*'.
An example of his style is: '*A prating barber asked Archelaus how he would be
trimmed. He answered "In silence".*'

GAIUS SUETONIUS TRANQUILLUS
c.69-c.122 CE

'The Ides of March have come'

'Several victims were then sacrificed, and despite consistently unfavourable omens, he (Julius Caesar) entered the House, deriding Spurinna as a false prophet. "The Ides of March have come," he said. "Yes, they have come," replied Spurinna, "but they have not yet gone."'

The Lives of the Caesars – Julius Caesar, Chapter 81, c.121 CE

This eminent Roman historian was the contemporary of Tacitus and Pliny the Younger, and to him we owe the account of *The Lives of the Caesars*.

Suetonius' father was a military tribune, and Suetonius was the Magister Epistolarum (private secretary in charge of imperial correspondence) to Emperor Hadrian from 117–138 CE. In this position he had unrivalled access to the imperial archives and other information. He also served under Emperor Trajan. It seems he was dismissed by Hadrian for not showing enough respect to Hadrian's wife when the Emperor was in Britain. *The Lives* is full of personal anecdotes, which add to their fascination, and covers ground that Tacitus omits. Some of Suetonius' other works are still extant, but many have been lost.

Regarding Emperor Claudius (41–54 CE) and the Riot of Rome in 49 CE, Suetonius wrote '*As the Jews were making constant disturbances at the instigation of Chrestus (Christ), he (Claudius) expelled them from Rome*'. He also wrote about the great fire of Rome in 64 CE: '*Punishment by Nero was inflicted on the Christians, a class of men given to a new and mischievous superstition.*' From Suetonius we have some of the wonderful stories of vice and virtue of the times. He describes Caligula's plan to make his horse a consul, Nero singing while Rome burns and Tiberius' vices in the swimming pool, as well as descriptions of Augustus' redevelopment of Rome: '*He found a city built of brick; he left it built of marble.*'

DECIMUS IUNIUS IUVENALIS (JUVENAL)
c.65–c.128 CE

'Quis custodiet ipsos custodes?'
(Who will guard the guards themselves?)

"'Bolt her in, keep her indoors.' But who will guard the guards
themselves? Your wife arranges accordingly and begins with them.'

Satires

This passage shows Juvenal's distaste with the declining morals of Rome.
He was the most powerful of all the Roman satirists, pouring his scorn on the
social vices of the early empire. To avoid censorship, Juvenal targeted people who
had lived a century before him, but was trying to describe the faults of his era.
Underlying all his writing is a strong dislike of the imperial system, and regret for
the loss of Republican Rome, run by Roman citizens with simple tastes. In his
later satires Juvenal combines, often with personal invective, many passages of
great beauty describing the ideal life of virtue and simple manners.

Juvenal did not dedicate his work, so probably did not have a patron. He was sent
against his will to Egypt, and lived for some time at Aquinum in Latium. We know
little more of his life than that he endured the reign of Domitian, and was still
alive under Hadrian. The *Satires* consist of 16 satires, varying in length from
60 to 660 lines, on all aspects of life, and some of his phrases are still used today:

'A rare bird upon the earth, and exceedingly like a black swan'

'Our prayers should be for a sound mind in a healthy body'

'Everything is Greek, when it is more shameful to be ignorant
of Latin'

'Revenge is always the weak pleasure of a little and narrow mind'

'Ask not what your country can do for you, ask what you can do for
your country'

AKIBA BEN JOSEPH
c.50–c.135 CE

'The paper burns, but the words fly free'

His reputed last words

An illiterate shepherd, Akiba married late to a wealthy man's daughter, Rachel, who married him on condition that he devote himself to learning. Rachel was banished by her father for marrying the poverty-stricken Akiba. When their child started school, Akiba accompanied him and so learned to read. Aged 40 he was admitted to the rabbinical academy of a Pharisaic teacher, and found himself championing the poor against the rich. In 96 CE he went to Rome with other rabbis to petition the Emperor Domitian to revoke anti-Jewish laws. Fortunately Akiba received a bequest from a Jewish convert in Rome, which allowed him to set up an academy near Jaffa, where he attracted thousands of students.

Akiba developed a new method of textual interpretation which attached significance to every word of the Hebrew scriptures, and this allowed Akiba to adjust the law to the needs of the times. He also rearranged the haphazard organization of Oral Law. This system was further developed by his disciple, Rabbi Meir, and it was set up in its present form, the *Mishnah*, by Judah I around 200 CE. Akiba played an important role in the Bar Kochba revolt against Rome (132–135 CE) and insisted on continuing to teach the Law, though it was a capital offence. He was tortured and executed by the Romans, being burnt at the stake with the *Shema Yisroel* ('Hear O Israel', Deuteronomy 6.4), Israel's profession of faith, on his lips.

MARCUS AURELIUS
121–180 CE

'Nowhere can man find a quieter or more untroubled retreat than in his own soul'

'Men seek seclusion in the wilderness, by the seashore, or in the mountains – a dream you have cherished only too fondly yourself. Nowhere can man find a quieter or more untroubled retreat than in his own soul... Avail yourself often, then, of this retirement, and so continually renew yourself.'

Meditations

Roman Emperor from 161–180 CE, he was born Marcus Annius Catilius Severus, and renamed when Emperor as Marcus Antoninus Aurelius Augustus. His *Vita* in the *Historia Augusta* records that '*Plato's judgment was always on his lips, that states flourished if philosophers ruled or rulers were philosophers*'. He embodied Plato's ideal of the philosopher king, defending Rome for his entire rule, but also concerned with social justice and welfare. He sold his own possessions to alleviate people's suffering from famine and plague (from which he died), and left behind a corpus of writing which offers us some timeless wisdom. His charitable *Meditations of Stoic Philosophy* were written when he was campaigning on the borders of the empire, against the Parthians, Gauls and others. In it we read:

'*Receive wealth or prosperity without arrogance; and be ready to let it go*'

'*Time is a sort of river of passing events, and strong is its current; no sooner is a thing brought to sight than it is swept by and another takes its place, and this too will be swept away*'

'*It is not death that a man should fear, but he should fear never beginning to live*'

'*When you arise in the morning, think of what a precious privilege it is to be alive – to breathe, to think, to enjoy, to love*'

QUINTUS SEPTIMIUS FLORENS TERTULLIANUS (TERTULLIAN)
155/160–222/230 CE

'Out of the frying pan into the fire'

This quote is a translation of a sarcastic note by Tertullian, '*De calcaria in carbonariam*', regarding the belief of Apelles that Christ had an astral body made of superior substance, and comparing the Incarnation to the appearance of the angel to Abraham.

Quintus Septimius Florens Tertullianus was born in Carthage. Possibly the son of a centurion in the consular service, he was struck by the courage that Christians showed when they were executed or attacked and killed by wild animals in the games. He became a Christian around 197 CE and his conversion was decisive, transforming his personality. He thus said that '*Christians are made, not born*'. Tertullian was the first Christian writer to write in Latin, in his defence of the religion, so is sometimes known as the 'Father of the Latin Church'. He wrote that '*It is no religion to compel religion*' and '*As often as we are mown down by you, the more we shall grow in numbers; the blood of Christians is seed*'. He depicted Rome as '*the Babylon of the Apocalypse*', drunk with the blood of martyred saints.

St Jerome said that Tertullian was also a brilliant speaker and lived to an old age. Thirty-one of his works still exist, but many of his books are recorded as being lost, including all those he wrote in Greek. His most important work is the *Apologeticum*, in defence of the Christians. In his *Adversus Praxean*, the doctrine of the Trinity comes into clear focus for the first time. At this time he was a successful lawyer in Rome, in the reign of Marcus Aurelius. Tertullian has been called '*the first Protestant*', as he noted that the real church was not a conclave of bishops, but the people who possessed the Holy Spirit.

ST AUGUSTINE OF HIPPO
354–430 CE

'There is no salvation outside the church'

On Baptism: Against the Donatists IV, c.400 CE

St Augustine was born Aurelius Augustinus in the Roman-controlled Numidia (now Algeria); his mother was St Monica and his father a pagan. Augustine lost his faith, leading a dissolute life and living with a Carthaginian woman from the ages of 15 to 30, by whom he had a son. He wrote in his *Confessions* of 397/398 CE, '*God give me chastity and continence, but not yet*'. He taught rhetoric at Carthage and Milan, and became a Manichean until he was baptized by St Ambrose of Milan. On his mother's death Augustine returned to Africa, gave all his possessions to the poor and founded a monastery at Hippo, becoming its bishop in 396 CE at the age of 42.

From this point he became the leading theologian of the orthodox Catholic Church, and more than anyone is responsible for the centralization of Christian power in Rome. He wanted one central source with one central message for the infant religion, and in his *Sermons* of c.400 CE stated: '*Rome has spoken. The case is concluded.*' The Briton Pelagius had threatened to break up the church with his teachings that man could be good of his own free will, and could go to heaven without needing the power structure of the Roman church. Pelagius was condemned by Pope Innocent I, and then re-instated by Pope Zosimus. Augustine refused to accept the judgment of Zosimus, and ultimately won the day against the Pelagian Heresy, giving Catholicism a rigidity that ensured its survival. However, this inflexibility to new ideas and thoughts held back scientific advance until the Renaissance.

Augustus wrote '*The good Christian should beware of mathematicians, and all those who make empty prophecies. The danger already exists that mathematicians have made a covenant with the Devil to darken the spirit and to confine man in the bonds of Hell.*'

'Christ in the heart of everyone who thinks of me'

'I bind to myself to-day
The strong virtue of the Invocation
of the Trinity:
I believe the Trinity in the Unity
The Creator of the Universe.

I bind to myself to-day
The virtue of the Incarnation of
Christ with His Baptism,
The virtue of His crucifixion with
His burial,
The virtue of His Resurrection with
His Ascension,
The virtue of His coming on the
Judgment Day.

I bind to myself to-day
The power of Heaven,
The light of the sun,
The brightness of the moon,
The splendour of fire,

The flashing of lightning,
The swiftness of wind,
The depth of sea,
The stability of earth,
The compactness of rocks.

Christ with me, Christ
before me,
Christ behind me, Christ
within me,
Christ beneath me, Christ above me,
Christ at my right, Christ at my left,
Christ in the fort,
Christ in the chariot seat,
Christ in the poopdeck,
Christ in the heart of everyone who
thinks of me,
Christ in the mouth of everyone
who speaks to me,
Christ in every eye that sees me,
Christ in every ear that hears me.'

St Patrick's Lorica (Breastplate), *c*.433

Born a Christian in Wales or south-west Scotland, St Patrick was captured by Irish pirates as a 16-year-old and treated as a slave for six years before escaping to Wales. He received priestly training at Llanilltud Fawr (Llantwit Major) before returning to Ireland around 431–433 and evangelizing the barbarian Irish from a base in Armagh. The druids and magicians fought to maintain their control over the Irish, but Patrick's prayer and faith triumphed. On Easter Day 433, after winning the Irish clan chieftains over to Christianity, St Patrick is said to have plucked a shamrock and explained by its triple leaf and single stem the Blessed Trinity. This trefoil, called 'Patrick's Cross', became the symbol both of the saint and of Ireland itself. St Patrick's prayer is believed to have been composed in preparation for his victory over paganism.

GILDAS BADONICUS
*c.*498–*c.*570 or 583 CE

'Death has entered through the windows of their pride'

'Abstinence from bodily food is useless without charity.
Those who do not fast unduly or obtain overmuch from God's
creation, while being careful within the sight of God to preserve
within them a clean heart (on which, as they know, their life
ultimately depends), are better than those who do not eat flesh
or take pleasure in the food of this world, or travel in carriages
or on horseback, and so regard themselves as superior to the
rest of men: to these death has entered through the windows
of their pride.'

Letter fragment

The first British historian, Gildas is regarded as a saint
in the Celtic and Breton churches. He castigated the five
remaining British Christian kings of Wales and the West
Country for their failure against the invading Barbarian
Germanic tribes, in *De Excidio et Conquesta Britanniae*
(*Concerning the Ruin and Conquest of Britain*), written in about
540 BCE. Gildas described the heathen attack: '*In the midst of
the streets lay the tops of lofty towers, tumbled to the ground, stones
of high walls, holy altars, fragments of human bodies, covered
with livid clots of coagulated blood, looking as if they had been squeezed together
in a press; and with no chance of being buried, save in the ruins of houses, or in the
ravening bellies of wild beasts and birds.*'

Gildas studied at Llanilltud Fawr (Llantwit Major) in Wales with the Welsh saints
David, Paul and Samson, and had helped develop the Irish Church. With many
others, he fled to Brittany, France, where he is remembered as a saint with many
church dedications, and where he built a great monastery at Gildas-de-Rhuys in
the Morbihan district.

THE VENERABLE BEDE
672/673–735 CE

'This life of man appears for a short space but of what went before or what is to follow we are ignorant'

'The present life of man, O king, seems to me, in comparison with that time which is unknown to us, like to the swift flight of a sparrow through the room wherein you sit at supper in winter amid your officers and ministers, with a good fire in the midst whilst the storms of rain and snow prevail abroad; the sparrow, I say, flying in at one door and immediately out of another, whilst he is within is safe from the wintry storm but after a short space of fair weather he immediately vanishes out of your sight into the dark winter from which he has emerged. So this life of man appears for a short space but of what went before or what is to follow we are ignorant. If, therefore, this new doctrine contains something more certain, it seems justly to deserve to be followed'

Historia Ecclesiastica Gentis Anglorum (Ecclesiastical History of the English People), passage on The Conversion of Northumbria, 731 CE

One of King Edwin of Northumbria's chief ministers is arguing that the Barbarian king should convert to Christianity. His image of a bird flitting through a feasting hall has been copied by other writers such as Turgenev. For many of the events of these Dark Ages in England, Bede is our only source. He was an Anglo-Saxon chronicler and theologian, and a monk at Jarrow, who is notable also as the first person to date events from the birth of Christ.

OMAR KHAYYÁM
1048–1122 CE

'The moving finger writes'

'The Moving Finger writes; and, having writ,
Moves on: nor all thy Piety nor Wit
Shall lure it back to cancel half a Line
Nor all thy Tears wash out a Word of it.'

The Rubáiyát of Omar Khayyám

Ghiyas Od-Din Abol-Fath Omar ibn Ebrahim Khayyám Neyshaburi was a Persian mathematician, astronomer, philosopher and poet. He is best known for the poem translated as *The Rubáiyát of Omar Khayyám*, made popular by the translation into English by Edward Fitzgerald (1809–1883). It appears that as an astronomer, Khayyám proposed that the Earth was not the centre of the universe centuries before Copernicus, and he contributed to the reform of the calendar. His *Treatise on Demonstration of Problems of Algebra* gave a geometric method for the solution of cubic equations, and helped make his name as a leading mathematician.

Khayyám also built an observatory, and measured the solar year to a precision of a one-hour error every 5,500 years. The Gregorian Calendar, 400 years later, has a 24-hour error every 3,330 years. His famous star chart has been lost, but it appears that many of his ideas have passed down to other scholars over the centuries. Another well-known quatrain of his reads:

'Here with a loaf of bread beneath the bough,
A Flask of Wine, a Book of Verse – and Thou
Beside me singing in the Wilderness –
And Wilderness is Paradise enow.'

'Of all the wretched women I am the most wretched and amongst the unhappy I am the unhappiest'

'O merciless mercy!... Of all the wretched women I am the most wretched and amongst the unhappy I am the unhappiest. The higher I was exulted when you preferred me above all other women, the greater my suffering over my own fall and yours, when I was flung down; for the higher the ascent the heavier the fall. Has fortune ever set any great or noble woman over me and made her my equal, only to be similarly cast down and crushed with grief?... To make me the saddest of all women she first made me blessed above all, so that when I thought how much I had lost, my consuming grief would match my crushing loss, and my sorrow for what was taken from me would be the greater for the fuller joy of possession which had gone before; and so that the happiness of supreme ecstasy would end in the supreme bitterness of sorrow.'

Part of love letter written to Peter Abelard (1079–1142),
probably written between 1132 and 1142

Aged 37, Peter Abelard, one of the most brilliant philosophers and theologians of his day, met Heloise. In 1117 Heloise was his private pupil, half his age, and they fell in love but she became pregnant. They married secretly as he would otherwise lose his post as Canon at Notre Dame Cathedral. He was beaten, castrated and sent to a monastery, whilst Heloise was sent to a convent, eventually becoming an abbess. In her letters, she relates her fear of outliving her only true love. Upon her death, she was buried next to him, and they are in a single tomb in the Père Lachaise Cemetery in Paris.

'For the name of Jesus and the protection of the church I am ready to embrace death'

His last words

The last words of Thomas Becket (later known as a'Becket) have also been recorded as '*I commend myself to God, the Blessed Mary, St Denis, and the patron saints of this Church*'.

Appointed Chancellor of England by Henry II in 1154, he was an excellent administrator and a loyal friend, and when the Archbishop of Canterbury died in 1161, Henry believed that Becket would be the ideal man to give him an agreeable and pliable church. Henry petitioned the Pope who agreed with Becket's appointment. However, Becket, busy at court, had never been ordained, so Becket was first invested as a priest. The next day he was ordained a bishop, and that afternoon, 2 June 1162, he was made Archbishop of Canterbury. Becket now took the church's side in disputes, infuriating Henry, who had no real power to remove him.

However, Becket was forced to flee to France in 1164 and was exiled there until 1170. He was reconciled with King Henry, but returning to Canterbury, he refused to absolve two bishops who had supported Henry. The king was still in France when he raged: '*What sluggards, what cowards have I brought up in my court, who care nothing for their allegiance to their lord? Who will rid me of this meddlesome priest?*' Four of his knights then rode to Canterbury Cathedral and cut Becket to death when he sought refuge in the cathedral. Becket is said to have told them: '*If all the swords in England were pointed against my head, your threats would not move me.*' On his death, Becket was declared a martyr and Henry was threatened with excommunication and forced to do public penance, walking barefoot through Canterbury while being beaten by monks with sticks.

ST FRANCIS
1182–1226

'Where there is hatred, let me sow love; where there is injury, pardon; where there is doubt, faith'

'Lord, make me an instrument of your peace,
where there is hatred, let me sow love;
where there is injury, pardon;
where there is doubt, faith;
where there is despair, hope;
where there is darkness, light;
where there is sadness, joy.
O Divine Master, grant that I may not so much seek to be
consoled as to console;
to be understood as to understand;
to be loved as to love.
For it is in giving that we receive;
it is in pardoning that we are pardoned;
and it is in dying that we are born to eternal life.'

Prayer of St Francis, 1205

St Francis was born Giovanni Bernadone at Assisi. His merchant father named him Francesco (little Frenchman) on his return from a trading visit to France, having missed his son's birth. In 1201, Francesco spent a year in prison after being captured on a military expedition to Perugia. After a carefree youth as a troubadour, he turned his back upon his inherited wealth and gave himself to God. Francesco had been troubled by his conscience for some time, and had a religious experience in 1205 in Spoleto, on his way to again enlist in the army. He next nursed lepers, and upon a pilgrimage to Rome had another vision at the Church of San Damiano. The Icon of Christ Crucified came to life and told Francesco to 'repair His house'. The saint understood the message to be to take the church back to Christ's ways of simplicity and humility.

Known for his simple ways and as the patron saint of animals and Italy, Francesco established the Order of Friars Minor, now known as the Franciscans. A mystic and poet, he is possibly the most loved of all the Catholic saints.

WILLIAM WALLACE
c.1270–1305

'I have brought you to the ring, now dance if you can'

Statement about Edward I before the Battle of Falkirk, quoted in
The Story of England, Samuel B. Harding, 1909

In 1296, King Edward I of England summoned 2,000 Scottish landowners and senior clergy to Berwick to sign an oath of loyalty to him, having taken the kingship of Scotland from John Balliol. Wallace joined with Andrew Murray to free the country from the new and unwanted English domination. The Battle of Stirling Bridge in 1297 was Wallace's greatest triumph, when the Earl of Surrey's army fled the field. In 1298, Edward I met Wallace's forces at Falkirk, where Welsh archers tipped the balance of the fighting in favour of the English. Wallace escaped and became a fugitive, taking part in a number of minor battles, but was betrayed and captured in 1305. He was denied a defence and accused of treason, to which he responded:

'I can not be a traitor, for I owe him no allegiance. He is not my Sovereign; he never received my homage; and whilst life is in this persecuted body, he never shall receive it. To the other points whereof I am accused, I freely confess them all. As Governor of my country I have been an enemy to its enemies; I have slain the English; I have mortally opposed the English King; I have stormed and taken the towns and castles which he unjustly claimed as his own. If I or my soldiers have plundered or done injury to the houses or ministers of religion, I repent me of my sin; but it is not of Edward of England I shall ask pardon.'

Wallace was then pulled by horses and hung, drawn and quartered. His clan's motto is 'For Freedom'.

JACQUES DEMOLAY
c.1245–1314

'Let evil swiftly befall those who have wrongly condemned us – God will avenge us'

His last words at the stake

Jacques DeMolay was elected Master of the Knights Templar shortly after the order had been defeated by the Muslims and expelled from the Holy Land. The Templars' headquarters was temporarily established in Cyprus, and many Templars returned to the continent, while DeMolay sought support for a new Crusade to recapture Jerusalem. In 1307, he was summoned to France by Pope Clement V, the French puppet that Philippe IV had installed at Avignon, ostensibly to discuss combining with the Knights Hospitaller for a new crusade. Philippe IV and other French nobles were jealous of the wealth and lands of the Templars, and Clement informed DeMolay that Philippe had made charges of Templar homosexuality, heresy and blasphemy. Philippe had previously seized all the wealth of French Jews. DeMolay challenged the King to make the charges public, and after weeks of secret plotting Philippe suddenly arrested almost 5,000 Templars. Clement initially chose not to intervene, but eventually sided with the King.

The next seven years of Templar imprisonment included continuous torture, confessions and executions until Philippe felt he had enough power to kill DeMolay. During years of torture, DeMolay continued to be loyal to his order, refusing to disclose the location of its funds. With Geoffroy de Charney, he was slowly roasted to death over a hot, smokeless fire. All Templar lands and known wealth were confiscated. A month later, Pope Clement V died of cancer, and within seven months, Philippe died in a hunting accident: the last Grand Master's dying words had come true. In 2002, a document from 1308 confirming Pope Clement's absolution for DeMolay and other Templars was found in the Vatican Secret Archives.

DANTE
1265–1321

'Abandon hope, all ye who enter here'

The supposed inscription at the entrance to Hell,
The Divine Comedy c.1307/1308–c.1320/1321

Dante was born in Florence to a noble but impoverished family, and became a poet, moral philosopher, prose writer, literary theorist, political thinker and one of the great figures of world literature. His work was inspired by the Florentine noblewoman Beatrice Portinari – Dante was nine when he first met her in 1274, and saw her only twice more before her death 16 years later, but never spoke to her. He sought distraction from his adoration by writing *La Vita Nuova* (*The New Life*) soon after her death. It tells of the course of his love for Beatrice, her death, and his wish to write a work to her memory, and is one of the greatest verse sequences in European literature.

His epic masterpiece, *La Divina Commedia* (*The Divine Comedy*) recounts the poet's imaginary journey through Hell, Purgatory and Heaven. Beatrice is an instrument of the Divine Will, and his guide through Heaven – '*L'esperienza de questa dolce vita*' (*The experience of this sweet life*). It is thus an optimistic work, leading him to his beloved Beatrice in Paradise, but begins bleakly, as evidenced by the above inscription at the entrance to Hell – '*The darkest places in hell are reserved for those who maintain their neutrality in times of moral crisis*'. He wrote in a new language he called 'Italian', based on Tuscan dialect, breaking from the custom of publishing in only Latin.

Dante became involved in the war between the Guelphs and the Ghibellines, becoming a leading White Guelph (who opposed Pope Boniface VIII's influence). When the Black Guelphs assumed power in 1302, Dante was condemned to exile from his beloved Florence. He lived in Verona and wandered across Europe before settling in Ravenna, where he is buried.

'I have not told half of what I saw'

Remark made in 1324, quoted in *The Story of Civilization*, William Durant, 1935

Marco Polo was born into a wealthy Venetian merchant family. His father and uncle, both jewel merchants, left Venice in 1260 and met the Mongol Emperor of China, Kublai Khan, who allowed them to return in 1269 to persuade the Pope to send Christian scholars back to him. In 1271, they set off again with Marco and two missionaries, reaching Kublai Khan's summer court in 1275. For 17 years they lived in his empire, and Marco was sent on missions across China. In 1292, the Polo family offered to accompany a Mongol princess to Persia and the party sailed from China to the Persian Gulf. After leaving the princess, the Polos travelled overland to Constantinople and then to Venice, arriving home in 1295.

In 1298, Marco was captured by the Genoese in a naval battle between Venice and Genoa. In prison, his stories caught the imagination of a prisoner from Pisa, Rustichello, who began to write them down. The resulting book was wildly popular and was translated into many languages, usually as *The Travels of Marco Polo*. On his eventual release, Marco Polo returned to Venice, where he remained for the rest of his life. Of Kublai Khan, the *Travels* tell us: '*He is the most potent man, as regards forces and lands and treasure that exists in the world.*' Polo stated that the capital of China, Cambaluc (now Beijing) was '*arrayed in squares just like a chessboard*' and that in the Khan's palace there was '*nothing to be seen anywhere but gold and pictures*'. This description inspired Coleridge's poem beginning '*In Xanadu did Kubla Khan a stately pleasure-dome decree*'.

GIOVANNI BOCCACCIO
1313–1375

'Do as we say, and not as we do'

The Decameron, Third Day, Story VII, *c.*1348–*c.*1353

Born in Paris, the illegitimate son of a merchant, Boccaccio moved to Florence as a child. Aged 23, he met Maria d'Aquino, the illegitimate daughter of King Robert in Naples, with whom he fell in love. Although she was married, they had an affair and she inspired him to write in prose. The next year, 1338, he was recalled to Florence by his ageing father, and carried on writing. In 1344 he obtained his father's permission to return to Naples and wrote *La Fiammetta*, dedicated to his mistress, who died in the Black Death of 1348.

Returning to Florence, Boccaccio became a leading humanist, meeting Petrarch and Dante, and wrote *The Decameron*, a collection of 100 novellas. It is an allegory dealing with all aspects of love, beginning with a description of the Black Death that killed his greatest love, and following a group of seven men and three women who flee from Florence to a rural villa. To pass the time, each person tells one story for each day in the villa, so 100 tales are recounted in 10 days. Almost all the plots were borrowed, from France, Persia, Spain, second-century Ephesus and Latin and Sanskrit sources. Boccaccio is accounted one of the founders of the Renaissance, and his use of the vernacular influenced later writers, including Chaucer. The quotation represents an attack upon the impious friars and churchmen of Boccaccio's day: '*And when they are taken to task for these things, and many other unseemly things that they do, they think that they have sufficiently discharged all their grave burdens to reply "Do as we say and not as we do" – as if it were possible for the sheep to be more constant and stouter against temptation than the shepherds.*'

THOMAS À KEMPIS
c.1379/80-1471

'O quam cito transit gloria mundi'
(O how quickly passes away the glory of the earth)
The Imitation of Christ, 1414–c.1424

This line, usually misquoted as '*Sic transit Gloria mundi*' (*thus passes the glory of the world*) has been spoken at the coronation of popes since 1409.

Thomas à Kempis (originally Thomas Haemerkken) was a Catholic monk and author of *The Imitation of Christ*, one of the best-known Christian books of devotion. He was born in Cleves and buried in Utrecht. It seems he was buried alive, as splinters were later found embedded under the fingernails of his corpse, and he was denied canonization on the grounds that a saint would not fight death in this way. He received priest's orders at Zwolle in 1413 and was made sub-prior in 1429, spending his life in devotion and copying out the Bible at least four times.

His writings are all of a devotional character, including letters, sermons and biographies. *The Imitation of Christ* instructed the reader to emulate Christ in order to achieve spiritual perfection. In it, we read:

'*For man proposeth, but God disposeth*'

'*At the Day of Judgment we shall not be asked what we have read but what we have done*'

'*If, however, you seek Jesus in all things, you will surely find Him*'

'*But when he [man] shall have been taken from sight, he quickly goes also out of mind*'

'*Of two evils, the lesser is always to be chosen*'

JOAN OF ARC
c.1412–1431

'Hold the cross high so I may see it through the flames!'

Her attributed last words at the stake

At her trial in 1431, Joan of Arc said, '*I was in my thirteenth year when God sent a voice to guide me. At first, I was very much frightened. The voice came towards the hour of noon, in summer, in my father's garden... If I said that God did not send me, I should condemn myself; truly God did send me.*'

The voices told her to serve France against the English, and she convinced the Dauphin to allow her to lead the army, lifting the Siege of Orleans and winning at Troyes and Patay. The victory allowed the Dauphin to be crowned Charles VII, with Joan at his side at Rheims Cathedral. She was captured in 1430 by Burgundians, possibly by Charles' treachery, and handed over to the English. She was interrogated for over a year, tried for heresy and witchcraft, and promised never to wear a man's clothes again. However, while still in prison with not enough evidence to kill her, she again wore men's clothing, probably having been tricked into doing so as there was nothing else to wear. She was declared a heretic and burned in Rouen marketplace, and her ashes thrown in the Seine. Charles VII did not attempt to come to her assistance. Twenty-five years later, the Pope declared her innocent, and she was canonized in 1920.

SIR THOMAS MALORY
c.1405–1471

'Whoso pulleth out this sword of this stone and anvil, is rightwise King born of all England'

Le Morte d'Arthur, Book I, Chapter V, c.1451–1469 (first published 1485)

Le Morte d'Arthur was written during Malory's long imprisonment in Newgate Prison from 1451. A follower of the Earl of Warwick, he had been captured during the Wars of the Roses and was seemingly a violent, rather than a chivalrous, individual. His prose epic recounts the legends of King Arthur and his Knights of the Round Table, the search for the Holy Grail, the betrayal of Sir Lancelot and Guinevere, the bravery of Sir Galahad, the Sword in the Stone, the Lady of the Lake, the Fisher King, the court at Camelot, the Round Table, Tristan and Isolde, Merlin the magician and Morgan le Fay the enchantress. It is generally a free translation of various French romances, themselves based on Breton and Welsh sources in the *Mabinogion*. They are the most powerful set of legends in Western literature, and the inspiration of countless films, paintings and books:

> 'Through this man [Launcelot] and me [Guenevere] hath all this war been wrought, and the death of the most noblest knights of the world; for through our love that we have loved together is my most noble lord slain.'

> 'In the midst of the lake Arthur was aware of an arm clothed in white samite, that held a fair sword in that hand.'

Malory's original manuscript was called *The Book of King Arthur and His Noble Knights of the Round Table*, made up of eight more or less separate romances. William Caxton printed it in 1485 and gave it the misleading title of *Le Morte d'Arthur* (*The Death of Arthur*). It is generally regarded as the most significant accomplishment in English literature between the works of Chaucer and those of Shakespeare.

DESIDERIUS ERASMUS
1466/1469–1536

'In the country of the blind, the one-eyed man is king'

Adagia, Book 3, Century 4, No. 96, 1500

Born Gerrit Gerritszoon in Rotterdam, Erasmus was illegitimate, and on his parents' death his guardians insisted upon him entering a monastery. He was so disenchanted with the behaviour of the monks that he criticized so-called 'men of God' and academics for the rest of his life. He took priest's orders, teaching for a living in Paris, and lived at Oxford for two years before returning to Paris in 1500. He published *Adagia*, his collection of Greek and Latin adages, and *Enchiridion Militis Christiani* (*The Handbook of the Christian Soldier*), and in 1506 visited England, Padua and Rome. He made England his home once more, becoming Professor of Greek and Divinity at Cambridge, and published the satire *Encomium Moriae* (1509), mocking kings and churchmen alike. From 1514 he lived in Basel and England, then moved to Louvain (Leuven) in 1517. In the first edition of *Adagia*, there were only 800 Greek and Latin adages, which had expanded to 4,658 by the time of Erasmus' death. In the same passage of the *Adagia* is a variant: '*Among the blind, the squinter rules*'. Thomas Fielding (Lord Chesterfield) in 1824 used the saying as the basis for his '*A little wit, among foolish people, will pass a man for a great genius*'.

His masterpiece, *Colloquia*, was published in 1519, criticizing the abuses of the Church. With the Lutheran Revolution he was heavily criticized by Lutherans for not wholeheartedly siding with them, and by Catholics for inspiring Luther's schism. He left Louvain in 1521 and spent the rest of his life in Freiburg and Basel.

MICHELANGELO
1475-1564

'I've finished that chapel I was painting. The Pope is quite satisfied.'

Letter to his father on the completion of the ceiling of the Sistine
Chapel in the Vatican, October 1512

Michelangelo resented this commission for Pope Julius II, as he believed that it was serving the aggrandisement of that Pope. From 1508 to 1512 he painted 12,000 square feet of ceiling, including the iconic image of God creating Adam with touching fingertips at its centre. He said: '*After four tortured years, more than 400 over life-sized figures, I felt as old and as weary as Jeremiah. I was only 37, yet friends did not recognize the old man I had become.*'

He had completed his astonishing Pietà sculpture, showing Jesus with his head on his mother Mary's lap after the Crucifixion, when he was just 24. His statue of David was finished before he was 30, and is one of the most admired sculptures in the world. Another sculptor had tried to work the solid block of Carrera marble before Michelangelo succeeded, who commented: '*I saw the angel in the marble and I carved until I set him free.*'

Michelangelo was not only possibly the greatest painter and sculptor of all time, but also an architect and poet. His thirty-eighth sonnet includes the lines:

'*Love is a beautiful image
Imagined or seen within the heart,
The friend of virtue and gentility.*'

His fifteenth sonnet tells us about his ideas on sculpture:

'*The marble not yet carved can hold the form
Of every thought the greatest artist has.*'

NICCOLÒ MACHIAVELLI
1469–1527

'There is nothing more difficult to take in hand, more perilous to conduct, or more uncertain in its success, than to take the lead in the introduction of a new order of things'

'It ought to be remembered that there is nothing more difficult to take in hand, more perilous to conduct, or more uncertain in its success, than to take the lead in the introduction of a new order of things. Because the innovator has for enemies all those who have done well under the old conditions, and lukewarm defenders in those who may do well under the new. This coolness arises partly from fear of the opponents, who have the laws on their side, and partly from the incredulity of men, who do not readily believe in new things until they have had a long experience of them.'

The Prince, 1513

 In 1498, Machiavelli began his career as an active politician in the city-state of Florence, but after more than a decade of public service, he was driven from his post when the republic collapsed. Repeated efforts to win the confidence and approval of the new regime were unsuccessful, and Machiavelli was forced into retirement. *The Prince* was written in the hope of securing an appointment with the ruling Medici family, a practical guide to the exercise of political power over a principality.

Machiavelli argued that it is primarily the character of the Prince that determines the success of any state: *'Politics have no relation to morals'*. His *The Art of War* (1520) and *Discourses on Livy* (1531) were also influential books. Whatever the form of government, Machiavelli held, only success and glory really matter – *'A prince never lacks legitimate reasons to break his promise'*. His works still have relevance today, as evinced in his thoughts upon change in organizations.

LEONARDO DA VINCI
1452–1519

'Iron rusts from disuse; stagnant water loses its purity and in cold weather becomes frozen; even so does inaction sap the vigour of the mind'

The Notebooks, 1519

Da Vinci, a restless polymath, was always conscious of the value of using his time wisely, writing that '*Learning never exhausts the mind*' and '*As a well-spent day brings happy sleep, so a life well spent brings happy death*'. However, he was acutely aware that he could not achieve all that he wanted to achieve in his lifetime: '*I have wasted my hours*'. Thus hours were important to him, not days or months, in his constant struggle for self-improvement.

Da Vinci was possibly the greatest genius in known history, moving easily between painting, architecture, anatomy, sculpture, music, geometry, science and engineering. Aged 17, he was in Florence, and apprenticed to Verrochio, whose artistry he soon surpassed. In 1481, he moved to Milan, where he painted the *Virgin of the Rocks* and *The Last Supper*. He consulted on architecture in Venice from 1495 to 1499, became a military engineer for Cesare Borgia, and returned to Florence, where he painted the *Mona Lisa*. Back again in Milan, he concentrated on scientific studies, and in Rome came into contact with Michelangelo and Raphael.

Leonardo set out to write the first systematic explanations of how machines work and how the elements of machines can be combined. Five hundred years after they were put on paper, many of the sketches in his surviving notebooks can be used as blueprints to create perfect working models. Among his ideas were tanks, helicopters, solar power, calculators, engines and double hulls. He even developed a rudimentary theory of plate tectonics, and as a scientist this amazing polymath advanced knowledge in the fields of hydrodynamics, optics, civil engineering and anatomy.

ANNE BOLEYN
1500/09–1536

'Oh God, have pity on my soul.
Oh God, have pity on my soul.'

Her last words

From the scaffold, Anne Boleyn said: *'Good Christian people, I am come hither to die, for according to the law, and by the law I am judged to die, and therefore I will speak nothing against it. I am come hither to accuse no man, nor to speak anything of that, whereof I am accused and condemned to die, but I pray God save the king and send him long to reign over you, for a gentler nor a more merciful prince was there never: and to me he was ever a good, a gentle and sovereign lord... O Lord have mercy on me, to God I commend my soul.'*

She was then blindfolded and led to the block, where she prayed, *'To Jesus Christ I commend my soul. Lord Jesu receive my soul.'* As she placed her head on the stone, she began to cry and spoke her last words.

Born sometime between 1500 and 1509, Anne spent time at the French court, but returned to England in 1521 and followed her sister Mary in Henry VIII's affections. However, it seems that she wished marriage before consummation of the relationship, so Henry sought an annulment of his marriage to Catherine of Aragon, to be free to marry Anne.

Near the end of 1532, Anne finally succumbed to Henry, and by December she was pregnant. Henry was forced into action, and in January 1533 they were secretly married. On 23 May, the Archbishop of Canterbury officially proclaimed that the marriage of Henry and Catherine was invalid. Henry desperately wanted a male heir, but in September Princess Elizabeth Tudor was born. Anne had two miscarriages, and Henry started to court one of her ladies-in-waiting, Jane Seymour. Five men, including Anne's brother, were gruesomely tortured to falsely confess sexual relations with Anne, then executed.

NICOLAUS COPERNICUS
1473–1543

'Face the facts'

'Finally we shall place the Sun himself at the centre of the Universe. All this is suggested by the systematic procession of events and the harmony of the whole Universe, if only we face the facts, as they say, "with both eyes open".'

On the Revolutions of the Heavenly Spheres
(De Revolutionibus Orbium Coelestium), 1543

Copernicus was the Polish proponent of the theory that the Sun, and not the Earth, is in the centre of our universe, first proposed by Aristarchus. Copernicus studied in Italy and then practised medicine in Poland, but was officially employed as a canon in Olstzyn Cathedral. In about 1513, he wrote a short account of his Sun-centred cosmology for friends he had met in Rome. A full account of the theory, *De Revolutionibus*, was not published until he was near the end of his life. He is said to have received a copy of the printed book on his deathbed.

Copernicus' heliocentric system was thought implausible by the vast majority of his contemporaries, and by most other astronomers and natural philosophers, until the middle of the 17th century. Its main defenders included Johannes Kepler and Galileo Galilei, but there was strong opposition from the Church. Conclusive theoretical underpinning for the Copernican theory was provided by Sir Isaac Newton's theory of universal gravitation in 1687.

FRANÇOIS RABELAIS
c.1494–c.1553

'*Je n'ai rien vaillant; je dois beaucoup; je donne le reste aux pauvres*'
(I have nothing, owe a great deal, and the rest I leave to the poor)

The single statement in the last will and testament of Rabelais 1553

Rabelais was a Franciscan monk, humanist and doctor, whose series of comic novels, *Gargantua and Pantagruel*, are classics of literature, and whose protagonists are giants travelling in a world full of greed and stupidity. From him we have the adjective Rabelaisian, meaning something coarsely humorous.

Rabelais' works were banned by the Catholic Church, and later placed on its Index of Forbidden Books. Symptomatic of his relationship with the Church is the following anti-Inquisition passage:

> 'Yet these devilish heretics refuse to learn and know it. Burn 'em, tear 'em, nip 'em with hot pincers, drown 'em, hang 'em, spit 'em at the bunghole, pelt 'em, paut 'em, bruise 'em, beat 'em, cripple 'em, dismember 'em, cut 'em, gut 'em, bowel 'em, paunch 'em, thrash 'em, slash 'em, gash 'em, chop 'em, slice 'em, slit 'em, carve 'em, saw 'em, bethwack 'em, pare 'em, hack 'em, hew 'em, mince 'em, flay 'em, boil 'em, broil 'em, roast 'em, toast 'em, bake 'em, fry 'em, crucify 'em, crush 'em, squeeze 'em, grind 'em, batter 'em, burst 'em, quarter 'em, unlimb 'em, behump 'em, bethump 'em, belam 'em, belabour 'em, pepper 'em, spatchcock 'em, and carbonnade 'em on gridirons, these wicked heretics! decretalifuges, decretalicides, worse than homicides, worse than patricides, decretalictones of the devil of hell.'

Rabelais also said, '*Nature abhors a vacuum*', when requiring a drink of wine to cure thirst, *Plain as the nose in a man's face*' and '*Looking as like... as one pea does like another*'.

NOSTRADAMUS
1503–1566

'The blood of the just will be demanded of London
burnt by fire in three times twenty plus six.
The ancient lady will fall from her high position,
and many of the same denomination will be killed.'

The Prophecies of Nostradamus, Century 2, Stanza 51

This quote is believed to refer to the Great Fire of London in 1666. The 'ancient lady' is interpreted as the Cathedral of St Paul's, destroyed in the fire.

Michel de Nostredame was the son of Jewish parents who were forced to become Catholics by the Inquisition in France. He became an astrologer, linguist and a skilled physician, treating plague victims, but gained fame as a seer and prophet in his lifetime. His wife and two children died of the plague and he was forced by the Inquisition to leave Montpellier, travelling for six years before returning to France in 1554, where he had a second family.

In 1555, he wrote his first collection of *Centuries* – a set of 100 quatrains foretelling the future. Over the next few years he completed 10 Centuries, describing the years from the mid-1500s to 3797, the 'end of the world'. He plotted the horoscopes of Queen Catherine and her husband Henry II, and later was appointed Royal Physician to King Charles IX. On 1 July 1566, Nostradamus gave his final prediction to his priest. In response to the priest's farewell of '*Until tomorrow*', Nostradamus is said to have answered: '*You will not find me alive at sunrise*' and died that night. The following quatrain is thought to refer to the abdication of Edward VIII: '*For not wanting to consent to the divorce, which then afterwards will be recognized as unworthy, the King of the islands will be forced to flee, and one put in his place who has no sign of kingship.*'

EMPEROR CHARLES V
1500–1558

'To God I speak Spanish, to women Italian, to men French, and to my horse – German'

Attributed

Charles I was King of Spain from 1516 to 1556 and became Holy Roman Emperor from 1519 to 1558 after bribing the electors. He was faced with dynastic conflict from King Francis I of France, who also wanted to rule Italy. Charles said *'My cousin Francis and I are in perfect accord – he wants Milan, and so do I'*. In 1521, Charles invaded northern Italy, then controlled by France. Asked by his advisers to stay away from the fighting, Charles retorted: *'Name me an emperor who was ever struck by a cannonball.'*

Charles' reign was focused upon expanding his empire and ruling it justly – it was he who first used the phrase *'an iron fist in a velvet glove'*, when faced with a Spanish revolt against his taxes to pay for the Italian wars. Regarding his battles, Charles wrote: *'I came, I saw, God conquered.'* Faced with Martin Luther and the Protestant Reformation in Germany, he noted *'A single friar who goes counter to all Christianity for a thousand years must be wrong'*. In 1521 he signed the Edict of Worms, outlawing Lutherans. When later advised, in 1546, to hang Luther's corpse on the gallows, he retorted: *'I make war on the living, not the dead'*.

Charles captured Francis at the Battle of Pavia in 1525, and sacked Rome in 1527, extorting money from Pope Clement VII. Faced with religious revolts in Germany, he was also confronted by Francis allying with the Turks, and had to make a humiliating peace. In his final years, he abdicated some of his kingdoms to other members of the House of Habsburg. Charles instructed his son, Philip II of Spain, to: *'Exterminate heresy, lest it take root and overturn the state and social order'*, leading to Spain's virtual bankruptcy in the wars against England and the Netherlands.

LUÍS VAZ DE CAMÕES
1525–1580

'He who, solely to oppress,
Employs or martials force, or pow'r, achieves
No victory; but a true victory
Is gain'd, when justice triumphs and prevails'

Os Lusiadas, Canto 10, 1572

The national poet of Portugal, Camões was the master of a great variety of poetic styles, but was virtually unrecognized in his lifetime. *Os Lusiadas (The Lusiads)* is his masterpiece, an epic poem about the travels of Vasco da Gama. Camões fought in India, losing an eye, and after returning to Lisbon was imprisoned for injuring a member of the Royal Stables in 1552. He was released, fined and made to serve three years in the militia in Goa. There he was imprisoned for debt, and took part in several skirmishes before finishing his military service.

He became a chief warrant officer in Macao, but was charged with mismanagement and summoned to a tribunal in Goa. For some years he had been working on *Os Lusiadas*, and he took the unfinished manuscript with him. Shipwrecked off the Mekong Delta, it is said that he managed to reach shore holding his manuscript out of the waters. In 1570 he was back in Lisbon, and in 1572 *Os Lusiadas* was published. He then lived on a tiny pension granted by King Sebastian.

One of his better-known sonnets is *'Amor é fogo que arde sem se ver'*:

'Love is a fire that burns unseen,
A wound that aches yet isn't felt,
An always discontent contentment,
A pain that rages without hurting,
A longing for nothing but to long,
A loneliness in the midst of people,
A never feeling pleased when pleased,
A passion that gains when lost in thought.'

'I know I have but the body of a weak and feeble woman, but I have the heart and stomach of a king, and of a king of England, too'

'I know I have the body of a weak and feeble woman, but I have the heart and stomach of a king, and of a king of England too; and think foul scorn that Parma or Spain, or any prince of Europe, should dare to invade the borders of my realm.'

Address to the English army at Tilbury Fort, 1588

This speech by the Virgin Queen was made when there was an expectation of an imminent invasion by the Spanish Armada. Spain planned to secure a landing area on the Kent coast, and then ferry the army of the Duke of Parma across from the Netherlands. That year, the English fleet left Plymouth to chase the Spanish Armada east along the English Channel. The Spanish anchored off Calais, which enabled the English to disperse the fleet by a fire-ship attack, and strong winds blew it into the North Sea. The failure of the Armada shattered the image of the invincibility of Spanish arms. The efficiency of Elizabeth's government in the crisis and the queen's public appearance among her troops boosted her prestige across the nation.

Elizabeth Tudor was known as Gloriana, since her rule saw English expansion overseas and the renaissance of architecture and literature, the so-called Golden Age of the monarchy. The only daughter of Henry VIII and Anne Boleyn, she sacrificed her prospects of marriage to keep the country at peace during her 44-year reign – she told Parliament, '*I have already joined myself in marriage to a husband, namely the kingdom of England*'. As a young woman, Elizabeth had been under threat of execution, and wisely avoided committing herself on the relative merits of Protestantism and Catholicism, saying: '*There is only one Christ, Jesus, one faith. All else is a dispute over trifles.*'

EDMUND SPENSER
1552–1599

'The noblest mind the best contentment has'

The Faerie Queene, Book I, Canto I, Stanza 35, 1596

Spenser was a profound moral poet and a master of metre and language. He fought and held lands in Ireland, and in 1589, Sir Walter Raleigh encouraged him to return to London to seek court preferment and a pension, and to publish the first three books of *The Faerie Queene*. He was only partially successful in his pension claims, writing in *Lines on his Promised Pension*:

'I was promised on a time
To have reason for my rhyme;
From that time unto this season,
I received nor rhyme nor reason.'

Spenser had first published 12 pastoral eclogues of *The Shepheardes Calender* (1579), treating the shepherd as a rustic priest and poet. After more publications, *Amoretti*, his sonnet sequence on his courtship of Elizabeth Boyle, and '*Epithalamion*', a beautiful wedding poem in honour of his marriage in 1594, were printed. In 1596 the first six books of *The Faerie Queene*, Spenser's unfinished masterpiece, appeared. For this he invented the Spenserian stanza (nine lines, eight of iambic pentameter followed by one of iambic hexameter, rhyming ababbcbcc). *The Faerie Queene* is an allegory in praise of Elizabeth I:

'Her angel's face,
As the great eye of heaven, shined bright,
And made a sunshine in the shady place'

The work symbolically follows several knights in an examination of different virtues:

'Who will not mercy unto others show,
How can he mercy ever hope to have?
Ill can he rule the great that cannot reach the small.'

Spenser seems to have died in poverty, and is buried in Westminster Abbey next to Chaucer. He was known by his contemporaries as 'the prince of poets', as great in English as Virgil was in Latin, and Milton claimed that Spenser was 'a better teacher than Aquinas'.

SIR FRANCIS BACON
1561–1626

'Ipsa scientia potestas est'
(Knowledge is power)

Sacred Meditations. From The 11th Meditation: Of Heresies, 1597

Bacon, an English author, statesman, courtier and philosopher, was later Viscount St Albans. He joined Gray's Inn to study law in 1576, was called to the Bar in 1582, and began writing philosophical tracts in Latin. From 1584 he was an MP and later was Attorney-General, Solicitor-General and a Queen's Counsel. Bacon was knighted on the accession of James in 1603, becoming Lord Chancellor in 1621, but because of debts had succumbed to political and judicial corruption. He could not defend himself against 23 counts of corruption in 1621, the case was so conclusive. He begged mercy and was forced to pay a huge fine of £40,000 to the King (this was later commuted), and banned from holding any office. Despite his huge intellect, proven by his many publications and lasting influence, he died £22,000 in debt – the equivalent of over £3 million today. His death was caused by his experimentations with the preservative powers of snow. Some of his works tell us:

'A wise man will make more opportunities than he finds'

'By far the best proof is experience'

'Discretion in speech is more than eloquence'

'He of whom many are afraid ought to fear many'

'Silence is the virtue of fools'

Bacon was also the originator of the phrase about Mahomet and the mountain:

'Mahomet made the people believe that he would call a hill to him, and from the top of it offer up his prayers for the observers of his law. The people assembled. Mahomet called the hill to come to him, again and again; and when the hill stood still he was never a whit abashed, but said, "If the hill will not come to Mahomet, Mahomet will go to the hill."'

WILLIAM SHAKESPEARE
1564–1616

'Once more unto the breach, dear friends, once more'

'Once more unto the breach, dear friends, once more,
Or close the wall up with our English dead!
In peace there's nothing so becomes a man
As modest stillness and humility;
But when the blast of war blows in our ears,
Then imitate the action of the tiger:
Stiffen the sinews, summon up the blood.'

Henry V, Act III, Scene I, 1599

These lines are based upon Henry's exhortation to his troops at the siege of Harfleur. On 13 August 1414, English forces landed on the Seine estuary and attacked the port with 2,000 men-at-arms and 6,000 archers from Wales and its borders. The town was encircled and a French supply convoy captured. The walls were badly damaged by 12 'great guns' and the French asked to parley. Terms were agreed that if the relieving French army did not arrive before 23 September, the town would surrender honourably. On 22 September Harfleur surrendered and Henry left a small garrison there. His army had been incapacitated by 'the bloody flux' (dysentery), and he headed for Calais for safety and embarkation back to England. However, the French army blocked his route and he was forced to fight at Agincourt, gaining a glorious victory because of his superb longbow men. This is Shakespeare's account of Henry's speech before the battle:

'We few, we happy few, we band of brothers;
For he to-day that sheds his blood with me
Shall be my brother; be he ne'er so vile,
This day shall gentle his condition;
And gentlemen in England now-a-bed
Shall think themselves accurs'd they were not here,
And hold their manhoods cheap while any speaks
That fought with us upon Saint Crispin's day.'

WILLIAM SHAKESPEARE
1564–1616

'To be, or not to be: that is the question'

'To be, or not to be: that is the question:
Whether 'tis nobler in the mind to suffer
The slings and arrows of outrageous fortune,
Or to take arms against a sea of troubles,
And by opposing end them? To die: to sleep;
No more; and by a sleep to say we end
The heart-ache and the thousand natural shocks
That flesh is heir to, 'tis a consummation
Devoutly to be wish'd. To die, to sleep;
To sleep: perchance to dream: ay, there's the rub;
For in that sleep of death what dreams may come
When we have shuffled off this mortal coil,
Must give us pause'

Hamlet, Act III, Scene I, 1601

These lines, Hamlet's soliloquy on the nature of action and being, the meaning of life and death, are probably the best-known lines in English literature. Hamlet, the young prince of Denmark, is musing on his way to a meeting with Ophelia, after discovering that his beloved father has been poisoned by his new stepfather. His musings seem to give us Shakespeare's own ideas on the meaning of life and death, in one of the greatest speeches in literature.

CHRISTOPHER MARLOWE
1564–1593

'Was this the face that launch'd a thousand ships And burnt the topless towers of Ilium?'

'Was this the face that launch'd a thousand ships
And burnt the topless towers of Ilium?
Sweet Helen, make me immortal with a kiss!
Her lips suck forth my soul: see, where it flies!
Come Helen, come give me my soul again.
Here I will dwell, for heaven be in these lips,
And all is dross that is not Helena.'

Dr Faustus, 1604

This quote is uttered by Faustus before surrendering himself to the possessor of 'this face', Helen of Troy. Marlowe, the contemporary of Shakespeare, was stabbed in a mysterious tavern brawl, aged only 29. His killer was pardoned by Queen Elizabeth I. Marlowe had been a government spy and possibly an *agent provocateur*. However, he was named as a Catholic by his fellow playwright, Thomas Kyd, when Kyd was under torture. A warrant was put out for Marlowe's arrest, but days later Marlowe was killed. Only four years previously, Marlowe had been charged with murder and imprisoned, but was released after two weeks. In 1582 he was reported for being involved in another death, and was also deported from the Netherlands for counterfeiting.

Nothing is definitive, but it is thought that Marlowe wrote the plays *Tamburlaine the Great, The Jew of Malta, The Tragical History of Dr Faustus* (to give *Dr Faustus* its full title), *Edward II* and the poetry *Hero and Leander* and *The Passionate Shepherd*. Another line from *Dr Faustus* is: '*O thou art fairer than the evening air clad in the beauty of a thousand stars.*' A famous response from Barabas in *The Jew of Malta* to Barnadine's '*Thou hast committed –*' is: '*Fornication? But that was in another / country: and besides, the wench is dead.*' Many people believe that Marlowe did not die, but took another identity and is the 'real' author of Shakespeare's works.

GUY (GUIDO) FAWKES
1570–1606

'A desperate disease requires a desperate remedy'

Answer under interrogation to King James and captors on 5 November 1606

When being questioned immediately after his capture during his attempt to blow up the Houses of Parliament, Fawkes also said that he wanted to '*blow the Scots back into Scotland*'.

After Queen Elizabeth I died in 1603, English Catholics hoped that her successor, James VI of Scotland (James I of England), would be more tolerant. However, their hopes were thwarted and in 1605 Robert Catesby and others began plotting to kill King James. They decided to blow up the King when he was in Parliament, and Guy Fawkes bought and stored 36 barrels of gunpowder under the House of Lords. An anonymous letter was sent to Lord Mounteagle, urging him to stay away from Parliament on 5 November 1606. It seems to have been a forgery written by the King's spies, who had been informed of the Gunpowder Plot by Francis Tresham, one of the 13 conspirators. Thus Fawkes was found in the cellars on the morning of 5 November, hours before Parliament assembled, and taken before the King.

For two days, Fawkes was the only suspect in custody, so his name became synonymous with the Gunpowder Plot. Soon, however, the other plotters were caught, and Catesby was killed in a siege. The others were all tortured, then hanged, drawn and quartered publicly in 1606. Francis Tresham was probably poisoned, and died in prison. The government used the treason to justify anti-Catholic repression, including the execution of at least two Jesuit leaders. On 5 November, bonfires were set alight to celebrate the safety of the King. The day is now known as Bonfire Night, with effigies of Guy Fawkes being burnt.

CERVANTES
c. 1547–1616

'There are only two families in the world, my old grandmother used to say, The Haves and Have-Nots'

Don Quixote, Part II, Chapter 20, 1605–1615

Miguel de Cervantes Saavedra was born to poor nobility, and is the most well-known Spanish novelist and playwright, most famous for *Don Quixote*. He was injured in the great Mediterranean Battle of Lepanto (1571) and later captured and taken to Algiers as a slave in 1575. It was five years before his family could raise enough money to pay his ransom. During the next 20 years he led a nomadic existence, suffered bankruptcy and was imprisoned at least twice.

According to Cervantes, he wrote 20 to 30 plays, but only two copies have survived. It is said that he wrote *Don Quixote* in prison in La Mancha. His use of everyday speech was acclaimed by the general public and it brought him international appreciation as a man of letters. It is often called 'the first modern novel', and was originally conceived as a comic satire against the chivalric romances. It gives a panoramic view of 17th-century Spanish society, and from Cervantes we have an incredible number of modern sayings:

'I shall be as secret as the grave'

'Many count their chickens before they are hatched'

'The pot calls the kettle black'

'When thou art in Rome, do as they do in Rome'

'Too much of a good thing'

'Tell me the company thou keepest, and I'll tell thee what thou art'

'He has an oar in every man's boat, and a finger in every pie'

**'Good Friend for Jesus Sake Forbeare
To Dig the Dust Encloased Heare.
Blest Be Ye Man That Spares Thes Stones
And Curst Be He That Moves My Bones'**

Shakespeare's epitaph tells us nothing of the greatest writer in the English language. Rather, it functions as a plea, ostensibly written by Shakespeare himself, for his grave to remain undisturbed – overcrowding in graveyards was a common problem at the time. A poet and actor, he is considered by many to be the greatest dramatist of all time. Some of his plays, such as *Hamlet, Macbeth* and *Romeo and Juliet*, are among the most famous literary works in the world.

Shakespeare possessed a huge vocabulary for his day, using over 29,000 different words in his plays. Today the average English-speaking person uses something like 2,000 words in everyday speech. His erudition is such that there are many other, more learned claimants to the authorship of Shakespeare's works, such as Christopher Marlowe, Edward de Vere, Francis Bacon, Ben Jonson, Sir Walter Raleigh, the Earl of Southampton or even Queen Elizabeth I. By 1584, the actor Shakespeare had emerged as a rising playwright in London, and soon became a central figure in London's leading theatre company, the Lord Chamberlain's Company, renamed later as the King's Men. He wrote many great plays for the group, which from 1599 performed in a new theatre, the Globe. In 1623 there appeared a folio edition of Shakespeare's collected works, the *First Edition*, which cemented his place in literary history.

BEN JONSON
c.1573–1637

'Drink to me, only, with thine eyes'

'Drink to me, only, with thine eyes,
And I will pledge with mine;
Or leave a kiss but in the cup,
And I'll not look for wine.
The thirst that from the soul doth
  rise,
Doth ask a drink divine:
But might I of Jove's nectar sup,
I would not change for thine.

I sent thee, late, a rosy wreath,
Not so much honouring thee,
As giving it a hope, that there
It could not wither'd be.
But thou thereon didst only breathe,
And sent'st it back to me:
Since when it grows, and smells,
  I swear,
Not of itself, but thee.'

'To Celia', 1616

The son of a clergyman (who died before Jonson was born), Ben Jonson worked as a brick-layer, then served in Flanders in the army. By 1597 he was an actor and playwright, and in that year killed another actor in a duel. Convicted of murder, he was spared execution on pleading 'benefit of the clergy', as he was literate, but was branded on his thumb as a felon and all his possessions were confiscated. His play, *Every Man in His Humour*, was performed in 1598 at the Globe, with William Shakespeare in the cast. His satirical comedies made Jonson a celebrity, but he was imprisoned on charges of 'popery and treason' for *Sejanus*, and later for anti-Scots sentiments in *Eastward Ho* (King James was Scottish). He was also suspected of involvement in the Gunpowder Plot.

Volpone, published in 1607, is his masterpiece, and he was made Poet Laureate in 1616. He was idolized in his day, and he is buried in Westminster Abbey. Some lines we remember from his works include: '*I have it here in black and white*', '*Alas, all the castles I have, are built on air*' and '*Boldly nominate a spade a spade*'. Scholars have suggested – though it remains unproven – that the 'Celia' to whom the above poem is addressed may have been fellow poet Lady Mary Roth.

JOHANNES KEPLER
1571–1630

'Nature uses as little as possible of anything'

Harmonices Mundi (Harmonies of the Worlds), 1619

'But before mankind could be ripe for a science which takes in the whole of reality, a second fundamental truth was needed, which only became common property among philosophers with the advent of Kepler and Galileo. Pure logical thinking cannot yield us any knowledge of the empirical world; all knowledge of reality starts from experience and ends in it. Propositions arrived at by purely logical means are completely empty as regards reality. Because Galileo saw this, and particularly because he drummed it into the scientific world, he is the father of modern physics – indeed, of modern science altogether.' Albert Einstein, *Ideas and Opinions*

Along with Galileo Galilei, Johannes Kepler is the founding father of empirical science. It was believed throughout history that planetary orbits were perfect circles. From Tycho Brahe (1546–1601), Kepler derived astronomical data of Mars, the planet that least fitted with the findings of either Ptolemy or Copernicus. Kepler believed that he could work out Mars' orbit in a week, but after five years of trying combinations of circular orbits, none matched the data with the necessary accuracy. He was forced to give up circles, the only proposed shape for orbits (the perfection proposed by Plato and Pythagoras), deciding that planetary orbits must be elliptical. Thus he developed three laws of planetary motion, which he first explained in his *Harmonices Mundi*. Expanding on these laws in *Astronomia Nova* (1609), He wrote '*I was almost driven to madness in considering and calculating this matter*', as it was such a revolutionary step. Furthermore, Kepler insisted that planetary motion was the result of real physical force emanating from the Sun, prefiguring Newton's work on gravity a century later.

ROBERT BURTON
1577–1640

'See one and you've seen them all'

The Anatomy of Melancholy, 1621

This quote is in fact a paraphrase of Burton's actual statement in *The Anatomy*: '*See one promontory (said Socrates of old), one mountain, one sea, one river, and we see all.*' A clergyman and scholar who spent most of his life at Oxford, Burton wrote the book to help deal with his own lifelong sufferering from melancholia. The treatise itself was intended as self-treatment: '*I write of melancholy, by being busy to avoid melancholy. There is no greater cause of melancholy than idleness, no better cure than business.*' Later authors used the work without attribution. For many years, Burton told everyone he would die aged 63, which he did. Some of the many, many well-known lines that originated with Burton are:

'*I call a spade a spade*'

'*One was never married, and that's his hell: another is, and that's his plague*'

'*Where God hath a temple, the Devil will have a chapel*'

'*Going as if he trod upon eggs*'

'*Rob Peter and pay Paul*'

'*Birds of a feather will gather together*'

'*Diogenes struck the father when the child swore*'

Burton also wrote: '*I may not here omit those two main plagues, and common dotages of human kind, wine and women, which have infatuated and besotted myriads of people. They commonly go together.*'

JOHN DONNE
1572–1631

'No man is an island'

'No man is an island, entire of itself; every man is a piece of the continent, a part of the main. If a clod be washed away by the sea, Europe is the less, as well as if a promontory were, as well as if a manor of thy friend's or of thine own were. Any man's death diminishes me, because I am involved in mankind; and therefore never send to know for whom the bell tolls; it tolls for thee...'

Meditation 17, *Devotions upon Emergent Occasions*, 1624

John Donne was born into a Catholic family at a time of difficulties for that religion in England. First taught by Jesuits, Donne entered Oxford but did not take a degree, for that would have meant swearing the Oath of Supremacy to the King and Protestantism. He studied law, and his brother was imprisoned for sheltering a Catholic priest and died in gaol. Donne began to question his faith, leading him to become perhaps the greatest of the Metaphysical Poets. A friend of Ben Jonson, he served on expeditions under the Earl of Essex, but his career was ruined by a secret marriage for which he was thrown into the Fleet Prison and dismissed from his post.

Later, King James insisted that he took Anglican orders and Donne was appointed a Royal Chaplain in 1607, and later Dean of St Paul's. Donne was grief-stricken when his wife died and her demise led to his finest poetry, his *Meditations* on illness and death. In his *Elegies*, he wrote: '*Love built on beauty, soon as beauty, dies*' and '*She and comparisons are odious*', and in *Holy Sonnets*: '*One short sleep past, we wake eternally, And Death shall be no more; Death, thou shalt die.*'

WILLIAM HARVEY
1578–1657

'[The heart] is the household divinity which, discharging its function, nourishes, cherishes, quickens the whole body, and is indeed the foundation of life, the source of all action'

Exercitatio Anatomica, 1628

William Harvey was an English physician who was the first man to describe accurately how blood was pumped around the body by the heart. Educated at Cambridge University, he then studied medicine at the University of Padua under the surgeon Hieronymus Fabricius. Fabricius knew that blood veins had one-way valves but did not know their function, and Harvey discovered what part the valves played in the circulation of blood through the body.

In 1607, Harvey became a fellow of the Royal College of Physicians and in 1618 was physician to James I and then Charles I. Harvey's research was assisted through the dissection of animals, and in 1628 he published his theories in *Exercitatio Anatomica de Motu Cordis et Sanguinis in Animalibus (An Anatomical Study of the Motion of the Heart and of the Blood in Animals)*, showing how the heart propelled the blood in a circular course through the body. In doing so he was ridiculed, as this argued against Galen's teachings of the previous 1,400 years that the liver was the most important organ in the blood-vascular system, with blood ebbing and flowing like the tides. From direct observation Harvey had concluded that venous blood would only travel in one direction, towards the heart.

Harvey was also the first to suggest that humans and other mammals reproduced via the fertilization of an egg by sperm. It took a further two centuries before a mammalian egg was finally observed. An inveterate experimenter, Harvey wrote: *'There is no perfect knowledge which can be entitled ours, that is innate; none but what has been obtained from experience, or derived in some way from our senses.'*

GALILEO GALILEI
1564–1642

'I do not feel obliged to believe that same God who endowed us with sense, reason, and intellect had intended for us to forgo their use'

Dialogue Concerning the Two Chief World Systems, 1632

Galileo was an Italian scientist who formulated the basic law of falling bodies, which he verified by careful measurements. His work in dynamics assisted Newton and Kepler in formulating their Laws of Motion. He also discovered that the time for pendulums to swing is always the same, regardless of amplitude, allowing more precise clocks to be built. The 'Father of Modern Astronomy', Galileo pioneered the 'experimental scientific method'. In 1609 he learned of the invention of the telescope in Holland and constructed a vastly superior model with double the magnification to 20×. Galileo was the first to use a refracting telescope to make important astronomical findings, and made a series of profound discoveries, including the moons of the planet Jupiter and the phases of the planet Venus. He was also the first Westerner to discover sunspots.

As a professor of astronomy at the University of Pisa, Galileo was required to teach the accepted theory of his time that the Sun and all the planets revolved around the Earth. Later, at the University of Padua, he was exposed to a new theory, proposed by Nicolaus Copernicus, that the Earth and all the other planets revolved around the Sun. Galileo's observations with his new telescope convinced him that Copernicus' Sun-centred (heliocentric) theory was correct, and he confirmed it in his *Dialogue* published in 1632. The Catholic Church responded quickly to the publication and its threat to Catholic orthodoxy that the Earth was the centre of God's universe. In 1633, aged 69, Galileo was subject to a 'show trial' by the Inquisition, after being threatened with torture and the stake. The Inquisition convicted him of heresy, forcing him to recant his support of Copernicus. He was sentenced to lifelong house arrest, becoming blind from 1638, and his *Dialogue* was placed on the Vatican's blacklist of banned books, the Index Librorum Prohibitorum. In 1992, Pope John Paul II finally lifted the Edict of the Inquisition from Galileo.

GEORGE HERBERT
1593–1633

'Let all the world in every corner sing, My God and King!'

'Let all the world in every corner sing, My God and King!
The heavens are not too high, His praise may thither fly;
The earth is not too low, His praises there may grow.
Let all the world in every corner sing, My God and King!'

The Temple: Sacred Poems and Private Ejaculations, 1633

A Welsh Metaphysical Poet, orator and priest, George was the brother of Baron Herbert of Cherbury. After studying at Cambridge, he was a public orator for eight years, and in 1630 was ordained and made a rector. Herbert's devotional poems are marked by a quiet tone, precise language and versatile use of metre. None was published, but after Herbert's death his friend, Nicholas Ferrar, had them published as *The Temple*, a magnificent paean to the wonders of God's universe.

Herbert had instructed Ferrar to burn the poems if they would not *'turn to the advantage of any dejected poor soul'*, but Ferrar was deeply moved by the poems, describing them as a *'rich jewel and most worthy to be in the hands and hearts of all true Christians that feared God and loved the Church of England'*. Four have found their way into *The New English Hymnal*, each with a 19th-century tune. Of these, *'Let all the world in every corner sing'* is the most majestic, and *'The God of love my shepherd is'* the most beautiful and moving. Herbert also said: *'He that is not handsome at 20, nor strong at 30, nor rich at 40, nor wise at 50, will never be handsome, strong, rich or wise'* and *'One enemy is too much'*.

RENÉ DESCARTES
1596–1650

'Ego cogito, ergo sum'
(I think, therefore I am)

Principles of Philosophy, 1644
(Also 'Je pense donc je suis' *A Discourse on Method, 1637*)

'I think, therefore I am' is a fundamental element of Western philosophy – if someone wonders if he exists, that in itself is proof of his existence. Descartes is sometimes called the 'founder of modern philosophy'. After studying mathematics and law in France, he volunteered for the Dutch army, and after 11 years of travelling across Europe, he settled in the Netherlands. In 1641 he published *A Discourse on Method, Meditations on First Philosophy*, trying to devise a method for seeking the truth in times of rapid discovery and change. His methodology of systematic doubt impacted on the development of philosophy and science. He thought that everything should be doubted unless it can be proven to be true under all circumstances, and all subsequent knowledge should be based on this 'true' knowledge.

Systematic doubt was applied to empirical science to create experimental science. Controlled experience allows for an experience to be repeated; if the repetition of the experience leads to the same knowledge, then the original knowledge is confirmed. Following Cartesian logic, we are bound to doubt all knowledge until it is proven to be true. He believed that the universe was created by God, who resembled the human mind in that both think, but have no physical being. However, God is infinite and does not depend on a creator for His existence. Descartes was also a superb mathematician, inventing analytic geometry. He wrote: *'If you would be a real seeker after truth, it is necessary that at least once in your life you doubt, as far as possible, all things.'*

EVANGELISTA TORRICELLI
1608–1647

'Is it a surprise that into the vessel, in which the mercury has no inclination and no repugnance, not even the slightest, to being there, it should enter and should rise in a column high enough to make equilibrium with the weight of the external air which forces it up?'

After his invention of the barometer in 1643–45

Torricelli, an Italian physicist, was the secretary and companion of Galileo in the last three months of Galileo's life. He developed the concepts of momentum and impetus, and was asked to succeed Galileo in the Florence Academy, solving some of the great mathematical problems of the day, such as the finding of the area and centre of gravity of the cycloid. Pump-makers of the Grand Duke of Tuscany attempted to raise water to a height of 40 feet or more in mines, but found that 32 feet was the limit to which it would rise in the suction pump. Galileo believed Aristotle's proposition that 'nature abhors a vacuum', so he had modified the law by stating that the 'horror' extended only to about 32 feet. Torricelli did not believe that vacuum-abhorrence was responsible for raising the water, reasoning that it was the result of the pressure exerted on the liquid by the surrounding air. To prove his theory, he filled a glass tube, sealed it at one end, filled it with mercury and up-ended it into a dish also containing mercury. Only a portion of the tube emptied. As the mercury emptied, the first man-made vacuum was created at the top of the tube, effectively proving the existence of vacuums in nature. Torricelli conceived that the height of mercury was only 1/14 that of a water barometer, owing to the fact that mercury is 14 times as dense as water. He also noticed that the level of mercury varied from day to day, and so constructed the world's first mercury barometer.

He wrote: '*The Geometer has the special privilege to carry out, by abstraction, all constructions by means of the intellect. Who, then, would wish to prevent me from freely considering figures hanging on a balance imagined to be at an infinite distance beyond the confines of the world?*'

JOHN FLETCHER
1579–1625

'Man is his own star'

'Man is his own star, and the soul that can
Render an honest and a perfect man
Commands all light, all influence, all fate.
Nothing to him falls early, or too late.
Our acts our angels are, or good or ill,
Our fatal shadows that walk by us still.'

The Honest Man's Fortune, Epilogue, 1647

At one time Fletcher ranked alongside Shakespeare and Ben Jonson as a playwright, succeeding Shakespeare as the chief dramatist for the King's Men on Shakespeare's death. Fletcher was known as one of the literary men frequenting the Mermaid Tavern – the London pub famous for hosting the 'Friday Street Club' of leading literary figures – from around 1606 onwards, and began to collaborate with Shakespeare, Jonson and Francis Beaumont. His preferred genre was comedy, which he wrote with Beaumont from 1607 until Beaumont's death in 1616, and their plays are still performed today. *The Honest Man's Fortune* is thought to have been written in collaboration with Philip Massinger and Nathan Field, and was included in the second *Beaumont and Fletcher Folio*. Fletcher's *The Tamer Tamed* answered Shakespeare's *The Taming of the Shrew*, and he seems to have collaborated with Shakespeare on *The Two Noble Kinsmen* and *The Life of King Henry VIII*. His *Knight of the Burning Pestle* was a satire of Cervantes. The salaried playwrights of the day had to agree not to publish their plays without permission of their company, so only nine of Fletcher's 42 plays were published in his lifetime. With Beaumont, he has given us a host of sayings:

'Hit the nail on the head'
'I find the medicine worse than the malady'
'He went away with a flea in 's ear'
'Deeds, not words'
'All your better deeds, Shall be in water writ, but this in marble'
'It shew'd discretion, the best part of valour'
'Kiss till the cow comes home'
'Beggars must be no choosers'
'One foot in the grave'
'What's one man's poison, signor, Is another's meat or drink'

RICHARD LOVELACE
1618–1657

'Stone walls do not a prison make, Nor iron bars a cage'

'When Love with unconfined wings
Hovers within my gates,
And my divine Althea brings
To whisper at the grates;
When I lie tangled in her hair,
And fettered to her eye,
The gods that wanton in the air
Know no such liberty.
When flowing cups run swiftly
   round
With no allaying Thames,
Our careless heads with roses
   bound,
Our hearts with loyal flames;
When thirsty grief in wine we steep,
When healths and draughts go free,
Fishes that tipple in the deep,

Know no such liberty.
When, like committed linnets, I
With shriller throat shall sing
The sweetness, mercy, majesty,
And glories of my king;
When I shall voice aloud how good
He is, how great should be,
Enlarged winds, that curl the flood,
Know no such liberty.
Stone walls do not a prison make,
Nor iron bars a cage;
Minds innocent and quiet take
That for an hermitage;
If I have freedom in my love,
And in my soul am free,
Angels alone that soar above,
Enjoy such liberty.'

'To Althea, from Prison' written 1642 published in 'To Lucasta' 1649

Lovelace was an attractive, handsome and witty courtier, one of the Cavalier
Poets. Close to Charles I, he took part in the King's military expeditions to Scotland
in 1639–40. In 1642, Lovelace presented a Royalist petition to Parliament,
favouring the restoration of the Anglican bishops to Parliament. He was
imprisoned, and while in prison he wrote the above poem to Lucy Sacheverelle
(Lucasta). He declared that, although a prisoner, he can still think and dream about
her. Released, Lovelace was wounded at the battle of Dunkirk and returned to
Cromwell's England in 1647, only to be imprisoned again. Released from prison in
1649, he published the poetry collection To Lucasta. However, hearing that Lovelace
had died of the wounds he received, Lucasta had married another. Financially
ruined by his support of the Royalist cause, Lovelace died in poverty in 1657.

THOMAS HOBBES
1588–1679

'No arts, no letters, no society, and which is worst of all, continual fear and danger of violent death, and the life of man solitary, poor, nasty, brutish, and short'

Leviathan, or The Matter, Forme and Power of a Common Wealth Ecclesiasticall and Civil, 1651

In his Leviathan, Hobbes develops the theory of a 'social contract' between man and the legitimate government. Politics is based on the desire for power and the fear of death, and the social contract gives up the rights of man to an authorized sovereign authority to act on man's behalf. He believes that only absolute sovereignty will prevent the anarchy and consequent wars described above. *'The sovereign must be absolute to overcome the haunting fear of death that man has in a state of nature, and a government's sole reason for existence is for the safety of the people.'* Hobbes believed that in the normal 'state of nature', men's dispositions prevail towards anarchy, with three basic causes of conflict – competition, diffidence and glory. *'The first maketh men invade for gain; the second, for safety; and the third, for reputation.'* '*Bellum omnium contra omnes*' (the war of all against all) can only be averted by a strong central government represented by the monarchy, and there can be no right of rebellion towards this social contract.

Hobbes' philosophy was a reaction against the decentralizing ideas of the Reformation, which he believed brought anarchy. However, he believed that all men were born equal. His ideas were much influenced by his times, as he lived through the two English Civil Wars. After Oxford University, he spent most of his life as a tutor for rich families, including as the tutor of Charles II when he was exiled in Paris in 1646. On his trips to the Continent, he met Francis Bacon, Galileo and Descartes, and from his growing interest in mathematics believed that he could deduce the behaviour of men using scientific principles. He also wrote on mechanics, law, psychology and a history of the English Civil War.

ANDREW MARVELL
1621–1678

'But at my back I always hear Time's winged Chariot hurrying near'

'Had we but World enough, and
    Time,
This coyness, Lady, were no crime.
We would sit down and think
    which way
To walk, and pass our long love's day.

An hundred years should go to praise
Thine Eyes, and on thy Forehead
    Gaze.
Two hundred to adore each Breast,
But thirty thousand to the rest.
An Age at least to every part,
And the last Age should show your
    Heart.
For Lady you deserve this State,
Nor would I love at lower rate.

But at my back I always hear
Time's winged Chariot hurrying near:
And yonder all before us lie
Deserts of vast Eternity.

Thy Beauty shall no more be found;
Nor, in thy marble Vault, shall
    sound
My echoing Song: then Worms
    shall try
That long preserved Virginity:
And your quaint Honour turn to
    dust;
And into ashes all my Lust.

The Grave's a fine and private place,
But none I think do there embrace.

Let us roll all our strength and all
Our sweetness up into one Ball:
And tear our Pleasures with rough
    strife,
Thorough the Iron gates of Life:
Thus, though we cannot make our
    Sun
Stand still, yet we will make him
    run.'

Abridged version of 'To His Coy Mistress', c.1650–1653

Marvell was a committed Parliamentarian who became tutor to the children of Sir Thomas Fairfax from 1650 to 1653. It appears that the young Mary Fairfax (1638–1704) inspired the love-struck Marvell to write this poem when she was around 12 to 15, and Marvell 29 to 32, but the relationship appears to have been unrequited. Marvell later became an MP for Hull. The poem was published three years after Marvell's death.

OLIVER CROMWELL
1599–1658

'Warts and all'

'Mr Lely, I desire that you would use all your skill to paint my picture truly like me, and not flatter me at all; but remark all these roughnesses, pimples, warts, and everything as you see me, otherwise I will never pay a farthing for it.'

Attributed by Horace Walpole, *Anecdotes of Painting in England*, 1763

This quote apparently came from Cromwell's instruction to the portrait painter Peter Lely in 1653. Cromwell became an MP in 1628 and later had a religious experience which convinced him that he would be guided to carry out God's purpose. Civil war broke out between King Charles I and Parliament in 1642, and Cromwell created a superb force of cavalry, the 'Ironsides', and convinced Parliament to establish a professional army – the New Model Army – which won the decisive victory over the King's forces at Naseby in 1645.

Cromwell was a prime mover in the trial and execution of Charles I in 1649, and became Army Commander and Lord Lieutenant of Ireland, where he crushed resistance. Cromwell next defeated the supporters of the King's son, Charles II, at Dunbar in 1650 and Worcester in 1651, effectively ending the Second Civil War. In 1653, he dissolved the Long Parliament and, after the failure of his Puritan Convention, made himself Lord Protector. In 1657 Cromwell refused the offer of the crown, seeing it as vanity. Instead he reorganized the national church, establishing Puritanism, and allowed some degree of religious tolerance. He ended the wars with Portugal in 1653 and Holland in 1654 and allied with France against Spain, winning at the Battle of the Dunes in 1658. After the Restoration of Charles II, Cromwell's body was dug up and hanged.

HENRY VAUGHAN
1622–1695

'I saw Eternity the other night'

'I saw Eternity the other night,
Like a great ring of pure and endless
      light,
All calm, as it was bright;
And round beneath it, Time in
      hours, days, years,
Driv'n by the spheres
Like a vast shadow moved; in which
      the world
And all her train were hurled.
The doting lover in his quaintest strain
Did there complain;
Near him, his lute, his fancy, and his
      flights,
Wit's sour delights,
With gloves, and knots, the silly
      snares of pleasure,
Yet his dear treasure
All scattered lay, while he his eyes
      did pour
Upon a flow'r.'

'The World', *Silex Scintillans*, 1650–1655

This Welsh mystic and poet was the twin brother of Thomas Vaughan, the celebrated hermetic philosopher and alchemist. Henry took the King's side in the Civil War, and his religious poetic masterwork was *Silex Scintillans* (*The Flashing Flint*), referring to 'the stony hardness of his heart, from which divine steel strikes fire'. He is one of the major Metaphysical Poets, and the poem 'Peace' from *Silex Scintillans* is demonstrative of his search for a personal relationship with God:

'My soul, there is a country
Far beyond the stars,
Where stands a wingèd sentry
All skilful in the wars:
There, above noise and danger,
Sweet Peace sits crown'd with smiles,
And One born in a manger
Commands the beauteous files.
He is thy gracious Friend,
And – O my soul, awake! –
Did in pure love descend
To die here for thy sake.
If thou canst get but thither,
There grows the flower of Peace,
The Rose that cannot wither,
Thy fortress, and thy ease.
Leave then thy foolish ranges;
For none can thee secure
But One who never changes –
Thy God, thy life, thy cure.'

SAMUEL PEPYS
1633–1703

'And so to bed'

Samuel Pepys wrote about his life and times in Restoration England, keeping his thoughts in his diary between 1660 and 1669, and this phrase was regularly his last entry for the day. Pepys seems to have been prompted by vanity to record his achievements, but stopped as he feared he was losing his eyesight. The diary is in shorthand, and ranges from private observations to recording events such as the fall of the Commonwealth, Charles II's coronation (1661), the Great Plague (1665) and the Great Fire of London (1666), and gives insights into the lives of such luminaries as Sir Christopher Wren and Sir Isaac Newton.

His diary entry for 16 September 1665 records the Plague: '*Thence I walked to the Tower; but Lord! how empty the streets are and how melancholy, so many sick poor people in the streets full of sores... in Westminster, there is never a physician and but one apothecary left, all being dead.*' Pepys also describes the punishments of the day: '*I went out to Charing Cross to see Major General Harrison hanged, drawn, and quartered; which was done there, he looking as cheerful as any man could in that condition.*' His was a dyspeptic view of marriage, especially after his wife caught him having an affair with her companion: '*Saw a wedding in the church. It was strange to see what delight we married people have to see these poor fools decoyed into our condition*' and '*I find my wife hath something in her gizzard, that only waits an opportunity of being provoked to bring up; but I will not, for my content-sake, give it*'. Pepys was also a naval administrator and MP.

ROBERT BOYLE
1626–1691

'I use the Scriptures... as a matchless temple'

'I use the Scriptures, not as an arsenal to be resorted to only for arms and weapons, but as a matchless temple, where I delight to be, to contemplate the beauty, the symmetry, and the magnificence of the structure, and to increase my awe, and excite my devotion to the Deity there preached and adored.'

Some Consideration Touching the Style of the Holy Scriptures, 1664

Robert Boyle, "The Father of Chemistry', was the 14th son of the wealthy Earl of Cork, and discovered 'Boyle's Law', describing the relationship between the elasticity and pressure of gases. He is regarded as the first modern chemist and as such one of the founders of modern chemistry, but thought himself as much a theologian as a scientist: '*As the moon, though darkened with spots, gives us a much greater light than the stars that seem all-luminous, so do the Scriptures afford more light than the brightest human authors. In the Bible the ignorant may learn all requisite knowledge, and the most knowing may learn to discern their ignorance.*'

Also a physicist, inventor and philosopher, Boyle wrote in his cornerstone book *The Sceptical Chymist* of 1691: '*It is my intent to beget a good understanding between the chymists and the natural philosophers who have hitherto been too little acquainted with one another's learning.*' In this work, he used the word 'element' in its modern sense for the first time and speculated about the existence of atoms. He inspired his assistants, such as the polymath, Robert Hooke, and Dennis Pain, who invented the pressure cooker and proposed the principles for developing steam engines.

FRANÇOIS LE DUC DE LA ROCHEFOUCAULD, LE PRINCE DE MARCILLAC
1613–1680

<hr>

'Absence diminishes small loves and increases great ones, as the wind blows out the candle and fans the bonfire'

Maximes, 1665

Born into one of the leading aristocratic families in France, La Rochefoucauld studied Latin, mathematics, fencing, dancing, heraldry and etiquette, entering military service as the commander of a regiment aged only 15. He seemed destined for great influence at Court. However, in 1836 he involved himself in an abortive political intrigue against Richelieu with the French Queen Anne of Austria. He was detected and imprisoned in the Bastille for some days, then banished from Paris to his country estates. A series of ill-fated political and sexual affairs followed, he was gravely wounded and later almost blinded during wars, and one of his country estates was razed, ruining him financially.

His bitter experiences taught him that friendship, loyalty and love were nothing more than elaborate façades built to protect and disguise the ego, the self-centred core of every personality that La Rochefoucauld called *Amour-Propre* (self-love). He believed that we only compare each other, in a society based on wealth and social standing, on an insubstantial and harmful basis. He wrote: '*We are so accustomed to disguise ourselves to others, that in the end we become disguised to ourselves.*' He became what he termed a 'melancholic', with a pessimistic view of human motivations. In 1659 he was back in Paris, spending time at the salon of Madame de Sablé, and he often played a game called '*sentences*', where random ideas were discussed. He spent hours polishing these ideas into his *Maximes*, which are still in print, such as: '*There is no disguise which can hide love for long where it exists, or simulate it where it does not*' and '*If we had no faults, we should not take so much pleasure in noting those of others*'.

MOLIÈRE
1622–1673

'We must eat to live, not live to eat'

'Know, Master Jacques, you and people like you, that a table
overloaded with eatables is a real cut-throat; that, to be the true
friends of those we invite, frugality should reign throughout the
repast we give, and that according to the saying of one of the
ancients, "We must eat to live, and not live to eat."'

L'Avare (The Miser), 1668

Jean-Baptiste Poquelin (Molière) was the son of
one of Louis XIII's upholsterers, and showed a talent for
mimicry as a child. Living near the two main theatres in
Paris, aged 21 he decided to make his career in the
theatre. He fell in love with an actress, and with her and
some others founded a dramatic troupe, changing his
name to spare his family the embarrassment of having
an actor in the family. The troupe was unsuccessful
in two years in Paris, so toured the provinces for the next
12 years, when Molière began writing plays such as *The Blunderer*. By 1658 they
were back in Paris, and his comedy *The Love-Sick Doctor* impressed Louis XIV.
His company was now allowed to perform at one of the three best Paris theatres,
and Louis became their unofficial patron.

Molière usually directed his own plays and often played the leading role. He
suffered a haemorrhage while performing *The Imaginary Invalid* but insisted on
completing the performance and died that night. No priest would take his
confession, as all actors were excommunicated, and he was not allowed to be
buried in holy ground until Louis XIV intervened and he was buried under cover
of darkness. His comedy has influenced the work of other dramatists the world
over, with plays like *The School for Wives*, *Tartuffe* and *The Misanthrope* still
amusing audiences today.

JEAN DE LA FONTAINE
1621–1695

'Beware, as long as you live, of judging people by appearances'

Fables Choisies Mises en Vers, Book VI, Fable 5, 1668

La Fontaine's *Fables* rank among the masterpieces of world literature, published from 1668 to 1694. Each tale has a moral of how to behave correctly, or how life should be lived. The use of animals in the stories gave La Fontaine distance from contemporary issues and protection from the bad feelings of those he mocked in reality. He was considered a lover of pleasure, drifting from one patron to another rather than applying himself to a vocation. He went to Paris to study medicine and theology, but qualified as a lawyer. He then held a number of government posts but they did not pay much money, so he decided to become a writer in Paris, and in 1683 he was elected to the Académie Française in recognition of his contribution to French literature. At the age of 71 La Fontaine became ill, and he started to think seriously about his previous dissolute life, wearing a hair shirt, and again embracing Catholicism. His friends were not convinced of his redemption, as he had taught that pleasure is one's *'primal and congenital good'*. Among his precepts are:

'Help yourself, and heaven will help you'

'A hungry stomach has no ears'

'I bend but do not break'

'He knows the universe, and himself he does not know'

'Never sell the bear's skin before one has killed the beast'

'Patience and time do more than strength or passion'

'People who make no noise are dangerous'

'On the wings of Time grief flies away'

BLAISE PASCAL
1623–1662

'"God is or He is not." But to which side shall we incline?'

'"God is or He is not." But to which side shall we incline?...
Let us weigh the gain and the loss in wagering that God is.
Let us estimate the two chances. If you gain, you gain all;
if you lose, you lose nothing. Wager then without any hesitation
that He is.'

Pensées (Thoughts), 1670

This proposition is known as 'Pascal's wager'. A contemporary of Descartes, Pascal was a mathematician, inventing the first accurate mechanical calculator, but it was not successful as it was feared it would put accountants out of business. The basic design of his 'Pascaline' lived on in mechanical calculators for over 300 years, and as a counting machine it was not superseded until the invention of the electronic calculator.

Pascal was also a physicist and moralist, and devoted most of his life to the exercise of religion, otherwise his legacy may have been even greater. Before he was 13 he discovered an error in the geometry of Descartes. Aged 27, he temporarily abandoned all science to '*contemplate the greatness and the misery of man*', but in 1653 invented the arithmetical triangle and with Fermat created the calculus of probabilities. In 1654 he fortunately survived a coach crash, and believed it was again a call for him to abandon all but the religious life. He was depressed about the lack of commercial success of his Pascaline, so generally turned his back on science. Pascal is best known for his posthumous collection of essays, *Pensées*, in which we read: '*If Cleopatra's nose had been shorter, the whole face of the world would have changed*' and '*We shall die alone*'.

JOHN MILTON
1608–1674

'Eyeless in Gaza at the Mill with slaves'

'Why was my breeding ordered and
    prescribed
As of a person separate to God,
Designed for great exploits; if I must die
Betrayed, Captived, and both my Eyes
    put out,
Made of my Enemies the scorn and
    gaze;
To grind in Brazen Fetters under task
With this Heav'n-gifted strength? O
    glorious strength
Put to the labour of a Beast, debased
Lower than bondslave! Promise was
    that I
Should Israel from Philistian yoke
    deliver;
Ask for this great Deliverer now, and
    find him
Eyeless in Gaza at the Mill with slaves,
Himself in bonds under Philistian yoke;
Yet stay, let me not rashly call in doubt
Divine Prediction; what if all foretold
Had been fulfilled but through mine
    own default,
Whom have I to complain of but my
    self?
Who this high gift of strength
    committed to me,

In what part lodged, how easily
    bereft me,
Under the Seal of silence could not keep,
But weakly to a woman must reveal it
O'ercome with importunity and tears.

God, when he gave me strength, to
    show withal
How slight the gift was, hung it in my
    Hair.
But peace, I must not quarrel with the
    will
Of highest dispensation, which herein
Happ'ly had ends above my reach to
    know:
Suffices that to me strength is my bane,
And proves the source of all my
    miseries;
So many, and so huge, that each apart
Would ask a life to wail, but of all,
O loss of sight, of thee I most complain!
Blind among enemies, O worse than
    chains,
Dungeon, or beggary, or decrepit age!

O dark, dark, dark, dark, dark, amid
    the blaze of noon,
Irrecoverably dark, total Eclipse
Without all hope of day!'

Samson Agonistes, 1671

This verse play about the Biblical Samson superbly evokes Milton's anguish about his own blindness. The titular quote was popularized in the 20th century by Aldous Huxley, who used it as a title for one of his most famous novels.

JOHN MILTON
1608–1674

'They also serve who only stand and wait'

'When I consider how my light is spent,
Ere half my days in this dark world and wide,
And that one talent which is death to hide
Lodged with me useless, though my soul more bent
To serve therewith my Maker, and present
My true account, lest He returning chide;
"Doth God exact day-labour, light denied?"
I fondly ask. But Patience, to prevent
That murmur, soon replies, "God doth not need
Either man's work or His own gifts. Who best
Bear His mild yoke, they serve Him best. His state
Is kingly: thousands at His bidding speed,
And post o'er land and ocean without rest;
They also serve who only stand and wait."'

'When I Consider How My Light Is Spent' ('On His Blindness'), 1673

After Cambridge University, Milton decided against becoming a clergy-man and secluded himself at his father's house for years, studying and writing. In 1638 he toured Europe, meeting Galileo and other scholars. In 1642, aged 36, he married the 17-year-old Mary Powell, but within weeks they were estranged, partially stimulating him to write the epic *Paradise Lost*, printed in 1667. It is an inspirational work, considered one of the greatest pieces of writing in the history of literature. Slowly going blind, Milton worked as a languages secretary for the Commonwealth, so was thrown into gaol during the Restoration. He expresses his fear in the above poem that blindness has robbed him of his usefulness, and that he will be cast aside by society. It ends on a hopeful note, though: that he must wait for his reward. Milton also published *Paradise Regain'd* (1671) and the superb *Samson Agonistes* (1671). A devout Christian, he wrote in *Christmas*: '*Ring out ye crystal spheres! Once bless our human ears, If ye have power to touch our senses so; And let your silver chime Move in melodious time, And let the bass of Heaven's deep organ blow; And with your ninefold harmony Make up full consort to the angelic symphony.*'

THOMAS TRAHERNE
c.1637–1674

'You never enjoy the world aright, till the Sea itself floweth in your veins'

'You never enjoy the world aright, till the Sea itself floweth in your veins, till you are clothed with the heavens, and crowned with the stars: and perceive yourself to be the sole heir of the whole world, and more than so, because men are in it who are every one sole heirs as well as you. Till you can sing and rejoice and delight in God, as misers do in gold, and Kings in sceptres, you never enjoy the world.

Till your spirit filleth the whole world, and the stars are your jewels; till you are as familiar with the ways of God in all Ages as with your walk and table; till you are intimately acquainted with that shady nothing out of which the world was made; till you love men so as to desire their happiness, with a thirst equal to the zeal of your own; till you delight in God for being good to all: you never enjoy the world.'

Centuries of Meditation: First Century, Part 29

Thomas Traherne was ordained as an Anglican clergyman in 1660. In his lifetime, he published only one work, *Roman Forgeries* (1673) – *Christian Ethicks*, his most important prose work, was published posthumously. His *Thanksgivings* appeared anonymously in 1699. In 1896, two of his manuscripts were discovered by chance on a London bookstall. *Poetical Works* was first published in 1903, followed in 1908 by *Centuries of Meditations*, a series of some 410 short passages which explore morality, spirituality and creation. More of his manuscripts have been found since, including one on fire in a rubbish tip. Traherne is often considered as the last of the Metaphysical Poets, who included such major figures as George Herbert, John Donne and Henry Vaughan. Traherne also gave us: *'The world is a mirror of Infinite Beauty, yet no man sees it.'*

BARUCH SPINOZA
1632–1677

'Man is a social animal'

Ethics, 1677

Spinoza's regard for his fellow man was such that Bertrand Russell called him *'the noblest and most lovable of the great philosophers... As a natural consequence, he was considered, during his lifetime and for a century after his death, a man of appalling wickedness'.*

Spinoza was born in Amsterdam to a family of Jewish emigrants fleeing persecution in Portugal. His views were so heretical that in 1656 he was excommunicated from Judaism by a rabbinical court and Latinized his name to Benedict de Spinoza. He then earned his living as a simple lens-grinder, refusing academic posts. His philosophy was that the highest good was knowledge of God. This gave us true blessedness, freedom from tyranny by the passions, resignation to destiny and freedom from fear. To Spinoza, truth is like geometry, following from first principles, and is accessible to the logical mind. Spinoza regarded mind and body (or ideas and the physical universe) as merely different aspects of a single substance, which he called alternately God and Nature, God being Nature in its fullness. This pantheism was considered blasphemous by the religious and political authorities of his day. Of his works, only *A Treatise on Religious and Political Philosophy* (1670) was published during his lifetime. *Ethics, Political Treatise* and *Hebrew Grammar* are among his works published posthumously (in 1677). Spinoza tells us:

'Those who wish to seek out the cause of miracles, and to understand the things of nature as philosophers, and not to stare at them in astonishment like fools, are soon considered heretical and impious, and proclaimed as such by those whom the mob adores as the interpreters of nature and the gods. For these men know that once ignorance is put aside, that wonderment would be taken away which is the only means by which their authority is preserved.'

JOHN BUNYAN
1628–1688

'Hanging is too good for him, said Mr Cruelty'

The Pilgrim's Progress, 1678

Bunyan's father was a brazier who made and sold brass articles, and Bunyan was brought up in his trade. From 1644 to 1646 he fought in the English Civil War: *'When I was a soldier, I with others were drawn out to go to such a place to besiege it; but when I was just ready to go one of the company desired to go in my room, to which when I had consented, he took my place; and coming to the siege, as he stood sentinel he was shot into the head with a musket bullet and died.'*

Bunyan described himself as the worst of sinners, having indulged in *'swearing, lying, and blaspheming'*. In 1653 he began to preach, gaining great success, but on the 1660 Restoration of the Monarchy, his church was given back to the Established Church. Late that year, Bunyan was arrested for unlicensed preaching, and was again arrested in 1661. Refusing to abstain from his evangelical preaching, he was kept in prison with one short interval until 1672, when he was released at the Declaration of Indulgence.

Bunyan wrote and published several books of meditations whilst in prison, including his remarkable autobiography, *Grace Abounding to the Chief of Sinners* (1666). Still preaching, he was imprisoned again in the winter of 1675–6, and mainly in Bedford Gaol composed the religious allegory *The Pilgrim's Progress*. The work was hugely successful and has been translated into more than 100 languages. The opening lines are: *'As I walked through the wilderness of this world'*, and lines include *'dark as pitch'*, *'the name of the slough was Despond'* and *'an ornament to her profession'*.

JOHN BUNYAN
1628–1688

'Who would true Valour see'

'Who would true Valour see
Let him come hither;
One here will Constant be,
Come Wind, come Weather.
There's no Discouragement,
Shall make him once Relent,
His first avowed Intent,
To be a Pilgrim.

Who so beset him round,
With dismal Stories,
Do but themselves Confound;
His Strength the more is.

No Lyon can him fright,
He'll with a Giant Fight,
But he will have a right,
To be a Pilgrim.

Hobgoblin, nor foul Fiend,
Can daunt his Spirit:
He knows, he at the end,
Shall Life Inherit.
Then Fancies fly away,
He'll fear not what men say,
He'll labour Night and Day,
To be a Pilgrim.'

The Pilgrim's Progress, Part II, 1684

This is the only hymn in popular use today by the Baptist minister John
Bunyan. The words are spoken by Mr Valiant-for-Truth, relating the story of his
pilgrimage to Mr Greatheart. *The Pilgrim's Progress* is probably the most widely
read Christian allegory in the world. Bunyan's evangelical conversion came about
after he married a woman named Mary when he was just 21. Her only dowry was
two religious books, Lewis Bayly's *Practice of Piety* and Arthur Dent's *Plain Man's
Pathway to Heaven*. Bunyan began to feel guilt for having been profane, and for
bell-ringing and dancing as a youngster, and his Christianity was reinforced when
he narrowly escaped being killed in the Civil War. He believed he had been saved
to carry out religious works.

JEAN DE LA BRUYÈRE
1645–1696

'There are but three events in a man's life: birth, life and death. He is not conscious of being born, he dies in pain, and he forgets to live.'

Characters, or Manners of the Age, 1688

One of the major French writers, La Bruyère was a satirist and moralist who became famous with his misanthropic *Les Caractères*, which described a wide variety of leading people of his era. He was admitted to the Bar in 1665, but spent around 20 years in Paris reading, meditating and living the life of a recluse. At this time he wrote *'There are some who speak one moment before they think'*. From 1684 until the end of his life, he worked for the family of the Duc de Bourbon as a tutor, secretary and librarian at Chantilly, but was dissatisfied with his low status in the household. La Bruyère's *Characters* made him instantly famous, appearing as an appendage to his translation of the *Characters of Theophrastus*, but also made him enemies among powerful persons, who felt that they were being ridiculed. Gradually the book expanded massively from 30 character sketches to over 1300, and eight successive editions were published in his lifetime. His is a disillusioned view of human nature in the time of Louis XIV:

> 'Nothing more clearly show how little God esteems his gift to men of wealth, money, position and other wordly goods, than the way he distributes these, and the sort of men who are most amply provided with them… If we heard it said of Orientals that they habitually drank a liquor which went to their heads, deprived them of reason, and made them vomit, we should say "How very barbarous!"'

JOHN LOCKE
1632–1704

'Though the familiar use of the Things about us, takes off our Wonder; yet it cures not our Ignorance'

An Essay Concerning Human Understanding (III. vi. 9), 1690

Possibly the greatest philosopher in the English language, Locke's work defined English political thought for over a century. He trained as a doctor before becoming tutor in the family of the Earl of Shaftesbury, who was himself imprisoned for opposition to the government in the 1670s. Locke was in exile in Holland from 1683 to 1688, when the accession of William III made it possible for him to return. Locke's *Two Treatises of Government* was written in the throes of the Whig revolutionary plots against Charles II in the early 1680s. In this work, Locke gives us a theory of natural law and natural rights, which he uses to distinguish between legitimate and illegitimate civil governments, and to argue for the legitimacy of revolt against tyrannical governments:

'Whenever the Legislators endeavour to take away, and destroy the Property of the People, or to reduce them to Slavery under Arbitrary Power, they put themselves into a state of War with the People, who are thereupon absolved from any farther Obedience... (Power then) devolves to the People, who have a Right to resume their original Liberty, and, by the Establishment of a new Legislative (such as they shall think fit) provide for their own Safety and Security, which is the end for which they are in Society.'

In his *An Essay Concerning Human Understanding*, Locke expressed his ideas of human nature and his understanding of it. He believed that at birth our minds are a tabula rasa, a blank slate, upon which experience would write. Ideas are not innate, but come from sensation and reflection of experiences. His aim was to measure the abilities of our understanding so that we are fully aware of our ability to know. Only by understanding can we be aware of that of which we are ignorant, and can knowledge be progressed.

WILLIAM CONGREVE
1670–1729

'Musick has charms to soothe a savage breast'

The Mourning Bride, 1697

Educated at Trinity College, Dublin, Congreve then studied law and was helped by John Dryden to write plays. His first, *The Old Bachelor* (1693), was a success when it was produced at the Theatre Royal, Drury Lane. He writes: *'Thus grief still treads upon the heels of pleasure; Married in haste, we may repent at leisure.'* 1694 saw *The Double Dealer*, from where we get the line *'She lays it on with a trowel'*. In 1697, Congreve wrote his only tragedy, *The Mourning Bride*, in which we read *'Musick has charms to soothe a savage breast – To soften rocks, or bend a knotted oak'* and *'Heav'n hath no rage like love to hatred turn'd, Nor Hell a fury, like a woman scorn'd'*.

Other plays were followed by Congreve's comedy masterpiece, his 'comedy of bad manners', *The Way of the World* (1700). The story revolves around a pair of lovers who establish a rather unconventional marriage arrangement based on their knowledge of the way of the world, which is full of fops and fools. Congreve tells us: *'Beauty is the lover's gift'* and that Lady Wishfort is *'the antidote to desire'*. His wit and his characters' sexual freedom offended moralists of the day, and he found it increasingly difficult to get a play produced. He was forced to give up playwriting completely at the age of 30, and for the next 29 years he lived on his reputation and the royalties from his plays, suffering from gout and cataracts. He is buried in Westminster Abbey.

DANIEL DEFOE
1660–1731

'The best of men cannot suspend their fate:
The good die early, and the bad die late.'

'The Character of the Late Dr Samuel Annesley', 1697

Daniel Foe was trained under the influence of the clergyman Annesley, but did not pass into the ministry, becoming a hose factor (cloth merchant) aged 18. He then joined Monmouth's rebels to overthrow the Catholic James II and fought at Sedgmoor. Somehow he escaped the trials of Judge Jeffreys and altered his name to Daniel Defoe. Aged 31, Defoe published 'An Essay on Projects', with a view of women's rights three centuries before its time: '*I have often thought of it as one of the most barbarous customs in the world, considering us as a civilized and a Christian country, that we deny the advantages of learning to women.*' A 1702 pamphlet upon Dissenters was deemed critical of the Anglican Church, so Defoe was fined, pilloried and imprisoned. In 1703 he started a newspaper, *The Review*, reporting on politics and social issues, and was imprisoned again. In 1719 he began a new career, writing a stream of novels including *Robinson Crusoe* (1719), *Journal of the Plague Year* (1722), *Moll Flanders* (1722) and *Roxana* (1724).

Though Defoe was not generally known for his poetry, in 1697 he wrote an elegy for Dr Samuel Annesley, who had been the minister of Defoe's parish for many years. Defoe published over 560 books and pamphlets, many under pseudonyms, and is considered the founder of British journalism. In *Roxana*, he returned to his theme on the inequality of women:

'I thought that a woman was a free agent, as well as a man, and that she was born free, and could she manage herself suitably, might enjoy that liberty to as much purpose as the men do; that the laws of matrimony were indeed otherwise... and those such that a woman gave herself entirely away from herself, in marriage, and capitulated only to be, at least, but an upper servant.'

SIR RICHARD STEELE
1672–1729

'Reading is to the mind what exercise is to the body'

Tatler, 18 March 1710

Richard Steele was an excellent publicist, for his new concept of regular publications with well-written articles. Previously, papers only existed for news transmission, and his new 'magazines' were designed to appeal to the gentry with discretionary spending power. He founded and published the *Tatler* in 1709, followed by the *Spectator* in 1711 and the *Guardian* in 1713. Noted for his working relationships with Joseph Addison and Alexander Pope, Steele had left Oxford without taking a degree, to join the Horse Guards. In 1707 he married Mary Scurlock, whom he had met at his first wife's funeral four months earlier, and they lived in a small house named The Hovel in Hampton. He borrowed money from Addison, using the house as security, and had to sell it when Addison called in the debt in 1709.

Extravagant throughout his life, Steele was elected to Parliament in 1713, but was expelled the following year for seditious libel. Restored to favour in 1715 he was knighted, and appointed Inspector of the Royal Stables and Commissioner of Drury Lane Theatre. There, in 1722, he produced *The Conscious Lovers*, his best comedy. His wife became domiciled in Wales, and Steele ended a 1708 letter to her with '*A little in drink, but at all times your faithful husband*'. In another letter to her in 1717, he complains of his landlady's demand for rent: '*I have had much struggle by reason of ill-payments, and unreasonable, hasty, severe people; among the rest, that hag Lady Vandeput. I have paid her to the end of last quarter.*' In the *Spectator*, Steele noted: '*There are so few who can grow old with a good grace.*'

ALEXANDER POPE
1688–1744

'For fools rush in where angels fear to tread'

'No Place so Sacred from such Fops is barr'd,
Nor is Paul's Church more safe than Paul's Church-yard:
Nay, fly to Altars; there they'll talk you dead;
For Fools rush in where Angels fear to tread.'

An Essay on Criticism, 1711

Pope was an essayist, critic, satirist and one of the greatest poets in the English language, dominating the literary world of his time. His family's Catholic faith meant that his schooling was severely disrupted, since at that time Catholics were not allowed in universities or public employment. However, he could use his father's library, so became enamoured of Homer. Pope was mercilessly mocked for his height of 4 feet 6 inches, being called a 'hunchbacked toad', as tuberculosis had affected his bone development as a teenager.

Pope began writing verse aged 12, but his breakthrough was with his extended poem *An Essay on Criticism* in 1711, a collection of his thoughts on the state of criticism and of literature as a whole. In it we read: '*Good nature and good sense must ever join; To err is human, to forgive divine*'; '*A little learning is a dang'rous thing*'; and '*Hope springs eternal in the human breast*'. In 1712 to 1714 two versions of *The Rape of the Lock*, a wonderful satire about the battle between the sexes, based on a real incident, confirmed Pope's pre-eminence. He had become one of the first professional poets and writers to live off his earnings. Words relevant to all of us are: '*A man should never be ashamed to own he has been in the wrong, which is but saying, in other words, that he is wiser today than he was yesterday.*'

JOSEPH ADDISON
1672–1719

'Cheerfulness keeps up a kind of day-light in the mind'

'Mirth is like a flash of lightning that breaks through a gloom of clouds, and glitters for a moment: cheerfulness keeps up a kind of day-light in the mind'

Spectator, 17 May 1712

Addison was the son of the Dean of Lichfield and was educated at Oxford, beginning his literary career in 1693 with a poetical address to Dryden. In 1694 there followed his *Account of the Greatest English Poets*. In 1699, with the help of the Earl of Halifax, he obtained a pension of £300 a year and went on to spend four years in France, Italy, Austria, Germany and Holland. In 1704 his long poem, *The Campaign*, celebrated the victory of Blenheim, and secured him a post as Commissioner of Excise. He was elected an MP, and contributed hugely to the *Tatler*, started by his friend Richard Steele in 1709. In March 1711 Addison and Steele founded the *Spectator* (as distinct from the modern magazine of the same name, which dates from 1812) and 274 numbers are attributed to Addison.

In his *Cato* (1713) we read: '*The woman who hesitates is lost*' and '*Sweet are the slumbers of the virtuous man*'. Addison was made a Commissioner for Trade and the Colonies, and in 1716 married the Countess of Warwick. His near-contemporary, Samuel Johnson, highly regarded the writings of this poet, essayist, statesman and dramatist: '*Whoever wishes to attain an English style, familiar but not coarse and elegant but not ostentatious, must give his days and nights to the volumes of Addison.*'

DR ISAAC WATTS
1674–1748

'Our God, our help in ages past'

'Our God, our help in ages past,
Our hope for years to come;
Be Thou our guard while life shall last,
And our perpetual Home.'

'Our Help in Ages Past: The Psalms of David Imitated', 1719

John Wesley altered 'Our God' to 'O God' in 1748. This hymn has been called 'The Church's National Anthem', and Watts is the real father of modern hymns. John's brother Charles is mainly remembered for the thousands of hymns he wrote, but before Watts' time hymns were hardly used in public worship. Aged just 18, Isaac Watts complained to his father, the Deacon of a congregational chapel in Southampton, that existing renditions of the psalms lacked harmony and taste. His father asked him to find something better, and that evening the service in the chapel ended with a new hymn:

'Behold the glories of the Lamb
Amidst His Father's throne;
Prepare new honours for His Name
And songs before unknown.'

From that day onwards, Watts brought a fresh hymn to the chapel each Sunday, writing hundreds of hymns throughout a life racked by ill-health. Some think his finest hymn is: '*When I survey the wondrous cross / On which the Prince of Glory died*'. Many of Dr Watts' hymns were written to be sung after his sermons, and so they are full of the teaching he had been trying to enforce. Among his children's hymns is:

'How doth the little busy bee
Improve each shining hour,
And gather honey all the day
From every opening flower!

How skilfully she builds her cell,
How neat she spreads the wax!

And labours hard to store it well
With the sweet food she makes.

In works of labour, or of skill,
I would be busy too;
For Satan finds some mischief still
For idle hands to do.'

BLACK BART
1682–1722

'A merry life and a short one shall be my motto'

'In an honest service there is thin rations [poor food and drink], low wages, and hard labour; in this, plenty, satiety, pleasure and ease, liberty and power; and who would not balance creditor on this side, when all the hazard that is run for it, at worst, is only a sour look or two at choking [dying]? No, a merry life and a short one shall be my motto.'

Quoted in *A General History of the Robberies and Murders of the Most Notorious Pirates*, Captain Charles Johnson (Daniel Defoe), 1724

Known as Bartholomew Roberts, but born as John Robert in Wales, Black Bart was called by *Newsweek* '*The last and most lethal pirate*' and was known across the globe as the 'Black Pirate'. This most formidable pirate in history captured an amazing 400 ships between 1719 and 1722, bringing commerce in North America, the West Indies, West Africa and the whole Atlantic almost to a standstill.

He was captured by the Welsh pirate, Hywel Davis, and asked to join him. Within six weeks, Hywel Davis was dead in an ambush by the Portuguese, and Roberts was voted the new captain by the men. Accepting, he said: '*If I must be a pirate, it is better to be a commander than a common man*'. He swiftly avenged Davis' death, then sailed to Brazil and attacked a Portuguese fleet of 42 merchant ships protected by two men-of-war. Roberts escaped with the richest merchantman in the fleet. He wore for the rest of his career a jewelled golden cross made for the King of Portugal. The band played Black Bart into battle – he dressed in red damasks and velvet from head to toe, with a three-cornered red hat with a huge scarlet plume, and was armed with cutlasses and pistols. His demeanour and scarlet dress were such that French traders called him 'Le Joli Rouge' ('the pretty man in red'), the origin of the 'Jolly Roger'. Roberts' crew was drunk when he was finally killed by Royal Navy cannon fire. Two hundred and fifty-four pirates were captured, and the bodies of the 18 worst offenders, the members of the famous *House of Lords*, were dipped in tar, bound with metal strips and hung in chains from gibbets on three prominent hills overlooking the sea-lanes off what was known as the Gold Coast, now Ghana.

EPITAPH OF SIR CHRISTOPHER WREN
1632–1723

'Lector, si monumentum requiris circumspice'
(Reader, if you seek his monument look around you)

This inscription is on Wren's tomb in St Paul's Cathedral, London – he was the first person to be buried there. This scientist, mathematician and inventor became one of Europe's finest architects, and by the age of 17 he had invented an instrument that wrote in the dark, a pneumatic engine, a weather clock and a new deaf and dumb language. At the age of 25 he was Professor of Astronomy at Gresham College, and aged 29 held the same post at Oxford University. At Gresham College he carried out experiments on the Laws of Motion, and Isaac Newton pointed out that Wren was his precursor in the development of the Law of Gravity.

At Oxford, Wren showed it was possible to send people to sleep for operations by injecting them with opium, and successfully used a syringe to transfer blood between dogs. A founding member of the Royal Society in 1662, he designed the Sheldonian Theatre in Oxford. After the 1666 Great Fire of London, Wren presented Charles II with detailed plans for its rebuilding, and designed 51 new churches as well as St Paul's Cathedral. St Paul's took 35 years to build, and its dome was the largest in the world after St Paul's Basilica in Rome. Wren's other works include the Royal Observatory at Greenwich, the Royal Exchange, Drury Lane Theatre, Chelsea Hospital and the façade of Hampton Court Palace. Wren died in his ninety-first year, as he said, *'Worn out (by God's mercy) a long life in the Royal Service, and having made some figure in the world'*.

EPITAPH OF ISAAC NEWTON
1642–1727

'Nature and Nature's laws lay hid in night: God said, "Let Newton be!" and all was light'

20 March 1727 Composed by Alexander Pope

These words are engraved on the elaborate tomb of Sir Isaac Newton (1642–1727) in Westminster Abbey. Recently voted the most influential scientist of all time, Newton always gave credit to the mathematicians and scientists whose work he developed: *'If I have seen further it is by standing on the shoulders of giants.'* In mathematics, optics and physics, Newton laid the foundations for modern science and revolutionized the world. Newton invented integral calculus and (jointly with Leibniz) differential calculus.

Newton also developed theoretical astronomy, defining the laws of motion and universal gravitation which he used to predict the motions of stars, and the planets around the Sun. Using his discoveries in optics, he also constructed the first reflecting telescope. He developed science from a mélange of isolated facts and laws, capable of describing some phenomena, but predicting only a few. His work gave science a unified system of laws that can be applied to an enormous range of physical phenomena, and can be used to make exact predictions. His two major works were *Opticks* and *Principia*. Newton was the first scientist to be buried in Westminster Abbey.

ISAAC NEWTON
1642–1727

'The great ocean of truth lay all undiscovered before me'

'I do not know what I may appear to the world; but to myself I seem to have been only like a boy playing on the seashore, and diverting myself in now and then finding a smoother pebble or a prettier shell than ordinary, whilst the great ocean of truth lay all undiscovered before me.'

Memoirs of the Life, Writings, and Discoveries of Sir Isaac Newton,
Sir David Brewster, 1855

Newton's remark was made to a young relative, who scribbled it down later, and shows the characteristic modesty of a man who some have called the greatest scientist of all time. Nothing was outside the scope of his enquiring mind, and Louis Figuier recorded that '*He lived the life of a solitary, and like all men who are occupied with profound meditation, he acted strangely. Sometimes, in getting out of bed, an idea would come to him, and he would sit on the edge of the bed, half dressed, for hours at a time.*'

Newton wrote: '*No great discovery was ever made without a bold guess*', and in 1726 he was paid a visit by William Stukely, who recorded: '*I paid a visit to Sir Isaac... he told me he was just in the same situation as when, formerly, the notion of gravitation came into his mind. It was occasioned by the fall of an apple, as he sat in a contemplative mood.*' A committed Christian, Newton refuted attacks from atheistic scientists, telling them, '*This most beautiful system [the universe] could only proceed from the dominion of an intelligent and powerful Being.*' In some of his notes, written in Latin, we see Newton's driving force: '*Plato is my friend – Aristotle is my friend – but my greatest friend is truth.*'

'HERE continueth to rot
The Body of FRANCIS CHARTRES'

'HERE continueth to rot
The Body of FRANCIS CHARTRES,
Who with an INFLEXIBLE CONSTANCY,
And INIMITABLE UNIFORMITY of Life
   PERSISTED
In spite of AGE and INFIRMITIES,
In the Practice of EVERY HUMAN VICE;
Excepting PRODIGALITY and
   HYPOCRISY:
His insatiable AVARICE exempted him
   from the first,
His matchless IMPUDENCE from the
   second.
Nor was he more singular
In the undeviating (De)pravity of his Manners
Than successful
In Accumulating WEALTH.
For without TRADE or PROFESSION,
Without TRUST of PUBLIC MONEY,
And without BRIBE-WORTHY Service
He acquired, or more properly created

A MINISTERIAL ESTATE.
He was the only Person of his Time
Who could cheat without the Mask of
   HONESTY,
Retain his Primeval MEANNESS
When possess'd of TEN THOUSAND a Year.
And having daily deserved the GIBBETT
   for what he did,
Was at last condemn'd to it for what he
   could not do.
Oh Indignant Reader!
Think not his Life useless to Mankind!
PROVIDENCE conniv'd at his execrable
   Designs,
To give to After-ages
A conspicuous PROOF and EXAMPLE,
Of how small Estimation is EXORBITANT
   WEALTH
In the sight of GOD,
By his bestowing it on the most Unworthy
   of ALL MORTALS.'

Written by Dr John Arbuthnot, 1732

Colonel Chartres was an English rake, gambler, brothel-keeper and money-lender, detested by society. The Earl of Chesterfield noted: '*By-gones are by-gones, as Chartres, when he was dying, said of his sins: let us look forwards.*' William Hogarth depicted Chartres as a lecherous old man in *The Harlot's Progress*, behind the procuress, looking libidinously at the unsuspecting country girl new to London. Pope called Chartres '*a man infamous for all manner of vices*' and he was nicknamed 'The Rape-Master General of Great Britain'. In 1730 sensational newspaper reports tell of his being sentenced to death for 'a rape on the body of one Anne Bond, his servant maid'. He paid her £800 to petition for his pardon, with which she married, and bought a tavern with the sign of Colonel Chartres' head. The author of the epitaph, Dr John Arbuthnot, was a well-known satirist, mathematician and physician, who created the cartoon figure of John Bull.

DAVID HUME
1711–1776

'Never literary attempt was more unfortunate than my
Treatise of Human Nature. **It fell dead-born from the**
press, without reaching such distinction, as even to cause
a murmur among the zealots'

'My Own Life', *Essays, Moral and Political*, 1741

According to *The Stanford Encyclopedia of Philosophy,* Hume is *'the most important philosopher ever to write in English',* but he was also a historian and essayist. Born David Home, he attended the University of Edinburgh and refused to follow his expected career in law, turning instead to philosophy. His major works were the poor-selling *A Treatise of Human Nature* (1739–1740), the *Enquiries concerning Human Understanding* (1748) and *Concerning the Principles of Morals* (1751). These books, and his posthumously published *Dialogues concerning Natural Religion* (1779) remain extremely influential. In his *Treatise,* he claimed that *'the errors in religion are dangerous; those in philosophy only ridiculous'* and *'Grief and disappointment give rise to anger, anger to envy, envy to malice, and malice to grief again, till the whole circle be completed'.* His contemporaries denounced his writings as sceptical and atheistic, but he strongly influenced his friend Adam Smith, Immanuel Kant, Jeremy Bentham, Charles Darwin and T.H. Huxley.

Hume is now seen as a precursor of cognitive science, and a champion of philosophical naturalism. In 1752, Hume had published the *Political Discourses* which made his name in wider intellectual circles, and in 1754 began publishing his *History of England,* which brought recognition in Europe. In America, he influenced Benjamin Franklin, Alexander Hamilton and James Madison. As his death approached, crowds gathered to see whether Hume would turn to Christianity. James Boswell recounts that Hume *'said he never had entertained any belief in Religion since he began to read Locke and Clarke... He then said flatly that the Morality of every Religion was bad, and... that when he heard a man was religious, he concluded he was a rascal, though he had known some instances of very good men being religious'.*

EDWARD YOUNG
1683–1765

'Procrastination is the thief of time'

'Procrastination is the thief of time:
Year after year it steals, till all are fled,
And to the mercies of a moment leaves
The vast concerns of an eternal scene.'

The Complaint, or Night Thoughts on Life, Death and Immortality, 1742–45

Disappointed in his political career, Young, a poet and dramatist, took holy orders around 1724, serving for a time as the Royal Chaplain. He wrote: '*I had looked for happiness in fast living, but it was not there. I tried to find it in money, but it was not there either.*'

In 1726, the Prime Minister Walpole awarded him a pension of £200 a year for life. From 1725 to 1728 he had written a set of satires, *The Universal Passion*, and he was the author of three tragedies, *Busiris* (1719), *The Revenge* (1721) and *The Brothers* (1753). His last important work was his prose work *Conjectures on Original Composition* (1759).

The long poem *The Complaint* was inspired by the deaths of his wife, step-daughter and step-daughter's husband between 1736 and 1740, and made him famous across Europe. Young had not married until 1731 when he was 48, and never recovered from the death of his wife in 1740.

Other lines from *The Complaint* include:

'All men think all men mortal, but themselves'

'Tomorrow is the day when idlers work, and fools reform'

'A God all mercy is a God unjust'

'By night an atheist half believes in God'

CHARLES-LOUIS DE SECONDAT, BARON DE LA BRÈDE ET DE MONTESQUIEU
1689–1755

'Liberty is the right to do everything which the laws allow'

The Spirit of the Laws, 1748

Montesquieu was an eminent social commentator and political philosopher of the Age of Enlightenment, famed for his theory of separation of powers, which has been implemented in many democratic constitutions such as that of the USA. He accounted for various forms of government, and the causes for their development, using his thesis to explain how governments could be preserved from corruption. Despotism was a permanent threat to any other type of government, and it was best prevented by a system in which different bodies exercised legislative, executive and judicial power, all bound by the rule of law.

In 1721, Montesquieu published the *Persian Letters*, becoming a literary celebrity. After other publications, in 1728 he was elected to the Académie Française, and in 1731, he began work on his masterpiece, *The Spirit of the Laws*. During this time he also wrote *Considerations on the Causes of the Greatness of the Romans and of their Decline*, which he published anonymously in 1734. In it he tried to work out the application of his views to the particular case of Rome, to discourage the use of Rome as a model for contemporary governments. The Roman Catholic Church placed *The Spirit of the Laws* on the Index of Forbidden Books in 1751, possibly for statements such as '*No kingdom has ever had so many civil wars as the kingdom of Christ*'. In the light of today's distribution of wealth in democratic Western societies, he tells us that '*Luxury is ever in proportion to the inequality of fortunes*' and '*The less luxury there is in a republic, the more it is perfect*'.

HENRY FIELDING
1707-1754

'His designs were strictly honourable'

'His designs were strictly honourable, as the phrase is; that is,
to rob the lady of her fortune by way of marriage.'

The History of Tom Jones, A Foundling, 1749

 The picaresque story of the eponymous foundling's accrual of a fortune, *Tom Jones* was a real breakthrough in comedic writing and from it we get the lines: *'What is commonly called love, namely the desire of satisfying a voracious appetite with a certain quantity of delicate white human flesh'* and *'When children are doing nothing, they are doing mischief'*. Fielding was an eminent writer and playwright as well as a novelist, born in Somerset and at one time a theatre manager. His plays satirizing Walpole's government, however, led to the Theatrical Licensing Act, and Fielding was forced to move to the legal profession.

In the novel *Amelia*, he wrote: *'It hath been often said that it is not death, but dying, which is terrible'*; *'When widows exclaim loudly against second marriages, I would always lay a wager that the man, if not the wedding-day, is absolutely fixed on'* and *'Guilt hath very quick ears to an accusation'*. Also, with his brother John, Fielding organized Britain's first professional police force, the Bow Street Runners, which later developed into Scotland Yard. As a JP at court in Bow Street, he broke up several crime gangs in London. Always suffering from poor health, Fielding went to Lisbon to recuperate but died there.

THOMAS GRAY
1716–1771

'The curfew tolls the knell of parting day'

'The curfew tolls the knell of parting day,
The lowing herd winds slowly o'er the lea,
The ploughman homeward plods his weary way,
And leaves the world to darkness and to me.

Now fades the glimmering landscape on the sight,
And all the air a solemn stillness holds,
Save where the beetle wheels his droning flight,
And drowsy tinklings lull the distant folds:

Save that from yonder ivy-mantled tower
The moping owl does to the moon complain
Of such as, wandering near her secret bower,
Molest her ancient solitary reign.
. . .
The boast of heraldry, the pomp of power,
And all that beauty, all that wealth e'er gave,
Awaits alike th' inevitable hour.
The paths of glory lead but to the grave.

Elegy Written in a Country Churchyard, 1742–50

Thomas Gray was the only child in his family of eight to survive infancy, and one of the most important poets of the 18th century. His mother ran a millinery business to earn money for his education, sending him to Eton where he and his three friends – Horace Walpole, Thomas Ashton and Richard West – formed the Quadruple Alliance. In 1741 Gray's father died. His mother, aunt and he moved to the village of Stoke Poges, where the *Elegy* was written over a period of eight years. In 1742, Gray lost his best friend, Richard West, which inspired him to begin writing poetry seriously. Gray's poems made his reputation, and in 1768 he became Professor of Modern History at Cambridge. He is buried at Stoke Poges churchyard, the scene of the *Elegy*, next to his aunt and mother. Gray's line *'Far from the madding crowd's ignoble strife'* was borrowed by Hardy for his book title, and Gray also wrote: *'Where ignorance is bliss, 'Tis folly to be wise'*.

PHILIP DORMER STANHOPE, EARL OF CHESTERFIELD
1694–1773

‘**Old Mr Lowndes, the famous Secretary of the Treasury, used to say "Take care of the pence, and the pounds will take care of themselves".**’

Letters, 5 February 1750

Chesterfield succeeded to the earldom in 1726, and was a shrewd politician noted for his fine oratory, who became an opponent of Walpole and George II and an admired Lord Lieutenant of Ireland. A patron of literature who offended Dr Johnson, Chesterfield was an ardent Francophile and an intimate friend of Montesquieu and Alexander Pope, and an urbane man of the world whose stoic philosophy and belief in the cultivation of the graces are enshrined in the celebrated *Letters to his Son*, published after his death. As the title suggests, the *Letters* collect Chesterfield's dispatches to his natural son, Philip, and reflect his desire to pass on the political wit and wisdom he accrued in his lifetime. Robert Burns described Chesterfield as *'one of the ablest judges of men, and himself one of the ablest men who ever lived'*. The following are excerpts from his *Letters*:

'I recommend you take care of the minutes: for hours take care of themselves'

'Despatch is the soul of business'

'A chapter of accidents'

'Advice is seldom welcome; and those who want it the most always like it the least'

'In matters of religion or marriage I never give any advice; because I will not have anybody's torments in this world or the next laid to my charge'

DENIS DIDEROT
1713–1784

'There are three principal means of acquiring knowledge available to us'

'There are three principal means of acquiring knowledge available to us: observation of nature, reflection, and experimentation. Observation collects facts; reflection combines them; experimentation verifies the result of that combination. Our observation of nature must be diligent, our reflection profound, and our experiments exact. We rarely see these three means combined; and for this reason, creative geniuses are not common.'

'On the Interpretation of Nature', Essay no. 15, 1753, from *L'Encyclopédie ou Dictionnaire raisonné des sciences, des arts et des métiers, par une Société de Gens de lettres (The Encyclopedia or A Systematic Dictionary of the Sciences, Arts and Crafts)*, 1751–1772

Denis Diderot explained the goal of the *Encyclopedia* thus: '*All things must be examined, debated, investigated without exception and without regard for anyone's feelings.*' The *Encyclopedia* was published under the direction of Diderot and d'Alembert, and contains 72,000 articles written by more than 140 contributors, a massive reference work for the arts and sciences, which served to propagate the ideas of the French Enlightenment. Through its attempt to classify learning and to open all domains of human activity to its readers, the *Encyclopedia* gave expression to many of the most important intellectual and social developments of its time.

Diderot studied history and developed a fear that knowledge would continue to be destroyed by Christians, and his books were proscribed by the Church. He said: '*The philosopher has never killed any priests, whereas the priest has killed a great many philosophers*' and '*From fanaticism to barbarism is only one step*'. His attacks on the political system of France were among the most potent causes of the Revolution, and his criticisms of the morality of the day led to his imprisonment.

VOLTAIRE (FRANÇOIS MARIE AROUET)
1694–1778

Pour encourager les autres
(To encourage the others)

'In this country [England] it is thought well to kill an admiral
from time to time to encourage the others'

Candide, Chapter 23, 1759

Voltaire wrote this two years after the execution of Admiral John Byng (1704–1757). At the start of the Seven Years' War, the French fleet had captured Minorca, with the exception of the castle of St Philip where General Blakeney was besieged. Admiral Byng's ships were in poor condition, and his engagement with the French fleet was inconclusive. In a council of war of his captains, it was decided that the state of the fleet militated against further action, which the admiral accepted. Blakeney surrendered the island and on his return to England Byng was arrested and imprisoned, the scapegoat for a government that had not given him an adequate force to attack. He was found guilty of neglect of duty for not doing his utmost to take, sink, burn and destroy the enemy ships. The court made a strong recommendation for clemency on the grounds of Byng's personal courage in the action, but the German-born King George II refused to grant it. And when the Leader of the House of Commons, William Pitt the Elder, told the Hanoverian king: '*The House of Commons, Sir, is inclined to mercy*', the King rudely answered: '*You have taught me to look for the sense of my people elsewhere than in the House of Commons.*' All the men-of-war at Spithead were ordered to send their boats, with their captains and all the officers of each ship, accompanied by a party of Marines under arms, to attend Byng's execution on his former flagship, the *Monarch*. The *Monarch*'s log records the execution: '*At 12 Mr Byng was shot dead by 6 Marines and put into his coffin*'.

JEAN-JACQUES ROUSSEAU
1712–1778

'Man was born free, and everywhere he is in chains'
The Social Contract, 1762

Rousseau's first major philosophical work, *A Discourse on the Sciences and Arts*, argued that the progression of the sciences and arts caused the corruption of virtue and morality. His next work, *The Discourse on the Origin of Inequality*, rationalized that human beings are basically good by nature, but have been corrupted by the historical events that resulted in present-day society. Rousseau's praise of nature continues throughout all his books, the most significant of which include one on the philosophy of education, *Emile, or On Education*, and his masterpiece on political philosophy, *The Social Contract*, both published in 1762. These works caused great controversy in France and were immediately banned by Paris authorities.

Rousseau believed that it was impossible to return to the moral innocence of 'the noble savage', so individuals would have to contract with each other to enter society. From the isolated selves of individuals a collective entity is therefore formed which can both legislate for and embody its individual members. The nature of freedom is changed by the act of contract. Before contracting, man's freedom lies in pursuing his individual interests, but afterwards freedom consists in obeying 'the general will'. Rousseau fled from France (helped by David Hume) and settled in Switzerland, but he continued to find difficulties with the authorities and quarrel with friends. The end of his life was marked in large part by his growing paranoia and his continued attempts to justify his life and his work. His writings inspired many of the leaders of the French Revolution, leading Napoléon to comment at Rousseau's tomb: '*Maybe it would have been better if neither of us had been born.*'

LAURENCE STERNE
1713–1768

'Of all the cants which are canted in this canting world, though the cant of hypocrites may be the worst, the cant of criticism is the most tormenting!'

Tristram Shandy, Volume iii, Chapter xii, 1759–1767

Educated at Cambridge, Sterne was ordained in the Church of England in 1738. He spent the next 21 years as a vicar in Yorkshire, preaching eccentrically, and despite the fact that he was married, having various affairs throughout his life. It was reported that as soon as he mounted the pulpit, *'half of the congregation usually left the church, as his delivery and voice [were] so very disagreeable'*. In 1760 Sterne moved to London, where he lived a gregarious, dissolute life despite suffering from consumption. The nine volumes of his masterpiece, the comically Rabelaisian novel *The Life and Opinions of Tristram Shandy, Gentleman*, became a literary sensation.

Tristram Shandy was a ground-breaking 'stream of consciousness' novel. Tristram is not born until halfway through the novel, and the account of his life never manages to progress beyond his third year. As a child, when asked his name, Tristram replies: *'Don't puzzle me!... I wish either my father or my mother, or indeed both of them, as they were in duty equally bound to it, had minded what they were about when they begot me.'* Unlike any book in English ever written, we find terms like *'the corregiescity of Corregio'*. The novel was so obscure and unfathomable that the following passage has given us the term 'a cock and bull story': *'Said my mother, "what is this story all about?" – "A Cock and a Bull" said Yorick'*. For health reasons, from 1762 to 1764 Sterne lived in Toulouse with his wife, who was mentally ill, and their daughter. In 1765 he made a tour of France and Italy, which he recorded in *A Sentimental Journey Through France and Italy* (1768).

OLIVER GOLDSMITH
1730–1774

'Ask me no questions and I'll tell you no lies'

She Stoops to Conquer, 1773

After a miserable time at Trinity College, Dublin, because of his lack of 'gentlemanly' manners, Goldsmith missed his ship to emigrate to America. After beginning to study law, but gambling away his money, he started to study medicine before taking a walking tour through Europe, supporting himself by flute-playing. He arrived in England, penniless, in 1756 and began writing to earn a living. Of these difficult times, he wrote: *'Our greatest glory consists not in never falling, but in rising every time we fall'.* He rapidly became popular, and joined the eminent circle of Johnson, Burke and Reynolds. He was established as a poet and writer when his novel *The Vicar of Wakefield* really made his name in 1766. In this, we read: *'To what happy accident is it that we owe so unexpected a visit?'*; *'And his best riches, ignorance of wealth'* and *'Handsome is that handsome does'*. In 1770 there followed his poem, 'The Deserted Village', and in 1773 his dramatic masterpiece, *She Stoops to Conquer*, a comedy of manners whose appeal has lasted into the modern era, spawning a number of film and stage adaptations. In this, Goldsmith noted: *'The first blow is half the battle'* and: *'Let schoolmasters puzzle their brain, With grammar, and nonsense, and learning; Good liquor, I stoutly maintain, Gives genius a better discerning.'*

Goldsmith's mission was to make natural the comedy of his time, breaking away from the genteel genre of other works. However, his drunkenness and gambling brought him massive debts and broke his health. Some other quotes of his are:

> *'A modest woman, dressed out in all her finery, is the most tremendous object of the whole creation'*

> *'I'll be with you in the squeezing of a lemon'*

> *'Honour sinks where commerce long prevails'*

> *'The man recover'd of the bite, The dog it was that died'*

In his *Art of Poetry on a New Plan* (1761), Goldsmith improvised on an old saying of Demosthenes (*see page 33*): *'For he who fights and runs away / May live to fight another day; /But he who is in battle slain / Can never rise and fight again'.*

'Don't Tread on Me'

Motto on the 'Gadsden Flag', c.1775

In 1751, Benjamin Franklin (1706–1790) made a suggestion in his *Pennsylvania Gazette*, responding to the British government's policy of sending convicted felons to America. In exchange, he said, the American colonists should send rattlesnakes to England. In 1754, Franklin sketched and published the first political cartoon in an American newspaper, the image of a snake cut into eight sections. The separate sections represented eight colonies and the curves of the snake the coastline. The original colonies (now States) were combined as the head of the snake, and South Carolina was the tail segment. Beneath the snake were the words '*Join, or Die*'. By 1775, the snake symbol was appearing all over the colonies, and transformed over the years into a coiled rattlesnake, with the warning '*Don't Tread on Me*'.

In 1775, when the Continental Army was desperately short of munitions, it was discovered that munitions ships were on their way to supply the British Army. The Continental Congress decided to create a Continental Navy to capture the ships, accompanied by five companies of Marines. Some of the Marines that enlisted that month in Philadelphia carried drums painted yellow and decorated with a rattlesnake, coiled and ready to strike. The 13 rattles in its tail represented all 13 founder colonies, and the drums carried the motto '*Don't Tread on Me*'. Christopher Gadsden, the leader of the Sons of Liberty in South Carolina, decided that the commander of the new navy, Esek Hopkins, needed his own personal flag. Gadsden gave him a yellow flag with the same coiled rattlesnake and motto that the Marines were using. The rattlesnake was used on many flags over the years, and Benjamin Franklin is attributed with writing: why a snake might be chosen as a symbol for America:

> 'She never begins an attack, nor, when once engaged, ever surrenders: She is therefore an emblem of magnanimity and true courage… she never wounds till she has generously given notice, even to her enemy, and cautions him against the danger of treading on her.'

THOMAS JEFFERSON
1743–1826

'We hold these truths to be self-evident: that all men are created equal; that they are endowed by their Creator with certain inalienable rights; that among these are life, liberty, and the pursuit of happiness'

Draft of The Declaration of Independence, 11–28 June 1776

Probably the most brilliant of all US presidents, and one of the ablest politicians of all time, Jefferson drafted The Declaration of Independence, the document that formally announced and explained the decision of Congress to proceed with the cessation of the American colonies from the British Empire, aged only 33. Jefferson originally wrote '*We hold these truths to be sacred and undeniable*' – '*self evident*' was substituted by Benjamin Franklin. Jefferson later wrote: '*I know of no safe depository of the ultimate power of the society but the people themselves*'. A proponent of religious freedom, Jefferson was Minister to France from 1785 and gradually assumed leadership of the Republicans, who sympathized with the revolutionary cause in France. Attacking Federalist policies, he opposed a strong centralized government and championed the rights of states.

A reluctant candidate for President in 1796, Jefferson came within three votes of election. He became Vice President, although an opponent of President Adams, and in 1800 Jefferson assumed the presidency. He slashed army and navy expenditures, cut the budget, eliminated the tax on whisky so unpopular in the West, yet reduced the national debt by a third. He also sent a naval squadron to fight the Barbary pirates, who were harassing American commerce in the Mediterranean. Further, although the Constitution made no provision for the acquisition of new land, Jefferson suppressed his qualms over constitutionality when he had the opportunity to acquire the Louisiana Territory from Napoléon in 1803. Jefferson retired to the house he built in Monticello to ponder such projects as his grand designs for the University of Virginia.

JOHN ADAMS
1735–1826

'These United Colonies are, and of right ought to be, free and independent States'

'Yesterday, the greatest question was decided which was ever debated in America, and a greater perhaps never was nor will be decided among men. A resolution was passed without one dissenting colony, that "these United Colonies are, and of right ought to be, free and independent States".'

Letter to his wife, Abigail, 3 July 1776

The Continental Congress voted for independence from Britain on 2 July 1776, but 4 July was later chosen as the commemorative date. In another letter sent to his wife, Adams forecast the 4 July celebrations to come: '*The second day of July 1776 will be the most memorable epoch in the history of America... It ought to be solemnised with pomp and parade, with shows, games, sports, guns, bells, bonfires and illuminations from one end of this continent to the other, from this time forward, forevermore.*'

A Harvard-educated lawyer, Adams was always identified with the independence movement, being a delegate to the First and Second Continental Congresses. He was known as a political philosopher as well as a politician and during the Revolutionary War he served in France and Holland in diplomatic roles, and helped negotiate the treaty of peace. From 1785 to 1788 he was minister to the Court of St James's, returning to be elected Vice President under George Washington, and he served as President from 1797 to 1801. In 1800, Adams arrived in the new capital city to take up his residence in the White House. On his second evening in its damp, unfinished rooms, he wrote to his wife: '*Before I end my letter, I pray Heaven to bestow the best of Blessings on this House and all that shall hereafter inhabit it. May none but honest and wise Men ever rule under this roof.*'

ADAM SMITH
1723–1790

'With the great part of rich people, the chief enjoyment of riches consists in the parade of riches'

An Inquiry into the Nature and Causes of the Wealth of Nations, Book 1,
Chapter 11, 1776

From 1751, Smith was Professor of Logic and then of Moral Philosophy at Glasgow University. In 1759 he published a work on the ethics that hold society together – his *Theory of Moral Sentiments*. In 1776, he moved to London and in that year published the book upon which his fame is based – known generally today as *The Wealth of Nations*. It was the first book which established 'economics' as a separate area of study, so he is known as the 'Father of Economics'. Smith formulated the doctrine of 'free enterprise' creating wealth, leading to today's libertarian markets being ruled by market forces. From Smith we also have the concepts of economic self-interest, the division of labour and 'laissez-faire' international trade.

Smith stated that each of us tries to gain wealth, but we must exchange what we own or produce with others who sufficiently value what we have to offer. Thus, by division of labour and a free market, the public interest is rewarded. His expression 'the invisible hand' shows how self-interest guides the most efficient and effective use of resources in any nation's economy. With the extra production and productivity, surplus wealth can fund social welfare. The market should rule economies, not the state, and his works guided right-wing economic thinkers in the second half of the 20th century to influence politicians to dismantle governmental constraints upon business and trade: '*There is no art which one government sooner learns of another than that of draining money from the pockets of the people.*'

VOLTAIRE (FRANÇOIS MARIE AROUET)
1694-1778

'This is no time to make new enemies'

The response of Voltaire on his deathbed, when asked to forswear Satan

François Marie Arouet took the pen name of Voltaire, and was one of France's greatest writers and philosophers. He was briefly imprisoned in the Bastille in 1717 for writing a satire of the government, and while there wrote *Oedipe*. In 1726 he insulted the Chevalier de Rohan and was forced to choose between the Bastille and exile, so he lived in England for three years where he was influenced by the works of Locke and Newton. Back in Paris, he wrote a book praising English institutions, and was forced to leave Paris again as it was interpreted as a criticism of the government.

Voltaire also studied the natural sciences and was voted into the Académie Française in 1746. At his estate at Ferney, he worked continuously, producing a constant flow of books such as *Candide*, plays and letters. He was an outspoken critic of religious intolerance and persecution. Voltaire at last returned to a hero's welcome in Paris aged 83, but because of the excitement of his return he soon died there. In one of his works, he wrote: '*If God did not exist, it would be necessary to invent Him.*' Other statements attributed to him on his deathbed are: '*I am abandoned by God and man*' and '*For God's sake, let me die in peace*'. In 1791 his remains were moved to a resting place at the Panthéon in Paris, but in 1814 a group of 'ultras', a right-wing religious group, stole them and threw them on a rubbish dump.

WILLIAM COWPER
1731–1800

'God moves in a mysterious way
His wonders to perform'

'God moves in a mysterious way
His wonders to perform;
He plants His footsteps in the sea,
And rides upon the storm.

Deep in unfathomable mines
Of never-failing skill
He treasures up His bright
    designs,
And works His sovereign will.

Ye fearful saints, fresh courage
    take,
The clouds ye so much dread
Are big with mercy, and shall
    break
In blessings on your head.

Judge not the Lord by feeble
    sense,
But trust Him for His grace;
Behind a frowning providence
He hides a smiling face.

His purposes will ripen fast,
Unfolding every hour;
The bud may have a bitter
    taste,
But sweet will be the flower.

Blind unbelief is sure to err,
And scan his work in vain;
God is His own interpreter,
And He will make it plain.'

'Light Shining Out of Darkness', *Olney Hymns*, 1779

Cowper was called to the Bar but had to retire because of depression. With his partial recovery, he converted to Christian evangelism. It may be that *'God moves in a mysterious way'* was his rationale for the illness which converted him to a life dedicated to writing. He spent 18 years at Olney in Buckinghamshire, and despite periods of melancholia wrote hymns, poems, translations and letters. He collaborated with Newton on the *Olney Hymns*, found some fame with his ballad 'The Diverting History of John Gilpin', and *The Task* influenced poets such as Wordsworth. In *The Task*, Cowper gave us the couplet:

'Variety's the very spice of life / That gives it all its flavour'

SAMUEL JOHNSON
1709–1784

'Resolve not to be poor: whatever you have, spend less.'

'Resolve not to be poor: whatever you have, spend less. Poverty is a great enemy to human happiness; it certainly destroys liberty, and makes some virtues impracticable and others extremely difficult.'

Letter to James Boswell, 7 December 1782

Johnson had known relative poverty, not being able to afford to finish his degree at Oxford. Scarred from scrofula and blind in one eye, he was lucky to live to old age and become one of the most famous men of his era. In 1735, aged 25, he married the 46-year-old Elizabeth Porter to stabilize his finances. He wrote book reviews in London, then worked on his massive *Dictionary* (1755), then his *Rambler* essays (1750–52), *Idler* essays (1758–60) and *Rasselas, Prince of Abyssinia* (1759). His wife died in 1752, causing him grief for the rest of his life.

He received a government pension in 1762, giving him relief from the threat of a debtors' prison, and in 1763 he met a young Scot named James Boswell and they became fast friends. Boswell took notes of their conversations, and used them in his landmark biography *The Life of Samuel Johnson* (1791). Johnson's *Dictionary* definitions are sometimes superb – '*Network: Anything reticulated or decussated at regular distances, with interstices between the intersections*' – and often humorous, as in this description of himself: '*Lexicographer: A writer of dictionaries, a harmless drudge*'. Johnson's wit was recorded by Boswell in phrases such as: '*A woman's preaching is like a dog's walking on his hinder legs. It is not done well; but you are surprised that it is done at all*' and '*the noblest prospect a Scotchman ever sees, is the high road that leads him to England!*'.

PIERRE AMBROISE FRANÇOIS CHODERLOS DE LACLOS
1741–1803

'A man enjoys the happiness he feels, a woman the happiness she gives'

Les Liaisons Dangereuses, 1782

In Les Liaisons Dangereuses, Laclos gives us a classic work of 18th-century literature, exploring the amorous intrigues and machinations of French aristocracy. The Marquise de Merteuil and the Vicomte de Valmont concoct a plan of seduction to entrap members of high society, but eventually their plotting leads to their undoing: *'Monsieur de Valmont, with an illustrious name, a large fortune, and many agreeable qualities, early realized that to achieve influence in society no more is required than to practise the arts of adulation and ridicule with equal skill.'* The work explores seduction, revenge and malice in the form of letters collected and published by a fictional author, and caused a scandal on its publication, with memorable lines such as: *'He cannot rate me very high if he thinks he is worth my fidelity!'*

Laclos' low social position had prevented him from progressing as an officer in the French army, so he wrote *Les Liaisons Dangereuses*, basing it on the libertine attitudes of the time. In his portrayal of decadence, no doubt exacerbated by his feelings of being an outsider not considered for promotion, Laclos argued that women could not be equal to men as long as they were kept ignorant. It seems that Laclos was challenging his readers to reject the immoral lifestyle of his characters, and to come to understand the limitations of such a life: *'Our intentions make blackguards of us all; our weakness in carrying them out we call probity'*. Laclos did rejoin the army, but his public letter attacking its bureaucracy and workings lost him his commission. He next entered politics, as secretary to the Duc d'Orléans, then again joined the army in 1792, rising to become a general under Napoléon and serving in the Rhine and Italian campaigns.

THOMAS JEFFERSON
1743–1826

'All men shall be free to profess, and by argument to maintain, their opinions in matters of religion'

'Be it therefore enacted by the General Assembly, That no man shall be compelled to frequent or support any religious worship, place, or ministry whatsoever, nor shall be enforced, restrained, molested, or burdened in his body or goods, nor shall otherwise suffer on account of his religious opinions or belief; but that all men shall be free to profess, and by argument to maintain, their opinions in matters of religion, and that the same shall in nowise diminish, enlarge, or affect their civil capacities.

And though we well know this Assembly, elected by the people for the ordinary purposes of legislation only, have no powers equal to our own and that therefore to declare this act irrevocable would be of no effect in law, yet we are free to declare, and do declare, that the rights hereby asserted are of the natural rights of mankind, and that if any act shall be hereafter passed to repeal the present or to narrow its operation, such act will be an infringement of natural right.'

The Virginia Act For Establishing Religious Freedom, 1786

Thomas Jefferson was possibly the greatest statesman and political thinker of all time, and this ground-breaking act was later enshrined in the First Amendment to the United States Constitution: *'Congress shall make no law respecting an establishment of religion, or prohibiting the free exercise thereof; or abridging the freedom of speech, or of the press; or the right of the people peaceably to assemble, and to petition the Government for a redress of grievances.'* Jefferson wrote his own understated epitaph, and it can be seen today on his gravestone in the family cemetery at the house he designed at Monticello:

'THOMAS JEFFERSON
Author of the Declaration of American Independence,
Of the Statute of Virginia for Religious Freedom,
And Father of the University of Virginia.'

EPITAPH OF LADY MARY WORTLEY MONTAGU
1689–1762

'Sacred to the memory
Of
The Right Honourable
Lady Mary Wortley Montagu,
Who happily introduc'd from Turkey,
Into this Country,
The Salutary Art
Of inoculating the Small-Pox.
Convinc'd of its Efficacy
She first tried it with success
On her own Children;
And then recommended the
   practice of it
To her fellow-Citizens.
Thus by her Example and Advice,
We have soften'd the Virulence,
And escap'd the danger of this
   malignant Disease,
To perpetuate the Memory of such
   Benevolence;
And to express her Gratitude
For the benefit She herself has receiv'd
From this alleviating Art,
This Monument is erected
By
HENRIETTA INGE
Relict of THEODORE WILLIAM
   INGE ESQ.
And daughter of Sir JOHN
   WROTTESLEY Baronet
In the Year of Our Lord
MDCCLXXXIX'

This 1789 memorial can be found in Lichfield Cathedral. Lady Mary Wortley Montagu suffered smallpox badly while accompanying her husband to Constantinople, where he was ambassador. She introduced inoculation, which paved the way for Edward Jenner to pioneer vaccination in Britain. Montagu also introduced 'the language of flowers' into England, using flowers to express emotions, and she was a distinguished letter-writer, diarist, essayist and poet. Alexander Pope fell in love with her, but she rebuffed him, earning his lasting enmity – she wrote: 'Some called Pope little Nightingale – all sound and no sense.' She has been called 'the most interesting Englishwoman of her century' and her wit is shown in her remark: 'The one thing that reconciles me to the fact of being a woman is the reflexion that it delivers me from the necessity of being married to one.' There is also a story that she was told at the opera that her hands were dirty, and she answered: 'You should see my feet!' She is buried in London, and her dying words are supposed to have been: 'It has all been most interesting.'

'The body of Benjamin Franklin, printer
(like the cover of an old book, its contents worn out,
and stript of its lettering and gilding)
Lies here, food for worms.
Yet the work itself shall not be lost,
for it will, as he believed, appear once more
In a new and more beautiful edition, corrected and
amended by its Author Benjamin Franklin R.I.P.'

Benjamin Franklin became famous as a scientist, inventor, printer, philosopher, musician, economist and philosopher. This polymath's achievements are too vast to be recounted here, but among his inventions were bifocal glasses, a flexible urinary catheter, the Franklin stove for heating homes more safely, an odometer and the lightning conductor. He started the *Pennsylvania Gazette*, and pioneered lending libraries in the United States.

In the War of Independence, Franklin was ambassador to Europe for the colonies, negotiating French help for America. When he signed the Constitution of the United States of America in 1787, he was the only Founding Father to have signed all five documents that established American independence, the others being the Declaration of Independence, the Treaty of Amity and Commerce with France, the Treaty of Alliance with France, and the Treaty of Peace with Great Britain.

BENJAMIN BANNEKER
1731–1806

'The colour of the skin is in no way connected with the strength of the mind or intellectual powers'

Preface to Almanac 2, 1792

Born the son of a slave and the grandson of a slave, Benjamin Banneker became a mathematician and amateur astronomer. His father had bought his freedom and Benjamin lived on a Maryland homestead for most of his life, working as a tobacco planter. With no formal education, aged 30 he took apart a pocket watch and from it designed and constructed a striking wooden clock, which operated successfully from 1761 at least until his death in 1806. Aged 58 he taught himself astronomy, making projections of eclipses and computing, for almanacs he published from 1791 to 1802, and predicted an eclipse in 1789 that no other scientist in America had foreseen.

In 1791, Thomas Jefferson recommended Banneker to help in surveying Federal Territory for the new capital of Washington. Banneker had sent a copy of his first *Almanac* to Jefferson, then Secretary of State, and in an enclosed letter he petitioned Jefferson to help get rid of '*absurd and false ideas*' that one race was superior to another: '*We have long been considered rather as brutish than human, and scarcely capable of mental endowments.*' He wished Jefferson's sentiments to be the same as his, in other words that '*one Universal Father... afforded us all the same sensations and endowed us all with the same faculties*'. He proudly added: '*I am of the African race, and in the colour which is natural to them of the deepest dye; and it is under a sense of the most profound gratitude to the Supreme Ruler of the Universe.*' Jefferson responded with praise for Banneker's accomplishments.

MARIE ANTOINETTE
1755–1793

'I am calm, as one is when one's conscience reproaches one with nothing.'

'It is to you, my sister, that I write for the last time. I have just been condemned, not to a shameful death, for such is only for criminals, but to go and rejoin your brother. Innocent like him, I hope to show the same firmness in my last moments. I am calm, as one is when one's conscience reproaches one with nothing. I feel profound sorrow in leaving my poor children: you know that I only lived for them and for you, my good and tender sister. You who out of love have sacrificed everything to be with us, in what a position do I leave you! I have learned from the proceedings at my trial that my daughter was separated from you… Let my son never forget the last words of his father, which I repeat emphatically; let him never seek to avenge our deaths. I have to speak to you of one thing which is very painful to my heart, I know how much pain the child must have caused you. Forgive him, my dear sister; think of his age, and how easy it is to make a child say whatever one wishes, especially when he does not understand it. It will come to pass one day, I hope, that he will better feel the value of your kindness and of your tender affection for both of them. It remains to confide to you my last thoughts. I should have wished to write them at the beginning of my trial; but, besides that they did not leave me any means of writing, events have passed so rapidly that I really have not had time…'

The last letter of Marie Antoinette, written hours before her execution,
to her sister-in-law Princess Elizabeth Philippine Marie Helene of France,
at 4.30 a.m., 16 October 1793

This tear-stained letter was passed to Robespierre and hidden, so it never reached Marie Antoinette's sister-in-law, the sister of Louis XVI. Marie Antoinette's son had been forced in the trial to accuse his mother of incest. Madame Elizabeth was guillotined in 1794 in the midst of the French Revolution, having also been found guilty of treason.

WILLIAM BLAKE
1757–1827

'Tyger! Tyger! burning bright'

'Tyger! Tyger! burning bright
In the forest of the night,
What immortal hand or eye
Could frame thy fearful
symmetry?

In what distant deeps or skies
Burnt the fire of thine eyes?
On what wings dare he aspire?
What the hand dare seize the
fire?

And what shoulder, and what
art,
Could twist the sinews of thy
heart?
And when thy heart began to
beat,
What dread hand? and what
dread feet?

What the hammer? what the
chain?
In what furnace was thy brain?
What the anvil? what dread
grasp
Dare its deadly terrors clasp?

When the stars threw down their
spears,
And watered heaven with their
tears,
Did he smile his work to see?
Did he who made the Lamb
make thee?

Tyger! Tyger! burning bright
In the forests of the night,
What immortal hand or eye
Dare frame thy fearful
symmetry?'

'The Tyger', *Songs of Experience*, c.1794

Blake was a superb artist and engraver, a mystic, and one of the finest poets in the English language. Part of one of his longer poems is used for the hymn 'Jerusalem', and he told us: '*If the doors of perception were cleansed everything would appear to man as it is, infinite*'. Blake was an unknown genius in his lifetime, dying in obscurity and his body consigned to an unmarked grave. T. S. Eliot wrote of Blake: '*He approached everything with a mind unclouded by current opinions. There was nothing of the superior person about him. This makes him terrifying*', and the critic William Hazlitt noted: '*He attempts impossibles*'.

THOMAS PAINE
1737–1809

'The most formidable weapon against errors of every kind is reason. I have never used any other, and I trust I never shall.'

'You will do me the justice to remember that I have always supported the right of every man to his opinion, however different that opinion might be to mine. He who denies to another this right makes a slave of himself to present opinion because he precludes himself the right of changing it. The most formidable weapon against errors of every kind is reason. I have never used any other, and I trust I never shall.'

The Age of Reason, 1794

Born in Norfolk, England, Thomas Paine left for America in 1774, and became a journalist for the *Pennsylvania Magazine*. His 1776 pamphlet, 'Common Sense', established his reputation – he committed himself to American independence, and urged the establishment of a Republican constitution. In 'Common Sense', he says: *'Government, even in its best state, is but a necessary evil; in its worst state, an intolerable one.'*

Paine's most influential work was *The Rights of Man* (1791–92), in which he argued for political rights for all men because of their natural equality in the sight of God. Paine also argued for a programme of social legislation to deal with the condition of the poor. In 1792, he was made a French citizen and a month later was elected to the National Convention. He declared: *'A share in two revolutions is living to some purpose.'* From 1793 until 1794, he was in Luxembourg prison, where he wrote *The Age of Reason*. Paine denied that the Bible was the revealed word of God and condemned many of the Old Testament stories as immoral. His political influence was important in England as well as in France and America.

MARY WOLLSTONECRAFT
1759–1797

'You know not how much tenderness for you may escape in a voluptuous sigh'

'I would have liked to have dined with you today, after finishing your essay – that my eyes, and lips, I do not exactly mean my voice, might have told you that they had raised you in my esteem. What a cold word! I would say love, if you will promise not to dispute about its propriety, when I want to express an increasing affection, founded on a more intimate acquaintance with your heart and understanding. I shall cork up all my kindness – yet the fine volatile essence may fly off in my walk – you know not how much tenderness for you may escape in a voluptuous sigh, should the air, as is often the case, give a pleasurable movement to the sensations, that have been clustering round my heart, as I read this morning – reminding myself, every now and then, that the writer loved me... I have felt it in your arms – hush! Let not the light see, I was going to say hear it – these confessions should only be uttered – you know where, when the curtains are up – and all the world shut out – Ah me! I wish I may find you at home when I carry this letter to drop it in the box – that I may drop a kiss with it into your heart, to be embalmed, till we meet, closer.'

Love letter written to William Godwin, 4 October 1796

An early feminist, in 1790 she wrote *A Vindication Of The Rights Of Men* in response to Edmund Burke's *Reflections on The Revolution In France*. In 1792, her *A Vindication of The Rights of Woman* was published. In 1793, she began living with Gilbert Imlay, an American businessman, had a daughter and later tried to commit suicide because of his infidelity. After more publications, she met the philosopher William Godwin in 1796 and the two became lovers. In March 1797 they married owing to her pregnancy, and in August Mary Wollstonecraft Godwin was born, later to marry Shelley and write *Frankenstein*. Just 11 days after the birth, Mary Wollstonecraft died of 'childbed fever', aged only 38.

ROBERT (RABBIE) BURNS
1759–1796

**'My luve is like a red, red rose
That's newly sprung in June;
My luve is like the melodie
That's sweetly played in tune'**

'A Red, Red Rose' (derived from many folk songs), 1796

Born in Ayrshire, Scotland, to a poor tenant farmer, Robert Burns (born Burnes) spent his youth working his father's farm, but in spite of his poverty he was extremely well read. Aged 15, Burns penned his first verse, an ode to the non-farming subjects that dominated his life: whisky and women. Later, after having several illegitimate children, he planned to escape from subsistence-level farming to the safer environment of the West Indies. However, his first collection, *Poems, Chiefly in the Scottish Dialect* (known as the *Kilmarnock Edition*), was published and received critical acclaim. He moved to Edinburgh, where society was amazed at the writing of the 'Ploughman Poet'. He quickly became a national celebrity, and married the mother of two of his children. He worked as an excise-man to supplement his writing income, and continued to write.

More than 400 of Burns' songs are still in existence. His last years were spent writing poems which are now famous, such as 'Tam O'Shanter' and 'A Red, Red Rose'. He died aged 37 on the same day as his wife gave birth to his last son. More than 10,000 people came to his burial to pay their respects. Since 1801, on the anniversary of his birth, Scots both at home and abroad celebrate 'Burns Night' with a supper, where they address the haggis, the ladies and whisky. His 'Auld Lang Syne' is traditionally sung at New Year, and begins: '*Should auld acquaintance be forgot / And never brought to mind?*' Burns was also the first to coin the phrases '*Man's inhumanity to man*' and '*The best-laid plans of mice and men*'.

THOMAS MALTHUS
1766–1834

'Population, when unchecked, increases in a geometric ratio. Subsistence only increases in a mathematical ratio.'

Essay on the Principle of Population, 1798

Malthus' *Essay* was the first serious economic study of the welfare of the lower classes, and in it he predicted a *'perpetual struggle for room and food'* caused by exponential growth of population but linear growth of food. However, it may be that he was writing 200 years before his time. The fulfilment of his prediction has been delayed because of increases in the productivity of mechanization in agriculture, but we are now in the midst of a global population explosion, led by China, India and the Islamic nations.

Malthus believed that actual population has a tendency to push above the food supply. Therefore, increasing the incomes of poorer classes would be useless, as this would boost population. In his much-expanded 1803 edition of the *Essay*, he used empirical evidence to prove this hypothesis. He wanted the lower classes to gain middle-class virtues (and have smaller families) by the introduction of universal suffrage, state-run education for the poor, the elimination of the Poor Laws and the establishment of a nationwide labour market. He argued that once the poor had a taste for luxury, they would demand a higher standard of living for themselves before starting a family. Unknown to Malthus at the time, however, farmland deteriorates with use, so the current situation may be more serious than economists understand. We can now see enormous pressure building on water and food supplies across the globe.

'Here lies in the horizontal position'

'Here lies in the horizontal
   position
The outside *case* of
GEORGE ROUTLEIGH,
   Watchmaker,
Whose abilities in that line were
   an honour
To his profession:
Integrity was the *main-spring*,
And prudence the *regulator*
Of all the *actions* of his life:
Humane, generous and liberal,
His *hand* never stopped
Till he had relieved distress;
So nicely regulated were all his
   movements
That he never went wrong
Except when *set-a-going*
By people
Who did not know his *key*;

Even then, he was easily
Set right again:
He had the art of disposing of his
   time
So well
That his *hours* glided away
In one continual round
Of pleasure and delight,
Till an unlucky *moment* put a
   period to
His existence;
He departed this life
November 14, 1802
Wound up,
In hopes of being taken in *hand*
By his Maker,
And of being
Thoroughly *cleaned*, *repaired* and
   set-a-going
In the World to come.'

These words were marked on the grave of George Routleigh, a watchmaker
buried in St Petroc's Church, Lydford, Devon in 1802. However, they were first
published in an American almanac in 1797, the work of the black American
astronomer and clockmaker, Benjamin Banneker. An earlier version has also been
discovered printed for 'Peter Pendulum' in the *Derby Mercury* in 1786. The stone
grave lid bearing Routleigh's inscription now hangs inside St Petroc's Church.

LUDWIG VAN BEETHOVEN
1770–1827

'I carry my ideas a long time'

'I carry my ideas a long time, rejecting and rewriting until I am satisfied. Since I am conscious of what I want, I never lose sight of the fundamental idea. It rises higher and higher until I see the image of it, rounded and complete, standing there before my mental vision.'

Sketchbooks, 1802

Denis Matthews wrote in his 1988 biography, *Beethoven*: '*The sketchbooks of Beethoven are among the most remarkable documents of human endeavour in existence. They are the private workings of Beethoven's mind – the laboratory or workshop in which his compositions were built up the hard way, as it were stone upon stone...*' Beethoven kept the private notes found in his *Sketchbooks* all his working life, and they show the painful growth of each composition through constant revision, until he achieved his finished opus. The American music critic and music historian Irving Kolodin (1908–1988) said: '*He helps us to understand how the bare bones of a group of notes on a single stave were fleshed out to become a titanic exercise in the use of orchestral power.*'

After having music published in Bonn at the age of just 12, Beethoven moved to Vienna in 1792, finding success and patrons as a piano virtuoso. He began an immense workload of composition, of piano sonatas, symphonies, choral symphonies and string quartets, innovating both in style and in musical content. As early as 1802 he discovered his hearing to be impaired and he soon became profoundly deaf, but carried on composing at a tremendous pace. When a violinist complained about an 'unplayable passage', Beethoven answered: '*When I composed that, I was conscious of being inspired by God Almighty. Do you think I can consider your puny little fiddle when He speaks to me?*' He also wrote: '*Music should strike fire from the heart of man, and bring tears from the eyes of woman.*'

'In overthrowing me, you have cut down in Saint Dominique only the trunk of the tree of liberty. It will spring up by the roots for they are numerous and deep.'

Spoken in June 1802, quoted in *The Black Jacobins*, C.L.R. James, 1938

Born François-Dominique Breda, this slave became known as 'the Black Napoléon' for leading a slave revolt that threw France out of Saint Dominique (later known as Haiti). He was fortunate to have a master who had recognized his intelligence and trained him as a house servant, teaching him to read and write. Toussaint read everything he could, admiring the advocacy of individual rights and equality of the French Enlightenment philosophers. In 1789, the French Revolution changed France and men such as Jean-Jacques Rousseau questioned slavery. Plantation owners in the colonies reacted against proposed changes, which were abandoned, triggering a slave rebellion led by Toussaint. He became known as Toussaint L'Ouverture ('the one who finds an opening') and brilliantly led his ragtag slave army, successfully fighting the French (who helped by succumbing to yellow fever in large numbers) as well as the invading Spanish and British. Robespierre's Jacobins came to power and agreed to abandon slavery, and Toussaint agreed to help the French army eject the British and Spanish. He proved to be a brilliant general, winning seven battles in seven days.

Toussaint became a de facto governor of Haiti, but when Napoléon came to power he reinstated slavery, plunging the colony into war once more. Napoléon then invited Toussaint to a meeting under safe conduct and took him to France in 1802, placing him in a dungeon to die of cold, starvation, torture and neglect. Six months later Napoléon gave Haiti independence. In exile on St Helena, asked about his treatment of Toussaint, Napoléon answered, '*What could the death of one wretched Negro mean to me?*'

WILLIAM WORDSWORTH
1770–1850

'My heart leaps up when I behold
A rainbow in the sky'

'My heart leaps up when I behold
A rainbow in the sky:
So was it when my life began;
So is it now I am a man;
So be it when I shall grow old,
Or let me die!
The Child is father of the Man;
I could wish my days to be
Bound each to each by natural piety.'

'The Rainbow', from the third edition of *The Lyrical Ballads*, 1802

Wordsworth changed the nature of English language poetry for all time. He was a member of the English Romantic Movement, and his personality and poetry were deeply influenced by his love of nature, especially by the scenery of the Lake District, where he lived. His home was frequented by Britain's key writers, poets and artists, such as Robert Southey, Thomas de Quincey and Samuel Taylor Coleridge. A profoundly earnest thinker, Wordsworth simplified poetry to make it understandable to those without classical educations. Other lines from his poems include:

'Come forth into the light of things, let nature be your teacher'

'That best portion of a man's life, his little, nameless, unremembered acts of kindness and love'

'Our birth is but a sleep and a forgetting. Not in entire forgetfulness, and not in utter nakedness, but trailing clouds of glory do we come'

'What though the radiance which was once so bright / Be now forever taken from my sight / Though nothing can bring back the hour / Of splendour in the grass, glory in the flower / We will grieve not, rather find / Strength in what remains behind'

WILLIAM BLAKE
1757–1827

'To see a world in a grain of sand'

'To see a world in a grain of sand,
And a heaven in a wild flower,
Hold infinity in the palm of your hand,
And eternity in an hour.'

*Auguries of Innocence, c.*1803

Poetry has always been concerned with revealing God, man and nature, and Blake uses metaphors to give us an insight into the wonders of life. His poetry conquers time and space, emphasizing our relationship with the universe.

The son of a Westminster draper, aged 11 he entered a drawing school, and aged 14 was apprenticed as an engraver. He mixed with the radical set of Priestley, Paine, William Godwin and Mary Wollstonecraft, and experimented with new methods of engraving. He linked his poems with these new coloured engravings, and published *Political Sketches* (1783) and *There is No Natural Religion* (1788). These works were followed by *Songs of Innocence* (1789), *Marriage of Heaven and Hell* (1790) and *Songs of Experience* (1794), a book that deals with topics of corruption and social injustice.

In his books *The French Revolution* (1791), *America: A Prophecy* (1793) and *Visions of the Daughters of Albion* (1793), Blake developed his attitude of revolt against authority, combining his beliefs with visionary ecstasy. Blake feared government persecution and some of his work was printed anonymously, being only distributed to political sympathizers. From 1800 he worked on his epic poems, *Milton* and *Jerusalem*. They were a potent mixture of prophecy, social criticism and biblical legend. He was charged with high treason on the evidence of a soldier in 1803, but acquitted. In 1809, an exhibition of his work at the Royal Academy was not a success, and he sank into obscurity, for the last 18 years of his life living in poverty, and being buried in an unmarked grave. Blake is now recognized as one of the greatest poets and artists that England has ever produced, a truly radical visionary.

HORATIO NELSON
1758–1805

'Kiss me, Hardy'

Nelson's attributed dying words, spoken to his Flag Captain,
Thomas Masterman Hardy, who kissed his cheek and then his forehead.
Battle of Trafalgar, 1805

Among Nelson's other final words at the Battle of Trafalgar, he apparently also said: '*Thank God, I have done my duty*'. His signal to the fleet before attacking the French and Spanish had been '*England expects every officer and man to do his duty this day*'. As a Vice Admiral of the Royal Navy, the Viscount Nelson was revered in his day for his patriotism and courage. At the attack on Bastin in 1794, he remarked: '*Our country will, I believe, sooner forgive an officer for attacking an enemy than for letting it alone.*' In 1795, he prophesized the death he wished: '*My character and good name are in my own keeping. Life with disgrace is dreadful. A glorious death is to be envied.*' Before the Battle of the Nile in 1797, he told his officers: '*Before this time to-morrow I shall have gained a peerage, or Westminster Abbey.*'

Nelson was badly wounded during the failed attack on Santa Cruz de Tenerife in 1797, and said: '*Let me alone: I have yet my legs and one arm. Tell the surgeon to make haste and (bring) his instruments. I know I must lose my right arm, so the sooner it's off the better.*' Also in 1797, at the Battle of St Vincent, he was asked by his officers not to wear his medals as he was such a conspicuous target. He responded: '*In honour I gained them, and in honour I will die with them*'. In 1801, he refused to see the signal from his admiral to call off his attack at the Battle of Copenhagen, putting the telescope to his blind eye – '*I have only one eye – I have a right to be blind sometimes... I really do not see the signal!*'

JOHANN WOLFGANG VON GOETHE
1749–1832

'Words are mere sound and smoke, dimming the heavenly light'

Faust: A Tragedy, Part I, 1808

This is a paraphrase of one of Faust's speeches to Margaret in her garden:

> 'Call it, then, what thou wilt –
> Call it Bliss! Heart! Love! God!
> I have no name to give it!
> Feeling is all in all:
> The Name is sound and smoke,
> Obscuring Heaven's clear glow.'

Goethe was a German courtier, novelist, poet, playwright and natural philosopher, and is as important in German literature as Shakespeare is in English. Aged only 25, he gained fame with *The Sorrows of Young Werther*, but his most famous work is the poetic drama in two parts, *Faust*. Goethe also made important discoveries in connection with plant and animal life, and evolved a non-Newtonian theory of the character of light and colour, influencing abstract painters such as Mondrian and Kandinsky. Aged 74 Goethe fell in love with the 19-year-old Ulrike von Levetzow, following her from Marienbad to Karlsbad, hoping to marry her. Bitterly disappointed, he wrote *The Marienbad Elegy*. Its last stanza reads:

> 'To me is all, I to myself am lost,
> Who the immortals' fav'rite erst was thought;
> They, tempting, sent Pandoras to my cost,
> So rich in wealth, with danger far more fraught;
> They urged me to those lips, with rapture crown'd,
> Deserted me, and hurl'd me to the ground.'

JOHANN WOLFGANG VON GOETHE
1749–1832

'Omniscient I am not, but well-informed'

Spoken by Mephistopheles in *Faust: A Tragedy*, Part 1, 1808

In Goethe's tragic poem, Faust sells his soul in a pact with a devil named Mephistopheles. Mephistopheles has made a bet with God that he can deflect God's favourite human being, Faust, from righteous pursuits. The poem became a drama and has inspired literature, music and art over the centuries.

Goethe was a precocious youngster, studying Greek, Latin, French and Italian by the age of eight, and became Germany's pre-eminent author. A polymath, he was also a painter, scientist and philosopher. In 1771 Goethe was in Frankfurt, expected to practise law, but instead began writing a hugely successful drama, *Götz von Berlichingen*, which symbolized his wish for intellectual freedom and established his name. He was invited in 1775 to the Duke Karl August's court at Weimar and became manager of his Court Theatre, and thereafter spent most of his life writing his masterpiece, *Faust*. Part 1 was completed in 1808 and Part 2 in 1832, when Goethe was 81. On learning of his son's death in 1830, Goethe remarked: '*I was not unaware that I had begotten a mortal*'. His other works include *Clavigo, Egmont, Stella, Iphigenia in Tauris* and *Torquato Tasso*. His *The Sorrows of Young Werther* initiated a suicide cult, so Napoléon banned the work. In *Faust*, Goethe also writes. '*All extraordinary men, who have accomplished great and astonishing actions, have ever been decried by the world as drunken or insane... Misunderstandings and neglect occasion more mischief in the world than even malice and wickedness.*'

RICHARD BRINSLEY SHERIDAN
1751–1816

'A man may surely be allowed to take a glass of wine by his own fireside'

Spoken in a coffee-house in 1809 as Sheridan watched Drury Lane Theatre burn down, quoted in *Memoirs of the Life of the Rt. Hon. Richard Brinsley Sheridan*, T. Moore, 1825

Sheridan is remembered as the witty writer of *The Rivals* (1775) and *The School for Scandal* (1777), both acute observations of Georgian manners. From 1776 he managed Drury Lane, one of the largest theatres in Europe, until it burnt to the ground in 1809. The fire, combined with his losing his seat in Parliament in 1812 after 32 years as an MP, caused Sheridan to be imprisoned for debt in 1814, as he no longer had Parliamentary immunity. However, the Prince of Wales ensured his early release.

In Parliament Sheridan had been a strong advocate of reform, and the general public thought him to be the most honest MP. A superb orator, in one speech he retorted: '*The Right Honourable Gentleman is indebted to his memory for his jests, and to his imagination for his facts.*' The young Lord Byron idolised 'Sherry', but debts overshadowed Sheridan's later years. To a tailor who asked him to pay off an old debt, or at least pay some interest on it, Sheridan answered: '*It is not in my interest to pay the principal, nor my principle to pay the interest.*' His son Tom, on being told he was to be cut off and left only a shilling by his father, asked him, '*I'm sorry to hear that, sir, you don't happen to have the shilling about you now, do you?*' And when asked by a friend to pay back a loan of £500, Sheridan asked for a further loan of £25, saying, '*My dear fellow, be reasonable; the sum you ask me for is a very considerable one, whereas I only ask you for £25.*'

NAPOLÉON BONAPARTE
1769–1821

'Du sublime au ridicule il n'y a qu'un pas'
(There is only one step from the sublime to the ridiculous)

Born Napolcone di Buonaparte, he said this to the Polish Ambassador in 1812 after his disastrous retreat from Moscow. A soldier from Corsica, Napoléon was rapidly promoted, becoming Commander of the French forces in Italy, and defeating Austria and its allies. In 1798 he took Egypt to hit British trade routes with India, but was isolated when the British fleet destroyed the French at the Battle of the Nile. Britain then allied with Russia and Austria against France, causing a crisis in Paris, and Napoléon seized power. He reformed the law and French institutions, and in 1800 defeated Austria at Marengo. He planned to invade Britain but his fleet was defeated at Trafalgar in 1805. Napoléon next beat a Russo-Austrian army at Austerlitz, and virtually took control of Europe from Sweden to Spain and Italy.

From 1808, Napoléon was engaged in the Peninsular War against Spanish guerrillas and the armies of Portugal and Britain, and his Russian invasion in 1812 led to the weakening of France and the fall of Paris in 1814. Imprisoned on the Isle of Elba off Italy, he escaped in 1815. Marshall Ney was sent with the Fifth Regiment to arrest him, but Napoléon dismounted and walked towards him, shouting that any man could shoot his emperor if he wished. The troops shouted back: '*Vive l'Empereur!*' His 'One Hundred Days' of rule were ended at Waterloo in 1815 by the forces of Wellington and Blucher. Napoléon also gave us the phrase '*An army marches on its stomach*', but his '*England is a nation of shopkeepers*' was in fact first coined by Samuel Adams – one of the founding fathers of the United States.

JANE AUSTEN
1775–1817

'It is a truth universally acknowledged, that a single man in possession of a good fortune, must be in want of a wife'

The opening lines of *Pride and Prejudice*, 1813

The above remark is followed up in *Mansfield Park* (1814), with the observation that '*There certainly are not so many men of large fortune in the world as there are pretty women to deserve them*', and also in a letter Austen wrote dated 13 March 1817: '*Single women have a dreadful propensity for being poor – which is one very strong argument in favour of matrimony*'.

Jane Austen's novels were witty insights into the lives of the upper classes of her day, especially focusing upon relationships and the need for people to make 'the right match' in 'polite society'. She was one of eight children of a clergyman and began to write as a teenager. Her brother Henry helped her find a publisher, and her first novel, *Sense and Sensibility*, appeared in 1811. *Pride and Prejudice* next received excellent reviews, but Austen was relatively unknown until her death. She described it as her '*own darling child*', and its romantic hero Fitzwilliam Darcy's uneven romance with Elizabeth Bennet is a marvellous story. However, her themes of realism and irony run throughout the book: '*Happiness in marriage is entirely a matter of chance*'. *Mansfield Park* was published in 1814, followed by *Emma* in 1816, which was dedicated to the Prince Regent, an admirer of her work. All of Austen's novels were published anonymously, and *Persuasion* and *Northanger Abbey* were published posthumously. In the latter, Austen notes:

'*It would be mortifying to the feelings of many ladies, could they be made to understand how little the heart of man is affected by what is costly or new in their attire*'. Suffering from Addison's disease, she wrote out her will in April 1817, and died in the arms of her sister Cassandra on Friday 18 July 1817, aged only 41.

ROBERT OWEN
1771–1858

> **'Women will be no longer made the slaves of, or dependent upon men... They will be equal in education, rights, privileges and personal liberty.'**
>
> *A New View of Society, 1813*

Montgomeryshire in Wales produced a man who changed society across the world with his thoughts and actions. Karl Marx and Friedrich Engels both paid generous tribute to Robert Owen in the development of their theories – Engels wrote that *'English socialism arose with Owen'*. Aged 29, Owen had become part-owner of a Manchester cotton mill, then took over cotton mills in New Lanark in Scotland. He improved housing and sanitation, provided medical supervision, set up a co-operative shop, selling at little more than cost price, and established the first infant school in Great Britain. He reasoned that character was moulded by circumstances, and that improved circumstances would lead to goodness. The *Gentleman's Magazine* recorded: *'The children live with their parents in neat comfortable habitation, receiving wages for their labour... The regulations here to preserve health of body and mind, present a striking contrast to those of most large manufactories in this kingdom.'* Owen's factories not only enhanced the workers' environment, but received international interest as they actually also increased productivity and profits.

1813 saw the publication of Owen's *A New View of Society*, which pleaded for education for all as the key to social reform and improving working conditions. He was largely responsible for bringing about The Factory Acts of 1819, and in 1833 formed the Grand National Consolidated Trades Union. He wanted to use the unions to change the economic system, to destroy capitalism and break the overwhelming power of the state. In 1835 he founded the Association of All Classes of All Nations, for which he is known as the founder of the Socialist movement. Those that followed his teachings, who called themselves Owenites, gradually changed their name to Socialists, the first recorded use of the term.

WILLIAM WILBERFORCE
1759–1833

'They charge me with fanaticism. If to be feelingly alive to the sufferings of my fellow-creatures is to be a fanatic, I am one of the most incurable fanatics ever permitted to be at large.'

Speech in the House of Commons, 19 June 1816

William Wilberforce was a deeply religious MP and social reformer who fought for the abolition of the slave trade, and eventually slavery itself across the British Empire. At Cambridge University he began a lasting friendship with the future Prime Minister, William Pitt the Younger. Wilberforce's dissolute lifestyle changed completely when he became an evangelical Christian, and his faith caused him to become interested in social reforms and the improvement of factory conditions in Britain.

Thomas Clarkson and others were campaigning for an end to the slave trade, in which British ships were carrying black slaves from Africa to the West Indies and Americas. For 18 years Wilberforce regularly introduced anti-slavery motions in Parliament. He said: 'Never, never will we desist till we... extinguish every trace of this bloody traffic, of which our posterity, looking back to the history of these enlightened times will scarce believe that it has been suffered to exist so long a disgrace and dishonour to this country.' In 1807 the slave trade was abolished, but this did not free those who were already slaves. In 1833 an act was passed giving freedom to all slaves in the British Empire. Shortly after Wilberforce died, his mission finally accomplished. Wilberforce also worked to provide all children with regular education in reading, personal hygiene and religion.

JOHN KEATS
1795–1821

'A thing of beauty is a joy for ever'

'A thing of beauty is a joy for ever:
Its loveliness increases; it will never
Pass into nothingness; but still will keep
A bower quiet for us, and a sleep
Full of sweet dreams, and health, and quiet breathing.
Therefore, on every morrow, are we wreathing
A flowery band to bind us to the earth,
Spite of despondence, of the inhuman dearth
Of noble natures, of the gloomy days,
Of all the unhealthy and o'er-darkened ways
Made for our searching: yes, in spite of all,
Some shape of beauty moves away the pall
From our dark spirits. Such the sun, the moon,
Trees old, and young, sprouting a shady boon
For simple sheep; and such are daffodils
With the green world they live in; and clear rills
That for themselves a cooling covert make
'Gainst the hot season; the mid-forest brake,
Rich with a sprinkling of fair musk-rose blooms:
And such too is the grandeur of the dooms
We have imagined for the mighty dead;
All lovely tales that we have heard or read:
An endless fountain of immortal drink,
Pouring unto us from the heaven's brink.'

Endymion, 1818

The 23-year-old Keats' visual, sensuous poem was a dramatic departure from the poetry of his day. Aware that this opened him to criticism, in its preface he spoke openly of perceived flaws. The criticism was so vicious that it was thought to have helped kill Keats, who died of tuberculosis three years later (*see pages 176-177*).

JOHN KEATS
1795–1821

'Season of mists and mellow fruitfulness'

'Season of mists and mellow fruitfulness,
Close bosom-friend of the maturing sun;
Conspiring with him how to load and bless
With fruit the vines that round the thatch-eaves run;
To bend with apples the mossed cottage trees,
And fill all fruit with ripeness to the core;
To swell the gourd, and plump the hazel shells
With a sweet kernel; to set budding more,
And still more, later flowers for the bees,
Until they think warm days will never cease,
For Summer has o'erbrimmed their clammy cells.'

'Ode to Autumn', 1819

After studying at Guy's Hospital, Keats became an apothecary and was allowed to practise surgery. However, he became one of the best of the lyrical Romantic poets, but suffered from harsh criticism of his poems until after his death. Too poor to marry the love of his life, Fanny Brawne, he contracted tuberculosis while caring for his brother and eventually succumbed to the disease in Rome. His last request was to be buried in an unnamed grave in Rome's Protestant Cemetery.

John Hamilton Reynolds (1796–1852) was a friend and poet and correspondent of Keats, and in his letter of September 1819, Keats writes to him: 'How beautiful the season is now – How fine the air... Somehow a stubble field looks warm as in the same way that some pictures look warm. This struck me so much on my Sunday's walk that I composed upon it.'

JOHN KEATS
1795–1821

'Here lies One Whose Name was writ in Water'

'This Grave contains
all that was Mortal of
a Young English Poet
Who
on his Death Bed
in the Bitterness of his Heart
at the Malicious Power of his Enemies
Desired these words to be engraven
on his Tomb Stone
"Here lies One Whose Name
was writ in Water".'

Keats' self-penned epitaph

Keats suffered a lingering death from tuberculosis, aged only 26. He had asked that one phrase be put upon his tombstone: '*Here lies one whose name was writ in water.*' It was taken from Beaumont and Fletcher's *Philaster: 'all your better deeds / Shall be in water writ.*' He had written to his love Fanny Brawne in 1820 *"If I should die", said I to myself, "I have left no immortal work behind me – nothing to make my friends proud of my memory – but I have loved the principle of beauty in all things, and if I had had time I would have made myself remembered."*

His great friends, Percy Bysshe Shelley and Lord Byron, believed that the final straw for the poet had been an incredibly cruel review in *Blackwood's Edinburgh Magazine* of his epic poem *Endymion*. Keats was told: '*It is a better and a wiser thing to be a starved apothecary than a starved poet; so back to the shop Mr John, back to "plasters, pills and ointment boxes".*' Byron referred to his friend's demise in *Don Juan*: '*Tis strange the mind, that very fiery particle, Should let itself be snuffed out by an article.*'

PERCY BYSSHE SHELLEY
1792–1822

'Hail to thee, blithe Spirit!'

'Hail to thee, blithe Spirit!
Bird thou never wert—
That from Heaven, or near it,
Pourest thy full heart
In profuse strains of unpremeditated
   art.
Higher still and higher
From the earth thou springest
Like a cloud of fire;

The blue deep thou wingest,
And singing still dost soar, and
   soaring ever singest.
In the golden lightning
Of the sunken Sun—
O'er which clouds are brightening,
Thou dost float and run;
Like an unbodied joy whose race is
   just begun.

'To a Skylark', 1820

A radical and a great friend of Lord Byron, Shelley is one of the most lauded poets of English Romanticism. He was inspired to write this poem by a skylark he saw whilst walking near Livorno in Italy with his wife, the author Mary Shelley. Italy would prove to be his final resting place: the 30-year-old poet was drowned in the Mediterranean and cremated on a beach because of quarantine laws to protect against the plague restrictions. His ashes are in the Protestant Cemetery in Rome, but his heart was taken to Bournemouth. Shelley's heart was given to his wife, who carried it with her in a silken shroud everywhere she went for the rest of her life. His most famous short poem, *Ozymandias*, reminds us of the transient glories of life:

'And on the pedestal these words appear:
"My name is Ozymandias, King of Kings:
Look on my works, ye mighty, and despair!"
Nothing beside remains. Round the decay
Of that colossal wreck, boundless and bare,
The lone and level sands stretch far away.'

LORD BYRON
1788–1824

'Tis strange, but true; for truth is always strange; Stranger than fiction.'

Don Juan, 1819–1824

George Gordon Noel, 6th Baron Byron, led a scandalous life, and is the epitome of the English Romantic poet. In 1812, the first two cantos of *Childe Harold's Pilgrimage* were published and after its instant success, Lord Byron noted: '*I awoke one morning and found myself famous*'. In 1814, his half-sister had a daughter who was almost certainly his, and he married the next year and had another daughter, but separated from his wife in 1816. Because of huge debts and public pressure over his unorthodox love life, including a famous affair with Lady Caroline Lamb, he fled overseas in 1816. He initially stayed with Shelley at Lake Geneva, and had another daughter with Shelley's wife's half-sister. Byron then moved to Italy for six years where he composed some of his best works, including *Don Juan*, an unfinished satirical epic that turns the traditional story on its head, by portraying the hero as the innocent victim of a strict upbringing who is repeatedly seduced by women. The first two cantos were published anonymously in 1819, and the poem was criticized for its 'immoral content', but Byron managed to complete 16 cantos, leaving an unfinished 17th canto.

In 1823, Byron left Italy to join the Greek insurgents in their war of independence against the Ottoman Empire. In 1824 he died from fever at Missolonghi, in modern-day Greece, and his death was mourned throughout Britain. His body lies in the family vault in Nottinghamshire. Other lines Byron gave us include:

'*Always laugh when you can. It is cheap medicine*'

'*Society is now one polished horde / Formed of two mighty tribes, the Bores and Bored*'

'*Now hatred is by far the longest pleasure: Men love in haste, but they repent at leisure*'

'I recognize you in all the beauty that surrounds me'

'If only I were a clever woman, I could describe to you my gorgeous bird, how you unite in yourself the beauties of form, plumage, and song! I would tell you that you are the greatest marvel of all ages, and I should only be speaking the simple truth. But to put all this into suitable words, my superb one, I should require a voice far more harmonious than that which is bestowed upon my species – for I am the humble owl that you mocked at only lately, therefore, it cannot be. I will not tell you to what degree you are dazzling and to the birds of sweet song who, as you know, are none the less beautiful and appreciative. I am content to delegate to them the duty of watching, listening and admiring, while to myself I reserve the right of loving; this may be less attractive to the ear, but it is sweeter far to the heart. I love you, I love you, my Victor; I cannot reiterate it too often; I can never express it as much as I feel it. I recognize you in all the beauty that surrounds me – in form, in colour, in perfume, in harmonious sound: all of these mean you to me. You are superior to all. I see and admire – you are all! You are not only the solar spectrum with the seven luminous colours, but the sun himself, that illumines, warms, and revivifies! This is what you are, and I am the lowly woman that adores you.'

Love letter to Victor Hugo, 1831

Born Julienne Gauvain, she was orphaned before she was two years old, and raised by her uncle, René Drouet. She was a French actress and lived with the sculptor James Pradier from 1825. He represented her in a statue symbolizing Strasbourg in the Place de la Concorde in Paris. She had a daughter by Pradier and began acting in 1829. In 1833 she abandoned her theatrical career to dedicate her life to her Victor Hugo, becoming his secretary and travelling companion. For years she lived a cloistered life, leaving home only in his company. Drouet wrote thousands of passionate and lyrical love letters to Hugo for over 50 years. She died just two years before Hugo, and this letter dates from the first year of their everlasting affair.

EVARISTE GALOIS
1811–1832

‘Don't cry, I need all my courage to die at twenty’

His last words to his brother

The 'Father of Modern Algebra' was born near Paris, and died of gunshot wounds before he was 21. He failed the École Polytechnique's mathematics entry examination twice because his answers were 'odd'. He was then expelled from the École Normale for attacking the director in a letter to the press. He was arrested for making a threatening speech against the King, acquitted, and then imprisoned for illegally wearing a uniform and carrying weapons. Some of Galois' work was published, so eminent scientists like Gauss and Fourier knew of him. Released after six months, Galois had a disastrous love affair before being challenged to a duel by a political enemy. He could not refuse 'an affair of honour' and knew he had little chance of winning at dawn the next day. He therefore spent the night writing all the mathematics he did not want to die with him, often writing in the margin '*I have not time*' to prove some of his equations. He sent the results to his friend Auguste Chevalier before duelling with pistols at 25 paces. He was shot in the intestines and taken to hospital, telling his brother: '*Don't cry, I need all my courage to die at twenty*'. He died the day after the duel and was buried in a common grave.

E.T. Bell commented: '*In all the history of science there is no completer example of the triumph of crass stupidity over untameable genius than is afforded by the all too brief life of Evariste Galois.*' Twenty-four years after his death, the mathematician Joseph Liouville discovered 'the complete correctness' of Galois' advanced algebraic theorems.

CHIEF BLACK HAWK
1767–1838

'May the Great Spirit shed light on yours'

'May the Great Spirit shed light on yours – and that you may never experience the humility that the power of the American government has reduced me to, is the wish of him, who, in his native forests, was once as proud and bold as yourself.'

Remark made to General Henry Atkinson in 1833, in reference to the Bad Axe Massacre of Native American Indians by US Army forces, quoted in Touch the Earth, T.C. McLuhan, 1971

Chief Black Hawk's Indian name was Ma-ka-tae-mish-kia-kiak (Black Sparrow Hawk), and his Sauk tribe signed a treaty of friendship and protection with the US in 1795. However, in 1804 their leaders were given alcohol and signed a treaty giving away 15,000,000 acres of their lands in Illinois, Wisconsin and Missouri for $2,274.50. Black Hawk argued that the treaty was not valid because most of the Sauk Nation was not told of the treaty, but the government insisted the treaty was binding. In the 1812 War between Britain and the US, Black Hawk sided with the British to try to regain his lands, and even after the war ended, he kept fighting, saying, '*I have fought the Big Knives and will continue to fight them till they are off our lands*'.

Black Hawk tried to escape over the Mississippi, but his way was blocked so he tried to surrender. The next day, US soldiers caught up with the Sauk and killed dozens of their number, including women, children and the elderly. Of the 500 Sauk with Black Hawk, only about 150 survived. At his surrender after this, the Bad Axe Massacre, he said: '*His heart is dead, and no longer beats quick in his bosom. He is now a prisoner to the white men; they will do with him as they wish. But he can stand torture and is not afraid of death. He is no coward. Black Hawk is an Indian.*'

HONORÉ DE BALZAC
1799–1850

'Our love will bloom always fairer, fresher, more gracious, because it is a true love'

'Our love will bloom always fairer, fresher, more gracious, because it is a true love, and because genuine love is ever increasing. It is a beautiful plant growing from year to year in the heart, ever extending its palms and branches, doubling every season its glorious clusters and perfumes; and, my dear life, tell me, repeat to me always, that nothing will bruise its bark or its delicate leaves, that it will grow larger in both our hearts, loved, free, watched over, like a life within our life...'

Love letter to Madame Evelina Hanska, 6 October 1833

 Balzac was a French novelist and playwright, and this letter was to his long-time lover whom he finally married in 1850, just six months before he died. He had probably preferred to be a lover than a husband, writing elsewhere: '*The majority of husbands remind me of an orangutan trying to play the violin*'. His magnum opus, a sequence of almost 100 novels and plays collectively entitled *La Comédie Humaine*, presents a broad panorama of French life in the years after the fall of Napoléon Bonaparte in 1815. Balzac is one of the founding fathers of Realism in European literature, due to his extensive use of detail and precise representation of society. He failed in attempts at different careers, from politician to printer, from publisher to critic, and his fiction reflects his real-life difficulties and includes scenes taken directly from his experience. Balzac influenced Émile Zola, Charles Dickens, Gustave Flaubert, Henry James and many others.

GENERAL KARL VON CLAUSEWITZ
1780–1831

'War is nothing but the continuation of politics with the admixture of other means'

On War, Book 8, 1832–1834

This phrase is commonly misquoted as '*War is the continuation of politics by other means*', and reflects von Clausewitz's statement that '*It is politics which begets war. Politics represents the intelligence, war merely its instrument, not the other way around. The only possible course in war is to subordinate the military viewpoint to the political.*' His book was the first treatise on the art of modern warfare, where he looked beyond the battlefield to war's place in the broader political context, not as simply an end in itself.

Von Clausewitz was a strategic thinker, most influenced by the Napoleonic Wars in which he fought. He entered the Prussian Army in 1792, and was commissioned during the Rhine campaign of 1793–94 against the French Revolutionary army. On Napoléon's invasion of Russia, he resigned his commission and joined the Russian army. Then he rejoined the Prussian army, and fought at Waterloo after helping negotiate the alliance of Prussia, Britain and Russia against Napoléon. Von Clausewitz stressed the need to strive for the most complete military victories possible, using whatever reasonable resources were available, and his theories still influence military strategists. He stated that all strategy should aim at three targets: the enemy's forces, his resources and his will to fight. Among his beliefs were: '*Pursue one great decisive aim with force and determination*'; '*The bloody solution of the crisis, the effort for the destruction of the enemy's forces, is the first-born son of war*'; and '*Blood is the price of victory*'. He argued that defensive warfare is militarily and politically the stronger position. Of relevance to today's conflicts in Iraq and Afghanistan, Von Clausewitz also wrote: '*No one starts a war – or rather, no one in his senses ought to do so – without first being clear in his mind what he intends to achieve by that war and how he intends to conduct it.*'

RALPH WALDO EMERSON
1803–1882

'The shot heard round the world'

'By the rude bridge that arched the flood,
Their flag to April's breeze unfurled,
Here once the embattled farmers stood,
And fired the shot heard round the world.

The foe long since in silence slept;
Alike the conqueror silent sleeps;
And Time the ruined bridge has swept
Down the dark stream that seaward creeps.

On this green bank, by this soft stream,
We set to-day a votive stone;
That memory may their deeds redeem,
When, like our sires, our sons are gone.

Spirit, that made those heroes dare
To die, and leave their children free,
Bid Time and Nature gently spare
The shaft we raise to them and thee.'

'The Concord Hymn', 1836

This poem was sung as a hymn on 4 July 1837 to mark the completion of the North Bridge Obelisk (the Concord Monument). The Obelisk immortalized the resistance of American Minutemen to British forces at the Battle of North Bridge, Concord, on 19 April 1775. It was the first Battle of the American Revolution, and 'The shot heard round the world' is symbolic of the first revolt by a colonial nation against the mighty British Empire. The phrase was subsequently reappropriated to describe the assassination of Archduke Franz Ferdinand, which led to the Great War. Emerson was raised in The Old Manse not far from the North Bridge, and wrote this poem whilst living there. His grandfather, the Reverend William Emerson, had been a witness to the battle.

NATHANIEL HAWTHORNE
1804–1864

'Our souls went far away among the sunset clouds'

'Belovedest little wife – sweetest Sophie Hawthorne – what a delicious walk that was, last Thursday! It seems to me, now, as if I could really remember every footstep of it. It is almost as distinct as the recollection of those walks, in which my earthly form did really tread beside your own, and my arm uphold you; and, indeed, it has the same character as those heavenly ramblings; for did we tread on earth even then?... Oh no – our souls went far away among the sunset clouds, and wherever there was ethereal beauty, there were we, our true selves; and it was there that we grew into each other, and became a married pair... Perhaps not a single pressure of the hand, not a glance, not a sweet and tender tone, not one kiss, but will be repeated sometime or other in our memory. Oh, dearest blessed Dove, I never felt sure of going to Heaven, till I knew that you loved me; but now I am conscious of God's love in your own... Dove, come to my bosom – it yearns for you as it never did before. I shall fold my arms together, after I am in bed, and try to imagine that you are close to my heart. Naughty wife, what right have you to be anywhere else? How many sweet words I should breathe into your ear, in the quiet night – how many holy kisses would I press upon your lips...'

Love letter to his fiancée, Sophia Peabody, 23 September 1839, 6.30 a.m.

Hawthorne was one of the great figures of American literature, composing his most famous novel, *The Scarlet Letter*, in 1850. Before they were married, Hawthorne and his fiancée created a game in their letters by referring to Sophia Hawthorne, as she would be, as if she were a third person. Their wedding took place on 9 July 1842 and they celebrated their love affair in letters throughout their marriage.

ALEXIS DE TOCQUEVILLE
1805–1859

'Democracy and socialism have nothing in common but one word: equality. But notice the difference: while democracy seeks equality in liberty, socialism seeks equality in restraint and servitude.'

Democracy in America, Volume I, 1835 and Volume II, 1840

De Tocqueville's treatise looked to America's flourishing democracy in the early 19th century and the progressive model it offered 'old' Europe. He was a French aristocrat who went to the USA in 1831, aged 25, after studying law in Paris, when the July Revolution of 1830 had meant that his position in France had become difficult. De Tocqueville had increasingly liberal sympathies, believing that the decline of the aristocracy was inevitable. He returned to France, convinced that the model of democracy in the USA should be applicable to his native country.

In 1835, the first part of *Democracy in America*, a positive account of American government and society, was published, and was read throughout Europe. It is one of the most comprehensive and insightful books ever written about the US. In 1839 De Tocqueville was elected to the Chamber of Deputies and later to the Constituent Assembly and Legislative Assembly. He also briefly served as Minister of Foreign Affairs. Published in 1840, the second part of his treatise was more pessimistic, warning of the dangers of despotism and governmental centralization. *Democracy in America* deals with issues like the role of government, the judicial system, religion, the press, financial systems, class structure and racism:

'The first who attracts the eye, the first in enlightenment, in power and in happiness, is the white man, the European, man par excellence; below him appear the Negro and the Indian. These two unfortunate races have neither birth, nor face, nor language, nor mores in common; only their misfortunes look alike. Both occupy an equally inferior position in the country that they inhabit; both experience the effects of tyranny; and if their miseries are different, they can accuse the same author for them.'

ROBERT BROWNING
1812–1889

'God's in His heaven – All's right with the world!'

'The year's at the spring,
And day's at the morn;
Morning's at seven;
The hill-side's dew-pearl'd;

The lark's on the wing;
The snail's on the thorn;
God's in His heaven –
All's right with the world!'

'Pippa Passes', 1841

Robert Browning was sent by his father to oversee a West Indies sugar plantation, but he was disgusted with slavery and instead became a clerk in the Bank of England. Beginning with his *Bells and Pomegranates* series, from which 'Pippa Passes' is taken, Browning became an established poet and in 1845 he contrived to meet the poetess Elizabeth Barrett after reading her work. They married in 1846, eloping to Florence to escape her domineering father. They were extremely happy despite her illness, and both of them were respected as major poets in their lifetimes. Browning's finest poetry, in *Men and Women*, was written in Italy. Deeply in love, he wrote:

'So, I gave her eyes my own eyes to take,
My hand sought hers as in earnest need,
And round she turned for my noble sake,
And gave me herself indeed.'

Browning's best-known poem is probably 'The Pied Piper of Hamelin' (1842) where he recounts the legend:

'Rats!
They fought the dogs and killed
    the cats,
And bit the babies in the cradles,
And ate the cheeses out of the vats,
And licked the soup from the
    cooks' own ladles,

Split open the kegs of salted sprats,
Made nests inside men's Sunday
    hats,
And even spoiled the women's chats
By drowning their speaking
With shrieking and squeaking
In fifty different sharps and flats.'

THOMAS CARLYLE
1795–1881

'The greatest scene in Modern European history'

'The Diet of Worms. Luther's appearing there on 17ᵗʰ April 1521 may be considered as the greatest scene in Modern European history, the point, indeed, from which the whole subsequent history of civilization takes its rise.'

Carlyle's description of Luther's influence on history: *On Heroes, Hero-Worship, and the Heroic in History*, 1841

Carlyle's works inspired social reformers such as Ruskin, Dickens and William Morris. Luther's appearance at Worms, under a pass of safe conduct, and his refusal to accept the power of Rome in doctrinal matters, solidified the schism between Catholicism and Protestantism across Europe.

Martin Luther (1483–1546) was ordained an Augustinian friar in 1507, and was Doctor in Theology at the University of Wittenberg from 1512. In 1510 he had visited Rome, and was disgusted by its corruption. He said: *'And I myself, in Rome, heard it said openly in the streets, "If there is a hell, then Rome is built on it." That is, "After the devil himself, there is no worse folk than the pope and his followers."'* He was also angered by the selling of 'indulgences', remission from punishments for sin, which could be bought both for the living and the dead. In 1517 Luther published 95 *Theses*, an attack on indulgences and papal abuses, believing that Christians could be saved by faith rather than the Church. He wrote: *'The Mass is the greatest blasphemy of God, and the highest idolatry upon earth'*. A series of pamphlets followed, and aided by the spread of printing presses, his teachings spread across Europe.

In January 1521, Pope Leo X excommunicated Luther, who was summoned to appear at the Diet of Worms, an assembly of the Holy Roman Empire. Luther would not recant – he said: *'Here I stand; I can do no otherwise. God help me. Amen!'* – so Emperor Charles V declared him a heretic and he was forced into hiding at Wartburg Castle. Luther was also involved in the controversy surrounding the Peasants' War (1524–1526), the leaders of which had used his arguments to justify their revolt, but Luther backed the authorities. In 1534, he published a translation of the Bible into German. The rise of Protestantism began with Luther's refusal to recant.

RALPH WALDO EMERSON
1803–1882

'A foolish consistency is the hobgoblin of little minds'

'Self Reliance', *Essays*, 1841

A preacher, philosopher and poet, known as the 'Sage of Concord', Emerson was at the intellectual centre of the American Renaissance. An original thinker, he embodied the finest spirit and highest ideals of the age. After Harvard he became a Unitarian minister in 1829, but experienced a religious crisis after the death from tuberculosis of his first wife after only 18 months of marriage. He resigned from the Church and became a lecturer, remarrying and settling in Concord, Massachusetts. In 1836, he published his first major essay, 'Nature'. A circle of poets, reformers, artists and thinkers revolved around him, including the Alcott family, Henry Thoreau and Nathaniel Hawthorne.

Emerson wrote on the mystical harmonies of man and nature, the essential perfectibility of the human spirit, the values of non-conformity, self-reliance and utopian friendship. An Abolitionist, he also championed Native Americans, and crusaded for educational reform and peace. After several family tragedies, in 1872 his home was burnt to the ground. He was depressed, so his friends arranged for him to travel abroad and, unknown to him, whilst he was on his travels they raised funds, rebuilt his house in Concord and reconstructed his library. Emerson also gave us the saying: '*If a man write a better book, preach a better sermon, or make a better mouse-trap than his neighbour, though he build his house in the woods, the world will make a beaten path to his door.*'

THOMAS HOOD
1799–1845

'With fingers weary and worn,
With eyelids heavy and red'

'With fingers weary and worn,
With eyelids heavy and red,
A woman sat, in unwomanly rags,
Plying her needle and thread
Stitch! stitch! stitch!
In poverty, hunger, and dirt,
And still with a voice of dolorous pitch
She sang the "Song of the Shirt".

Work! work! work!
While the cock is crowing aloof!
And work work work,
Till the stars shine through the roof!
It's Oh! to be a slave
Along with the barbarous Turk,
Where woman has never a soul to save,
If this is Christian work!'

'The Song of the Shirt', *first two stanzas, 1843*

A journalist, humorist, essayist, novelist, publisher, poet and co-founder of the radical weekly journal the *Examiner* (1808), Thomas Hood mixed with such notable writers as Thomas de Quincey, Charles Lamb, William Hazlitt, Samuel Taylor Coleridge, Alfred, Lord Tennyson and John Clare. Hood founded *The Comic Annual* (1830–42), but losses as a publisher compelled him to live overseas from 1835. In 1840 he returned to England and began writing for *The New Monthly Magazine*, becoming its editor in 1841. Despite his reputation as a humorist, Hood is best known as the author of 'The Song of the Shirt', which he published anonymously in *Punch* in 1843. The poem is grimly realistic about the plight of the working classes, in this case the seamstress.

GEORGE IV
1762–1830

'Harris, I am not well. Get me a brandy.'

Diaries and Correspondence, Earl of Malmesbury, 1844

Famous for his dissolute ways and his Royal Pavilion in Brighton, 'Prinny' became Prince Regent in 1811 and King in 1820. His extravagant lifestyle caused his father, George III, to regard him with contempt. The dandy Beau Brummell famously remarked to an acquaintance of the Prince: *'Who's your fat friend?'* as 'Prinny's' excesses of food and drink had made him huge. In 1812, Leigh Hunt described the Prince Regent thus: *'This Adonis in loveliness was a corpulent man of fifty.'*

In 1785, George had secretly and illegally married a Roman Catholic, Maria Fitzherbert, but in 1795 he was officially married to Princess Caroline of Brunswick, in exchange for Parliament paying off his massive debts. Caroline had arrived in Gravesend that year to marry him, and travelled to Greenwich to meet an official delegation to take her to meet the Prince, but no delegation appeared. The Prince eventually had to meet her, and when he entered the room, she knelt in obedience. He then embraced her, released her immediately and hurried to a far corner of the room, beckoning James Harris, Earl of Malmesbury, to follow. Here, he exclaimed: *'Harris, I am not well. Get me a brandy.'* Malmesbury replied, *'Sir, had you better have a glass of water?'* The Prince said angrily, *'No! I will go directly to the Queen'*, and left the room to head for the palace. Caroline responded, *'My God! Does the Prince always act like that? I think he is very fat and he is nothing like as handsome as his portrait.'* The marriage was a disaster and George tried unsuccessfully to divorce Caroline after his accession. W.S. Landor summed up his reign thus:

> 'George the First was always reckoned
> Vile, but viler George the Second
> And what mortal ever heard
> Any good of George the Third?
> When from earth the Fourth descended
> God be praised the Georges ended!'

EDWARD EVERETT
1794–1865

'**If this boy passes the examinations he will be admitted and if the white students choose to withdraw, all the income of the college will be devoted to his education**'

On admitting the first black student to Harvard University, 1847

The student in question was Beverly Williams, who had been in the same preparatory school as Everett's son, and whom Everett claimed was a superb Latinist. However, Williams died of tuberculosis before his 18th birthday and never took the place. (The first black pupil to study at Harvard was in fact Richard Greener in 1865.)

Everett was from 1846 to 1849 President of Harvard College (now University). He was a Whig politician who was also a professor of Greek literature, a congressman, senator, Ambassador to Britain, Governor of Massachusetts, failed Vice-Presidential candidate and President Fillmore's Secretary of State. He was also the first American to receive a PhD. Everett was considered the nation's greatest orator, so was invited to give the main speech at the dedication of the Soldiers' National Cemetery at Gettysburg on 23 September 1863. He asked for a postponement to prepare a suitable speech, and on 19 November gave a well-received two-hour address. Almost as an afterthought, President Lincoln was asked to make '*a few appropriate remarks*'. Lincoln's impromptu speech, now known as The Gettysburg Address, lasted just two minutes. The next day Everett wrote to Lincoln: '*I should be glad, if I could flatter myself that I came as near the central idea of the occasion in two hours, as you did in two minutes.*'

EMILY JANE BRONTË
1818–1848

'I cannot live without my soul!'

'Catherine Earnshaw, may you not rest as long as I am living! You said I killed you – haunt me, then! The murdered do haunt their murderers, I believe – I know that ghosts have wandered on earth. Be with me always – take any form – drive me mad! only do not leave me in this abyss, where I cannot find you! Oh, God! It is unutterable! I cannot live without my life! I cannot live without my soul!'

Wuthering Heights, Heathcliff's soliloquy, 1847

 **Emily Brontë was a** teacher at Law Hill School from 1838, but her health broke under the strain of teaching from 6 a.m. to 11 p.m. with only a 30-minute break each day. In 1839 she returned to Haworth Parsonage and never looked for another post. In 1842 her sister Charlotte compelled Emily to attend school in Brussels, but she returned home as quickly as possible. A stark depiction of destructive romance, her *Wuthering Heights* was condemned as being too shocking for anyone to read, and was partly responsible for people thinking that men wrote the Brontë sisters' novels – it was believed that no woman could write about such matters. Emily would not admit that she was suffering from consumption, and refused to take medicine or to see doctors until she collapsed, three months after her brother Branwell's death. She said, '*If you will send for a doctor, I will see him now*', but died that afternoon. It is thought that Charlotte destroyed the novel that Emily had been working on before her death, in order to protect Emily's reputation after the furore that *Wuthering Heights* provoked.

CHARLOTTE BRONTË
1816–1855

'Reader, I married him'

'Reader, I married him. A quiet wedding we had: he and I, the parson and clerk, were alone present. When we got back from church, I went into the kitchen of the manor-house, where Mary was cooking the dinner and John cleaning the knives, and I said – "Mary, I have been married to Mr. Rochester this morning."'

Jane Eyre, final chapter, 1847

Charlotte Brontë's birth in 1816 was quickly followed by that of brother, (Patrick) Branwell Brontë, in 1817, and her sisters Emily and Anne in 1818 and 1820. In 1820 the family moved to Haworth, where Mrs Brontë died the following year. In 1825, Charlotte's other sisters Maria and Elizabeth died. The remaining four children were very close all their lives, and all had an interest in writing. Together they wrote tiny manuscripts about fantasy worlds such as Angria and Gondal. In 1831, Charlotte became a school pupil, but left in 1832 to teach her sisters at home. She returned to Roe Head School as a teacher from 1835 to 1838, prior to becoming a governess. On returning to Haworth, the three sisters, led by Charlotte, decided to open their own school, but advertisements did not elicit any responses for students. Charlotte next discovered Emily's poems, and decided to publish a selection of the three sisters' poetry. Thus in 1846 their *Poems* were printed under the pen-names of Currer, Ellis and Acton Bell. Charlotte also completed *The Professor*, which was rejected for publication, but was published after her death.

In 1847, however, Charlotte's *Jane Eyre*, Emily's *Wuthering Heights* and Anne's *Agnes Grey* were all published, still under the Bell pseudonyms, and in 1848 Anne also had published *The Tenant of Wildfell Hall*. In that same year Charlotte and Anne visited their publishers, revealing the true identity of the Bell family, and Branwell Brontë died. Emily died shortly thereafter, and Anne died in 1849. In 1854, Charlotte married Arthur Bell Nicholls, her father's curate, but her health declined rapidly and she and her unborn child died in 1855.

THOMAS BABINGTON MACAULAY
1800–1859

'No man who is correctly informed as to the past, will be disposed to take a morose or desponding view of the present'

'Those who compare the age in which their lot has fallen with a golden age which exists only in imagination, may talk of degeneracy and decay; but no man who is correctly informed as to the past, will be disposed to take a morose or desponding view of the present.'

History of England, Volume I, Chapter 1, 1849

After Cambridge, Macaulay became a lawyer and in 1824 made an impressive speech at a meeting of the Anti-Slavery Society. A regular contributor to the *Edinburgh Review*, he became a Whig MP in 1830, supporting parliamentary reform. An excellent orator, as an MP he took a post on the Supreme Council of India, and so was able to pay off his father's debts. He was Secretary of War when the Melbourne government fell in 1841, and he could then devote more time to writing, beginning work on his non-pareil *History of England*.

In 1846, Macaulay became Postmaster-General in Lord Russell's government and the first two volumes of his *History* were published to great acclaim, their sales at the time rivalling those of the works of Sir Walter Scott and Charles Dickens. The third and fourth volumes were published in 1855 and sold over 26,000 copies in 10 weeks. Elsewhere in the *History* we read: '*The Puritan hated bear-baiting, not because it gave pain to the bear, but because it gave pleasure to the spectators.*' The work was also translated into German, Polish, Danish, Swedish, Italian, French, Dutch, Spanish, Hungarian, Russian, Bohemian and Persian. In 1857 Palmerston granted Macaulay the title Baron Macaulay of Rothley.

ELIZABETH BARRETT BROWNING
1806–1861

'How do I love thee? Let me count the ways'

'How do I love thee? Let me count the ways.
I love thee to the depth and breadth and height
My soul can reach, when feeling out of sight
For the ends of being and ideal grace.
I love thee to the level of every day's
Most quiet need, by sun and candle-light.
I love thee freely, as men strive for right.
I love thee purely, as they turn from praise.
I love thee with the passion put to use
In my old griefs, and with my childhood's faith.
I love thee with a love I seemed to lose
With my lost saints. I love thee with the breath,
Smiles, tears, of all my life; and, if God choose,
I shall but love thee better after death.'

Sonnets from the Portuguese, Number 43, 1850

Elizabeth Barrett was an English poet of the Romantic movement. Aged 14, she developed a lung ailment for which she was treated with morphine for the rest of her life. Then at 15, she injured her spine, giving her almost permanent pain. A devout Christian, she learned Hebrew and Greek, and published essays and poems. In the 1830s, her favourite brother's death and her father's tyrannical rule led to a breakdown, and she became a reclusive invalid. In 1844 she produced a collection entitled *Poems*, gaining the attention of the poet Robert Browning. They exchanged 574 letters over the next 20 months, a love affair immortalized in 1930 in the play *The Barretts of Wimpole Street*. They eloped and settled in Florence, Italy, where Elizabeth's health improved and she bore a son. Her *Sonnets from the Portuguese*, dedicated to her husband and written in secret before her marriage, was her best work.

CHARLES DICKENS
1812–1870

'Annual income £20, annual expenditure £19-19s-6d, result happiness. Annual income £20, annual expenditure £20-0s-6d, result misery.'

Spoken by Mr Micawber, *David Copperfield*, 1850

Charles Dickens is the essence of the Victorian author, with excellent characterization and epic stories. His father, the inspiration for the character Mr Micawber in *David Copperfield*, was imprisoned for debt, so Dickens had to miss three years of schooling to work in appalling, lonely conditions to help pay off the family debt. His experience was fictionalized in *David Copperfield* and *Great Expectations*. Dickens began his literary career as a journalist, then a parliamentary journalist, and was able to publish a series of sketches under the pseudonym 'Boz'. In 1836 he married and published the highly successful *Pickwick Papers*, which launched his career. From that point on he constantly wrote and toured, but was estranged from his wife in 1858 after the birth of their tenth child, maintaining relations with his mistress, the actress Ellen Ternan. The wonderful opening lines of his *The Tale of Two Cities* (1859) read as follows:

'It was the best of times, it was the worst of times; it was the age of wisdom, it was the age of foolishness; it was the epoch of belief, it was the epoch of incredulity; it was the season of Light, it was the season of Darkness; it was the spring of hope, it was the winter of despair; we had everything before us, we had nothing before us; we were all going directly to Heaven, we were all going the other way.'

HERMAN MELVILLE
1819–1891

'A whale ship was my college and my Harvard'

Moby Dick, 1851

Born Herman Melvill, he went to sea aged 20 as a cabin boy on a whaler, then later joined the US Navy before living among the Typee cannibals in the Marquesas Islands. He was rescued, and his fictionalized travel narrative *Typee* (1846) made Melville's name as a writer. Like most of his works, it was first published in Britain, and was followed by *Omoo*, about his experiences in the Polynesian Islands. Melville had almost finished *Moby Dick* when his neighbour and friend Nathaniel Hawthorne asked him to alter it from a whaling adventure to an allegorical novel.

Carl Jung called *Moby Dick* the '*greatest American novel*', but it was not a success until 30 years after Melville's death. Melville had dedicated the book to Hawthorne and worked all hours to finish it, writing to Hawthorne: '*I have written a wicked book and feel as spotless as the lamb.*' He was deeply depressed by the novel's reception, since public and critics did not understand his musings upon faith and the workings of God, such as the line '*Better sleep with a sober cannibal than a drunken Christian*'. In 1855 Melville had a breakdown, believing that he would never be successful with writing, and after 1857 he wrote only poetry. The unfinished manuscript, *Billy Budd, Foretopman* was found in his desk after his death. A wonderful passage from *Moby Dick* reads:

'All that most maddens and torments; all that stirs up the lees of things; all truth with malice in it; all that cracks the sinews and cakes the brain; all the subtle demonisms of life and thought; all evil, to crazy Ahab, were visibly personified, and made practically assailable in Moby Dick. He piled upon the whale's white hump the sum of all the general rage and hate felt by his whole race from Adam down; and then, as if chest had been a mortar, he burst his hot heart's shell upon it.'

VICTOR HUGO
1802–1885

'We must never forget those terrible, but so sweet, hours when you were close to me'

'You have been wonderful, my Juliette, all through these dark and violent days. If I needed love, you brought it to me, bless you! When, in my hiding places, always dangerous, after a night of waiting, I heard the key of my door trembling in your fingers, peril and darkness were no longer round me – what entered then was light! We must never forget those terrible, but so sweet, hours when you were close to me in the intervals of fighting. Let us remember all our lives that dark little room, the ancient hangings, the two armchairs, side by side, the meal we ate off the corner of the table, the cold chicken you had brought; our sweet converse, your caresses, your anxieties, your devotion. You were surprised to find me calm and serene. Do you know whence came both calmness and serenity? From you...'

Love letter to Juliette Drouet, 31 December 1851

The actress Juliette Drouet had become Hugo's mistress around 20 years before this letter, and they corresponded all their lives until her death in 1883. Hugo's wife began an affair in 1831, about the same time as he met Juliette, who became his lifelong companion. Hugo started to write poetry as a teenager, and went on to become a prolific and successful poet, dramatist and novelist, and the most celebrated author of his generation. His most famous works include *The Hunchback of Notre Dame* (1831), *Les Chants du Crepuscule* (1835) and *Les Misérables* (1862) (*see page 215*).

FREDERICK DOUGLASS
1818–1895

'What, to the American slave, is your Fourth of July? I answer: a day that reveals to him, more than all other days in the year, the gross injustice and cruelty to which he is the constant victim.'

Speech, Corinthian Hall, Rochester, New York, 5 July 1852

Born Frederick Augustus Washington Bailey, Douglass was an orator, reformer, editor, author, statesman and Abolitionist, one of the most eminent men in African-American history. His father was an unknown white man, probably a slave-owner, and he saw his mother only four or five times before he was orphaned aged seven. He said: '*I didn't know I was a slave until I found out I couldn't do the things I wanted*' and '*Slaves were expected to sing as well as to work. A silent slave was not liked, either by masters or overseers*'. Subjected to savage beatings, he was imprisoned for attempting to escape before finally succeeding in 1838 and changing his name to Douglass to avoid recapture. He claimed: '*I prayed for twenty years but received no answer until I prayed with my legs*'. He married and settled in Massachusetts, and in 1845 published his autobiography, the *Narrative of the Life of Frederick Douglass, an American Slave, Written By Himself.*

Douglass continually tried to better the lives of African Americans. Abraham Lincoln discussed abolition with him during the Civil War, and Douglass recruited northern blacks for the Union Army. After the Civil War he fought for the rights of women and African Americans alike, and in 1872 stood for Vice-Presidential candidate for the Equal Rights Party, supporting Victoria Woodhull as Presidential candidate. Douglass told us: '*The thing worse than rebellion is the thing that causes rebellion*' and '*The white man's happiness cannot be purchased by the black man's misery*'.

LEV NIKOLAYEVICH, COUNT TOLSTOY
1828–1910

'Can it be that there is not room for all men on this beautiful earth under these immeasurable starry heavens?'

'Can it be that there is not room for all men on this beautiful earth under these immeasurable starry heavens? Can it be possible that in the midst of this entrancing Nature feelings of hatred, vengeance, or the desire to exterminate their fellows can endure in the souls of men?'

The Raid, 1852

These lines are from one of Tolstoy's earliest published stories, based on a Russian military manoeuvre against the Chechen mountain tribesmen, in which Tolstoy's unit took part. After contracting heavy gambling debts, in 1851 Tolstoy accompanied his elder brother to the Caucasus, and joined an artillery regiment. During the Crimean War, he commanded a battery, witnessing the siege of Sebastopol (1854–55). In the 1850s, Tolstoy also began his literary career, publishing the autobiographical trilogy *Childhood* (1852), *Boyhood* (1854) and *Youth* (1857).

One of the greatest of all novelists, Tolstoy's major works include *War and Peace* (1863–69) and *Anna Karenina* (1875–77). *War and Peace* reflected his view that everything is predestined, but we cannot live unless we imagine that we have free will. This epic novel examines the hypocrisy and shallowness of war and aristocratic society, and comes to a climax during the Battle of Borodino. His other masterpiece *Anna Karenina* opens with the famous sentence: '*Happy families are all alike, every unhappy family is unhappy in its own way.*' Tolstoy's collected works, which were published in the Soviet Union between 1928 and 1958, consisted of 90 volumes. In 2007, *Anna Karenina* and *War and Peace* were placed on *Time* magazine's 10 greatest novels of all time, in first and third place respectively.

'I did not write it. God wrote it. I merely did His dictation.'

Reference to *Uncle Tom's Cabin*, 1852

Born Harriet Elizabeth Beecher, Stowe was the seventh child of a preacher and was originally a teacher. She wrote poems, travel books and ten novels, but is best known for *Uncle Tom's Cabin*, her first novel. One of the most influential American texts, it is possibly the first American social protest novel and it was originally serialized by Washington's *National Era*, an anti-slavery weekly. Stowe was spurred by her sister-in-law to write an Abolitionist novel, and she knew about slavery as she lived in Cincinatti, Ohio, just over the Ohio River from the slave state of Kentucky.

The huge sales of *Uncle Tom's Cabin* made Stowe a celebrity in America and Europe, and she gathered authentic evidence to speak against her pro-slavery critics wherever she went. She was blessed with an ability to communicate the slave culture to others, with realistic characters and local dialect. Sinclair Lewis said that 'Uncle Tom's Cabin *was the first evidence to America that no hurricane can be so disastrous to a country as a ruthlessly humanitarian woman'*. When Stowe met Abraham Lincoln in 1862, he allegedly exclaimed: '*So you're the little woman who wrote the book that made this big war!*'

NATHANIEL HAWTHORNE
1804–1864

'Caresses, expressions of one sort or another, are necessary to the life of the affections, as leaves are to the life of trees. If they are wholly restrained, love will die at the roots.'

American Note-Books, 9 March 1853

A central figure in the American Renaissance, Hawthorne's best-known works include *The Scarlet Letter* (1850) and *The House of the Seven Gables* (1851). The latter is based on a curse pronounced on Hawthorne's family by a woman condemned to death during the Salem witchcraft trials. In it, he tells us: *'Life is made up of marble and mud'* and *'the author has provided himself with a moral – the truth, namely, that the wrongdoing of one generation lives into the successive ones'.*

Hawthorne was pessimistic about human nature, possibly because his great-grandfather, John Hathorne, had been one of the judges in the Salem witchcraft trials of 1692. (Nathaniel Hawthorne, himself, added the 'w' to his name to distance himself from John Hathorne.) In *The Scarlet Letter*, an illicit love affair leads to an illegitimate child, so the mother wears the scarlet 'A' (for 'Adulteress') for years rather than reveal that her lover was the young village minister. The novel was a popular success, with the portrait it painted of sin-obsessed Puritans: *'The founders of a new colony, whatever Utopia of human virtue and happiness they might originally project, have invariably recognized it among their earliest practical necessities to allot a portion of the virgin soil as a cemetery, and another portion as the site of a prison.'*

Hawthorne also became friendly with Herman Melville, who dedicated *Moby Dick* to him. He was buried at Sleepy Hollow Cemetery in Concord, Massachusetts, and his mourners included Ralph Waldo Emerson, Bronson and Louisa May Alcott, Henry Wadsworth Longfellow, James Russell Lowell, Oliver Wendell Holmes, the scientist Louis Agassiz and his publisher, James T. Fields.

GUSTAVE FLAUBERT
1821–1880

'You can calculate the worth of a man by the number of his enemies, and the importance of a work of art by the harm that is spoken of it'

Letter to Louise Colet, 14 June 1853

The son of a surgeon, Flaubert was born in Rouen and expelled from school. He studied law in Paris, but was more committed to writing, stimulated by his friendship with Victor Hugo and an eight-year love affair with the poet Louise Colet. Flaubert seems to have been epileptic, failing his law exams, and his illness tended to make his works bleak and pessimistic. His father bought him a house, and on his father's death in 1846, Hugo's mother and sister came to live with him. He had rebelled against his family's wishes, and his hatred and contempt of bourgeois society is shown in his greatest work, *Madame Bovary* (1857). It took five years to write, as Flaubert was a perfectionist who constantly revised his work. In it, he turns a naïve provincial woman into a serial adulterer, and tortures her to death with poison. It was heavily criticized and then banned for a period. His next novel, *Salammbô*, took four years to write. In 1874, *The Temptation of St Anthony* was published.

Flaubert was bitter with his lot in life, a situation exacerbated by the death of his mother in 1872, the only woman to provide comfort to his troubled mind. Two weeks before his death from syphilis and other causes, he told his niece: '*Sometimes I think I'm liquefying like an old Camembert.*' The *Dictionary of Received Ideas* is a short satirical work published from 1911 to 1913 from Flaubert's notes in the last decade of his life. The entry for 'Money' is as follows: '*Cause of all evil... Politicians call it emoluments; lawyers, retainers; doctors, fees; employees, salary; workmen, pay; servants, wages.*'

ALFRED, LORD TENNYSON
1809–1892

'Cannon to right of them, Cannon to left of them, Cannon in front of them'

"'Forward, the Light Brigade!'"
Was there a man dismay'd?
Not tho' the soldier knew
Some one had blunder'd:
Theirs not to make reply,
Theirs not to reason why,
Theirs but to do and die:
Into the valley of Death
Rode the six hundred.

Cannon to right of them,
Cannon to left of them,
Cannon in front of them
Volley'd and thunder'd;
Storm'd at with shot and shell,
Boldly they rode and well,
Into the jaws of Death,
Into the mouth of Hell
Rode the six hundred.'

'The Charge of the Light Brigade', 9 December 1854

The Crimean War of 1854–56 saw the Russian Empire facing the Allied Army of Britain, France, Sardinia and the Ottoman Empire. The disastrous Charge of the Light Brigade took place on 25 October 1854, as part of the Battle of Balaclava. Of 673 men in the cavalry charge against cannon and overwhelming numbers, only 195 men came back with their horses. 157 men died, 122 were wounded and others were captured by the Russians. The French Field Marshall Bosquet commented on the futility of the order to charge: *'C'est magnifique, mais ce n'est pas la guerre. C'est de la folie.'* (*'It is magnificent, but it is not war. It is madness.'*) The Russian high command believed that the British must have been drunk to have attempted the assault.

Tennyson wrote *'The Charge of the Light Brigade'* almost immediately after the news of the disaster of 25 October reached England. The Crimean War in general was full of a series of errors by the English generals, and the public were desperate for good news. Thus the media made a heroine of 'The Lady of the Lamp', Florence Nightingale, and Tennyson made a heroic action of the destruction of the Light Brigade. Poet Laureate since 1850, Tennyson's works are often quoted, and he gave us the phrases *'better to have loved than lost'*, *'theirs is not to reason why, theirs is but to do and die'* (from 'The Charge of the Light Brigade') and *'nature, red in tooth and claw.'*

'Macaulay is like a book in breeches... He has occasional flashes of silence... that make his conversation perfectly delightful'

Reference to Lord Macaulay, quoted in *A Memoir of the Rev. Sydney Smith,* Lady Holland, 1855

The Reverend Sydney Smith was regarded as the wittiest man of his time. The historian Lord Thomas Babington Macaulay was a contributor to the *Edinburgh Review* and noted for his overlong sentences in conversation. Macaulay enjoyed Smith's wordplay, referring to him thus: *'In spite of innumerable affections and oddities, he is certainly one of the wittiest and most original writers of our times – the Smith of Smiths.'* In 1798, Smith had gone to Edinburgh as a tutor, and in 1802 he proposed the founding of the *Edinburgh Review*, superintending the first three numbers and writing for it for 25 years. In it he bravely promoted Catholics having voting rights, the abolition of slavery, criminal reforms and other radical humanitarian causes. This was at a time when the criticism of Parliament was considered as treason and sedition.

On leaving Edinburgh, Smith lectured in London, held curacies in Yorkshire and Somersetshire, and became Dean of St Paul's. Delightfully irreverent, when informed of a proposal to surround St Paul's Cathedral with a wooden pavement, he replied: *'Let the Dean and Canons put their heads together and the thing will be done'*. Because he loved eating, Smith's doctor asked him to lose weight and put him on a strict diet that excluded meat. One day Smith was heard to complain, *'I wish I were allowed even the wing of a roasted butterfly'*. His doctor had also advised he take walks, but on an empty stomach. *'Whose?'* asked Sydney. On shooting, he remarked *'The birds seem to consider the muzzle of my gun as their safest position'*, and he referred to one lady thus: *'[She] looked as if she had walked straight out of the ark'*.

WALT WHITMAN
1819–1892

**'I will not have in my writing any elegance, or effect...
to hang in the way between me and the rest like curtains...
What I tell I tell for precisely what it is'**

Preface to the first edition of *Leaves of Grass*, 1855

After working as a printer in New York, aged 17 the self-educated Whitman became a teacher, until he founded the weekly newspaper *Long-Islander* in 1841 and turned to journalism. After a time as editor of the *Brooklyn Daily Eagle*, in 1848 Whitman became editor of the *New Orleans Crescent* but was disgusted by the cruelty of the slave markets. That year he returned to found the *Brooklyn Freeman*, a 'free soil' newspaper. The Free Soil Party opposed the expansion of slavery into the western territories. In 1855, he published 12 untitled poems, *Leaves of Grass*, sending a copy to Ralph Waldo Emerson. The ever-supportive Emerson wrote that Whitman had written *'the most extraordinary piece of wit and wisdom that America has yet contributed'*. Emerson's letter was printed in the next edition of *Leaves of Grass*, this one with 33 poems, and the book was refined and published in several further editions.

During the Civil War, Whitman vowed to live a 'cleansed' life, and worked in hospitals and then as a clerk in Washington DC. He lived in poverty for most of his life, caring more for others than for himself. His last home, in Camden, New Jersey, is a National Historic Monument. The novelist David Lodge wrote that Whitman *'laid end to end words never seen in each other's company before outside of a dictionary'*. Whitman wrote: *'There is that indescribable freshness and unconsciousness about an illiterate person that humbles and mocks the power of the noblest expressive genius.'*

'Golden lie the meadows: golden run the streams'

'Away with Systems! Away with a corrupt World! Let us breathe the air of the Enchanted Island, Golden lie the meadows: golden run the streams; red gold is on the pine-stems. The sun is coming down to earth, and walks the fields and the waters.

The sun is coming down to earth, and the fields and the waters shout to him golden shouts. He comes, and his heralds run before him, and touch the leaves of oaks and planes and beeches lucid green, and the pine-stems redder gold; leaving brightest footprints upon thickly-weeded banks, where the foxglove's last upper-bells incline, and bramble-shoots wander amid moist rich herbage. The plumes of the woodland are alight; and beyond them, over the open, 'tis a race with the long-thrown shadows; a race across the heaths and up the hills, till, at the farthest bourne of mounted eastern cloud, the heralds of the sun lay rosy fingers, and rest... From silence into silence things move'

The Ordeal of Richard Feverel, 1859

A great novelist and poet, Meredith wrote complex and thought-provoking books that contain excellent psychological character studies. *The Ordeal of Richard Feverel* was his first, semi-autobiographical, novel. His wife had left him in 1858, and the passage quoted above shows his unblinking optimism when in a deep personal crisis. In the same book he also wrote: '*I expect that Woman will be the last thing civilized by Man.*' After an unhappy childhood, Meredith began a career as a freelance journalist, his first volume of poems appearing in 1851 and receiving the praises of Lord Tennyson. *Modern Love* (1862) was a series of 50 connected poems relating the sad dissolution of a marriage, again relating to his own life. His greatest novel was *The Egoist* (1879), and we can see in all his works a belief in life as a process of optimism and evolution.

JOHN BROWN
1800–1859

'I, John Brown, am now quite certain that the crimes of this guilty land will never be purged away but with blood'

Written on the morning of his execution in Virginia, 2 December 1859

Brown became an Abolitionist after the murder of the Abolitionist Presbyterian minister and journalist Elijah Parish Lovejoy in 1837 by a mob in Illinois. Increasingly Brown moved away from pacifism and advocated and practised armed insurrection, including the Pottawatomie Massacre in Kansas in 1856, where five supporters of slavery were killed. In 1859 he captured the Federal Armoury at Harper's Ferry, now in West Virginia, intending to arm black slaves and begin a rebellion. Within 36 hours he and his men had been killed, wounded or captured. The event is seen as a 'tipping point' in escalating the tensions leading to civil war. Brown was tried for treason and hung, but his impressive demeanour at his trial helped the Abolitionist cause. In his speech to the court on 2 November 1859, he said: '*Now, if it is deemed necessary that I should forfeit my life for the furtherance of the ends of justice, and mingle my blood further with the blood of my children and with the blood of millions in this slave country whose rights are disregarded by wicked, cruel, and unjust enactments, I submit; so let it be done!*'

Memorials were held in the North, church bells were rung, and Henry Thoreau and Ralph Waldo Emerson praised his actions. The 1861 song that includes the lines '*John Brown's Body lies a mould'ring in the grave, his soul is marching on*' was used as a marching song by Northern troops in the Civil War, which followed 16 months after his execution. At the end of the war, the noted black civil rights campaigner Frederick Douglass wrote: '*Did John Brown fail? John Brown began the war that ended American slavery and made this a free Republic. His zeal in the cause of freedom was infinitely superior to mine. Mine was as the taper light; his was as the burning sun. I could live for the slave; John Brown could die for him.*'

EMILY DICKINSON
1830–1886

'"Hope" is the thing with feathers'

'"Hope" is the thing with feathers –
That perches in the soul –
And sings the tune without the words –
And never stops – at all –

And sweetest – in the Gale – is heard –
And sore must be the storm –
That could abash the little Bird
That kept so many warm –

I've heard it in the chillest land –
And on the strangest Sea –
Yet, never, in Extremity,
It asked a crumb – of Me.'

'Poem 254', 1861

This is one of the most popular poems written by 'The Belle of Amherst', one of the most original of all American 19th-century poets. Dickinson innovated with metre and used hyphens and random capitals to create her own style. A sensitive woman, she questioned the puritanical background of her Calvinist family in often deeply personal poetry. Around 1864, she was told by an eye specialist to stop reading and writing, and by 1874 she had stopped going out in public. Dickinson kept corresponding from her seclusion, but eventually succumbed to chronic pain from Bright's disease (the historical name for kidney disease). There was no church service – she was buried in one of the white dresses she had taken to wearing, violets pinned to her collar by her sister, Lavinia. Only a handful of her poems had been published. Lavinia found over 400 tied into 'fascicles' stitched together by Emily's own hand. Some were written in pencil, only a few were titled, and many were unfinished. The above poem is number 254 in chronological order, with no known title.

HARRIET ANN JACOBS
c.1813–1897

'Cruelty is contagious in uncivilized communities'

Incidents in the Life of a Slave Girl, Written by Herself, 1861

Harriet Ann Jacobs was born a slave in North Carolina, and her autobiography was published under the pseudonym Linda Brent in 1861. It was probably the only slave narrative to deal with sexual oppression as well as the cruelty of conditions. Of her mother's death in 1819, she wrote, '*I was born a slave; but I never knew it till six years of happy childhood had passed away*.' Later, Harriet became the object of her owner Dr Norcom's unwanted sexual advances and his wife's vindictive jealousy: '*But I now entered on my fifteenth year – a sad epoch in the life of a slave girl. My master began to whisper foul words in my ear. Young as I was, I could not remain ignorant of their import*'.

In 1829 and 1833 she had children with Samuel Treadwell Sawyer ('*Always it gave me a pang that my children had no lawful claim to a name*'). The vengeful Dr Norcom sent her to a plantation to be broken in as a field-hand, but Jacobs ran away to her grandmother's house where she hid for seven years in a crawlspace under the front porch roof. In 1842, she escaped from Edenton by boat, becoming a nursemaid for the family of Abolitionist Nathaniel Parker Willis in New York. She was eventually reunited with her children, and the Willises bought Jacobs and gave her freedom in 1852. Elsewhere in her harrowing book, we read: '*The slave girl is reared in an atmosphere of licentiousness and fear*'; '*Death is better than slavery*'; and '*Everywhere the years bring to all enough of sin and sorrow; but in slavery the very dawn of life is darkened by these shadows*'.

HENRY DAVID THOREAU
1817-1862

'One world at a time'

*'"You seem so near the brink of the dark river, that I almost
wonder how the opposite shore may appear to you"* – Parker
Pillsbury to Thoreau a few days before Thoreau's death
"One world at a time." – Thoreau'

'Quoted in *Henry Thoreau: A Life of the Mind*, Robert D. Richardson, Jr, 1986

Parker Pillsbury was an old Abolitionist minister
who had left his church over the slavery issue and who
could not resist the impulse to peer into the future.
Thoreau's answer summed up his own life – he wished to
know about what was, not what might be. Thoreau always
looked to Nature for his ultimate truth; apparently one of
his first memories was *'looking through the stars to see if I
could see God through them'*. Born in Concord, Massachusetts, he was a naturalist, poet, writer and philosopher, and
his writings on natural history led a path for today's ecologists and environmen-
talists. A lifelong Abolitionist, Thoreau's philosophy of non-violent resistance
is said to have influenced Tolstoy, Gandhi and Martin Luther King. His civil
disobedience did not require the abolition of government – *'I ask for, not at once no
government, but at once a better government'*.

In 1845, wanting to write his first book, Thoreau went to Walden Pond and built
his cabin on land owned by Ralph Waldo Emerson. However, his self-published
A Week on the Concord and Merrimack Rivers pushed him into debt. He next
supported himself by surveying and making a few lectures, revising his new book,
Walden, or Life in the Woods, which was published in 1854. It told of the two years,
two months and two days he had spent at Walden Pond. The book compresses
the period into a single calendar year, and links human development to natural
simplicity and harmony, as a model for just social and cultural conditions.
Thoreau's attitude to life is summed up by his words: *'Our life is frittered away by
detail... Simplify, simplify'*.

OTTO VON BISMARCK
1815–1898

'Not by speeches and votes of the majority are the great questions of the time decided – that was the error of 1848 and 1849 – but by iron and blood'

Speech to the Prussian Diet, 30 September 1862

Otto Eduard Leopold von Bismarck, Prince of Bismarck, 'The Iron Chancellor', is considered the founder of the German Empire. For nearly three decades he shaped the fortunes of Germany, from 1862 to 1873 as Prime Minister of Prussia and from 1871 to 1890 as Germany's first Chancellor. In 1859 he was Ambassador to Russia, then Ambassador to France and in 1862 Prime Minister of Prussia, whence he devoted himself to the task of uniting Germany. In the War of 1866 he defeated Austria, and the Franco-Prussian War (1870–71) again ended with Prussian victory, both being geared towards German unification. This latter victory ensured the kingdoms of Bavaria, Württemberg, Baden and Hesse joined the North German Alliance of Prussia and 17 other German states created by Bismarck in 1866. This led to the declaration of the German Empire in 1870 and the proclamation of King William I of Prussia as German Emperor in Versailles in 1871. Under the new imperial constitution, Bismarck was appointed Imperial Chancellor – a system described at the time as a 'chancellor dictatorship'.

In 1848, a revolution had occurred in Prussia, during which King Frederick William IV refused to use his armed forces. He offered concessions, wore the revolutionary colours of red, yellow and black, and agreed to a constitution. Bismarck had tried to raise an army on his estates to march to Berlin and fight for the king. His offer of help was refused. In 1849, Parliament failed to unify the German states, and in 1850 Prussia was humiliated by Austria. Bismarck saw military action – *'iron and blood'*, rather than politics, as the way forward for a united Germany under Prussian domination. Bismarck's greatest achievements included administrative reforms, developing a common currency, a central bank, and a single code of commercial and civil law for Germany. He presided over the Congress of Berlin (1872) as mediator between the then great powers of Russia, Austria, France and Great Britain. He stated that politics was *'not an exact science'* but *'the art of the possible'*, and seemed to predict World War I and other conflicts: *'If ever there is another war in Europe, it will come out of some damned silly thing in the Balkans.'*

'There is always more misery among the lower classes than there is humanity in the higher'

Les Misérables, 1862

Victor Hugo grew up in Paris, the son of one of Napoléon's generals. His first collection of poems, *Odes et Poésies Diverses*, gained him a royal pension from Louis XVIII, and he soon began writing novels and dramas. He gained public and critical acclaim with his play *Hernani* (1830) and in 1831 with his novel *Notre-Dame de Paris* (*The Hunchback of Notre Dame*), which tells the moving story of a gypsy girl, Esmeralda, and the bell-ringer, Quasimodo, who loves her: '*Do you know what friendship is... it is to be brother and sister; two souls which touch without mingling, two fingers on one hand.*'

Hugo was elected to the Académie Française in 1841 and became involved in politics, gaining election to the Constitutional and Legislative Assemblies. He was embittered by the death of his daughter in 1843, and consequently stopped writing for a decade. He fled Paris after Louis Napoléon's coup d'état in 1851, living in Brussels and the Channel Islands for 20 years. During this time he wrote *Les Misérables*, his epic about social injustice in 19th-century Paris; another line from the novel is: '*To die is nothing; but it is terrible not to live.*'

The shortest correspondence in history was between Hugo and his publisher Hurst & Blackett, in 1862. Hugo was on holiday when *Les Misérables* was published. He telegraphed the single-character message '?' to his publisher. Sales were astonishing, and the publisher replied with a single '!'

'The world will little note nor long remember what we say here, but it can never forget what they did here'

'Fourscore and seven years ago our fathers brought forth on this continent a new nation, conceived in liberty and dedicated to the proposition that all men are created equal.

Now we are engaged in a great civil war, testing whether that nation or any nation so conceived and so dedicated can long endure. We are met on a great battlefield of that war.

We have come to dedicate a portion of that field as a final resting-place for those who here gave their lives that that nation might live. It is altogether fitting and proper that we should do this.

But in a larger sense, we cannot dedicate, we cannot consecrate, we cannot hallow this ground. The brave men, living and dead who struggled here have consecrated it far above our poor power to add or detract.

The world will little note nor long remember what we say here, but it can never forget what they did here. It is for us the living rather to be dedicated here to the unfinished work which they who fought here have thus far so nobly advanced.

It is rather for us to be here dedicated to the great task remaining before us – that from these honoured dead we take increased devotion to that cause for which they gave the last full measure of devotion – that we here highly resolve that these dead shall not have died in vain, that this nation under God shall have a new birth of freedom, and that government of the people, by the people, for the people shall not perish from the earth.

The Gettysburg Address, 19 November 1863

Little did Lincoln realize that this inspiring two-minute speech would be remembered as it is. It was his most famous oration, delivered at the dedication of the Soldiers' National Cemetery in Gettysburg, Pennsylvania, four and a half months after Union forces defeated the Confederate Army there.

CHARLES KINGSLEY
1819–1875

'Young blood must have its course, lad, and every dog its day'

The Water Babies, 1863

The son of a vicar, and Cambridge-educated, Kingsley became curate of Eversley in Hampshire in 1842. He was a fervent supporter of Chartism – voting rights for the working classes. After the government's rejection of the 1848 Chartist Petition, Kingsley helped form the Christian Socialist movement, writing pamphlets to further working-class causes and thereby prevent revolution. In 1850, his novel *Alton Locke* was published, exposing social injustice suffered by agricultural labourers and workers in the clothing trade. After a historical novel, *Hypatia*, in 1857 Kingsley published *Two Years Ago*, about how poor sanitary conditions and public apathy cause an outbreak of cholera.

The Water Babies is his most famous book and it tells the story of Tom, a young chimney-sweep, who runs away from his vicious employer. During his flight he falls into a river and is transformed into a water baby, meeting all sorts of creatures and learning a series of moral lessons. In the novel we read: '*Letting water-babies die is as bad as taking singing birds' eggs; for though there are thousands, ay, millions, of both of them in the world, yet there is not one too many*' and '*at that Tom cried so bitterly that the salt sea was swelled with his tears, and the tide was .3,954,620,819 of an inch higher than it had been the day before: but perhaps that was owing to the waxing of the moon*'. Kingsley also wrote *Westward Ho!* (1855) and *Hereward the Wake* (1866).

MAJOR-GENERAL JOHN SEDGEWICK
1813–1864

'They couldn't hit an elephant at this distance'

'At the same moment a sharp-shooter's bullet passed with a long shrill whistle very close, and the soldier, who was then just in front of the general, dodged to the ground. The general touched him gently with his foot, and said, "Why, my man, I am ashamed of you, dodging that way," and repeated the remark, "They couldn't hit an elephant at this distance.".... For a third time the same shrill whistle, closing with a dull, heavy stroke, interrupted our talk; when, as I was about to resume, the general's face turned slowly to me, the blood spurting from his left cheek under the eye in a steady stream. He fell in my direction; I was so close to him that my effort to support him failed, and I fell with him.'

His last words

Sedgewick was a teacher, career military officer and Union Army general in the American Civil War. He fought in the Seminole Wars, the Mexican-American War, the Utah War and the Indian Wars. A colonel at the beginning of the Civil War, he was promoted to brigadier – general, fighting in the Peninsula Campaign and at Yorktown and Seven Pines. He was wounded in the leg and arm at Glendale and promoted to major-general in 1862. Almost surrounded by 'Stonewall' Jackson's forces at Antietam, he was hit by three bullets and his division suffered 2,200 casualties. He also took part in the battles of Chancellorsville, Salem Church and the Battle of the Wilderness. At the Battle of Spotsylvania Court House, Sedgewick was directing artillery emplacements, with Confederate sharp-shooters causing his men to duck for cover. The passage quoted above is Brevet Major-General McMahon's eyewitness account of what occurred thereafter...

SIR WALTER SCOTT
1771–1832

'No, this right hand shall work it off'

On refusing offers to help after he was made bankrupt in 1826, referring to his
intention to write his way out of debt – *Century of Anecdote*, John Timbs, 1864

Lamed by polio, Scott studied law at Edinburgh University and practised all his life. When he was 23, his novel *Waverley*, based on the 1745 Jacobite Rising, established a new genre of historical novels and was a huge success. Over the next few years he wrote another 23 historical novels in a series called the *Waverley Novels*, each eagerly awaited, and all published anonymously. Not until a public dinner in 1827 did he reveal himself as the author. Scott's plots mix different classes, religions and politics, trying to show that people are fundamentally honest and moral, and many are about opposing cultures – for example, *Ivanhoe* puts Normans against Saxons, and *The Talisman* Christians against Muslims.

Scott's printing and publishing firm collapsed in 1826 and he vowed to pay off all £150,000 of the resultant debts, including those of his partner – and indeed, from the profits of his writings, all his debts were ultimately paid. Verses from his *The Lady of the Lake*, including '*Hail to the Chief who in triumph advances!*' were put to music by James Sanderson (1769–1841) and became the march traditionally played to honour the President of the United States. The critic William Hazlitt claimed that Scott's '*worse was better than any other person's best*', and from Scott's *Marmion* we have '*But search the land of living men / Where will we find their like agen?*' and '*O what a tangled web we weave / When first we practise to deceive!*'.

WILLIAM EWART GLADSTONE
1809–1898

'You cannot fight against the future. Time is on our side.'

Speech upon the Reform Bill, 1866

A Conservative MP, Gladstone became Chancellor of the Exchequer in the coalition government of Lord John Russell, and in 1859 was offered the same post under Lord Palmerston. He abolished paper duty to enable the publication of cheap newspapers, and advocated parliamentary reform, pointing out that only two per cent of the working classes had the right to vote. He was in a minority of 56, as against 272 MPs who voted against change. Chancellor under Russell again, as Leader of the House of Commons, in 1866 Gladstone introduced a new Reform Bill, but the bill foundered and the government collapsed. Gladstone's words proved prophetic – although his Conservative Party had voted against reform and the party had imploded, within a year time had proved him correct. In 1867 Disraeli proposed a new Reform Act and with Gladstone's support it was passed, enlarging the electorate from one million to two million.

In 1862 Gladstone introduced the Ballot Act, enforcing secret ballots. In 1868, he became Liberal Prime Minister, and in 1870 the Education Act was passed, establishing school boards. The Reform Act of 1884 added six million to the electoral rolls; Gladstone said: *'Justice delayed is justice denied'* and *'All the world over, I will back the masses against the classes'*. He tried to allow Irish independence, but was defeated: *'We are bound to lose Ireland in consequence of years of cruelty, stupidity and misgovernment and I would rather lose her as a friend than as a foe.'* He also presciently foretold troubles elsewhere in the world: *'Remember the rights of the savage, as we call him. Remember that the happiness of his humble home, remember that the sanctity of life in the hill villages of Afghanistan, among the winter snows, is as inviolable in the eye of Almighty God, as can be your own.'*

THOMAS CARLYLE
1795–1881

'Work is the grand cure of all the maladies and miseries that ever beset mankind'

Inaugural address as Rector of Edinburgh University, 2 April 1866

The son of a stonemason, Carlyle was raised as a strict Calvinist, then studied arts and mathematics at Edinburgh University, becoming a teacher at Kirkcaldy. He then returned to Edinburgh and began writing articles and translating German authors. On moving to London in 1826 he became a close friend of the philosopher John Stuart Mill and wrote *The French Revolution* (1837), *On Heroes, Hero Worship and the Heroic in History* (1841) and *Past and Present* (1843).

Driven by the 'puritan ethic', Carlyle was a workaholic, writing all his life, as the quote above demonstrates. His books and articles influenced social reformers such as John Ruskin, Charles Dickens and William Morris. In *Sartorius Resartus* he showed his mathematics training by stating: '*It is a mathematical fact that the casting of this pebble from my hand alters the centre of gravity of the universe.*' It was also Carlyle who first wrote of '*captains of industry*' and '*A witty statesman said, you might prove anything by figures*'. He called Robespierre '*the seagreen Incorruptible*' and political economy '*the Dismal Science*'.

'O Captain! My Captain! our fearful trip is done'

'O Captain! My Captain! our fearful trip is done;
The ship has weathered every rack, the prize we sought is won;
The port is near, the bells I hear, the people all exulting,
While follow eyes the stead keel, the vessel grim and daring.
But O heart! heart! heart!
O the bleeding drops of red!
Where on the deck my Captain lies,
Fallen cold and dead.

'O Captain! My Captain!', *Leaves of Grass*, 1867 edition

On Lincoln's assassination on 14 April 1865, Whitman immediately wrote two eulogies. The shorter poem, of which the first verse is shown above, represents Lincoln as the captain of the ship of the United States. The poem begins with a description of a ship returning safely to port. Crying out for his captain, the speaker realizes the captain has died at sea. The onlookers onshore celebrate the ship's safe return, but the speaker mourns the death of his captain.

The poem was so popular, and Whitman was requested to recite it so often, that he said '*I'm almost sorry I ever wrote it*'. His other poem, also written in the year of Lincoln's death, is the long, heartfelt elegy '*When Lilacs Last in the Dooryard Bloom'd*', of which the first verse is:

'When lilacs last in the dooryard bloom'd,
And the great star early droop'd in the western sky in the night,
I mourn'd, and yet shall mourn with ever-returning spring.
Ever-returning spring, trinity sure to me you bring,
Lilac blooming perennial and drooping star in the west,
And thought of him I love.'

RAMÓN MARÍA NÁRVAEZ
1800–1868

'I do not have to forgive my enemies, I have had them all shot'

When asked on his deathbed by a priest if he forgave his enemies, the Spanish leader gave this answer. A soldier and statesman, Nárvaez supported Isabel II on the death of Ferdinand VII, fighting for her forces from 1834 to 1839. He won a great victory over the Carlist forces of Miguel Gomez Damas at the Battle of Majaceite in 1836, then cleared La Mancha of bandits and was given military appointments.

Baldomero Espartero and the Progresista Party came to power in 1840, and for his part in the insurrection at Seville against them, Nárvaez was forced to flee to France where he joined the partisans of Maria Christina. He returned to Spain in 1843, having planned an expedition to overthrow Espartero, and became Prime Minister in 1844, then a field marshal and the first Duke of Valencia in 1845. His reactionary policies led to his removal in 1846, but he was back in Spain as President of the Council of Ministers in 1847. He resigned in 1848, but again became President from 1856 to 1857, and from 1866 until his death.

Known as the 'strong man' of Isabelline Spain, Nárvaez's authoritarian policies helped provoke the uprising shortly after his death, which led to the downfall of Queen Isabella.

JOHN STUART MILL
1806–1873

'The legal subordination of one sex to another – is wrong in itself'

'The principle which regulates the existing social relations between the two sexes – the legal subordination of one sex to another – is wrong in itself, and now one of the chief hindrances to human improvement.'

The Subjection of Women, 1869

John Stuart Mill was an economist and political theorist, and the most influential English-speaking philosopher of the 19th century. He was taught Greek, Latin, mathematics, philosophy and economics from an early age by his father, who kept him away from other children. After a mental breakdown in 1826–27 he moved away from a more right-wing philosophy to become a leading liberal thinker, sympathetic to Socialism and espousing women's rights. He also wanted proportional representation and was in favour of labour unions and farm co-operatives.

Mill was seen as a defender of individual liberty against the interference of state and society. His philosophy develops a positive view of the universe and the place of humans in it, leading to the progress of human knowledge, individual freedom and human well-being. His books *Utilitarianism* and *On Liberty* are still studied today, and in the latter, we read: *'If all mankind minus one were of one opinion, and only one person were of the contrary opinion, mankind would no more be justified in silencing that one person, than he, if he had the power, would be justified in silencing mankind.'*

JULES VERNE
1828–1905

'The sea is everything'

'The sea is everything. It covers seven tenths of the terrestrial globe. Its breath is pure and healthy. It is an immense desert, where man is never lonely, for he feels life stirring on all sides. The sea is only the embodiment of a supernatural and wonderful existence. It is nothing but love and emotion.'

Twenty Thousand Leagues Under the Sea, Part I, Chapter X:
'The Man of the Seas', 1869

 **Along with H.G. Wells,** Verne is considered the founding father of science fiction, but unlike Wells he always tried to ground his stories in scientific possibility rather than the imagination. Among his works are *Around the World in Eighty Days* (1873), *Journey to the Centre of the Earth* (1864) and *Twenty Thousand Leagues Under the Sea* (1869). He is the second most translated author of all time after Agatha Christie, with over 4,000 translations of his works.

Verne predicted the use of hydrogen as an energy source (in *From the Earth to the Moon*, 1865) and many inventions such as helicopters, aeroplanes, skyscrapers and submarines. He originally settled in Paris to study law, as his father had done, but upon obtaining his degree in 1850, he was much more interested in theatre. He lived a bohemian life, writing numerous plays, dramas and operettas before finding his niche in writing fiction. It may be that these lines from *The Mysterious Island* (1874) describe his reasons for becoming an author: '*The desire to perform a work which will endure, which will survive him, is the origin of man's superiority over all other living creatures here below. It is this which has established his dominion, and this it is which justifies it, over all the world.*'

CHARLES-MAURICE DE TALLEYRAND-PÉRIGORD
1754–1838

'This is the beginning of the end'

Said of Napoléon's Pyrrhic victory at Borodino in 1812,
quoted in M. de Talleyrand, *Sainte-Beuve*, 1870

Prince of Benevento and Bishop of Autun, this minister and ambassador is synonymous with French diplomacy. Charles-Maurice was regarded as an immoral and licentious unbeliever. However, his father, the Comte de Talleyrand, convinced King Louis XVI to give Charles-Maurice the bishopric of Autun in 1789. Elected a member of the États Généraux, Talleyrand-Périgord rapidly became one of the most important statesmen in Europe. As a member of the Constitutional Committee, he took part in the French Declaration of the Rights of Man, and resigned his bishopric, after which he was excommunicated in 1791. In 1792 he was sent to London to try to organize a Franco-English alliance, but only secured neutrality. Banished by the Convention, he escaped to the United States (where he found '*a country with thirty-two religions and only one sauce*') but was back in Paris in 1796, becoming Minister of Foreign Affairs.

He welcomed Napoléon as the man '*who would make everything smooth*', who nonetheless then compelled Talleyrand to marry his mistress. Then Talleyrand's opposition to the Spanish War in 1809 caused his downfall until Napoléon's defeat. In 1812, the bloody Battle of Borodino allowed Napoléon to take Moscow, but the Russian army was not destroyed and the French lost 30,000 men. The indecisive victory severely weakened Napoléon, and later that winter he was driven out of Russia. Talleyrand foresaw Napoléon's eventual downfall stemming from this battle. In 1814, as leader of the provisional government, Talleyrand gave power to Louis XVIII. However, of the Bourbons he remarked, '*They have learned nothing, and forgotten nothing.*' At the Congress of Vienna he secretly concluded a treaty with Austria and England; but after establishing this *entente cordiale*, he resigned office in 1834. In his *Mémoires*, he wrote that he '*never had betrayed a government which had not betrayed itself first*', nor ever put his '*own interests in the balance with those of France*'. On hearing of Napoléon's death in 1821, Talleyrand remarked: '*It is not an event. It is an item of news.*'

CHARLES DARWIN
1809–1892

'For my own part I would as soon be descended from that heroic little monkey'

'For my own part I would as soon be descended from that heroic little monkey, who braved his dreaded enemy in order to save the life of his keeper; or from that old baboon, who, descending from the mountains, carried away in triumph his young comrade from a crowd of astonished dogs – as from a savage who delights to torture his enemies, offers up bloody sacrifices, practises infanticide without remorse, treats his wives like slaves, knows no decency, and is haunted by the grossest superstitions.'

The Descent of Man, 1871

T.H. Huxley called Darwin *'the incorporated ideal of a man of science'.* At the beginning of *On the Origin of Species,* Darwin writes, *'We will now discuss in a little more detail the Struggle for Existence',* and towards the end of the book, he notes, *'The main conclusion arrived at in this work, namely, that man is descended from some lowly organized form, will, I regret, be highly distasteful to many. But there can be hardly any doubt that we are descended from barbarians.'*

In his *The Descent of Man,* Darwin is disparaging of females – some of their *'faculties are characteristic of the lower races; and therefore of a past and lower state of civilization.'* Darwin drew on the work on inherited genes by Lamarck (1744–1829), but even more so upon the findings of Alfred Russel Wallace (1823–1913), who first gave us the phrase *'the fittest would survive'.* Wallace independently discovered the theory of natural selection and evolution via fieldwork in the Amazon and Malaysia, but Darwin took most of the credit.

GEORGE ELIOT
1819–1880

'A woman dictates before marriage in order that she may have a habit for submission afterwards'

Middlemarch, 1871–1872

Mary Ann Evans used a masculine pseudonym to have her novels published and accepted, as women were usually only associated with romantic novels. When her mother died in 1836, Eliot left school to help run her father's household and lived with him until his death in 1849. She then travelled across Europe before settling in London. She began contributing to the *Westminster Review*, a journal for philosophical radicals, and became its editor. Then at the centre of a literary circle, she met George Henry Lewes and lived with him until his death in 1878 – but Lewes remained married and their relationship was considered scandalous. Lewes encouraged Eliot to write, and in 1856 she began *Scenes of Clerical Life*, stories about the people of her native Warwickshire. Her first novel, *Adam Bede* (1859), was a huge success, with its readers believing a man had written it; it contained lines such as '*I'm not denyin' the women are foolish. God made 'em to match the men.*'

Eliot's other novels include *The Mill on the Floss* (1860), in which we read '*The happiest women, like the happiest nations, have no history*'; *Silas Marner* (1861), containing the line '*Nothing is so good as it seems beforehand*'; *Romola* (1863); *Felix Holt: The Radical* (1866), in which she wrote '*An election is coming. Universal peace is declared, and the foxes have a sincere interest in prolonging the life of the poultry*'; *Middlemarch* (1872) and *Daniel Deronda* (1876). The realism and psychological insights of her novels finally brought her social acceptance, and the home she shared with Lewes became a meeting place for writers and intellectuals. Lewes died in 1878 and in 1880 Eliot married a man 20 years younger than herself, but she died that year of throat and kidney infections. She was not allowed burial in Westminster Abbey because of her denial of the Christian faith, and her long relationship with the married Lewes.

SAMUEL BUTLER
1835–1902

'Tis better to have loved and lost than never to have loved at all'

The Way of All Flesh, 1873–1884

This is an 18th-century proverb which Butler popularized and is still in common use today. Samuel Butler was expected to be a cleric like his forefathers, but while preparing for ordination after taking his degree at Cambridge, he worked in a poor school in London where he discovered that there was no difference in the morals or behaviour of the boys who had been baptized and those who had not. His father was furious about Butler's doubts, but in 1859 Butler sailed to New Zealand to become a sheep farmer instead of a priest.

Butler corresponded with Darwin after reading *On the Origin of Species* and became a convert to the theory of evolution. Returning to London, he enjoyed huge success with his Swiftian satire *Erewhon* (originally published anonymously in 1872), followed by *Erewhon Revisited* in 1900. He had begun *The Way of All Flesh*, an auto-biographical account of a harsh upbringing, in 1873, but did not publish it out of respect for his family. Instead it was edited, revised and published after his death, and received great critical and public acclaim. George Bernard Shaw called it '*One of the summits of human achievement*' and V.S. Pritchett '*One of the time-bombs of literature*'. Butler tells us that: '*Life is like playing a violin solo in public and learning the instrument as one goes on*'. Some of Butler's other memorable quotes include:

'*A hen is only an egg's way of making another egg*'

'*There's many a good tune played on an old fiddle*'

'*God cannot alter the past, though historians can*'

'*An Apology for the Devil: It must be remembered that we have only heard one side of the case. God has written all the books*'

'*It was very good of God to let Carlyle and Mrs Carlyle marry one another and so make only two people miserable instead of four, besides being very amusing*'

EPITAPH OF DAVID LIVINGSTONE
1813–1873

'Who will help heal this open sore of the world'

'Brought by faithful hands,
Over land and sea,
Here rests
David Livingstone,
Missionary,
Traveller,
Philanthropist.
Born March 19, 1813,
At Blantyre, Lanarkshire,
Died May 1, 1873, At Chitambo's
Village, Ulala.
For thirty years his life was spent
In an unwearied effort
To evangelise the native races,
To explore the undiscovered
secrets,
To abolish the desolating slave
trade
Of Central Africa,
Where with his last words he
wrote,
"All I can add in my solitude, is,
May Heaven's rich blessing come
down
On everyone, American, English
or Turk
– Who will help heal
This open sore of the world."'

This epitaph is on the tomb of David Livingstone in Westminster Abbey, where his embalmed body was laid 11 months after his death, identified by the lion wound in his left shoulder. Livingstone's heart had been buried in Africa, and his followers trekked for months through the jungle to take his embalmed body to a port. The quotation in the epitaph is taken from the last report Livingstone sent to the *New York Herald*.

Livingstone had studied theology and medicine in Glasgow before being ordained in 1840, and he decided to work in Africa to open up the interior for colonization, extend the gospel and abolish the slave trade. In 1849 he became the first European to cross the Kalahari Desert to reach Lake Ngami, and he discovered and named the Victoria Falls in 1855. When he was found by Henry Morton Stanley in 1871, Stanley greeted him with the famous words '*Dr Livingstone, I presume?*' Livingstone was ill but refused to leave his work, dying of dysentery soon after. Livingstone's efforts helped to stop slavery in Eastern Africa.

'Wild Bill, J.B. Hickok,
killed by the assassin Jack McCall in Deadwood, Black
Hills, August 2, 1876. Pard, we will meet again in the
happy hunting ground to part no more.
Good bye, Colorado Charlie, C.H. Utter.'

Charlie Utter, friend of James Butler 'Wild Bill' Hickok (1837–1876), wrote this on Wild Bill's wooden grave marker. He had previously placed a notice in the *Black Hills Pioneer* asking people to attend the funeral at 'Charlie Utter's Camp'. Wild Bill and the other denizens of Deadwood's original graveyard were moved to the Mount Moriah Cemetery in the 1880s, where Bill now has an imposing monument. According to her dying wish, Martha Jane Cannary – known popularly as Calamity Jane – was buried next to him, as was Potato Creek Johnny.

Hickok had been a skilled marksman and gunfighter, probably killing around 20 men, and had also scouted for General Custer, hunted buffalo, served as a lawman and gambled to excess. Because of his 'sweeping nose and protruding upper lip' Hickok was originally known as 'Duck Bill' Hickok, which he successfully transmuted over the years into something more suitable for a hard man of the Wild West. He always played poker in Nuttal & Mann's Saloon No. 10 in Deadwood, with his back to the wall to protect himself. Unfortunately, one day he arrived late for the game and his seat was already taken, so he sat with his back to one door and facing another, but Jack McCall shot him in the back of the head with a Colt 45. Hickock was holding aces and eights, which became known as the 'dead man's hand'. McCall was hung for his crime.

GERARD MANLEY HOPKINS
1844–1889

'Look at the stars! look, look up at the skies!'

'Look at the stars! look, look up at the skies!
O look at all the fire-folk sitting in the air!
The bright boroughs, the circle-citadels there!'

'The Starlight Night', 1877, from *Poems*, 1918

Gerard Manley Hopkins studied at Oxford, gaining a rare Double First, and was strongly influenced by the poetry of George Herbert and Christina Rossetti. Cardinal Newman was instrumental in Hopkins' conversion from Anglicanism to Roman Catholicism, and as a Jesuit priest Hopkins believed that his poetry was the fruit of personal ambition, so burnt all his early poems. He learned Welsh, and adapted the rhythms of Welsh poetry to his own verse, inventing 'sprung rhythm'. He began writing poetry again with 'The Wreck of the Deutschland', inspired by the story of nuns drowning, but for his time it was too radical in style to be printed. His friend, later the Poet Laureate, Robert Bridges was sent copies of Hopkins' poems, and almost 30 years after Hopkins' death arranged for them to be published. They are among the greatest poems of faith in the English language. The wonderful 'Pied Beauty' reads:

'Glory be to God for dappled things –
For skies of couple-colour as a brinded cow;
For rose-moles all in stipple upon trout that swim;
Fresh-firecoal chestnut-falls; finches' wings;
Landscape plotted and pieced – fold, fallow, and plough;
And áll trádes, their gear and tackle and trim.

All things counter, original, spare, strange;
Whatever is fickle, freckled (who knows how?)
With swift, slow; sweet, sour; adazzle, dim;
He fathers-forth whose beauty is past change:
Praise him.'

FYODOR DOSTOEVSKY
1821–1881

'If the devil doesn't exist, but man has created him, he has created him in his own image and likeness'

The Brothers Karamazov, 1879–1880

Albert Einstein remarked that '*Dostoevsky gives me more than any scientist, more than Gauss*', and the Russian author's intense, layered commentaries on religion, philosophy and psychology make him one of the greatest writers in world literature. Best known for his novels *Crime and Punishment* and *The Brothers Karamazov*, Dostoevsky attained profound philosophical and psychological insights. His own troubled life enabled him to portray with deep sympathy characters that were spiritually downtrodden – his father was murdered by his own serfs at the family's country estate before Dostoevsky embarked on a literary career. He published his first novel, *Poor Folk*, in 1846, and became an overnight celebrity when the most influential critic of the day declared him the literary successor of Gogol.

In 1848 Dostoevsky joined a group of young intellectuals to discuss literary and political issues. In 1849 the members were arrested and charged with subversion, and Dostoevsky was imprisoned and sentenced to death. As he and his friends were facing the firing squad, an imperial messenger arrived with the announcement that the Czar had commuted the death sentences to hard labour in Siberia. Dostoevsky described his life as a prisoner in *The House of the Dead* (1862), and while in prison he underwent a profound conversion, as the New Testament was the only book prisoners were allowed to read. He formed the conviction that redemption is possible only through suffering and faith, a belief which influenced all his later work. He was released but was forced to serve as a soldier in Siberia for another five years. When he returned to St Petersburg in 1859 he started up some journals, but they were closed down by the authorities, and both his wife and his brother died. It was during this difficult time that Dostoevsky wrote *Notes from the Underground* (1864) and *Crime and Punishment* (1866).

BENJAMIN DISRAELI
1808–1881

'There are three kinds of lies: lies, damned lies and statistics'

Attributed, according to Mark Twain's *Autobiography*

Twain's actual quote was '*The remark attributed to Disraeli would often apply with justice and force: "There are three kinds of lies: lies, damned lies, and statistics".*' The phrase is untraced among Disraeli's writings, but Leonard Henry Courtney, the British politician (1832–1918), gave a speech on proportional representation at New York, in 1895, in which he said: '*After all, facts are facts, and although we may quote one to another with a chuckle the words of the Wise Statesman, "Lies – damn lies – and statistics," still there are some easy figures the simplest must understand, and the astutest cannot wriggle out of.*' It seems that Twain understood its veiled attribution to a 'Wise Statesman' to be Disraeli. For some reason, allusions to, rather than outright quotations of, Disraeli were common at this time (he had died in 1881). We know of Disraeli's remark to an author who had sent him an unsolicited manuscript – '*Many thanks; I shall lose no time in reading it*'. However, this was merely ascribed to '*an eminent man on this side of the Atlantic*' by G.W.E. Russell in 1898. A renowned novelist, Disraeli said: '*When I want to read a novel, I write one*' and in the Darwinian controversy he cleverly sidestepped the issue, asking, '*Is man an ape or an angel? Now I am on the side of the angels.*' He also gave us the phrases '*a dark horse*', '*a peace I hope with honour*' and '*never take anything for granted*'. Disraeli was elected as an MP in 1837 but his first speech was barracked and he ended it with '*though I sit down now, the time will come when you will hear me*'.

A progressive Conservative politician, Disraeli championed the rights of the working class. He was Chancellor of the Exchequer in 1852, 1858 and 1866, and in 1867 he proposed the electoral Reform Act, which was supported by Gladstone's Liberal Party. In 1868 he became Prime Minister, but lost power to Gladstone in that year's election. Disraeli and Gladstone loathed each other, which in great part led to the polarization of Britain into two main political parties. In 1874 Disraeli was again elected Prime Minister and instituted social reforms, and in 1876 he was made Lord Beaconsfield by Queen Victoria.

DANTE GABRIEL ROSSETTI
1828–1882

'Eat thou and drink; to-morrow thou shalt die'

'Eat thou and drink; to-morrow thou shalt die.
Surely the earth, that's wise being very old,
Needs not our help. Then loose me, love, and hold
Thy sultry hair up from my face; that I
May pour for thee this golden wine, brim-high,
Till round the glass thy fingers glow like gold,
We'll drown all hours: thy song, while hours are toll'd,
Shall leap, as fountains veil the changing sky.'

'The Choice', *Ballads and Sonnets*, 1881

This poem reflects the alcoholic Rossetti's major health and drugs concerns towards the end of his life. He was never quite sure whether he was a poet or a painter, or of his role in society. In 'A Superscription' he wrote: '*Look in my face; my name is Might-have-been; / I am also called No-more, Too-late, Farewell.*' With six other artists he formed a 'secret society', the Pre-Raphaelite Brotherhood, to return to a purer, more symbolic style of painting. He married 'Lizzie' Siddal, the model for Millais' portrait *Ophelia*, but she became addicted to laudanum because of her poor health. When she died from an overdose, Rossetti threw his notebook, with most of his poems in it, into her casket. He became a stumbling drunk with failing eyesight, also addicted to laudanum. Six years after Lizzie's death, with the help of some friends he secretly retrieved the notebook and copied and published the poems. He hallucinated that he was surrounded by conspirators who would betray the secret of his poems, and in 1872 he attempted suicide by swallowing a whole bottle of laudanum. Nearing death, after some years of failing health, Rossetti refused to be buried next to his beloved Lizzie, possibly blaming his own predicament on her death.

KARL MARX
1818–1883

> **'Go on, get out. Last words are for fools who haven't said enough.'**
>
> On his deathbed

Karl Marx was born in Prussia but settled in London in 1849, where he lived in poverty while developing his economic and political theories. He believed that philosophy ought to be employed in practice, to change the world: '*The philosophers have only interpreted the world in various ways: the point is to change it*'. However, Marx is best known not as a philosopher but as a revolutionary Communist, inspiring the foundation of many Communist regimes. His theory of history, historical materialism, states that forms of society rise and fall as they improve, then impede, the development of human productive power. Marx saw in this process the inevitable breakdown of Capitalism, culminating in Communism. His economic analysis of Capitalism is based on his version of the labour theory of value, where he concludes that Capitalist profit is the extraction of surplus value from the exploited proletariat.

Marx's most famous works are *Das Kapital* (1867–1895) on economic theory, and, with Friedrich Engels, the *Communist Manifesto*, which details the class struggle. Its last three lines are: '*Let the ruling classes tremble at a communist revolution. The proletarians have nothing to lose but their chains. They have a world to win. Working men of all countries, unite!*' Other well-known statements by Marx include:

> '*A spectre is haunting Europe – the spectre of communism*'
>
> '*From each according to his abilities, to each according to his needs*'
>
> '*Religion is the opium of the masses*'
>
> '*Sell a man a fish, he eats for a day, teach a man how to fish, you ruin a wonderful business opportunity*'

It has often been said that Marx wrote so much that no individual has ever read all his writings, and, intriguingly, he once wrote to Engels: '*All I know is that I am not a Marxist.*'

EMMA LAZARUS
1849–1887

'Give me your tired, your poor, Your huddled masses yearning to breathe free'

'Not like the brazen giant of Greek fame
With conquering limbs astride from land to land;
Here at our sea-washed, sunset gates shall stand
A mighty woman with a torch, whose flame
Is the imprisoned lightning, and her name
Mother of Exiles. From her beacon-hand
Glows world-wide welcome; her mild eyes command
The air-bridged harbour that twin cities frame,

"Keep, ancient lands, your storied pomp!" cries she
With silent lips. "Give me your tired, your poor,
Your huddled masses yearning to breathe free,
The wretched refuse of your teeming shore,
Send these, the homeless, tempest-tossed to me,
I lift my lamp beside the golden door!"'

'The New Colossus', 1883

Born in New York to Sephardic Jewish parents, Emma Lazarus was the fourth of seven children. Between 1866 and 1882 she published poems and translations, but in the early 1880s, after learning about Russian pogroms against the Jews, she became more committed to Judaism and the plight of the poor, which led to her composition of 'The New Colossus'. This sonnet to the Statue of Liberty was hardly noticed until after her death, when it was found tucked into a small portfolio of poems she had written in 1883 to help raise money for the construction of the Statue of Liberty's pedestal. It was arranged to have the poem's last five lines become a permanent part of the statue itself and by 1945, the whole poem was engraved and placed over the Statue of Liberty's main entrance. Lazarus' words meant that the Statue of Liberty would forever be considered a beacon of hope for immigrants, leaving behind desperate conditions in their mother countries for the welcoming arms of America.

ELIZABETH CADY STANTON
1815–1902

ꞌThe Bible and the Church have been the greatest stumbling blocks in the way of woman's emancipationꞌ

Free Thought Magazine, September 1886

Elizabeth Cady married fellow Abolitionist Henry Brewster Stanton in 1840, and insisted that the word 'obey' was omitted from the ceremony. She stated: '*The prejudice against colour, of which we hear so much, is no stronger than that against sex. It is produced by the same cause, and manifested very much in the same way.*' She believed in universal suffrage, empowering blacks and whites, males and females alike. In 1848, she called for aꞌ women's rights convention at Seneca Falls, New York. Her 'Declaration of Sentiments' was approved there, and these events are credited with starting the long march to women's rights and female suffrage. With Susan B. Anthony she founded the National Woman Suffrage Association and became its first President, later becoming President of the National American Woman Suffrage Association. Apart from her autobiography and many speeches, she also wrote *The Woman's Bible*, in which we read:

> 'The Bible teaches that woman brought sin and death into the world, that she precipitated the fall of the race, that she was arraigned before the judgment seat of Heaven, tried, condemned and sentenced. Marriage for her was to be a condition of bondage, maternity a period of suffering and anguish, and in silence and subjection, she was to play the role of a dependent on man's bounty for all her material wants, and for all the information she might desire... Here is the Bible position of woman briefly summed up.'

GERONIMO
1829–1909

'Once I moved like the wind. Now I surrender to you, and that is all.'

Comment to General George Crook 27 March 1886

Goyathlay ('one who yawns') was born in what is today western New Mexico. As leader of the Apaches in Sonora, he showed such courage that the Mexicans called him Geronimo (Spanish for 'Jerome'), possibly because during his innumerable raids, he seemed invulnerable. Although he was not a hereditary leader of the Chiricahua Apache, he seemed to be so. His brother-in-law was their chief but had a speech impediment, so Geronimo often spoke for him. Geronimo was never a chief, but a medicine man.

In 1858, he returned home from trading in Mexico and found his wife, his mother and his three young children murdered by Spanish troops. This reportedly caused him to bear such a hatred of the whites that he vowed to kill as many as he could. In 1876, the US Army tried to move the Chiricahuas onto a reservation, but Geronimo fled to Mexico, eluding the troops for over a decade. The last few months of the campaign against him required over 5,000 American soldiers, 500 scouts and around 3,000 Mexican soldiers to track him down. In March 1886, Geronimo finally surrendered to General George Crook. However, he heard that the army planned to hang him and his followers, and Geronimo's group disappeared later that night into the drizzling rain. As a result of the incident, Crook resigned his command and a huge manhunt for Geronimo began. Not long after, Geronimo surrendered to Captain Henry Lawton of the 4th Cavalry, who had orders to capture him dead or alive. Geronimo gave credit to Lawton's tenacity for wearing the Apaches down in Mexico through constant pursuit. Completely exhausted, the small band of Apaches returned to the US with Lawton and officially surrendered to General Nelson Miles on 4 September 1886, at Skelton Canyon, Arizona. Geronimo agreed the same deal with Miles as he had with Crook, that his people would not be moved from their homelands. However, the government breached its agreement and transported Geronimo and nearly 450 Apache men, women and children to Florida for confinement in Forts Marion and Pickens. In 1894 the few remaining were removed to Fort Sill in Oklahoma. Geronimo died as a prisoner of war, unable to return to his homeland.

JOHN EMERICH EDWARD DALBERG-ACTON, 1ST BARON ACTON
1834–1902

'Power tends to corrupt, and absolute power corrupts absolutely'

'I cannot accept your canon that we are to judge Pope and King unlike other men with a favourable presumption that they did no wrong. If there is any presumption, it is the other way, against the holders of power, increasing as the power increases. Historic responsibility has to make up for the want of legal responsibility. Power tends to corrupt, and absolute power corrupts absolutely. Great men are almost always bad men... There is no worse heresy than that the office sanctifies the holder of it.'

Letter to Bishop Mandell Creighton, April 1887

Lord Acton was the most prominent Catholic layman in Britain, a historian and politician, and the closest and most influential adviser of Prime Minister Gladstone. This letter followed the crisis from 1870 onwards caused by Pope Pius IX promulgating the dogma of papal infallibility. Lord Acton had travelled to Rome to argue against it, but lost his case. Acton believed that no one was infallible, because power is a corrupting influence. He also sympathized with the Confederates in the American Civil War, in defence of states' rights against centralized power, writing to Robert E. Lee after the surrender: '*I mourn for the stake which was lost at Richmond more deeply than I rejoice over that which was saved at Waterloo.*' In a letter to Mary Gladstone in 1881, he wrote: '*The danger is not that a particular class is unfit to govern. Every class is unfit to govern.*'

ROBERT LOUIS BALFOUR STEVENSON
1850–1894

'Home is the sailor, home from the sea, And the hunter home from the hill'

'Under the wide and starry sky
Dig the grave and let me lie:
Glad did I live and gladly die,
And I laid me down with a will.
This be the verse you grave for me:
"Here he lies where he longed to be;
Home is the sailor, home from the sea,
And the hunter home from the hill."'

'Requiem', *Underwoods*, 1887

From childhood, Stevenson suffered from tuberculosis. He studied law at Edinburgh University and was called to the Scottish Bar in 1875. However, he began writing poems, travel sketches, essays and short stories, and his account of a canoe tour in Belgium and France appeared in 1878 as *An Inland Voyage*. *Travels With a Donkey In the Cervennes* was published in 1879, the year he moved to California with Fanny Osbourne, with whom he had fallen in love in France. Marrying in 1880, they returned to Scotland, then moved around the world looking for a better climate for Stevenson's illness.

Stevenson leapt to fame in 1883 with the adventure *Treasure Island*, from which many of us remember the pirate song '*Fifteen men on the dead man's chest – Yo-ho-ho, and a bottle of rum! Drink and the devil had done for the rest – Yo-ho-ho, and a bottle of rum!*' It was followed by *Kidnapped* (1886), *The Strange Case of Dr Jekyll and Mr Hyde* (1886), the story of which came to him in a dream, and *The Master of Ballantrae* (1889). *Underwoods* was a collection of his poetry, divided into two books: one in English, the other in Scots. His masterpiece, *Weir of Hermiston*, was unfinished, but was published in 1896, after his death. From the late 1880s Stevenson lived with his family in Samoa where he died and is buried.

FRIEDRICH NIETZSCHE
1844–1900

'Woman was God's second mistake'

'God created Woman. And boredom did indeed cease from that
moment – but many other things ceased as well! Woman was
God's second mistake.'

The Anti-Christ, Aphorism 48, 1888

The Anti-Christ can also be interpreted as the Anti-Christian. Far from
his Lutheran upbringing, Nietzsche had developed a thesis of the death of God.
His meaning of the world, as guaranteed by God, no longer existed, and morality
no longer had a moral basis. Good and evil were now subjective; simply matters of
opinion, and all of society's values were exposed as fake. This was a position of
absolute nihilism, so Nietzsche could either embrace this black void he had entered,
or create new values for mankind. Nietzsche here evokes an earlier quote by
Hannah Cowley (1743–1809) in her play *Who's the Dupe?*: '*But what is woman? –
only one of Nature's agreeable blunders.*' Friedrich Nietzsche was a German
philosopher who challenged the tenets of Christianity and the foundations of
traditional morality. He believed in the realities of the world we live in, rather than
those situated in an afterlife. Often referred to as one of the first existentialist
philosophers, Nietzsche's philosophy was focused on revitalizing our lives on Earth,
and has inspired leading figures including dancers, poets, novelists, painters,
psychologists, philosophers, sociologists and social revolutionaries. A friend of
Wagner, he also influenced Hitler to some extent with his atheism and the concept
of 'Superman' – '*I teach you the Superman. Man is something that is to be surpassed*'.

Famously, Nietzsche wrote: '*God is dead: but considering the state the species Man
is in, there will perhaps be caves, for ages yet, in which his shadow will be shown*' and
'*I call Christianity the one great curse... I call it the one immortal blemish of mankind*'.
He said that there were '*two great European narcotics, alcohol and Christianity*'.
Perhaps he foresaw the rise of Hitler and Stalin – focused psychopaths who
affected the thoughts of millions – '*Insanity in individuals is something rare –
but in groups, parties, nations and epochs, it is the rule*'. He also gave us: '*Whoever
fights monsters should see to it that in the process he does not become a monster.
And when you look into an abyss, the abyss also looks into you*' as well as '*What does
not destroy me, makes me stronger*'.

JEROME K. JEROME
1859–1927

'I like work: it fascinates me. I can sit and look at it for hours.'

'It always does seem to me that I am doing more work than I should do. It is not that I object to the work, mind you; I like work: it fascinates me. I can sit and look at it for hours. I love to keep it by me: the idea of getting rid of it nearly breaks my heart.'

Three Men in a Boat: To Say Nothing of the Dog, 1889

The humorist, novelist and playwright had the same name as his father, Jerome Clapp Jerome – not Jerome Klapka Jerome, as is sometimes thought. He left school at 14, becoming a clerk at Euston railway station in London. He failed as an actor, so tried teaching and journalism, his early humorous pieces becoming quite popular. The first of his books to be published were *On the Stage and Off* in 1885 and *Idle Thoughts of an Idle Fellow* in 1886, in which he writes: *'Love is like the measles; we all have to go through it'* and *'If there is one person I do despise more than another, it is the man who does not think exactly the same on all topics as I do'*. Three years later, his most famous work came with the story of a rowing holiday on the River Thames, *Three Men in a Boat*. In it we read: *'It is a most extraordinary thing, but I never read a patent medicine advertisement without being impelled to the conclusion that I am suffering from the particular disease therein dealt with in its most virulent form'*. From 1892 he edited and contributed to magazines such as the *Idler* and *Today*, but he was forced to sell his interests in 1897 following a libel action.

WILLIAM TOPAZ McGONAGALL
1830–1902

'Beautiful Railway Bridge of the Silv'ry Tay!'

'Beautiful Railway Bridge of the Silv'ry Tay!
Alas! I am very sorry to say
That ninety lives have been taken away
On the last Sabbath day of 1879,
Which will be remember'd for a very long time.
...
And the cry rang out all round the town,
Good heavens! The Tay Bridge has blown down.'

'The Tay Bridge Disaster', 1890

This book would not be complete without a contribution from one who is generally recognized as the worst poet in the English language. Of over 200 poems McGonagall left us, the most well remembered is 'The Tay Bridge Disaster', recounting the rail bridge collapsing in a gale in 1879 as a train was passing over it. McGonagall was a handloom weaver in Dundee, and wrote *'The most startling incident in my life was the time I discovered myself to be a poet, which was in the year 1877'*. God told him to *'Write! Write!'* so he sent an anonymous message in rhyme to the *Dundee Weekly News*, a tribute to a local vicar who *'has written the life of Sir Walter Scott / and while he lives he will never be forgot / nor when he is dead / because by his admirers it will be often read'*. The editor published it, and the teetotal McGonagall was on his prolific way.

McGonagall made his career giving readings of his poetry, and was paid 5 shillings a time. Audiences looked forward to jeering him and pelting him with rotten vegetables, behaviour that McGonagall blamed on the evils of alcohol. He hated alcohol and in *Scottish Gems* also bizarrely recounts: *'I don't like publicans. The first man to throw a plate of peas at me was a publican.'* Attempting a career as an actor, he paid in advance to play the title role in *Macbeth* and the show was a sell-out, the audience correctly presuming that it would be a comic disaster. Macbeth refused to die in the end, as McGonagall thought that the actor playing Macduff was trying to upstage him.

ANTON CHEKHOV
1860–1904

'In all the universe nothing remains permanent and unchanged but the spirit'

The Seagull, 1896

After his death, Anton Pavlovich Chekhov became recognized as the greatest Russian storyteller and dramatist of modern times. After graduating in medicine, Chekhov freelanced as a journalist and comic sketch-writer before going on to write full-length dramas. For most of his life he practised as a doctor: *'Medicine is my lawful wife, and literature is my mistress.'* Not until he was 37, with a Moscow production of *The Seagull*, did he enjoy any great success as a dramatist. A four-act ensemble drama that explores the theme of unrequited love, *The Seagull* is an exemplar of the 'Chekhovian' mood: heroic underdogs ground down by a hopeless society, with plot subservient to intense character development. Two years previously, in St Petersburg, the play had flopped so badly that Chekhov had vowed never to write for the theatre again, but in 1899 his *Uncle Vanya* was produced, followed by *The Three Sisters* (1901) and his masterpiece, *The Cherry Orchard* (1904). He had started a new genre of anti-heroic characters, and died of tuberculosis, aged only 44, in a Black Forest health spa.

Chekhov is now considered the most popular playwright in the English-speaking world after Shakespeare. However, some critics believe his short stories are an even greater achievement. Chekhov tells us: *'It is easier to ask of the poor than of the rich'* and in *Uncle Vanya* there is the following prophetic passage:

> 'Russian forests crash down under the axe, billions of trees are dying, the habitations of animals and birds are laid waste, rivers grow shallow and dry up, marvellous landscapes are disappearing forever... Man is endowed with creativity in order to multiply that which has been given him; he has not created, but destroyed. There are fewer and fewer forests, rivers are drying up, wildlife has become extinct, the climate is ruined, and the earth is becoming ever poorer and uglier.'

A.E. HOUSMAN
1859–1936

‘What are those blue remembered hills, What spires, what farms are those?’

'Into my heart an air that kills
From yon far country blows:
What are those blue remembered hills,
What spires, what farms are those?
That is the land of lost content,
I see it shining plain,
The happy highways where I went
And cannot come again.'

A Shropshire Lad, 'Poem XL', 1896

Alfred Edward Housman surprisingly failed his 'Greats' at Oxford, failing to get a degree but later taking a pass degree. He became a lowly clerk in the Patents Office, studied assiduously and published many scholarly articles in classical journals. On the basis of these, at the tender age of 33, he was astonishingly appointed Professor of Latin at University College London. Just four years later, in 1896, *A Shropshire Lad* was published: 63 nostalgic and simple verses that to some extent summarized his troubled life. One of the finest classical scholars of his day, in 1911 Housman was made Professor of Latin at Cambridge, and in 1922 his *Last Poems* was published. More poems were published posthumously. 'The Day of Battle' sums up the rueful mood of *A Shropshire Lad*:

'Far I hear the bugle blow
To call me where I would not go,
And the guns begin the song,
"Soldier, fly or stay for long."'
'Comrade, if to turn and fly
Made a soldier never die,
Fly I would, for who would not?
'Tis sure no pleasure to be shot.'
'But since the man that runs away
Lives to die another day,
And cowards' funerals, when
    they come
Are not wept so well at home.'
'Therefore, though the best is bad,
Stand and do the best my lad;
Stand and fight and see your slain,
And take the bullet in your brain.'

SIR HENRY JOHN NEWBOLT
1862–1933

'Play up! and play the game!'

'There's a breathless hush in the Close to-night –
Ten to make and the match to win –
A bumping pitch and a blinding light,
An hour to play and the last man in.
And it's not for the sake of a ribboned coat,
Or the selfish hope of a season's fame,
But his Captain's hand on his shoulder smote
"Play up! play up! and play the game!"

The sand of the desert is sodden red, –
Red with the wreck of a square that broke; –
The Gatling's jammed and the colonel dead,
And the regiment blind with dust and smoke.
The river of death has brimmed his banks,
And England's far, and Honour a name,
But the voice of a schoolboy rallies the ranks,
"Play up! play up! and play the game!"

This is the word that year by year
While in her place the School is set
Every one of her sons must hear,
And none that hears it dare forget.
This they all with a joyful mind
Bear through life like a torch in flame,
And falling fling to the host behind –
"Play up! play up! and play the game!"'

'Vitaï Lampada (Lantern of Life)', 1897

Newbolt wrote this poem after the British square infantry formation was broken in the Sudan, an event which shocked the nation, and is a clarion call for patriotism to everyone, making an analogy of schoolboys playing cricket with men fighting for their country. 'The Close' is a playing field at Clifton College, Bristol, where Newbolt was educated. The poem's popularity was long lived, and Newbolt was irritated by being continually asked to recite it while on a tour of Canada in the 1920s.

MARK TWAIN
1835–1910

'The report of my death was an exaggeration'

Telegram sent from London to the New York Journal on 2 June 1897,
after his obituary was mistakenly published

The original scrawled note given to the telegrapher still exists. It reads *'James Ross Clemens, a cousin of mine was seriously ill two to three weeks ago in London but is well now. The report of my illness grew out of his illness, and the report of my death was an exaggeration.'*

Born Samuel Langhorne Clemens, Twain's ambition, growing up in Missouri, was to be a riverboat pilot – hence his pseudonym, which means 'Mark Two Fathoms'. Twain was a writer, journalist and humorist who won a worldwide audience for his stories of the adventures of *Tom Sawyer* and *Huckleberry Finn*. He introduced colloquial speech into American fiction, and Ernest Hemingway wrote: *'All modern American literature comes from one book by Mark Twain called* Huckleberry Finn'. Aged 18, Twain headed east to New York City and Philadelphia where he worked on several different newspapers, but by 1857 he had returned home to be a riverboat pilot on the Mississippi River. In 1865 he had a short story published in papers across the USA. He went on to explore class relations in *The Prince and the Pauper* (1881) and *A Connecticut Yankee in King Arthur's Court* (1889), and in *The Adventures of Huckleberry Finn* (1884) he satirized slavery.

Twain's witticisms are legendary, for example: *'Total abstinence is so excellent a thing that it cannot be carried to too great an extent. In my passion for it I even carry it so far as to totally abstain from total abstinence itself.'* He also always pointed to moral truths: *'Man is a Religious Animal. He is the only Religious Animal. He is the only animal that has the True Religion – several of them. He is the only animal that loves his neighbor as himself and cuts his throat if his theology isn't straight. He has made a graveyard of the globe in trying his honest best to smooth his brother's path to happiness and heaven.'*

OSCAR WILDE
1854–1900

'Each man kills the thing he loves'

'Yet each man kills the thing he loves,
By each let this be heard,
Some do it with a bitter look,
Some with a flattering word.
The coward does it with a kiss,
The brave man with a sword!'

'The Ballad of Reading Gaol', 1898

Wilde effortlessly achieved a First Class degree at Oxford, and in 1881 published his first collection of poetry. In 1884, he married Constance Lloyd and his sons were born in 1885 and 1886. With a new family to support, Wilde worked from 1887 to 1889 for *Woman's World* magazine, and began writing seriously. Two collections of children's stories in 1888 and 1892 were followed by his only novel, *The Picture of Dorian Gray*. His first play, *Lady Windermere's Fan*, was a financial and critical success in 1892, prompting Wilde to concentrate on writing for the theatre. In it he defines a cynic as '*A man who knows the price of everything and the value of nothing*'. It was followed by *A Woman of No Importance* (1893), *An Ideal Husband* (1895) and *The Importance of Being Earnest* (1895).

Wilde was regarded as a leading literary figure, and known for his remarkable wit. In 1891 he met Lord Alfred 'Bosie' Douglas, a son of the Marquis of Queensberry. They became lovers and were inseparable until Wilde's arrest in 1895. Wilde had sued Bosie's father for libel, as the Marquis had accused him of homosexuality; Wilde withdrew his case but was himself arrested and convicted of gross indecency and sentenced to two years' hard labour. His wife deserted him, taking the children to Switzerland. Upon his release, the shattered Wilde wrote 'The Ballad of Reading Gaol', describing the agonies he had experienced in prison. His wife died shortly after, and Wilde spent the last three years of his life as a social outcast, wandering across Europe, staying with his few remaining friends and living in cheap hotels.

THOMAS HARDY
1840–1928

'I leant upon a coppice gate when Frost was spectre-grey'

'I leant upon a coppice gate
When Frost was spectre-grey,
And Winter's dregs made
    desolate
The weakening eye of day.
The tangled bine-stems scored
    the sky
Like strings of broken lyres,
And all mankind that haunted
    nigh
Had sought their household fires.

The land's sharp features seemed
    to be
The Century's corpse outleant,
His crypt the cloudy canopy,
The wind his death-lament.
The ancient pulse of germ and
    birth
Was shrunken hard and dry,
And every spirit upon earth
Seemed fervourless as I.

At once a voice arose among
The bleak twigs overhead
In a full-hearted evensong
Of joy illimited;
An aged thrush, frail, gaunt, and
    small,
In blast-beruffled plume,
Had chosen thus to fling his
    soul
Upon the growing gloom.

So little cause for carolings
Of such ecstatic sound
Was written on terrestrial
    things
Afar or nigh around,
That I could think there
    trembled through
His happy good-night air
Some blessed Hope, whereof he
    knew
And I was unaware.'

'The Darkling Thrush', 1900

Hardy was born in Dorset, and his second novel, *Under the Greenwood Tree,* brought him popular acclaim, as he used real places in Dorset as part of the plot. His fourth novel, *Far From the Madding Crowd,* was a great success, allowing him to give up his architectural practice and concentrate on writing. His other works include *Return of the Native, The Mayor of Casterbridge, The Woodlanders* and *Tess of the d'Urbervilles.* However, *Jude the Obscure* (1896) was seen as an attack upon the institution of marriage. Hardy was annoyed by this reaction, and thereafter focused on poetry, giving us this wonderful paean to hope, 'The Darkling Thrush'.

THEODORE (TEDDY) ROOSEVELT
1858–1919

'There is a homely adage which runs "Speak softly and carry a big stick, you will go far"'

Speech at Minnesota State Fair, 2 September 1901

In 1913, in his autobiography, Roosevelt added this codicil: '*Do not hit at all if it can be avoided, but never hit softly.*' A superb negotiator, more than anyone else Theodore Roosevelt made the United States a real world power. He was Vice President at the age of 42, and became the youngest ever President when McKinley was assassinated in 1901. Roosevelt spent his presidential career broadening executive power, equitably balancing the power of workers and big business and leading the American public towards progressive reforms. In the Spanish-American War, Roosevelt was Lieutenant Colonel of the Rough Rider Regiment, which he led on a charge at the battle of San Juan. He had been chosen as the Republican candidate for Governor of New York in 1898, and he enforced anti-trust suits and steered the United States more actively into world politics.

Roosevelt also ensured the construction of the Panama Canal for a trading shortcut between the Atlantic and the Pacific. He won the Nobel Peace Prize in 1906 for mediating the Russo-Japanese War, and added massively to the national forests in the American west, reserved lands for public use and sponsored huge irrigation projects. In 1910 he launched economic reforms: '*I stand for the "Square Deal"... I mean not that I stand for fair play under the present rules of the game, but that I stand for having those rules changed so as to work for a more substantial equality of opportunity and of reward for equally good service.*' He strongly wanted the USA to enter World War I, in 1917 calling Germany '*the most dangerous enemy of liberty now existing*'. Roosevelt was a historian, a biographer, a statesman, a naturalist and an orator, whose literary output includes 26 books, hundreds of magazine articles and thousands of speeches and letters.

THOMAS ALVA EDISON
1847–1931

'Genius is 1 per cent inspiration and 99 per cent perspiration'

Spoken in 1903, quoted in *Harper's Monthly*, 1932

Edison had only three months of formal education but became one of the greatest inventors in history. He obtained 1,093 United States patents, the most issued to any individual. His greatest contribution was the first practical electric lighting, and he experimented with over 3,000 filaments before he succeeded in making a practical light bulb. Far more importantly, perhaps, he also set up the first electrical power distribution company, which led to what has been called '*the miracle of the millennium*': providing light and power to the masses. He built the first central power station in Brockton, Massachusetts, and also invented the phonograph, made improvements to telegraph, telephone and motion picture technology, and founded the first modern research laboratory.

Edison encouraged Henry Ford to use the gasoline-powered engine for the automobile, and the two men not only became friends but were instrumental in creating American companies and exports across the globe. Edison was ruthless in business, however, going to extreme lengths to try to discredit Tesla's alternating current electrical distribution system, as Edison's inferior technology was based on the direct current. A hard and committed worker, he responded to criticism by answering, '*Hell, there are no rules here – we're trying to accomplish something!*' Edison believed that inventing useful products benefited society, while giving everyone the opportunity for fame and fortune. After Edison's death, Martin André Rosanoff – a Parisian chemist who had worked with Edison for 30 years – profiled him for *Harper's Monthly* magazine, where this quote was published.

GEORGE BERNARD SHAW
1856–1950

'The golden rule is that there are no golden rules'

Man and Superman, 'Maxims for Revolutionists', 1903

A leading figure in 20th-century theatre, this Irish dramatist was also a freethinker, literary critic, defender of women's rights, spokesman for Socialism and an advocate of equality of income and changes in the voting system. In 1925 he was awarded the Nobel Prize for Literature, accepting the honour but refusing the monetary award. As a young man he wrote pamphlets for the Fabian Society and began his career as a novelist, switching to plays as a criticism of the English theatre of the time. His earliest plays are strong attacks on social hypocrisy and he revolutionized stage dialogue, using the stage as a forum for the discussion of ideas, leavened with acute verbal wit.

Shaw's well-known works *Arms and the Man, Saint Joan, Androcles and the Lion* and *Major Barbara* were followed by *Pygmalion* in 1912, a witty treatment of class distinction and middle-class morality, known to filmgoers as *My Fair Lady*. The widow Mrs Patrick Campbell played the role of Liza Doolittle on the stage, causing some scandal as she uttered the line '*not bloody likely!*'. The vegetarian Shaw was largely self-educated (at the British Museum), and a lifelong teetotaller (he had an alcoholic father). His complete works appeared in 36 volumes between 1930 and 1950, the year of his death.

The above quote from *Man and Superman*, Shaw's drama based on the Don Juan theme, is just one example of what is known as 'Shavian wit', others being:

'*Democracy substitutes election by the incompetent many for appointment by the corrupt few*'

'*Better never than late*'

'*He who can, does. He who cannot, teaches*'

'*Marriage is popular because it combines the maximum of temptation with the maximum of opportunity*'

'Those who cannot remember the past are condemned to repeat it'

'Progress, far from consisting in change, depends on retentiveness. When change is absolute there remains no being to improve and no direction is set for possible improvement: and when experience is not retained, as among savages, infancy is perpetual. Those who cannot remember the past are condemned to repeat it. In the first stage of life the mind is frivolous and easily distracted, it misses progress by failing in consecutiveness and persistence. This is the condition of children and barbarians, in which instinct has learned nothing from experience.'

The Life of Reason, Volume 1, 1905

This is one of the finest pieces of prose by any philosopher, giving us the key to a peaceful future world. Born Jorge Augustín Nicolás Ruiz de Santayana, this principal figure in American philosophy was also a novelist, poet and a literary and cultural critic. He always retained his Spanish citizenship, and had an outsider's perspective of American life. He emphasized naturalism, multi-culturalism and spirituality, and his astonishing literary output rivals that of Ralph Waldo Emerson. His views on democracy in America have been compared to those of De Tocqueville – he tells us: '*America is a young country with an old mentality.*' Other memorable quotes of his include:

> '*A man's feet should be planted in his country, but his eyes should survey the world*'

> '*There is no cure for birth and death save to enjoy the interval*'

> '*Fanaticism consists of redoubling your effort when you have forgotten your aim*'

> '*The wisest mind has something yet to learn*'

JOSEPH CONRAD
1857–1924

'The terrorist and the policeman both come from the same basket'

The Secret Agent, 1907

Jósef Teodor Konrad Korzeniowski was born in the Ukraine, and his father's lands had been confiscated after a Polish uprising against the Russians who had taken their land. His aristocratic father had also been imprisoned, which led to his conclusion, quoted above, in *The Secret Agent*. After his parents died, Conrad persuaded his guardian uncle in Krakow to allow him to go to sea, and from 1875 to 1878 he made three voyages to the West Indies on French merchant ships. He then joined the English merchant navy for 16 years, rising through the ranks to achieve his Master's certificate in 1886 and command of his own ship, the *Otago*. He was given British citizenship, anglicized his name and sailed across the world, witnessing rebellions, killing and slavery in the Congo, and attempting to kill himself because of gambling debts.

In 1897 Conrad declared his goals as a writer: '*My task which I am trying to achieve is, by the power of the written word, to make you hear, to make you feel – it is, above all, to make you see. That – and no more, and it is everything.*' His best-known works are *Lord Jim* (1900) and *Heart of Darkness* (1902), the latter forming the basis for the anti-Vietnam War film *Apocalypse Now* (1979). In the film, Marlon Brando plays Kurtz, a man who has made himself the tribesmen's god and who has decorated the posts of his hut with human skulls. In the book Kurtz dies, his last words being '*The horror! The horror!*' Another famous phrase from the book is: '*We live as we dream – alone.*' Conrad declined honorary degrees from five universities, and refused the offer of a knighthood in 1924.

KENNETH GRAHAME
1859–1952

'There is nothing – absolutely nothing – half so much worth doing as simply messing about in boats'

The Wind in the Willows, Chapter I, 1908

This Scottish essayist and author wrote of Mr Toad, Ratty, Mr Badger and Mole in tales of riverbank life in a magically appealing style. Grahame grew up around Cookham and Cranbourne on the River Thames, but his guardian uncle could not afford for him to enter university, so he became a gentleman clerk at the Bank of England, becoming its Secretary 20 years later. During this time he became a respected writer, producing numerous essays, articles and short stories. *The Wind in the Willows* was adapted for the stage as *Toad of Toad Hall* by A.A. Milne in 1930, and is a classic of children's literature.

Aged 41, Grahame entered into an unhappy marriage, and his son Alastair arrived in 1900. Alastair was born with a congenital illness and blind in one eye, and had a poor relationship with his father. He was sent to boarding school, and his father hardly communicated with him or saw him, responding to his pleas for love and affection with the odd letter featuring himself as Mr Toad. Perhaps because of his own childhood, Grahame could not show Alastair any affection and ignored his pleas to visit him. Grahame's mother had died when he was only five, and elderly relatives had to take him away from his alcoholic father to bring him up. Alastair was eventually taken out of Rugby and went to Eton, where he had a breakdown. John O'Farrell, presenter of *Dreaming of Toad Hall* for BBC Radio 4 in 2008, claimed that Grahame '*wrote* Wind in the Willows *as a substitute for being a parent... It's his excuse for communicating with his son*'. Alastair had been subject to bullying at school, and probably also at Oxford University, and his increasingly poor eyesight and loneliness led him to lie down in front of a train aged just 20. Grahame was racked with guilt, profoundly grieved and became reclusive, spending months at a time in Italy.

RUDYARD KIPLING
1865–1936

'If you can keep your head when all about you Are losing theirs'

'If you can keep your head when all about you
Are losing theirs and blaming it on you,
If you can trust yourself when all men doubt you,
But make allowance for their doubting too;
If you can wait and not be tired by waiting,
Or being lied about, don't deal in lies,
Or being hated, don't give way to hating,
And yet don't look too good, nor talk too wise:
...
With sixty seconds' worth of distance run,
Yours is the Earth and everything that's in it,
And – which is more – you'll be a Man, my son!'

'If', *Rewards and Fairies*, 1909

These lines from Kipling's inspirational and motivational poem form a set of rules for adult behaviour that befits the values of Kipling's day. His life was a triumph of hope and perseverance over circumstance. He had been starved of love and attention, beaten and abused by his foster mother and hated the bullying atmosphere of public school. Even today '*If*' is also a model for ethical behaviour, self-development and personal integrity. Some lines appear over the players' entrance to Wimbledon's Centre Court – a reflection of the poem's timeless quality. In 1995, it was voted Britain's favourite poem. Kipling had wanted a military career, but had poor eyesight, and he encouraged his son John to join the army. John was killed in World War I, aged just 18, in the Battle of Loos. Kipling's epitaph to '*A Son*' reads '*My son was killed while laughing at some jest. I would I knew / What it was, and it might serve me in a time when jests are few*'. Combined with an unhappy marriage, and the loss of a 7-year-old daughter from pneumonia in 1899, this event caused Kipling to become depressed towards the end of his life. He was the first Englishman to receive the Nobel Prize in Literature in 1907, before '*If*' was written, '*in consider-ation of the power of observation, originality of imagination, virility of ideas and remarkable talent for narration, which characterise the creations of this world-famous author*'. Kipling is buried in Poets' Corner in Westminster Abbey.

RUDYARD KIPLING
1865–1936

'The female of the species is more deadly than the male'

'When the Himalayan peasant meets the he-bear in his pride,
He shouts to scare the monster, who will often turn aside.
But the she-bear thus accosted rends the peasant tooth and nail
For the female of the species is more deadly than the male'

'The Female of the Species', a song written for C.R.L. Fletcher,
'A History of England', 1911

Today this poem may be seen as anti-feminist, when the last verse says that woman *'must command but may not govern'*, but Kipling's thinking was typical of his age. He thought that woman *'must be deadlier than the male'*, as she is formed for the one purpose of motherhood. Woman, he believed, has the greater determination – the greater courage and single-mindedness in the pursuit of what is most important in life. We must remember that the poem was written well before the Great War, and the subsequent massive contribution of women in doing what had previously been regarded as 'man's work'. Not until 1918 did the Representation of the People Act give women of property over the age of 30 the right to vote – not all women, therefore, could vote – but it was a major start. Only in 1928 was there universal suffrage for women in Britain.

Kipling had achieved popular fame very quickly, based at first on his stories and poems, which were written in India. He refused honours including a knighthood, Poet Laureate and the Order of Merit, but accepted the Nobel Prize. Best known as a poet, 'Gunga Din' was his most famous poem of the time: *'You're a better man than I am, Gunga Din.'* He also wrote the novels *The Jungle Book* (1894), *Kim* (1901) and the *'Just So'* stories (1902). In conversation with Lord Beaverbrook, he once stated: *'Power without responsibility – the prerogative of the harlot throughout the ages.'*

W.H. DAVIES
1871–1940

'What is this life if, full of care, We have no time to stand and stare?'

'Leisure', *Songs of Joy*, 1911

William Henry Davies was adopted by his grandparents, who ran the Church House Inn, near Newport, Monmouthshire. A cousin of the actor Sir Henry Irving, he disliked school and was birched for being in a gang and stealing from a shop. Unable to settle into a job, in 1893 he left for the USA, and spent the next six years on the road, sometimes working, sometimes begging for a living.

After some time seeking his fortune in the Klondike Gold Rush, his foot was crushed trying to jump a train in Ontario, and his leg had to be amputated. With a heavy wooden peg-leg, he could no longer survive on intermittent work, and returned to London. After years of poverty, his poetry was slowly accepted for publication, and he achieved popular recognition when George Bernard Shaw came across a copy of his first book of poetry, *The Soul's Destroyer*. He wrote two novels and a harrowing account of his years of vagrancy, the *Autobiography of a Super-Tramp*. Aged 50, he married a London prostitute 30 years his junior, leaving the city to settle in Gloucestershire. His story of the marriage was eventually published after his wife's death, as *Young Emma* (1980).

CAPTAIN LAWRENCE EDWARD GRACE OATES
1880–1912

'I am just going outside and may be some time'

Robert Falcon Scott's journal entry, 16–17 March 1912

Educated at Eton, Captain Oates saw service in India, Egypt and South Africa with the Dragoons, and was badly wounded in the Boer War. In 1910, he volunteered to join Robert Scott's expedition to the Antarctic, hoping to be the first men to reach the South Pole. Despite malfunctioning equipment and terrible weather the party reached the South Pole on 17 January, only to find that Roald Amundsen had reached it a month earlier. On the same day, Captain Scott (1868–1912) wrote in his journal: '*The worst has happened*' and '*Great God! This is an awful place*'. Severe weather and lack of food and water hampered the 800-mile return trip to the base camp. Their progress was further hindered by Oates' Boer War wound, aggravated by scurvy, which slowed the whole party. On 16 March – the eve of his 32nd birthday – Oates, realizing he was a burden, left the tent and walked willingly to his death so as not to slow down his colleagues. The remaining party of Scott, Bowers and Wilson became trapped by blizzards within 11 miles of the base camp. Later explorers found Scott's journal, in which he wrote a Message to the Public on 29 March, presumably the day he died:

> 'We took risks, we knew we took them; things have come out against us, and therefore we have no cause for complaint, but bow to the will of Providence, determined still to do our best to the last… Had we lived, I should have had a tale to tell of the hardihood, endurance, and courage of my companions which would have stirred the heart of every Englishman. These rough notes and our dead bodies must tell the tale, but surely, surely, a great rich country like ours will see that those who are dependent on us are properly provided for.'

This final plea on behalf of the dependants of the dead led to the Mansion House Scott Memorial Fund, which closed at £75,000 (worth around £3.5 million in 2008). Scott's widow, son, mother and sisters received a total of £18,000. Wilson's widow had £8,500 and Bowers' mother £4,500. The widow and family of the first man to die in Scott's party, Edgar Evans, received only £1,500 between them.

JOHN JACOB ASTOR IV
1864–1912

'The ladies have to go first... Get in the lifeboat, to please me... Good-bye, dearie. I'll see you later.'

Said to his wife as the Titanic was sinking, 14–15th April 1912

John Jacob Astor was easily the richest man in the world. He owned over 700 prime Manhattan properties and was chairman of over 20 different companies. The family fortune had come from fur trading and real estate. In 1897 he built the Astoria, 'the world's most luxurious hotel', to adjoin his cousin William Waldorf Astor's Waldorf Hotel. The complex became known as the Waldorf Astoria.

After 19 years of marriage to a Philadelphia socialite, he divorced her in 1909, and in 1911, aged 47, married the 18-year-old Madeleine Talmadge Force, who was a year younger than his son, Vincent. To escape the resulting scandal, the Astors took a two-year holiday in Egypt and Europe, and when Madeleine became pregnant, the couple booked a passage from Cherbourg, France to New York on the maiden voyage of the *Titanic*. After the ship struck the iceberg, his wife was ushered to one of the last lifeboats. Astor asked if he could get into the lifeboat, on account of Madeleine's 'delicate condition', but was told to wait until all the women and children were taken off the sinking ship. He threw his gloves to Madeleine, who survived, saying that he would see her later. Astor died, along with 1,500 other passengers, when the ship sank.

STEPHEN BUTLER LEACOCK
1869–1944

'Personally, I would sooner have written *Alice in Wonderland* than the whole *Encyclopedia Britannica*'

'The writing of solid, instructive stuff fortified by facts and figures is easy enough. There is no trouble in writing a scientific treatise on the folk-lore of Central China, or a statistical enquiry into the declining population of Prince Edward Island. But to write something out of one's own mind, worth reading for its own sake, is an arduous contrivance only to be achieved in fortunate moments, few and far between. Personally, I would sooner have written *Alice in Wonderland* than the whole *Encyclopedia Britannica*.'

Sunshine Sketches of a Little Town, Preface, 1912

Born in England, this Canadian author had a difficult childhood, but found learning easy, becoming a full-time professor in political economy at McGill University in 1908. His first book, *Elements of Political Science*, became a standard university textbook. However, he had discovered a talent for writing gently humorous magazine articles, becoming from 1915–1925 the most popular humorist in the English-speaking world. Leacock published *Literary Lapses* in 1910, a compilation of the best of his previously published writings, but he is best remembered for the 1912 satirical book *Sunshine Sketches of a Little Town*. His material for this was mainly provided by gossip from his local barber, and the book propelled Leacock into international recognition. Of all his sayings, the most memorable is '*I am a great believer in luck, and I find the harder I work the more I have of it*'. Other 'Leacockisms' are: '*It is to be observed that "angling" is the name given to fishing by people who can't fish*'; '*Many a man in love with a dimple makes a mistake of marrying the whole girl*'; '*Lord Ronald said nothing; he flung himself from the room, flung himself upon his horse and rode madly off in all directions*'; and '*In ancient times they had no statistics so they had to fall back on lies*'.

WALTER DE LA MARE
1873–1956

❝"Is anybody there?" said the Traveller, Knocking on the moonlit door❞

"The Listeners', 1912

Born Walter John Delamere in Kent, to a wealthy family of Huguenot descent, he worked from the age of 16 to 35 in the accounts department of the Anglo-American Oil Company. De la Mere had published the story '*Kismet*' in 1895, and in 1902 a collection of poetry, *Songs of Childhood* appeared. He had little commercial success, but was awarded a yearly Civil List pension of £100 in 1908, so he resigned his job and devoted himself entirely to writing.

De la Mare's first successful book was *The Listeners*, and its title poem is his best-known work. The acclaim it attracted enabled him to write for the next four decades. In the poem, supernatural presences haunt the solitary traveller, and loneliness, death, dreams and silence were the themes to many of his works. His novels and short stories are also often melancholic, sometimes with a hidden malevolence that suits their inclusion in horror anthologies. De la Mare claimed that all children have a visionary imagination at first, but it is usually replaced at some point in their lives, and he tried to recapture this vivid imagination when he wrote. He received the Order of the Companions of Honour in 1948, the Order of Merit in 1953 and is buried in St Paul's Cathedral.

ALBERT SCHWEITZER
1875–1965

'Here, at whatever hour you come, you will find light and help and human kindness'

Inscription on the lamp outside his hospital in Lambaréné, Gabon

Albert Schweitzer began his theological studies in 1893 at the University of Strasbourg, receiving a PhD in 1899. He began preaching, and in 1906 published *The Quest of the Historical Jesus*, the foundation of his reputation as a theological scholar. He supported his education with piano and organ recitals. He decided he could do more good in Africa as a medical missionary than as a priest, so earned an MD and, in 1913, he founded his hospital at Lambaréné in French Equatorial Africa (now Gabon). In 1917 he and his wife were sent to a French internment camp as prisoners of war. After the war Schweitzer spent the next six years in Europe, preaching, giving lectures and concerts, taking medical courses and writing, before returning to Lambaréné in 1924 where he spent most of the rest of his life.

With the funds earned from his own literary royalties, concerts, personal appearance fees and donations, he expanded the hospital to 70 buildings. There he was a doctor and surgeon in the hospital, pastor of a congregation, administrator of a village, superintendent of buildings and grounds, and writer of scholarly books. He was awarded the 1952 Nobel Peace Prize a year later on 10 December 1953, and with the $33,000 prize money he started the leprosarium at Lambaréné. Schweitzer was buried at Lambaréné. This saintly man tells us: '*It is not enough merely to exist. It's not enough to say, "I'm earning enough to support my family. I do my work well. I'm a good father, husband, church-goer." That's all very well. But you must do something more. Seek always to do some good, somewhere.*'

RUPERT BROOKE
1887–1915

'If I should die, think only this of me'

'If I should die, think only this of me;
That there's some corner of a foreign field
That is for ever England. There shall be
In that rich earth a richer dust concealed;
A dust whom England bore, shaped, made aware,
Gave, once, her flowers to love, her ways to roam,
A body of England's breathing English air,
Washed by the rivers, blest by suns of home.

And think, this heart, all evil shed away,
A pulse in the eternal mind, no less
Gives somewhere back the thoughts by England given;
Her sights and sounds; dreams happy as her day;
And laughter, learnt of friends; and gentleness,
In hearts at peace, under an English heaven.'

'The Soldier', 1914

A marble plaque on the Greek island of Skyros, where he was buried in an olive grove, commemorates Brooke's most famous sonnet. A junior naval officer, Brooke was on his way to fight at the Dardanelles when he succumbed to acute food poisoning and died in his cabin off the island of Lemnos. On the white cross on his grave was originally written in pencil: '*Here lies the servant of God, Sub-Lieutenant in the English Navy, who died for the deliverance of Constantinople from the Turks.*' He also wrote the evocative poem about his home, 'The Old Vicarage, Grantchester', which contains the line: '*Stands the church clock at ten to three? And is there honey still for tea?*'

LAURENCE BINYON
1869–1943

'They shall grow not old, as we that are left grow old'

'For the Fallen' from *Poems for the Fallen*, 1914

Laurence Binyon won the Newdigate prize for poetry at Oxford University. Influenced by Wordsworth's works, he published two major volumes of poetry: *Lyric Poems* (1894) and *Odes* (1901). Binyon wrote '*Poems for the Fallen*' about the outbreak of the Great War, and it was published in *The Times* on 21 September 1914. The poem is still recited at every cenotaph in services on Remembrance Sunday, at 11 am on the nearest Sunday to 11 November. The eleventh hour of the eleventh day of the eleventh month was when World War I ended. Both world wars are now remembered with two minutes silence at this time. However, before World War II, everything stopped for two minutes on the actual date of 11 November at 11 am to commemorate the end of the slaughter – the cars and buses, factories, mines, shops and schools, trading and commerce all paused. Binyon had tried to enlist but was turned down because of his age. However, he went to the Western Front in 1916 as a medical orderly. After the war, Binyon returned to the British Museum where he had been in charge of Oriental prints and paintings. During the Munich Crisis in September 1939, Binyon made the following hopeful speech, as reported in *The Times* of the 26th of that month: '*We are living in a time of trouble and bewilderment, in a time when none of us can foresee or foretell the future. But surely it is in times like these, when so much that we cherish is threatened or in jeopardy, that we are impelled all the more to strengthen our inner resources, to turn to the things that have no news value because they will be the same to-morrow that they were to-day and yesterday – the things that last, the things that the wisest, the most farseeing of our race and kind have been inspired to utter in forms that can inspire ourselves in turn.*'

EDITH LOUISA CAVELL
1865–1915

'Patriotism is not enough. I must have no hatred or bitterness for anyone.'

'Standing, as I do, in view of God and eternity, I realize that patriotism is not enough. I must have no hatred or bitterness for anyone.'

Her last words, dawn, 12 October 1915

Edith Cavell's last words, to the English Chaplain in Brussels, were published in *The Times* in 1915 and are engraved as the epitaph on her statue near Trafalgar Square, London. Aged 20, Cavell entered the nursing profession, and in 1907 she became the matron of the Berkendael Institute in Brussels. During World War I the Germans occupied Belgium and Cavell sheltered British, French and Belgian soldiers at the Institute, from where hundreds were helped to escape to the Netherlands, which had remained neutral. A network was set up to help wounded soldiers get to the hospital for medical assistance, and then to freedom. As the soldiers were in disguise, the Germans shot any Allied soldiers that they found, together with the locals who sheltered them.

Cavell also treated injured German troops, as the Germans converted her hospital to a Red Cross hospital in 1914, but by 1915 she also had over 200 Allied soldiers secretly lodged there. Suspicions were aroused, and on 6 August 1915 Cavell was arrested by the German Secret Police. After 72 hours of questioning, the German interrogators told Edith that they already had the necessary information, and that she could save her friends from execution only if she made a full confession. She did so and was sentenced to death by firing squad. It was a major propaganda disaster for the Germans and the British exploited the execution, encouraging more men to enlist in the army, as there was no conscription at this time.

TSARINA ALEXANDRA
1872–1918

'I envy my flowers that will accompany you'

'Off you go again alone and it is with a very heavy heart I part from you. No more kisses and tender caresses, for ever so long – I want to bury myself in you, hold you tight in my arms, make you feel the intense love of mine. You are my very life Sweetheart, and every separation gives such endless heartache... Goodbye my Angel, Husband of my heart I envy my flowers that will accompany you. I press you tightly to my breast, kiss every sweet place with tender love... God bless and protect you, guard you from all harm, guide you safely and firmly into the new year. May it bring glory and sure peace, and the reward for all this war has cost you. I gently press my lips to yours and try to forget everything, gazing into your lovely eyes – I lay on your precious breast, rested my tired head upon it still. This morning I tried to gain calm and strength for the separation. Goodbye wee one, Lovebird, Sunshine, Huzy mine, Own!'

Love letter to Tsar Nicholas II of Russia (1868–1918), 30 December 1915

Born in Germany and orphaned at the age of six, Alexandra of Hesse married the Tsar in 1894 and gave him an heir, the haemophiliac Alexis, and four daughters. The Tsarina's anxious concern for her son's illness led her to embrace Rasputin, a debauched 'holy man', who proved able to stem Alexis' loss of blood (through hypnosis, it has been suggested), but her relationship with Rasputin made her unpopular at court. She and her family were bludgeoned and shot to death by the Bolsheviks on the night of 16 July 1918.

ROBERT FROST
1874–1963

'Two roads diverged in a wood, and I – I took the one less traveled by, And that has made all the difference'

Concluding lines of 'The Road Not Taken', *Mountain Interval*, 1916

In 1998, America's Poet Laureate Robert Pinsky launched a campaign to discover the nation's favourite poem. Nearly 40 years after his death, Frost's 'Stopping by Woods on a Snowy Evening' was voted third, and his 'The Road Not Taken' took first place in the hearts of the nation. (Second, fourth and fifth were Edgar Allan Poe's 'The Raven', Shel Silverstein's 'Sick' and Rudyard Kipling's 'If'.)

Many people refer to the poem as 'The Road Less Traveled', not realizing that the title was deliberately chosen to emphasize the conscious direction in which our lives are shaped. Frost claimed that he wrote this poem about his great friend, the poet Edward Thomas, with whom he walked many times in the woods when he lived in England. Frost said that they would come to different paths, and Thomas would always fret, wondering what they might have missed by not taking the other path. However, although this gave Frost the simple idea for the poem, it has a deeper meaning. As Frost himself wrote in one of his letters we read, *'You have to be careful of that one; it's a tricky poem – very tricky'*. Perhaps his decision to take *'the road less traveled'* is a confirmation of his individualistic choice, making an affirmative difference to his life. An inspirational poem, it exudes self-reliance upon making an inevitable choice, and tells us that we will never know the result of that choice until we have lived it.

WILFRED OWEN
1893–1918

'The old Lie: *Dulce et decorum est Pro patria mori*'

'Bent double, like old beggars under
    sacks,
Knock-kneed, coughing like hags, we
    cursed through sludge,
Till on the haunting flares we turned
    our backs,
And towards our distant rest began to
    trudge.
Men marched asleep. Many had lost
    their boots,
But limped on, blood-shod. All went
    lame, all blind;
Drunk with fatigue; deaf even to the
    hoots
Of gas-shells dropping softly behind.
Gas! GAS! Quick, boys! – An ecstasy
    of fumbling
Fitting the clumsy helmets just in time,
But someone still was yelling out and
    stumbling
And flound'ring like a man in fire or
    lime. –
Dim through the misty panes and
    thick green light,

As under a green sea, I saw him
    drowning.
In all my dreams before my helpless
    sight
He plunges at me, guttering, choking,
    drowning.
If in some smothering dreams, you
    too could pace
Behind the wagon that we flung him in,
And watch the white eyes writhing in
    his face,
His hanging face, like a devil's sick
    of sin,
If you could hear, at every jolt, the blood
Come gargling from the froth-
    corrupted lungs
Bitter as the cud
Of vile, incurable sores on innocent
    tongues, –
My friend, you would not tell with
    such high zest
To children ardent for some desperate
    glory,
The old Lie: Dulce et decorum est
Pro patria mori.'

'Dulce et Decorum Est', 1918

'The old Lie' **means** *'Sweet and fitting it is to die for one's country'* (taken from Horace's *Odes*, III. ii. 13). The war poet Wilfred Owen was machine-gunned to death on the Sambre Canal just seven days before the Armistice. The bells were ringing to celebrate the Armistice on 11 November 1918 in Shrewsbury, when the doorbell rang at Owen's parents' home, bringing them the telegram that told them their son was dead.

WALTER DE LA MARE
1873–1956

'Look thy last on all things lovely, Every hour'
'Fare Well', 1918

'*Fare Well*' begins with the lines '*When I lie where shades of darkness/ Shall no more assail mine eyes...*' and seems to be a valediction for the dead of the Great War. It is a warning to all of us that life is transitory, and that we must appreciate life as much as we can. It is a typical work of the man whom Vita Sackville-West called a '*poet of dusk*'.

De la Mare lived for part of World War II as a tenant in Southend House, Montpelier Row, overlooking the Thames, and had a habit of leaving his curtains open at night to watch the river. A police officer had to row across and rebuke him, because of the blackout that was enforced. On one of the house's windows, De la Mare's friend, the poet, artist and glass engraver Laurence Whistler has engraved the lines beginning '*Look thy last on all things lovely...*' De la Mare died here in 1956, much-loved and receiving friends until his final days. His inspiration for writing is summarized in his words: '*All day long the door of the sub-conscious remains just ajar; we slip through to the other side, and return again, as easily and secretly as a cat.*' A gentle and sensitive craftsman of poems and novels, including children's books,

De la Mare also gave us these memorable lines: '*Very old are we men; / Our dreams are tales / Told in dim Eden / By Eve's nightingales*'; '*Silence and sleep like fields / Of amaranth lie*'; and '*Oh, no man knows / Through what wild centuries / Roves back the rose*'.

JOSEF STALIN
1879–1953

'Our hand will not tremble'

Reply to a telegram from Lenin at the start of the 'Red Terror', September 1918,
urging him to be ruthless against the enemies of the Bolsheviks

Stalin was born Iosif Vissarionovich Dzhugashvili in Georgia, and
became one of the most brutal dictators in history. A Marxist activist, he helped
the Bolsheviks seize power in 1917, and by 1922 was General Secretary of the
Communist Party. After Lenin's death, he outmanoeuvred his rivals, killing some,
to take over the leadership of Russia. He said: '*You cannot make a revolution with
silk gloves*' and '*A single death is a tragedy; a million deaths is a statistic*'. His forced
collectivization of agriculture cost millions of lives, and his programme of rapid
industrialization achieved huge increases in economic growth but at great cost.

During the Great Terror of the 1930s, Stalin purged the party of '*enemies of the
people*', resulting in the execution of thousands and the exile of millions to the
gulag system of slave labour camps. Perhaps 10 million people died because of his
policies and actions. His purges, supervised by his secret police, severely depleted
the Red Army and Navy, so Stalin was not ready for Hitler's attack on the Soviet
Union in 1941. Between 1937 and 1939, the Commander-in-Chief of the Red Army,
seven leading generals, half the army's officers and all Russia's admirals were shot
or imprisoned. Stalin was assisted by the Russian winter and the country's vast
size, and at great human cost Hitler was repelled. After World War II, Stalin
became increasingly paranoid, leading to the raising of the 'Iron Curtain' and
the increased East–West tensions of the Cold War. He died in mysterious
circumstances in 1953, officially of a brain haemorrhage.

Stalin's disregard for human life is succinctly displayed in a remark quoted by his
successor Nikita Khrushchev in his 1956 'secret speech' to the 20th congress of
the Communist Party. Entitled 'On the Personality Cult and its Consequences',
Khrushchev's speech warned of the dangers of elevating one individual to a
position of supreme power, and served to distance him from the surviving Stalin
loyalists. According to the speech, Stalin's response when asked how best to
extract information from political prisoners was: '*Beat, beat and beat again!*'

VLADIMIR ILYICH LENIN
1870–1924

'The substitution of the proletarian for the bourgeois state is impossible without a violent revolution'

The State and Revolution, 1919

Born Vladimir Ilyich Ulyanov, Lenin was exposed to radical thinking at university and was influenced by the execution of his elder brother, a member of a revolutionary group. Expelled from university for political activities, he had to complete his law degree externally. Moving to St Petersburg, Lenin himself became a revolutionary and was exiled to Siberia. Upon his return in 1901 he adopted the pseudonym Lenin, then moved to Europe for 15 years, becoming the leader of the Bolsheviks. In 1917, assisted by Germany, he returned to Russia to work against the provisional government that had overthrown Tsar Nicholas.

Lenin then led the October Revolution, which began three years of brutal civil war. During this period of war and famine, he showed a chilling inhumanity towards the sufferings of the Russian people, mercilessly crushing any opposition to take control of Russia. In a 1918 directive to Bolshevik forces, he wrote: '*Do everything so that the people will see, tremble, and groan for miles and miles around... P.S. Search out hard people.*' The pamphlet *The State and Revolution* was one of Lenin's most important works, and served as a heavy influence on Marxist thinking. In his declining years, he worried about the bureaucratization of the regime and also the increasing power of Stalin. His corpse was embalmed and still lies in a mausoleum on Moscow's Red Square. Other famous quotes of his include: '*Capitalism has triumphed all over the world, but this triumph is only the prelude to the triumph of labour over capital*' and '*A lie told often enough becomes the truth*'.

SIR JAMES MATTHEW BARRIE
1860–1937

'I know I'm not clever but I'm always right'

Mary Rose, 1920

Most sources attribute this phrase to *Peter Pan* but it appears in Barrie's last successful play *Mary Rose*, a strange tale of a married couple (Simon and Mary Rose) who go on holiday in the Outer Hebrides. They have left their little son with a nurse, but he disappears, and in searching for him, Mary Rose eventually becomes a ghost. Even Barrie was unsure why and how he wrote the tragedy, which revisits the plot of the ageless child. In the play, Simon and Mary Rose are discussing the old place they used to sketch and Mary Rose informs him that they have found the spot because of the fir and the rowan tree there. He tells her that there were firs and rowan trees at other places they have seen, and she responds:

Mary Rose: *Not this fir, not this rowan.*
Simon: *You have me there.*
Mary Rose: *Simon, I know I'm not clever, but I'm always right. The rowan berries! I used to put them in my hair...'*

J.M. Barrie was the ninth child of a Scottish handloom worker, and completed a Master's degree at Edinburgh University in 1881. His childless marriage ended in divorce in 1909, but he became legal guardian to the five sons of Arthur and Sylvia Llewellyn Davies when they were orphaned. His best-known work was the play *Peter Pan*, the story of a boy who refuses to grow up and creates his own world of Indians, pirates and fairies. It is said the material for *Peter Pan* arose from the stories he told the Davies boys. Barrie rewrote the play as a novel, *Peter and Wendy*, in 1911, but the book also came to be known as *Peter Pan*.

Also notable among his early plays are *Quality Street* (1902) and *The Admirable Crichton* (1902), from which comes the line: '*I'm not young enough to know everything*'. In the play *What Every Woman Knows* (1908) he gives us the immortal line: '*There are few more impressive sights in the world than a Scotsman on the make.*' The honours of this modest man from humble beginnings included a baronetcy in 1913, the Order of Merit in 1922, the Rectorship of St Andrews University (1919–1922) and the Chancellorship of Edinburgh University (1930–1937).

WILLIAM BUTLER YEATS
1865–1939

'Things fall apart; the centre cannot hold'

'The Second Coming', *The Dial*, 1920

Yeats came to develop a cyclical theory of history and metaphysics, consisting of two conical spirals, one inside the other, which he articulated in *The Vision* (1925). He called these spirals 'gyres', and he claimed he received these ideas from spirits. He despaired over the decline of Europe's ruling classes and intellectuals (represented later in the poem by the head of the Sphinx), and the rise of the mob (symbolized by the Sphinx's body).

Yeats believed that Western civilization was nearing the end of a 2,000-year-old cycle, ending the poem with the question '... *what rough beast, its hour come at last, / Slouches towards Bethlehem to be born?*' Depressed by the Great War and the Russian Revolution, he believed that history was doomed to repeat itself, as humans never learn from their mistakes. Yeats was involved in the Celtic Revival, a movement against the cultural influences of English rule in Ireland, and was deeply involved in Irish politics. His verse often, as above, reflects pessimism about the political situation in Ireland and the rest of Europe. Yeats became an important cultural leader, a major playwright, and as one of the greatest poets of the century he was awarded the Nobel Prize for Literature in 1923.

HERBERT GEORGE WELLS
1866–1946

'Human history becomes more and more a race between education and catastrophe'

The Outline of History, Volume 2, 1920

After a basic education, H.G. Wells was apprenticed as a draper, then became a pupil-teacher before training to be a teacher. He dropped out of college, disliking the quality of teaching, but had been inspired by T.H. Huxley's teaching of evolution there. He turned to teaching and writing, and his essay on science, *'The Rediscovery of the Unique'*, was published. In 1895 *The Time Machine* established him as a novelist, and was followed by *The Island of Dr Moreau* (1896) and *The War of the Worlds* (1898). The latter predicted robotics, world wars, warfare tactics including aerial bombing, the use of tanks and chemical weapons, and nuclear power. Wells also wrote Socialist non-fiction books about politics, technology and the future, and was invited to join the Fabian Society.

Wells was horrified by the outbreak of World War I, collating his series of newspaper articles for the book *The War That Will End War* in 1914. In it, he says: *'We fight not to destroy a nation, but a nest of evil ideas... Our business is to kill ideas. The ultimate purpose of this war is propaganda, the destruction of certain beliefs, and the creation of others.'* A committed Socialist, he was encouraged by the news of the Communist revolution in Russia and visited the country, but was disillusioned and published *The Outline of History*. The main thesis of the book was that the world must be saved by education and not by revolution. By the time it was published, Wells was considered to be one of the world's most important political thinkers. In *The Shape of Things to Come* (1933), he writes of a world that has been devastated by war and is being rebuilt by humanistic technology. The penultimate line is: *'When the existing governments and ruling theories of life, the decaying religious and the decaying political forms of to-day, have sufficiently lost prestige through failure and catastrophe, then and then only will world-wide reconstruction be possible.'*

AGATHA CHRISTIE
1890–1976

'He tapped his forehead. "These little grey cells.
It is up to them."'

Hercule Poirot, *The Mysterious Affair at Styles*, 1920

Christie was born Agatha May Clarissa Miller in Devon, England, and was taught at home by a governess and tutors. In 1914 she married Archie Christie, a fighter pilot, and worked as a nurse during Word War I. While working in a hospital, she started writing a detective novel, but it was not published until 1920. *The Mysterious Affair at Styles* was the first of 30 novels featuring Hercule Poirot, a retired Belgian police officer who was to become one of the most enduring characters in fiction. Among many other books, he features in *Murder on the Orient Express* (1934) and *Death on the Nile* (1937).

In 1926, Archie asked for a divorce, and Christie disappeared. She was found three weeks later in a small hotel, claiming she had lost her memory. The second most well known of her characters was the elderly spinster Miss Jane Marple, first introduced in *Murder at the Vicarage* in 1930, and featuring in 11 further novels. Christie wrote over 66 novels in all, as well as numerous short stories and screenplays, and a series of romantic novels using the pen name Mary Westmacott. Several of her works became successful feature films. She is the best-selling novelist of all time with two billion books sold, and her work has been translated into more than 100 languages – no other novelist has had so many translations published. Of her dozen plays, *The Mousetrap* is the longest-running play in theatrical history, with over 23,000 performances in London's West End since 1952.

MICHAEL COLLINS
1890–1922

'Early this morning I signed my own death warrant'

'Think – what have I got for Ireland? Something which she has wanted these past 700 years... I tell you this – early this morning I signed my own death warrant.'

Letter to John O'Kane, 6 December 1921

When he wrote this letter, Collins had just signed the treaty with Great Britain that established the Irish Free State. The following year he was seven minutes late for the handover of British military jurisdiction to the Irish Free State and remarked: *'We've been waiting 700 years; you can have the seven minutes.'* Collins had fought in the Easter Rising of the Irish Republican Brotherhood in 1916, and was interned in Wales before becoming Commander-in-Chief of the Irish Republican Army (IRA) throughout the Irish War of Independence. He pioneered urban guerrilla tactics, provoking British counter-terror by the 'Black and Tans', which polarized popular opinion behind the Nationalist cause. Collins even penetrated British Intelligence HQ in Dublin Castle.

Along with Arthur Griffith, in 1921 Collins undertook the thankless task of negotiating the Anglo-Irish Treaty, which partitioned Ireland between a British Ulster and the semi-sovereign Irish Free State. Collins knew that the IRA had been severely weakened with internal dissention and losses of men and materiel by 1921, so control of the 26 Southern Counties was all that Nationalists could reasonably expect to obtain at that time. He defended the treaty against an IRA faction during a referendum campaign. Collins then led the Free State Army in the Irish Civil War against the dissident faction of the IRA led by Éamon de Valera. De Valera was enraged that Collins had allowed Britain to keep Ulster. The treaty was passed by a narrow margin in the Dáil and de Valera resigned as president. Collins was killed by the IRA in a rural ambush in August 1922, aged just 31.

MAHATMA GANDHI
1869–1948

'I am a man of peace. I believe in peace. But I do not want peace at any price'

'I am a man of peace. I believe in peace. But I do not want peace at any price. I do not want the peace that you find in stone; I do not want the peace that you find in the grave; but I do want the peace which you find embedded in the human breast, which is exposed to the arrows of the world, but which is protected from all harm by the power of Almighty God. The most heinous and the most cruel crimes of which history has record have been committed under the cover of religion or equally noble motives.'

Address to Ahmedabad Congress, 1921

Mohandas Karamchand Gandhi became known as 'Mahatma' (meaning 'great soul'). He was the leader of the Indian Nationalist movement against British rule, and is widely considered the father of his country. His doctrine of non-violent protest to achieve political and social progress has been hugely influential: '*I am prepared to die, but there is no cause for which I am prepared to kill*'. He developed the *satyagraha* ('devotion to truth'), a new non-violent way to redress wrongs. After 20 years fighting injustice in South Africa, he returned to India and by 1920 was the dominant figure in Indian politics. He transformed the Indian National Congress, and began a programme of peaceful non-cooperation with the British. In 1922 Gandhi was imprisoned. Later, he tried to improve Hindu-Muslim relations, which had worsened. He was opposed to the religious partition of the sub-continent into India and Pakistan ('*God has no religion*') and fasted in an attempt to bring calm, but was assassinated in Delhi by a Hindu fanatic.

MARCEL PROUST
1871–1922

'Everything great in the world is done by neurotics;
they alone founded our religions and created
our masterpieces'

À la Recherche du Temps Perdu: Le Côté de Guermantes II, 1921

Valentin Louis Georges Eugène Marcel Proust was from a rich Jewish family in Paris, and suffered from chronic asthma attacks all his life. He began to frequent literary salons and in 1896 his first book, *Les Plaisirs et les Jours*, was published with little success. He then began a novel which he never finished, and spent some years translating the works of the art historian John Ruskin. In 1907 he wrote an article for *Le Figaro* trying to analyse those elements of psychology – memory and guilt – which came to characterize his masterpiece. Increasingly neurotic, Proust continued writing articles and essays, which were subsumed into a single novel which he worked on for the rest of his days. In 1913 he titled it *À la Recherche du Temps Perdu* (*In Search of Lost Time*). The first part, *Du Côté de Chez Swann*, was published in 1913, and the second, *À l'Ombre des Jeunes Filles en Fleurs*, was published in 1919 and went on to win the Prix Goncourt.

Ill for most of his life, Proust died of pneumonia after spending his last three years working constantly and rarely leaving his cork-lined bedroom. He wrote: '*We are healed of a suffering only by experiencing it in full*'. He wrote the next two volumes of *À la Recherche...*, *Le Côté de Guermantes* and *Sodome et Gomorrhe*, between 1920 and 1922, and the remaining three volumes, which he had finished but not revised, were published between 1923 and 1927. The book is recognized as one of the major works in world literature. Proust was homosexual, and was one of the first European writers to treat the subject openly in this massive semi-autobiographical work with over 2,000 literary characters.

JAMES LANGSTON HUGHES
1902–1967

'My soul has grown deep like the rivers'

'The Negro Speaks of Rivers', 1921

Hughes' signature poem, is inscribed above his ashes in the foyer leading to the Langston Hughes Auditorium, in Harlem's Arthur Schomburg Centre for Research in Black Culture. Born in Missouri, Hughes' father wished to become a lawyer but was barred because of his colour, eventually going to Mexico to become a rancher. After an unsettled childhood, Hughes travelled to see his father, and on the train home wrote 'The Negro Speaks of Rivers'. First published in the African-American journal Crisis in 1921, the poem also appears in his first collection of poetry *The Weary Blues* in 1926.

Hughes began writing poetry when his family moved to Illinois and then Washington DC. He told the story of black suffering in his novels, plays and poems, reflecting actual black culture, and spearheaded what was known as the Harlem Renaissance of pride in black achievement. Hughes was probably the first man to write '*black and beautiful*', and sought equality for blacks. His essay entitled 'The Negro Artist and the Racial Mountain' appeared in the Nation in 1926: '*We younger Negro artists now intend to express our individual dark-skinned selves without fear or shame. If white people are pleased, we are glad. If they aren't, it doesn't matter. We know we are beautiful*'.

His writings led to Hughes appearing before a Senate Committee in 1953 testifying that he was not a communist. He was one of the first black authors to be able to support himself through his writing. In 1981, Landmark status was given to the Harlem home of Langston Hughes at 20 East 127th Street, and the street renamed Langston Hughes Place.

ROBERT ERSKINE CHILDERS
1870–1922

'Take a step forward, lads. It will be easier that way.'

His last words to the firing squad at his execution, 24 November 1922

Erskine Childers, a veteran of the Boer War and World War I, was an author and Irish Nationalist. A Londoner by birth and educated at Cambridge, he served as Clerk of the House of Commons from 1895 to 1910, and published the best-selling *The Riddle of the Sands* in 1903, which warned of the German menace and helped to create the spy novel genre. He converted to Irish home rule in 1908, and his yacht *Asgard* landed arms for the Irish Volunteers in 1914. Childers served with the Royal Navy Air Services from 1914 to 1919, but his support for home rule hardened into extreme Republicanism. He was appointed Director of Publicity for the IRA in 1919 and, elected to the Dáil (then the unofficial Republican parliament) in 1921, became its Minister for Propaganda. He had excellent capabilities in getting the IRA perspective into the English press.

Childers served as First Secretary to the Irish delegation in negotiations with the British government in 1921, but opposed the treaty that his colleagues agreed with the British. He was suspected by some Irish of being an English spy. Childers fought with the Republicans in the 1922 Civil War, and was captured by troops of the Free State government. He was court-martialled before a military court, found guilty of possessing an automatic pistol, and executed by firing squad at Beggars Bush Barracks. His son, Erskine Hamilton Childers (1905–1974), served as the fourth President of Ireland from 1973 until his death in 1974, after a distinguished career in government.

JAMES AUGUSTINE ALOYSIUS JOYCE
1882–1941

'Stately, plump Buck Mulligan came from the stairhead, bearing a bowl of lather on which a mirror and a razor lay crossed.'

Ulysses, 1922

These are the first lines from the strongly autobiographical Ulysses, written between 1914 and 1921 in Trieste, Zürich and Paris. It details a single day in Dublin in the life of the character Leopold Bloom, 16 June 1914. The date is significant, for it is the day upon which Joyce first dated Nora Barnacle, whom he had first met on 10 June. They later married, and 16 June is now celebrated across Dublin as 'Bloomsday'. Joyce told Frank Budgen in 1918 that in Ulysses: *'I want to give a picture of Dublin so complete that if the city suddenly disappeared from the earth it could be reconstructed out of my book.'*

Apart from a spell of 20 years in Paris, Joyce's life itself took on a peregrinatory nature. The eldest of 10 children, Joyce went to Paris after university to study medicine but was recalled to Dublin as his mother was ill. After his mother's death, he left Ireland to teach in Trieste in 1904, Joyce only made four return visits, the last of those in 1912, after which he never returned to Ireland.

Joyce revolutionized fiction writing with his 'stream of consciousness' approach. In 1914 Joyce's first novel, *A Portrait of the Artist as a Young Man*, began to appear in serial form and *Dubliners* was published. In 1922, he managed to get the first edition of the controversial *Ulysses* published. Joyce's last and most challenging work, *Finnegan's Wake* was published in 1939. He fled the Nazi invasion of France and died in Zürich, where he is buried. Joyce knew that his works were 'difficult', he said *'I've put in so many enigmas and puzzles that it will keep the professors busy for centuries arguing over what I meant, and that's the only way of insuring one's immortality'*. However, his last words in January 1941 were *'Does nobody understand?'*

HENRY FORD
1863–1947

'Any customer can have a car painted any colour that he wants so long as it is black'

My Life and Work, co-written with Samuel Crowther, 1922

Ford revolutionized production methods, leading to today's mass manufacturing and mass consumption, driving prices down so that the masses have purchasing power across the whole range of manufactured goods. Lee Iacocca, the ex-Ford manager who revived the Chrysler Corporation, wrote: '*He produced an affordable car, paid high wages and helped create a middle class. Not bad for an autocrat.*' In 1908, his black Model T Ford was a product of his unique vision. He realized that if he paid his factory workers a real living wage and they in turn produced more cars in less time for less money, everyone would buy them.

Ford's great strength was the manufacturing process. Previously, a team of workers would put together the whole car, but Ford organized teams that added parts to each Model T as it moved down a production line. By 1914, the world's first automatic conveyor belt could churn out a car every 93 minutes. He invented the dealer-franchise system to sell and service cars, and by 1912 there were 7,000 Ford dealers across America. He also lobbied for petrol stations across the country and for better roads for his 'tin lizzies' as they replaced horses. By the time production ended for the Model T in 1927, more than 15 million cars had been sold, half the world's output of automobiles.

In 1914, Ford shocked industrialists by instituting the $5-a-day minimum-wage scheme. (The average wage in the car industry was only $2.34 for a nine-hour shift.) Ford also cut the working day to eight hours. *The Wall Street Journal* called the plan '*an economic crime*', but Ford increased the wage later to a daily $10. He knew that because he had lowered his costs per car, the higher wages made no difference, except that they made his cars more affordable. His problem was that of living off his past success – he would not listen to plans for other models. The quote above ignored that General Motors was combining companies, and offering more models and prices, and Ford's Model A did not appear as a competitive product until 1927.

JOHN MAYNARD KEYNES
1883–1946

'This long run is a misleading guide to current affairs. In the long run we are all dead.'

A Tract on Monetary Reform, 1923

According to Robert Reich, Keynes' radical teaching, that governments should spend money they do not possess, may have saved Capitalism. Prior to Keynes, economists more or less believed in allowing the markets to dictate recessions and booms. Keynes had no patience with these theorists who assumed that everything would work out in the long run. Keynes believed that governments could beneficially affect their economies by borrowing money and spending it on investment projects, creating jobs. At Cambridge University, his lowest mark had been in economics, prompting him to later say: '*I evidently knew more about Economics than my examiners*'.

After World War I, Keynes published *The Economic Consequences of the Peace*, stating categorically that Germany could never pay the war reparations imposed upon it, and that the conditions would ultimately lead to massive unemployment and threaten all Europe once more. In 1936, he published *The General Theory of Employment, Interest and Money*. Keynes again told governments to run up deficits if the economy was slowing, to replace private investment and keep up full employment. After World War II, the Allies did not make the same mistake as three decades previously, assisting Germany, Japan and Italy to build up their economies, and thereby stifling Communist influence in many countries. Keynes was the most influential economist of all time. Unfortunately, world institutions that govern the global economy pay little attention to his work, and laissez-faire right-wing theories once again underpin national economies.

HILAIRE BELLOC
1870–1953

'When I am dead, I hope it may be said "His sins were scarlet, but his books were read".'

'On His Books', *Sonnets and Verse*, 1923

Hilaire Belloc lies in the family grave in West Grinstead, Sussex, but his self-penned epitaph, above, is unfortunately not inscribed there. Born near Paris, Belloc's family home was vandalized by Germans in the Franco-Prussian War, explaining his lifelong dislike of Germans. A devout Catholic, he became President of the Oxford Union, and started publishing in 1896. He wrote constantly: letters, poetry, criticisms, pamphlets, comic verse, and A.P. Herbert called him *'the man who wrote a library'*. A practising and proud Catholic, in his 1906 speech to voters, Belloc proclaimed: *'Gentlemen, I am a Catholic... If you reject me on account of my religion, I shall thank God that He has spared me the indignity of being your representative.'* Against all the odds, however, the electorate of South Salford voted for him. He became a Liberal, then Independent MP, but disillusioned with the party system, stood down – among other issues, he had demanded in Parliament that the finances of parties be subject to public audits. To some extent, his feelings about Westminster can be summarized by the following lines of his:

'The accursed power which stands on Privilege
(And goes with Women, and Champagne, and Bridge)
Broke – and democracy resumed her reign:
(Which goes with Bridge, and Women, and Champagne).'

In 1910 Belloc's beloved wife died, and he lost a son in each World War. His writings show his contempt for the political, literary and social establishments of the day, but he is now recognized first and foremost as one of the great writers of English prose and verse.

ROBERT FROST
1874–1963

'But I have promises to keep, And miles to go before I sleep.'

'Stopping by Woods on a Snowy Evening', *New Hampshire*, 1923

'**Stopping by Woods on a Snowy Evening**' was recently voted the third favourite poem in America. In 1920, Frost bought Stone House in rural Vermont where he wrote many of the poems contained in his fourth collection of poetry *New Hampshire* – which won the Pulitzer Prize for Poetry in 1923. In the poem, the speaker is on horseback and is entranced by the beauty of the scene, but knows he has to obligations to meet and must leave before he can rest for the night. Robert Frost claimed to write it almost spontaneously one evening.

Like most of Frost's poems, it can be read on several levels. There is a wonderfully evocative surface meaning, but there is an undercurrent of a gentle longing for sleep and death, which uses the images of night and winter. There is also the seduction of the restful, dark woodlands, and the pull of responsibility in civilization elsewhere. Again, perhaps the poem simply describes the temptation to sit and watch beauty, while all responsibilities are forgotten – to succumb to a contemplative mood and forget the worries of life. There is also a responsibility to his '*little horse*' which thinks it strange to have stopped, and becomes restless. The last two lines of the poem are intriguingly repeated, giving us at least two possible interpretations. Perhaps the second '*sleep*' indicates death in the future, or possibly that Frost, then aged 49, believed that he had many more poems left to write.

THOMAS EDWARD LAWRENCE
1888–1935

'All men dream: but not equally'

The Seven Pillars of Wisdom, Chapter I, 1926

As British liaison officer during the Arab Revolt against the Turks (1916–18), T.E. Lawrence masterminded military campaigns that ended with the triumphant march of the Arabs into Damascus. He did not wish to be remembered as a war hero, only as a writer, and *The Seven Pillars of Wisdom* is an epic account of his service in World War I. He completed the first draft in 1919, but the briefcase containing the manuscript was stolen the same year. He quickly wrote a second version, of 400,000 words, from memory, but in his own words it was *'hopelessly bad'*. He revised it and published a limited edition, printed by the *Oxford Times*, but he could not afford to have it proofed and reset, so this 'Oxford Text' had countless errors in it. He had six copies bound, and those who read them were extremely impressed. George Bernard Shaw wrote to the Prime Minister, Stanley Baldwin: *'The book is a masterpiece'*.

Lawrence suffered a breakdown from the stresses brought on by rewriting and publishing the book: *'nearly went off my head... heaving at that beastly book of mine'*. But admirers and friends wanted the book published, and convinced him to produce it for a subscription edition in an abridged form. He cut the Oxford Text by 25 per cent and the lavishly illustrated edition nearly bankrupted him and sold fewer than 200 copies. To recoup his investment, he authorized yet another abridgement for the general public. This appeared as *The Revolt in the Desert*, and launched the process by which he became known to the general public as 'Lawrence of Arabia'.

He was still extremely disillusioned by his failure to bring the Arabs self-rule. Still dogged by unwanted publicity, he left the RAF in February 1935 and died three months later in a motorcycle accident. Weeks later, the abbreviated *Subscribers' Edition* of *The Seven Pillars of Wisdom* was published for a general audience, with promises that the Oxford Text would reappear shortly. Unfortunately, the astonishing success of the *Subscribers' Edition* became an obstacle to the publication of the longer, superior version. In 1997, 75 years after it was completed, *The Seven Pillars of Wisdom* came out of copyright, and a complete edition, a corrected version of the Oxford Text, was finally published.

ALBERT EINSTEIN
1879–1955

'Imagination is more important than knowledge'

Interview in *The Saturday Evening Post*, 1929

Albert Einstein was born in Ulm, Wurttemberg, in Germany, and is probably the most important scientist since Sir Isaac Newton in his contribution to the understanding of physical reality. He graduated as a physics and mathematics teacher in Zurich in 1901, but could not find employment so worked as a technical assistant in the Swiss Patent Office from 1902 to 1909. Here, in his spare time, he worked tirelessly, writing papers on theoretical physics, outside the influence of academia or scientific colleagues.

In 1905 Einstein published a paper proposing 'the special theory of relativity', based on the principle that the laws of physics are in the same form in any frame of reference. He also assumed that the speed of light remained constant in all frames of reference. In that same year he showed how mass and energy were equivalent, expressed in the equation $E=mc^2$ (energy equals mass times the velocity of light squared), which became a building-block in the development of nuclear energy. Einstein received the Nobel Prize in 1921 for his 1905 work on the photoelectric effect, rather than for his contribution on relativity. In fact, 1905 saw four major papers which were each astounding breakthroughs. Einstein's special theory of relativity reconciled mechanics with electromagnetism; his general theory of relativity created a new theory of gravitation; he explained the Brownian movement of molecules; and he developed quantum theory. However, he said: '*Quantum mechanics is very impressive. But an inner voice tells me that it is not yet the real thing. The theory produces a good deal but hardly brings us closer to the secret of the Old One. I am at all events convinced that He does not play dice.*'

In 1932, in response to the growth of Fascism, Einstein emigrated to the USA and worked at Princeton University until the end of his life on an attempt to unify the laws of physics: '*The most incomprehensible thing about the Universe is that it is comprehensible.*' His first impression of Princeton was of '*A quaint ceremonious village of puny demigods on stilts*'. In 1999, *Time* magazine named him 'Person of the Century'.

AL CAPONE
1899–1947

'They can't collect legal taxes from illegal money.'

Internal Revenue Service, Narcotics-related Financial Investigations, 1930

Alphonsus Capone, known as 'Scarface', killed a man in 1918 and left New York to avoid charges, joining his old gangland mentor Johnny Torrio in Chicago. Capone became a contract killer and enforcer for Torrio, becoming head of the Chicago mafia after Torrio was seriously wounded in 1925. Capone's most fruitful period came during the Prohibition era, when he flooded a receptive market with illegal bootleg alcohol. Indeed, when Capone's mob was at its prime, he had city politicians, lawyers, governors, congressmen and over half the Chicago police force on his payroll. He said: '*My rackets are run on strictly American lines and they're going to stay that way*'. Another of his bons mots was: '*Vote early and vote often*'.

In 1929 Capone ordered the shooting of Bugs Moran in what became known as the St Valentine's Day Massacre, but Moran was not among the seven men killed. Two of Capone's quotes from around this time were: '*I have built my organization on fear*' and '*You can get much farther with a kind word and a gun than you can with a kind word alone*'. The IRS had been gathering tax evasion information on Capone for some time through a hired agent, and in 1932 he was sentenced to 11 years in Federal prison, fined $50,000, charged $7,692 for court costs and $215,000 in back taxes for tax evasion. He was released in 1939, after serving seven years and paying all his back taxes. His mental and physical condition had severely deteriorated.

FREDERICK EDWIN SMITH, 1ST EARL OF BIRKENHEAD
1872–1930

⟨"You are extremely offensive, young man." – Judge Willis "As a matter of fact, we both are, and the only difference between us is that I am trying to be, and you can't help it." – F. E. Smith⟩

Attributed to Smith by the 2nd Earl of Birkenhead, Frederick Edwin,
Earl of Birkenhead, 1933

As a young lawyer, F.E. Smith was legendary for his wit. To a judge who told him that he had listened to Smith's argument but was still none the wiser, Smith responded, *'Possibly not, My Lord, but far better informed'*. A superb orator, he became an MP and senior Conservative statesman, and was Winston Churchill's best friend until his early death. After Smith had been Solicitor-General and Attorney-General, David Lloyd George made him Lord Chancellor in 1919. Smith reformed the judiciary and the convoluted property laws, but is best remembered for his negotiations leading to the Anglo-Irish Treaty of 1921. Upon signing it, he remarked to the Irish leader Michael Collins, *'I may have just signed my political death warrant'*. Collins presciently replied, *'I may have just signed my actual death warrant'*.

In 1925, referring to the striking miners, Smith said: *'It would be possible to say without exaggeration that the miners' leaders were the stupidest men in England if we had not frequent occasion to meet the owners'* At the time, Somerset House was the repository of all birth and death records in Britain, and Smith wrote: *'We have the highest authority for believing that the meek shall inherit the earth; though I have never found any particular corroboration of this aphorism in the records of Somerset House.'*

'Would you be shocked if I changed into something more comfortable?'

Hells Angels, 1931

These lines made the young Jean Harlow the greatest sex symbol in the movies. Born Harlean Harlow Carpenter in Kansas City, Missouri, at the age of 16 Harlow ran away from home to marry a young businessman, Charles (Chuck) McGraw. They moved to Los Angeles, and from 1928 she found work as a film extra. Her marriage lasted only two years, and she said: '*I turned to motion pictures because I had to work or starve.*' After she appeared in Howard Hughes' war epic *Hell's Angels*, Hughes sold her contract to MGM for $60,000. By 1931 she had become the new star in Hollywood, appearing in *Platinum Blonde* before starring in six movies with Clark Gable. While filming *Red Dust* in 1932, she heard that her second husband, the MGM producer Paul Bern, had committed suicide.

Harlow made movies with Wallace Beery, Spencer Tracy, Lionel Barrymore and other screen legends, and began an affair with boxer Max Baer, who was separated but not divorced. His wife threatened divorce proceedings, citing Harlow, so MGM diffused the situation by hastily arranging her marriage to a studio cinematographer. Seven months later, Harlow quietly divorced her third husband at the age of 23, and became engaged to the film star William Powell. During the 1937 filming of *Saratoga* with Clark Gable, she was hospitalized with uremic poisoning, dying aged 26 of renal failure. Some other lines attributed to Harlow are:

> '*I like to wake up each morning feeling a new man*'

> '*I feel I can't breathe when I'm wearing a brassiere*'

> '*I'm not a great actress, and I never thought I was. But I happen to have something the public likes*'

> '*When you lie down with dogs, you get up with fleas*'

GROUCHO MARX
1890–1977

'Remember, men, we're fighting for this woman's honour, which is possibly more than she ever did'

Duck Soup, 1933

After a chequered start, Julius Henry Marx found success on the stage with his brothers in 1924 in the musical comedy *I'll Say She Is*. At one performance he arrived too late to glue on a moustache, so used grease-paint, and thereafter used a greasepaint moustache in all his performances. There were soon two more Broadway hits, *The Cocoanuts* in 1925 and *Animal Crackers* in 1928, where Groucho first played Captain Spaulding. Both plays became films, and Groucho also became a famous quiz show host on *You Bet Your Life*. A Liberal, he was investigated by the FBI in the 1950s.

Groucho made 14 films with his brothers Leonard (Chico) and Adolph (Harpo), and his other brothers Milton (Gummo) and Herbert (Zeppo) also appeared in some of them. Their films were anarchistic, attacking anyone in authority, wildly funny and riddled with some of the best one-liners in the history of comedy. The brothers wreaked havoc wherever they went, mainly uninvited, and in 1974 they received an Oscar for their achievements. Their superb films include *Monkey Business* (1931), *Horse Feathers* (1932), *Duck Soup* (1933), *A Night at the Opera* (1935), *A Day at the Races* (1937) and *A Night in Casablanca* (1946). Groucho was a wonderful performer, naturally quick-witted, and is possibly the funniest man to have appeared in the movies. In 1950 he resigned from the Friar's Club in Hollywood, writing: *'Please accept my resignation. I don't want to belong to any club that will accept me as a member.'* To a *Guardian* reporter in London in 1965, Groucho said: *'I never forget a face, but in your case I'll make an exception.'*

SIGMUND FREUD
1856–1939

'What progress we are making. In the Middle Ages they would have burned me. Now they are content with burning my books.'

Letter to Ernest Jones referring to the public burning of his books in Berlin, 1933

A brilliant child, Freud later chose to go to medical school, as options were limited for Jewish people in Vienna. He carried out research into neurophysiology, and his books and lectures brought him both fame and criticism from the medical community. He emigrated to England in 1937 to escape Fascism, and soon after died of cancer of the mouth and jaw. Freud had set up a private practice in the treatment of psychological disorders, which gave him much of the clinical material on which he based his theories. He had founded the 'Viennese school' of psychoanalysis, from which all subsequent developments in this field stemmed. With Breuer, Freud developed the idea that many neuroses had their origins in traumatic experiences which were now forgotten, hidden from consciousness. His treatment was to enable the patient to recall the experience to consciousness, to confront it deeply and remove the underlying psychological causes of the neurotic symptoms.

Many psychologists think that Freud overemphasized the sexual origins and content of neuroses – he believed that '*The sexual life of adult women is a "dark continent" for psychology*' – but his work has had an overwhelming influence on treatments. In 1900, Freud published *The Interpretation of Dreams*, regarded as his greatest work. This was followed by *The Psychopathology of Everyday Life* (1901) and in 1905 by *Three Essays on the Theory of Sexuality*. He also advanced the theory of a tripartite model of the mind – id, ego and super-ego – in 1923.

DAVID LLOYD GEORGE
1863–1945

'The world is becoming like a lunatic asylum run by lunatics'

Spoken in 1933 regarding the rise of Mussolini and Hitler,
quoted in the Observer, 8 January 1953

The son of a Welsh shoemaker, Lloyd George became a solicitor, MP –
'one of the greatest statesmen of the 20th century' (*Encyclopedia Brittanica*) – and *'the greatest Prime Minister since Pitt'* (John Barkham, *Saturday Review Syndicate*). In 1890, aged 27, be became the youngest member of the House of Commons, opposed the Boer War and advocated free schooling for all. As Minister for the Board of Trade (1905–1908) he was responsible for the passing of three important acts involving merchant shipping, the production census and patents. He introduced old age pensions (1908) and National Health Insurance (1911), and was Chancellor of the Exchequer from 1908 to 1915. A fierce opponent of the Poor Law, as Chancellor he wanted to *'lift the shadow of the workhouse from the homes of the poor'*. The rejection of his budget in 1909–1910 by the House of Lords, with its Conservative majority, led to parliamentary reform and a lessening of the power of the House of Lords. He was the first Prime Minister to come from outside the ruling classes.

Lloyd George toured the country, making speeches in working-class areas against the *'nobles with no nobility'*, who were using their privileged position to hurt the poor and stop old age pensions. The Conservative opposition and the House of Lords derided Lloyd George as a 'Socialist', but his measures eventually formed the basis of Britain's Welfare State. He did not want Britain to fight in World War I but was asked by Asquith not to resign. As Minister of War from 1915 to 1916, Lloyd George was put in charge of the total war effort, and found it difficult to control the poor and wasteful tactics of his generals of the Western Front. He argued strongly with the dinosaur Douglas Haig, Commander-in-Chief of the British Expeditionary Force, and with General Robertson, Chief of the Imperial General Staff, about their using men as cannon-fodder. When at last Lloyd George's proposal that the French and British forces fight under one joint commander was accepted, the war turned decisively the Allies' way, and he became Prime Minister of the Coalition Party that led Britain through World War I.

FRANKLIN DELANO ROOSEVELT
1882–1945

'The only thing we have to fear is fear itself'

'I am certain that my fellow Americans expect that on my induction into the Presidency I will address them with a candour and a decision which the present situation of our Nation impels. This is pre-eminently the time to speak the truth, the whole truth, frankly and boldly. Nor need we shrink from honestly facing conditions in our country today. This great Nation will endure as it has endured, will revive and will prosper. So, first of all, let me assert my firm belief that the only thing we have to fear is fear itself – nameless, unreasoning, unjustified terror which paralyzes needed efforts to convert retreat into advance. In every dark hour of our national life a leadership of frankness and vigour has met with that understanding and support of the people themselves which is essential to victory. I am convinced that you will again give that support to leadership in these critical days.'

Inaugural address, 4 March 1933

The Great Depression began with the Wall Street Crash of 4 October 1929, and Roosevelt's wonderful and uplifting speech marked America's recovery point. In the summer of 1921, when he was 39, Roosevelt was stricken with a paralytic illness, thought to be poliomyelitis, but now considered to be Guillaine-Barre Syndrome. He refused to be an invalid and hid his illness. In 1932, while the recession had damaged President Hoover, Roosevelt's efforts to combat it as Governor of New York had enhanced his reputation and he was elected Democratic President, the first of four terms. By the time of his inaugural address in 1933, there were 13,000,000 unemployed, and most banks were closed. Roosevelt faced the greatest crisis in American history since the Confederate States seceded, but his 'New Deal' and interventionist actions revived the American economy.

MARIE CURIE
1867–1934

'You cannot hope to build a better world without improving the individuals. To that end, each of us must work for our own improvement and, at the same time, share a general responsibility for all humanity, our particular duty being to aid those to whom we think we can be most useful.'

Quoted in *Philosophy and Organization*, John Sommers-Flanagan, 2002

Maria Sklodowska was born in Warsaw, Poland, and went on to become the first woman to win a Nobel Prize. She began studying at the Sorbonne in 1891, and was the first woman to teach there. She was also the first woman in France to earn a PhD and married Pierre Curie, who taught physics at the University of Paris. They found that the uranium ore, or pitchblende, contained much more radioactivity than could be explained solely by the uranium content. They then searched for the source of the radioactivity and discovered two highly radioactive elements, radium and polonium, which won them the 1903 Nobel Prize for Physics. Curie named polonium after her native country.

In 1906, Pierre died when he was run over by a horse-drawn wagon. Madame Curie next won the 1911 Nobel Prize for Chemistry for isolating radium. She said, *'We must not forget that when radium was discovered no one knew that it would prove useful in hospitals. The work was one of pure science. And this is a proof that scientific work must not be considered from the point of view of the direct usefulness of it. It must be done for itself, for the beauty of science, and then there is always the chance that a scientific discovery may become like the radium a benefit for humanity.'* When World War I broke out, Curie thought x-rays would help to locate bullets and facilitate surgery. It was important not to move the wounded, so she invented x-ray vans and trained 150 female attendants in how to use them. Curie died of leukaemia, brought on by exposure to the high levels of radiation involved in her research.

NIKOLA TESLA
1856–1943

'The scientists from Franklin to Morse were clear thinkers and did not produce erroneous theories. The scientists of today think deeply instead of clearly. One must be sane to think clearly, but one can think deeply and be quite insane.'

Modern Mechanics and Inventions, 1934

Born in Croatia, Nikola Tesla was a genius in electrical energy. His imagination enabled him to develop scientific hypotheses and put them into practice. After seeing a demonstration of a machine that operated in one direction as a generator, and in reverse as an electric motor, Tesla visualized a rotating magnetic field and applied the concept to develop plans for an induction motor. This electric motor was the first step towards the successful application of alternating current. He finished his education at the University of Prague, then worked as an electrical engineer in Germany, Hungary and France before emigrating to the United States in 1884.

Arriving in New York City with four cents in his pocket, Tesla worked for Thomas Edison in New Jersey. Differences between the two men soon led to Tesla leaving, and in 1885 George Westinghouse, founder of the Westinghouse Electric Company, bought patent rights to Tesla's system of alternating current, which killed off Edison's direct current technology. Tesla became a United States citizen in 1891 and developed the induction motor, new types of generators and transformers, a system of alternating-current power transmission, fluorescent lights and a new type of steam turbine. He ran out of funds to develop a wireless broadcasting company, but scientists still scour his notebooks for new ideas. A new company in California, making all-electric cars, is named Tesla Motors in his honour.

The quote above is taken from an article entitled 'Radio Power Will Revolutionize the World', which Tesla contributed to the magazine *Modern Mechanics and Inventions*. In it, he expounds on the possibilities afforded by wireless transmission of electrical power, a concept scientists are still working on to this day.

WILL ROGERS
1879–1935

'My ancestors didn't come over on the *Mayflower*, but they met the boat'

Quoted in *The Will Rogers Scrapbook*, Bryan W. Sterling, 1976

William Penn Adair Rogers was born in Cherokee Indian Territory, the son of a successful rancher, cattleman and banker. The Rogers ranch and his birthplace is now a tourist attraction near Oologah, Oklahoma. He was known as the 'Indian Cowboy' and became the best-loved American of his time. An expert horseman, he learned to lasso from an Indian, starring in Wild West shows, then on Broadway and in vaudeville around the world. Will started courting his wife in 1900, marrying her eight years later, and saying: '*When I roped her, that was the star performance of my life*'.

In 1918 Rogers went to Hollywood and was soon appearing in silent cinema, then with the advent of sound became an even bigger star. In 1934 he was voted the most popular male actor in Hollywood, and was also a brilliant broadcaster and an excellent writer. Rogers died in a plane crash near Point Barrow, Alaska, with his good friend, the legendary aviator Wiley Post. His credo was that of a simple Oklahoma cowboy, remarking: '*I never met a man I didn't like.*' He served as Mayor of Beverly Hills, and through his career made sublime comments upon politics and politicians, for example:

> '*I don't make jokes. I just watch the government and report the facts*'

> '*There's no trick to being a humorist when you have the whole government working for you*'

> '*If we got one-tenth of what was promised to us in these acceptance speeches there wouldn't be any inducement to go to heaven*'

> '*Everything is changing. People are taking the comedians seriously and the politicians as a joke*'

> '*If stupidity got us into this mess, then why can't it get us out?*'

'The stars are not wanted now: put out every one'

'Funeral Blues', 1936

W. H. Auden was known as a poet when studying at Oxford University, where he made lifelong friendships with Christopher Isherwood and Stephen Spender. In 1930, his *Poems* established his name, and thereafter he experimented successfully with almost every type of verse form. After serving in the Spanish Civil War, in 1939 he emigrated to the USA where he met his then 18-year-old long-term partner, the librettist Chester Kallman (1921–1975), and became an American citizen. They were together until Kallman's death 35 years later, which lends an extra resonance to the use of this poem in the funeral oration from a homosexual to his lover in the film *Four Weddings and a Funeral* (1994). The poem is a tribute to a dead lover, with the line '*I thought that love would last forever: I was wrong.*'

Auden was also a noted playwright, librettist, editor and essayist and is considered by many to be the greatest English poet of the 20th century. Many of his poems during the 1930s were inspired by unconsummated love, and in the 1950s he summarized his emotional life in a famous couplet: '*If equal affection cannot be / Let the more loving one be me.*' Homosexuality was not decriminalized in Britain until 1967, which gave Auden major difficulties. With his lover Christopher Isherwood, Auden sailed to New York in January 1939, hurting Auden's reputation. One of his most important poems was written in America at the start of the Second World War, '*September 1 1939*': '*The unmentionable odour of death/ Offends the September night...*' In 1972, Auden said '*It's frightfully important for a writer to be his age, not to be younger or older than he is. One might ask, "What should I write at the age of sixty-four," but never, "What should I write in 1940."*'

F. SCOTT FITZGERALD
1896–1940

'In the real dark night of the soul it is always three o'clock in the morning, day after day'

The Crack-Up, 1936

Unlikely to graduate from Princeton, in 1917 Fitzgerald joined the army. A fatalist, he believed he would die in World War I, and quickly wrote a novel. The letter of rejection he received in response to its submission asked that it be revised and resubmitted. In 1918 he fell in love with Zelda Sayre, a society belle and the youngest daughter of an Alabama Supreme Court judge. The novel was again rejected and Fitzgerald went to New York in 1919 to make enough money to marry Zelda, but she broke their engagement as she was unwilling to wait. In 1919, Fitzgerald rewrote his novel as *This Side of Paradise* and it was at last accepted, a story of career aspirations and disappointments in love which replicated his own life. He was writing short stories for the *Saturday Evening Post* when in 1920 the book was finally published, and it became an overnight success. Within a week he had married Zelda.

Fitzgerald's second novel was *The Beautiful and the Damned*, which was to some extent the story of the dissipated life he and Zelda were then living. Seeking quiet for Fitzgerald to concentrate on his writing, in 1924 they left the 'society set' for France, where *The Great Gatsby* was completed. Critics objected to Fitzgerald's concern with love, decadence, aspiration and success, and he answered: '*But, my God! It was my material, and it was all I had to deal with.*' It is now regarded as a classic American novel, and a symbol of the Jazz Age. Whilst they were in France, Fitzgerald's life was blighted by alcoholism and Zelda's increasing eccentricity – from 1930 she suffered a series of breakdowns. *Tender Is the Night* was published in 1934, but 1936 to 1937 is known as the 'crack-up' period of Fitzgerald's life – he was ill, in debt and drunk, and Zelda was hospitalized. He died believing himself a failure.

MARGARET MITCHELL
1900–1949

'Here in north Georgia, a lack of the niceties of classical education carried no shame, provided a man was smart in the things that mattered'

Gone With the Wind, Chapter I, 1936

In 1926, a fall meant that Margaret Mitchell had to give up her job as a reporter on the *Atlanta Journal*. Recuperating in a cramped apartment she called 'The Dump', she read so much that her husband bought her a typewriter and told her she should write a novel herself. She based the resultant story on local knowledge, and only her husband was allowed to read it. By 1929, she had almost finished it, but did not submit it for publishing as she thought it was *'lousy, I was ashamed of it'*.

By a series of accidents it was seen by a publisher nonetheless, but the first chapter had not been written and the publisher suggested renaming Pansy O'Hara, who became Scarlett. Eventually published in 1936, it became the most successful novel in history, with Clark Gable's last line of the film version – '*I wish I could care what you do or where you go, but I can't... Frankly, my dear, I don't give a damn*' – becoming world famous. Not until 1989 was it discovered that Rhett Butler's character was based on the Confederate blockade-runner, George Alfred Trenholm.

ADOLF HITLER
1889–1945

'The German people are not a warlike nation'

'The German people are not a warlike nation. It is a soldierly one, which means it does not want a war, but does not fear it. It loves peace but also loves its honour and freedom.'

Address to the Reichstag in Berlin, February 1936

It may be best to summarize Hitler's foul imprint upon the 20th century with a few sequential quotes:

'The broad mass of a nation... will more easily fall victim to a big lie than a small one.' (Mein Kampf, 1933)

'Germany will be either a world power or will not be at all.' (Mein Kampf, 1933)

'Before us stands the last problem that must be solved and will be solved. It is the last territorial claim which I have to make in Europe, but it is the claim from which I will not recede.' (Speech made at the Spoortspalast, Berlin, 1938, in reference to the Munich Agreement of three days later allowing Germany to annexe the Sudetenland.)

'We are going to destroy the Jews. They are not going to get away with what they did on November 19, 1918. The day of reckoning has come.' (Remark made in January 1939, in reference to the armistice that ended World War I.)

'In the West it is important to leave the responsibility for opening hostilities unmistakably to England and France.' (Remark made on the day the Allies declared war on Germany, 3 September 1939. Germany had attacked Poland on 1 September 1939.)

'For the last time our deadly enemies the Jewish Bolsheviks have launched their massive forces to the attack. Their aim is to reduce Germany to ruins and exterminate our people.' (Part of Hitler's final order stating that the Allies would 'bleed to death'. He committed suicide 15 days later, on 30 April 1945.)

'This Berlin-Rome connection is not so much a diaphragm as an axis, around which can revolve all those states of Europe with a will towards collaboration and peace'

Speech given in Milan on 1 November 1936, in reference to the German-Italian Treaty of Friendship, 25 October 1936

Benito Amilcare Andrea Mussolini, 'Il Duce', first conceptualized the 'Axis forces', and the term 'axis of evil' was subsequently used by President George W. Bush to describe terrorist nations. In May 1939, the Axis powers renamed their friendship as 'The Pact of Steel'. Japan, Hungary, Slovakia and Romania joined the Axis in 1940, and many Italian boys were named Roberto to celebrate (*Roma-Berlin-Tokyo*).

In the 1919 Italian election, Mussolini had won only 4,796 votes out of 315,165, but in 1922 he was appointed Prime Minister. Societal ills, fear of a Communist revolution, paralysis of Italy's liberal constitutional order and the violence inflicted by Fascist militia made the state eager to cooperate with him. (Similarly, Hitler's Nazi Party was placed ninth in the 1928 election with only 2.8 per cent of the popular vote, but achieved 37.2 per cent in 1932 because Storm Troopers intimidated enemies, Hitler delivered superb harangues and the Nazi Party became appealing to disillusioned Germans.) The need to keep citizens intoxicated by the dynamism and change of Fascism made both Mussolini and Hitler see war as both desirable and necessary. Mussolini stated: '*War is to men as maternity is to women.*' '*Il Duce is always right*' was the Fascist slogan, and in 1934 Mussolini claimed to '*have buried the putrid corpse of liberty*'. In *The Doctrine of Fascism* in 1935, Mussolini wrote: '*The Fascist conception of the State is all-embracing; outside of it no human or spiritual values can exist, much less have value.*'

T.S. ELIOT
1888–1965

'Human kind cannot bear very much reality'

Closing lines from 'Burnt Norton', 1936, Quartet I of *Four Quartets* (1943)

Thomas Stearns Eliot was born in Missouri, gained a doctorate at Harvard and settled in England in 1914. Ezra Pound encouraged his poetry, leading to the publication of 'The Love Song of Alfred J. Prufrock' in 1914. In 1917, Eliot's first book of poetry established him as a leading avant-garde poet. 'The Waste Land' (1922) may be the most influential poetic work of the 20th century. Eliot was also a noted playwright of verse dramas, and received the Nobel Prize for Literature in 1948.

Four Quartets was written over a period of eight years, following Eliot's conversion to the Church of England, the World War II and his naturalization as a British subject. Each of the four quartets considers spiritual existence and the relationship of the present to the past, being concerned with the conflict between individual mortality and the immortal span of human existence.

Burnt Norton is a ruined manor in Gloucestershire, famous for its rose garden, which Eliot visited in 1935. 'Burnt Norton' (1936) is a reminiscent meditation on Heraclitus' fragments on flux, change and time. In the poem, Eliot muses that the past and the future are always contained in the present. He combines his thoughts with a description of a rose garden where children hide, laughing. The children's laughter becomes almost mocking, scornful of our enslavement to time. The other three quartets are *'East Coker'* (1940), *'The Dry Salvages'* (1941) and *'Little Gidding'* (1942).

ERNEST RUTHERFORD
1871–1937

'In science, there is only physics; all the rest is stamp collecting'

Quoted in *Rutherford at Manchester*, J.B. Birks, 1962

In Rutherford's time, the only quantitatively predictive field was physics, all other sciences being mainly descriptive. His research was instrumental in the convening of the Manhattan Project to develop the first nuclear weapons, and he has been termed the 'Father of Nuclear Physics'. Ironically, in view of his love of physics, in 1908, he was awarded the Nobel Prize for Chemistry. He had demonstrated that radioactivity was the spontaneous disintegration of atoms. He studied the decay rate of radioactive material and found its 'half-life' to have a constant rate of decay, so could determine that the age of the Earth was much older than previously thought possible. Next, as Professor of Physics at Manchester University, he discovered the nuclear nature of atoms, and was said to be '*the world's first successful alchemist*', having converted nitrogen into oxygen.

Under Rutherford's supervision at the Cavendish Laboratory at Cambridge, four scientists shared three Nobel Prizes for Physics. (Cockroft and Walton split the atom using a particle accelerator, Chadwick discovered the neutron and Appleton demonstrated the existence of the ionosphere.) He pioneered the orbital theory of the atom, and with his gold foil experiment discovered the phenomenon now known as 'Rutherford scattering'. In 1931 he was made Baron Rutherford of Nelson. He went into hospital for a routine operation on an umbilical hernia, but as he was a lord, English protocol required a titled doctor to operate on him, and the delay in getting one proved fatal. He is buried in Westminster Abbey near Sir Isaac Newton.

DALE CARNEGIE
1888–1955

'Any fool can criticize, condemn, and complain – and most fools do'

How to Win Friends and Influence People, 1937

Dale Breckenridge Carnagey was an inspiring lecturer and creator of self-improvement, interpersonal skills and salesmanship courses. Born in poverty in Missouri, Carnagey changed his surname around 1922 to Carnegie, possibly to achieve a 'halo effect' from its association with the great philanthropist Andrew Carnegie (1835–1919). After giving up his successful sales job in 1911 and gaining little success as an actor, he then decided to teach public speaking. In his first lecture, he ran out of material and asked his audience to speak. No one would until he asked what made them angry, and he used this technique as the basis of building self-confidence in speaking in public.

By 1914 his courses had become extremely successful, and his book *How to Win Friends and Influence People* (1937), based on one of his 14-week seminars, was a best-seller. One of the first 'self-help' books, it has sold around 16 million copies to date, and his Dale Carnegie Institute still delivers courses based on his teachings. One of his insights was that one can change others' behaviour by changing your reaction to them. The book's sections are on handling people, making them like you, winning them to your way of thinking and changing them without causing resentment. He tells us: '*Most of the important things in the world have been accomplished by people who have kept on trying when there seemed to be no help at all.*'

DAVID MICHAEL JONES
1895–1974

'This all depriving darkness split now by crazy flashing'

'Starlight Order', *In Parenthesis*, 1937

David Jones' *In Parenthesis* describes the horrors of being on the front line in World War I, blending poetry, prose and other historical eras into one of the greatest poems of all time.

Jones left art college at the age of 20 to join the Royal Welsh Fusiliers and was badly wounded in the terrible Somme battle of Mametz Wood, which became the basis of *In Parenthesis*. Jones has been called 'the invisible poet', but T.S. Eliot described *In Parenthesis*, his first book, as '*a work of genius*'. Eliot also believed that Jones' *The Anathemata* put him on a par with James Joyce, Ezra Pound and Eliot himself as the key modernist masters. W.H. Auden declared *The Anathemata* (1952) to be '*very probably the finest long poem written in English this century*'.

When the Russian composer Igor Stravinsky made his last visit to England, he declared that it was largely a pilgrimage to visit David Jones. At this time, Jones' contemporary poets were lauding him for his rhythmic power and mastery of the patterns of sound. Jones' work as a painter is held by major collections, including the Tate, but nowadays he is unfortunately little known or read. He was deeply Catholic, a great war poet and a humble man, whose two works mentioned above and *The Sleeping Lord and Other Fragments* (1974) are among the most important poems of the 20th century.

GENERAL FRANCISCO FRANCO
1892–1975

'Our war is not a civil war... but a Crusade'

'Our war is not a civil war... but a Crusade... Yes, our war is a religious war. We who fight, whether Christians or Muslims, are soldiers of God and we are not fighting against men but against atheism and materialism.'

Spoken during the Spanish Civil War, 1937

Serving in Spanish Morocco from 1910 to 1927, Franco was known as a disciplinarian, executing two deserters in 1921 and remarking, '*If I didn't act with an iron hand, this would soon be chaos*'. Made a full general in 1927, he brutally suppressed a strike by Spanish coal miners. By 1936 he was Chief-of-Staff, appointed *generalissimo* of the right-wing Nationalist Spain and head of state. His slogan replicated Hitler's '*One Fatherland, One State, One Leader*', as he led right-wing factions in the terrible Civil War from 1936 to 1939. He did not believe in leaving any Popular Front left-wingers alive: '*In civil war, a systematic occupation of territory accompanied by the necessary purge is preferable to a rapid rout of the enemy armies which leaves the company still infested with enemies.*'

Nazi Germany and Fascist Italy supported Franco with arms in the war and afterwards recognized him as the legitimate ruler of Spain. From 1939 onwards, Franco was a dictator: his regime practised torture; opposition was ruthlessly suppressed; the secret police made lives miserable; and fair elections and political opposition were not tolerated. In 1947, a law made Franco head of state for life. When he died the monarchy was restored.

MAO ZEDONG
1893–1976

'Every Communist must grasp the truth: "Political power grows out of the barrel of a gun."'

Speech made on 6 November 1938

This quotation is taken from a collection of Mao's speeches, quotes and aphorisms entitled *Quotations from Chairman Mao Zedong*, which was staple reading during the Cultural Revolution, with an estimated six billion copies printed. Nicknamed the 'Little Red Book' in the West, it was small enough to be carried upon one's person, an act that was forcibly imposed by the Red Guards.

Via self-learning, Mao Zedong came to believe in Marxism-Leninism, and became a member of the Chinese Communist Party. By 1925 he was fleeing from the Nationalist Party of Chiang Kai-Shek, and from 1934 led the Long March of 8,000 miles (12,500 km) to escape the Nationalist Army. He became Chairman of the CCP, and after fighting to expel the Japanese, fought the Nationalists, assisted by Russia. His takeover of all of China except for Formosa (now Taiwan) enabled Mao to launch his disastrous Land Reform policy, the First Five-Year Plan and the Great Leap Forward, aimed at rapid industrialization in 1958. The latter resulted in a horrific famine that claimed 20 million lives. There followed his Cultural Revolution of 1966 to 1976, giving power directly to the Red Guards, who set up their own tribunals. Chaos reigned and millions were killed. Mao said: '*Letting a hundred flowers blossom, and a hundred schools of thought contend, is the policy for promoting progress in the arts and sciences and a flourishing socialist culture in our land.*' He also stated: '*Politics is war without bloodshed while war is politics with bloodshed.*'

Mao followed a policy of brinkmanship in his dealings with the USA, coming close to all-out war in Korea, and wrote: '*In waking a tiger, use a long stick... The atom bomb is a paper tiger which the United States reactionaries use to scare people. It looks terrible, but in fact it isn't... All reactionaries are paper tigers.*' In the reformist atmosphere following his death, the CCP acknowledged Mao had made errors.

GENERAL JOSEPH W. STILWELL
1883–1946

'Don't let the bastards grind you down'

Quoted 1939

'Illegitimis non carborundum' is the cod-Latin version of Stilwell's motto – 'Carborundum' is actually the name of a company that produced silicon carbide, an industrial grinding agent. The phrase endures to this day, and was further popularized by Barry Goldwater, whose outsider run for the American presidency in 1964 captured the public eye.

Stilwell was known as 'Uncle Joe' to his troops, but his alternative nickname was 'Vinegar Joe', as when he was Commander at Fort Benning, his fierce criticisms of men in field exercises led to a subordinate drawing his caricature rising out of a vinegar bottle. After serving in World War I, Stilwell completed three tours of duty in China and was there during the 1937 Japanese invasion. As Lieutenant-General he was sent to establish American army forces in China, Burma and India, but by his 1942 arrival in India, Burma and Singapore had been invaded. Chiang Kai-Shek, the Chinese leader, gave Stilwell permission to take over command of Chinese forces in Burma. General Alexander soon ordered all forces to retreat to India, but Stilwell refused to fly there for fear of the psychological effects on the Chinese troops among his forces, so instead took 22 days to travel overland to Delhi. Stilwell's courageous walkout from Burma and his honest assessment of the disaster (he called it 'a hell of a beating') captured the imagination of the American public, badly in need of an American hero at a difficult stage of the war. He was helped by Orde Wingate's Chindits and Merrill's Marauders, and in 1944 Stilwell was promoted to a full general and became Commander of the 10th Army.

JOHN ERNST STEINBECK
1902–1968

‘In the souls of the people the grapes of wrath are filling
and growing heavy, growing heavy for the vintage’

The Grapes of Wrath, 1939

John Steinbeck attended Stanford University intermittently, leaving in 1925 to pursue a writing career in New York. Unsuccessful, he returned to California where his first novel, *Cup of Gold*, was published in 1929, but attracted little attention. His two subsequent novels were also relative failures. Steinbeck married in 1930, living in Pacific Grove where he gathered material for *Tortilla Flat* (1935), *Of Mice and Men* (1937), *The Grapes of Wrath* (1939) and *Cannery Row* (1945): *'Cannery Row in Monterey in California is a poem, a stink, a grating noise, a quality of light, a tone, a habit, a nostalgia, a dream.'*

Steinbeck's acute personal observation of the human condition in the 1930s made his name, and *The Grapes of Wrath* won the Pulitzer Prize. It describes the uprooting of families, and the hunger and despair of desperately searching for work: *'The comfortable people in tight houses felt pity at first, and then distaste, and finally hatred for the migrant people'*; *'I'm learnin' one thing good... If you're in trouble or hurt or need – go to the poor people. They're the only ones that'll help – the only ones.'* After working as a war correspondent for the *New York Herald Tribune* in World War II, Steinbeck's next notable novel was *East of Eden* (1952). He was awarded the Nobel Prize for Literature in 1962, his citation stating the award was given: *'for his realistic as well as imaginative writings, distinguished by a sympathetic humour and a keen social perception'*.

WINSTON CHURCHILL
1874–1965

'I have nothing to offer but blood, toil, tears, and sweat'

'I have nothing to offer but blood, toil, tears, and sweat. We have before us an ordeal of the most grievous kind. We have before us many, many months of struggle and suffering.

You ask, what is our policy? I say it is to wage war by land, sea, and air. War with all our might and with all the strength God has given us, and to wage war against a monstrous tyranny never surpassed in the dark and lamentable catalogue of human crime. That is our policy.

You ask, what is our aim? I can answer in one word. It is victory. Victory at all costs – Victory in spite of all terrors – Victory, however long and hard the road may be, for without victory there is no survival.'

Speech made to the House of Commons on 13 May 1940

This is part of the address Churchill made after being appointed Prime Minister by King George VI to form a coalition government for the war against Germany. Germany had invaded France the day before, on 12 May. Churchill inspired the British people and its armed forces through the darkest days of World War II and worked closely with Franklin D. Roosevelt. He was awarded the Nobel Prize for Literature in 1955, and given a state funeral.

WINSTON CHURCHILL
1874–1965

'We shall fight on the beaches'

'I have, myself, full confidence that if all do their duty, if nothing is neglected, and if the best arrangements are made, as they are being made, we shall prove ourselves once again able to defend our Island home, to ride out the storm of war, and to outlive the menace of tyranny, if necessary for years, if necessary alone... Even though large tracts of Europe and many old and famous States have fallen or may fall into the grip of the Gestapo and all the odious apparatus of Nazi rule, we shall not flag or fail. We shall go on to the end, we shall fight in France, we shall fight on the seas and oceans, we shall fight with growing confidence and growing strength in the air, we shall defend our Island, whatever the cost may be, we shall fight on the beaches, we shall fight on the landing grounds, we shall fight in the fields and in the streets, we shall fight in the hills; we shall never surrender, and even if, which I do not for a moment believe, this Island or a large part of it were subjugated and starving, then our Empire beyond the seas, armed and guarded by the British Fleet, would carry on the struggle, until, in God's good time, the New World, with all its power and might, steps forth to the rescue and the liberation of the old.'

Speech made to the House of Commons on 4 June 1940

On 26 May 1940, the evacuation from Dunkirk began. Fortunately, the seas remained calm. The Royal Air Force bitterly defended the 'little ships' and over 338,000 Allied troops reached England, including 26,000 French soldiers (it had been estimated that only 45,000 would be saved). After Dunkirk, Churchill's speech is a clear appeal to the United States to assist in the battle for democracy.

WINSTON CHURCHILL
1874–1965

'This was their finest hour'

'What General Weygand has called the Battle of France is over. I expect that the Battle of Britain is about to begin. Upon this battle depends the survival of Christian civilization. Upon it depends our own British life, and the long continuity of our institutions and our Empire. The whole fury and might of the enemy must very soon be turned on us. Hitler knows that he will have to break us in this Island or lose the war. If we can stand up to him, all Europe may be freed and the life of the world may move forward into broad, sunlit uplands. But if we fail, then the whole world, including the United States, including all that we have known and cared for, will sink into the abyss of a new Dark Age made more sinister, and perhaps more protracted, by the lights of perverted science. Let us therefore brace ourselves to our duties, and so bear ourselves, that if the British Empire and its Commonwealth last for a thousand years, men will still say, "This was their finest hour."'

Speech made to the House of Commons on 18 June 1940

This is the concluding paragraph of the speech given shortly after Churchill was chosen as the Prime Minister of the coalition government on 10 May 1940. From 27 May to 4 June, Allied troops had been evacuating from Dunkirk. France was about to surrender after the Germans had broken through at Sedan and the Meuse, and that nation surrendered four days after this speech was made.

WINSTON CHURCHILL
1874–1965

'Never in the field of human conflict was so much owed by so many to so few'

'The enemy is, of course, far more numerous than we are…
We believe that we shall be able to continue the air struggle
indefinitely and as long as the enemy pleases, and the longer it
continues the more rapid will be our approach, first towards that
parity, and then into that superiority in the air, upon which in a
large measure the decision of the war depends. The gratitude of
every home in our Island, in our Empire, and indeed throughout
the world, except in the abodes of the guilty, goes out to the
British airmen who, undaunted by odds, unwearied in their
constant challenge and mortal danger, are turning the tide of the
world war by their prowess and by their devotion. Never in the
field of human conflict was so much owed by so many to so few.'

Speech made to the House of Commons on 20 August 1940

On 15 August 1940 the crisis of the Battle of Britain was reached. Britain was
the only country left facing the might of the Axis forces. All the resources of
Fighter Command in the south had been expended – there were no reserve planes
or pilots available. The most difficult and dangerous period of the Battle of Britain
came shortly after this speech was made, from 24 August to 6 September, when
the German attack was directed totally against the RAF airfields in the south of
England, with considerable success. In this speech Churchill first coined the
phrase 'the few' to describe the young RAF fighter pilots in their continual
dogfights against the attacking German bombers and fighters. If Germany
had achieved air supremacy, Hitler would have invaded Britain to complete the
conquest of Europe.

ANNA AKHMATOVA
1889–1966

'I learned to know how faces fall apart'

Requiem, Epilogue, 1935–1940

Anna Akhmatova was born Anna Gorenko in Odessa, in the Ukraine, and married the Russian poet Nikolai Gumilyov in 1910. Shortly after she also began publishing poetry, gaining fame along with her husband. He was unfaithful and they divorced in 1918. She was profoundly distressed, but worse was to come: in 1921 Gumilyov was executed by the Bolsheviks, who said he had betrayed the Revolution. To silence Akhmatova's protests, their son Lev was imprisoned in 1938, suffering 18 years in prison camps until the death of Stalin in 1956. Her third husband, Nikolai Punin, was imprisoned in 1949 and died in a Siberian prison camp in 1953.

Akhmatova's writing was banned from 1925 to 1940 and from 1945 onwards. She was persecuted by the Stalinist government as a dangerous enemy, but she had become so popular on the basis of her early poetry that even Stalin would not risk attacking her directly. Her greatest poem, *Requiem*, recounts the suffering of the Russian people under Stalinism, specifically the tribulations of the women with whom Akhmatova stood in line outside the prison walls. *Requiem* was not published in Russia in its entirety until 1987.

JOHN GILLESPIE MAGEE, JR
1922–1941

'Put out my hand, and touched the face of God'

'Where never lark, or ever eagle flew –
And, while with silent, lifting mind I've trod
The high untrespassed sanctity of space,
Put out my hand, and touched the face of God.'

'High Flight', 1941

Born in Shanghai, Magee was an American who at the age of 18 enlisted with the Royal Canadian Air Force, to be able to fight for freedom. After a year of flight training, he was posted to the Royal Canadian Air Force Fighter Squadron 412 in England, arriving in 1941. He was promoted to Pilot Officer after several missions over England and in France, and on 3 September 1941 he flew a high-altitude test flight in a newer model of the Spitfire V. As he climbed upwards, he was inspired to write a poem. Once back on the ground, he wrote a letter to his parents: '*I am enclosing a verse I wrote the other day. It started at 30,000 feet, and was finished soon after I landed.*' On the back of the letter, he jotted down his poem, *High Flight*. Just three months later, on 11 December 1941 (only three days after the US entered the war), he was killed in a collision in his beloved Spitfire V. This was the 19-year-old's only poem. 'High Flight' was quoted by President Reagan after the *Challenger* space shuttle disaster on 28 January 1988.

FRANKLIN DELANO ROOSEVELT
1882–1945

'In the future days, which we seek to make secure, we look forward to a world founded upon four essential human freedoms'

'Mr President, Mr Speaker, members of the 77th Congress:

I address you, the members of this new Congress, at a moment unprecedented in the history of the union. I use the word "unprecedented" because at no previous time has American security been as seriously threatened from without as it is today...

In the future days, which we seek to make secure, we look forward to a world founded upon four essential human freedoms.

The first is freedom of speech and expression – everywhere in the world.

The second is freedom of every person to worship God in his own way – everywhere in the world.

The third is freedom from want, which, translated into world terms, means economic understandings which will secure to every nation a healthy peacetime life for its inhabitants – everywhere in the world.

The fourth is freedom from fear, which, translated into world terms, means a worldwide reduction of armaments to such a point and in such a thorough fashion that no nation will be in a position to commit an act of physical aggression against any neighbour – anywhere in the world.

That is no vision of a distant millennium. It is a definite basis for a kind of world attainable in our own time and generation. That kind of world is the very antithesis of the so-called "new order" of tyranny which the dictators seek to create with the crash of a bomb.'

'The Four Freedoms' speech to Congress, 6 January 1941

The goals outlined in Roosevelt's State of the Union address proposed two extra freedoms – from want and from fear – that transcended those outlined in the First Amendment of the American Constitution. From this time American policy moved from protectionism to an internationalist perspective of human safety and security. A plaque commemorating this speech hangs inside the Statue of Liberty.

HERMANN GOERING
1893–1946

'A total solution of the Jewish question'

'I herewith commission you to carry out all preparations with regard to... a total solution of the Jewish question in those territories of Europe which are under German influence.'

Instructions to Reinhard Heydrich, 31 July 1941, quoted in *The Rise and Fall of the Third Reich*, W.L. Shirer, 1962

Commander-in-Chief of the Luftwaffe, President of the Reichstag and Prime Minister of Prussia, Goering was Hitler's designated successor, a World War I fighter pilot and war hero. Following the Kristallnacht (Crystal Night) pogrom of 9 November 1938, he fined the German Jewish community a billion marks and ordered the elimination of Jews from the German economy, the confiscation of their property and businesses, and their exclusion from schools and society. On 12 November 1938 he warned of a *'final reckoning with the Jews'* if Germany came into conflict with a foreign power. Goering instructed Reinhard Heydrich to prepare *'a general plan of the administrative material and financial measures necessary for carrying out the desired final solution [Endlösung] of the Jewish question'*. At the Wannsee Conference in 1942, Heydrich (1904–1942) convened 15 top Nazi bureaucrats to coordinate the Final Solution, in which the Nazis would exterminate 11 million Jews in Europe and the Soviet Union. There, on 20 January, Heydrich made a speech: *'Now the rough work has been done we begin the period of finer work. We need to work in harmony with the civil administration. We count on you gentlemen as far as the final solution is concerned.'* He told them that Europe would be *'combed of Jews from east to west'*. The minutes of the meeting were taken by Adolf Eichmann. By mid-1942, the mass gassing of Jews using hydrogen cyanide had begun at Auschwitz, with estimates of three million people killed there alone by gassing, starvation, disease, shooting and burning.

Goering's Luftwaffe progressively failed throughout the war, and he became marginalized by Hitler. To his surprise, he was put on trial at Nuremberg and found guilty on all four counts of the charges against him: of conspiracy to wage war, crimes against peace, war crimes and crimes against humanity. On 15 October 1946, two hours before he was due to hang, Goering committed suicide, taking a capsule of poison that he had succeeded in hiding from his guards.

FRANKLIN DELANO ROOSEVELT
1882–1945

'A date which will live in infamy'

'Yesterday, December 7, 1941 – a date which will live in infamy – the United States of America was suddenly and deliberately attacked by naval and air forces of the Empire of Japan. The United States was at peace with that nation, and, at the solicitation of Japan, was still in conversation with its government and its Emperor looking toward the maintenance of peace in the Pacific...

It will be recorded that the distance of Hawaii from Japan makes it obvious that the attack was deliberately planned many days or even weeks ago. During the intervening time the Japanese Government has deliberately sought to deceive the United States by false statements and expressions of hope for continued peace.

The attack yesterday on the Hawaiian Islands has caused severe damage to American naval and military forces. I regret to tell you that very many American lives have been lost. In addition, American ships have been reported torpedoed on the high seas between San Francisco and Honolulu.

Yesterday the Japanese Government also launched an attack against Malaya.
Last night Japanese forces attacked Hong Kong.
Last night Japanese forces attacked Guam.
Last night Japanese forces attacked the Philippine Islands.
Last night the Japanese attacked Wake Island.
And this morning the Japanese attacked Midway Island...
I ask that the Congress declare that since the unprovoked and dastardly attack by Japan on Sunday, December 7, 1941, a state of war has existed between the United States and the Japanese Empire.'

'Pearl Harbor Address to the Nation', Declaration of War upon Japan,
8 December 1941

The speech was delivered a day after the attack on Pearl Harbor and was deliberately kept brief for a more dramatic and emotional impact. Roosevelt transformed the speech into a collective statement on behalf of the shocked nation. He originally wrote 'a date which will live in *world history*' but replaced it with '*infamy*', and the passive wording was deliberate to contrast with Japan's aggression.

W.C. FIELDS
1880-1946

> **'I was in love with a beautiful blonde once, dear.
> She drove me to drink. It's the one thing
> I am indebted to her for.'**

Never Give a Sucker an Even Break, 1941

William Claude Dukenfield was the oldest child of a poor Philadelphia family, who ran away from home at the age of 11. Self-educated, he spent most of his time perfecting his juggling, and developed the technique of pretending to lose the things he was juggling. He moved to Atlantic City, where he developed his juggling act with comedic asides and became 'W.C. Fields – Tramp Juggler'. Appearing in vaudeville, by the early 1900s he was touring the world and was regularly called the world's greatest juggler. Aged 23 he was starring in London, and then at the Folies-Bergère. He made his Broadway debut in 1906, and altered his act into spoken comedy routines.

Fields appeared in silent films, then starred on Broadway in the musical *Poppy* in 1923. In 1925, the film of the musical established his reputation as a loveable con man. He settled into a mansion near Burbank, California and made most of his 37 films for Paramount. Fields' act was that of a misanthropic drunk who hated animals, women and children. He married in 1900, but was separated from 1907 until his alcohol-related death in 1946. His last starring role was as a version of himself in *Never Give a Sucker an Even Break*, which he also wrote. When asked why he drank alcohol, his politest answer was that '*I can't stand water because of the things fish do in it*'.

PAVEL FRIEDMANN
1921–1944

'I never saw another butterfly'

'Only I never saw another butterfly.
That butterfly was the last one.
Butterflies don't live here,
In the ghetto.'

'The Butterfly', 1942

A book with the title *I Never Saw Another Butterfly*, consisting of 'Children's Drawings and Poems from Theresienstadt concentration camp, 1942– 1944', was published in 1965. Theresienstadt, otherwise known as Terezín, was a Jewish ghetto set up in the Czech Republic, whose detainees – including, in 1942, Pavel Friedmann – were sent to Auschwitz and other concentration camps.

Of the 15,000 children under the age of 15 who went to the camp, around 100 survived Word War II. Can any statistic better tell us the horrors that man is capable of? Some pencilled notes from another victim, 15-year-old Petr Fischl, read: '*We got used to seeing undeserved slaps, blows and executions. We got accustomed to seeing people dying in their own excrement, to seeing piled-up coffins full of corpses, to seeing the sick amidst dirt and filth and to seeing helpless doctors. We got used to it that from time to time, one thousand unhappy souls would come here and that, from time to time another thousand unhappy souls would go away...*'

'The land was ours before we were the land's'

'The Gift Outright' from *A Witness Tree*, 1942

For John F. Kennedy's inauguration in 1961 as President of the United States, Robert Frost wrote a new poem entitled '*Dedication*'. In it, he conceived the new president as young and with the perfect combination of qualities to lead America into what he called:

'... *the glory of a next Augustan age*
Of a power leading from its strength and pride,
Of young ambition eager to be tried...'

However, Frost was 86, and could not read the words of his new poem because of his failing eyesight and the sun's glare on a cold January day. Instead, he put it down and recited perfectly '*The Gift Outright*' from memory. This original poem became a footnote in history until in 2006 an envelope unexpectedly arrived at the Kennedy Presidential Library in Boston. The envelope contained the original writing of the poem 'Dedication', in Robert Frost's handwriting. On the manuscript, Frost had added: '*To John F. Kennedy, At his inauguration to be president of this country. January 20th, 1961. With the Heart of the World*'. The archivist then noticed some pencil writing by Jacqueline Kennedy, noting that the handwritten poem was the first thing ever hung in President Kennedy's office, just three days after the inauguration. The faded pencil inscription from Jackie to Jack reads: '*For Jack, January 23, 1961. First thing I had framed to put in your office – first thing to be hung there.*'

Upon his death in Boston on 29 January 1963, Robert Frost was buried in the Old Bennington Cemetery, in Bennington, Vermont. In 1963 at Amherst College, President Kennedy said of the poet: '*The death of Robert Frost leaves a vacancy in the American spirit... His death impoverishes us all; but he has bequeathed his nation a body of imperishable verse from which Americans will forever gain joy and understanding.*'

GENERAL GEORGE S. PATTON
1885–1945

'America loves a winner'

'Men, this stuff some sources sling around about America wanting to stay out of the war and not wanting to fight is a lot of baloney! Americans love to fight, traditionally. All real Americans love the sting and clash of battle. America loves a winner. America will not tolerate a loser. Americans despise a coward; Americans play to win. That's why America has never lost and never will lose a war.

You are not all going to die. Only two percent of you, right here today, would be killed in a major battle.

Death must not be feared. Death, in time, comes to all of us. And every man is scared in his first action. If he says he's not, he's a goddamn liar. Some men are cowards, yes, but they fight just the same, or get the hell slammed out of them.

The real hero is the man who fights even though he's scared. Some get over their fright in a minute, under fire; others take an hour; for some it takes days; but a real man will never let the fear of death overpower his honour, his sense of duty, to his country and to his manhood.'

From Patton's final pep-talk to his troops in England on 17 May 1944,
before the Invasion of Europe

Patton also said: '*Don't be a fool and die for your country. Let the other sonofabitch die for his.*' He forced the Germans back at the Battle of the Bulge, and was badly hurt in a car crash. Paralysed from the neck down, he died of an embolism in 1945.

ANNELIESE MARIE FRANK
1929–1945

'Perhaps through Jewish suffering the world will learn good'

The Diary of a Young Girl, written 1942–44, published 1947

Between the ages of 13 and 15, when she and her family were hiding from the Nazis in Amsterdam, Anne Frank wrote short stories, began a novel and kept a diary. The diary, a 13th birthday present, begins just before the family retreated into their sealed-off flat, located in a spice warehouse. In 1933 the Frank family had fled from Frankfurt to the Netherlands. However, after the surrender of the Netherlands, the Nazis began their anti-Jewish programme and in 1942 Anne's sister was ordered to report to them. The Frank family of four immediately went into hiding, along with another family, the Van Pels.

Anne's diary tells of the constant terror they all suffered. Her entries on 25 March 1944 read: '*I felt nothing, nothing but fear; I could neither eat nor sleep – fear clawed at my mind and body and shook me*' and '*It was a terrible time through which I was living. The war raged about us, and nobody knew whether or not he would be alive the next hour*'. That same year the Gestapo was informed of the flat, and the Frank family was transported to Auschwitz. Anne's mother died there, and the children died in Belsen concentration camp. Anne's father's secretary searched the hiding place after the family had left and gave Otto Frank his daughter's diary after the war. It has been translated into 60 languages since its first publication. In it we read: '*I want to write, but more than that, I want to bring out all kinds of things that lie buried deep in my heart*' and '*I still believe, in spite of everything, that people are still truly good at heart*'. Her final entry was on 1 August 1944. On 4 August the family was arrested.

COMMANDER ANTHONY McAULIFFE
1898–1975

'NUTS!'

'To the German Commander, NUTS! –
The American Commander'

During the 1944 Allied invasion of Europe, a huge German offensive was ordered to break between the British and American forces. The surprise attack against a weak section of the advance succeeded because of Allied over-confidence and cloud cover preventing air strikes. This Battle of the Ardennes (lasting from 16 December 1944 to 25 January 1945) became known as the Battle of the Bulge, as the Wehrmacht Blitzkrieg offensive caused a huge indentation in the Allied line of advance.

The German plan was to drive through the Ardennes Forest, split Allied forces, take the main Allies' supply port of Antwerp, and circle around behind the Allies, causing their surrender. This simply had to be stopped for the invasion to succeed, and it became the bloodiest battle ever fought by American forces, with 19,000 ending up dying. In one battle alone, two US regiments were captured with the loss of up to 9,000 men. The town of Bastogne was on an important crossroads, and was quickly surrounded. The German commander sent a note asking for the town's surrender: '*If this proposal should be rejected one German Artillery Corps and six heavy A. A. Battalions are ready to annihilate the U.S.A. troops in and near Bastogne. The order for firing will be given immediately after this two hours' term.*' Commander McAuliffe of the 101st Airborne sent a typed note back containing the message quoted above, and Bastogne held out until the 4th Armoured Division arrived to support it.

JULIUS ROBERT OPPENHEIMER
1904–1967

'If the radiance of a thousand suns were to burst at once into the sky, that would be like the splendour of the mighty one... Now I am Death the destroyer of worlds'

Taken from the *Bhagavad-Gita (Song of God)*, c.500 BCE

Born of German parents in New York, Oppenheimer attended Harvard before taking his doctorate in Göttingen, Germany, in 1927. After further study at Cambridge University, he taught physics at Berkeley and California Tech from 1929. During World War II, President Roosevelt initiated the 'Manhattan Project' to develop nuclear weapons. In 1942, Oppenheimer was Scientific Director of the project, and as a result he became known as the 'Father of the Atomic Bomb'. The uranium bomb 'Little Boy' was dropped on Hiroshima on 6 August 1945, and the plutonium bomb 'Fat Man', which had been tested and observed on 16 July in New Mexico, was dropped on Nagasaki on 9 August 1945. This 'Trinity Test', of a bomb equivalent to 20 kilotons of TNT, caused the observing Oppenheimer to think of the above verses from the *Bhagavad-Gita*, which he had read in the original Sanskrit. They are the words of the god Krishna on the battlefield, and the ancient yoga text was described by Oppenheimer as shaping his personal philosophy.

As the post-war Chief Advisor of the US Atomic Energy Commission, Oppenheimer lobbied for international control of atomic energy to halt the nuclear arms race with Russia. He had seen the potential warlike consequences of nuclear arms spread. As a result of FBI and political pressure he was stripped of his security clearance in 1954, but was rehabilitated under President Kennedy a decade later. Oppenheimer is also remembered as the chief founder of the American school of theoretical physics whilst at the University of Berkeley, where he advanced theories on quantum mechanics, quantum fields, black holes and cosmic rays. The hydrogen bomb was first tested in 1952, and had 650 times the power of Oppenheimer's devices.

KING FAROUK I OF EGYPT
1921–1965

'The whole world is in revolt. Soon there will be only five Kings left – the King of England, the King of Spades, the King of Clubs, the King of Hearts and the King of Diamonds.'

Spoken at a conference in Cairo, 1948

Farouk was obviously aware of the dangers to his monarchy when he said this to Lord Boyd-Orr of the United Nations. Farouk was the tenth and penultimate ruler of the Muhammad Ali Dynasty, and during his reign Egypt was in a state of incomplete independence and suffered from chaos and corruption.

A kleptomaniac, Farouk was known by his subjects as 'the thief of Cairo', and criticized for his lavish lifestyle. On 23 July 1952, the revolution erupted and he was forced to abdicate the throne to his son Ahmed Fouad II, who was then still only a child. The abdication document was signed in Ras El Teen Palace on 26 July 1952, and Farouk left Egypt for Italy, where he put on a vast amount of weight and died in 1965, probably due to a weight-related heart attack. He weighed over 300 pounds (136 kg) and an acquaintance referred to him as '*a stomach with a head*'. His Majesty Farouk I – by the grace of God, King of Egypt and Sudan, Sovereign of Nubia, of Kordofan and of Darfur – also left behind a huge collection of pornography.

GEORGE ORWELL
1903–1950

'Big Brother is watching you'

Nineteen Eighty-Four, 1949

Eric Arthur Blair was born in India, educated at Eton and joined the Indian Imperial Police in Burma. He resigned in 1927, deciding to become a writer. In 1928 he moved to Paris, where lack of success forced him into a series of menial jobs, described in his first book, *Down and Out in Paris and London* (1933), for which he took the name George Orwell. It was followed in 1934 by his novel *Burmese Days*. A Socialist, Orwell was commissioned to write an account of poverty among unemployed miners, which became *The Road to Wigan Pier* (1937): '*It is brought home to you... that it is only because miners sweat their guts out that superior persons can remain superior*'.

In 1936, Orwell travelled to Spain to fight against Franco's Nationalists. He was forced to flee, and wrote a superb account of his experiences in *Homage to Catalonia*. His experience of Communists turning on Socialists made him vehemently anti-Stalinist – his novel *Animal Farm*, published in 1945, was set in a farmyard but based on Stalin's betrayal of the Russian Revolution, and became hugely popular. From it comes the famous line: '*All animals are equal, but some animals are more equal than others*'. *Nineteen Eighty-Four* followed, another diatribe against the totalitarianism seen in Russia, but set in the future. Many of the phrases within it, such as '*newspeak*' and '*doublethink*', passed into the English language, and well-known lines include: '*Who controls the past controls... the future: who controls the present controls the past*' and '*If you want a picture of the future, imagine a boot stamping on a human face – for ever... And remember that it is for ever*'.

SIMONE DE BEAUVOIR
1908–1986

'One is not born, but rather becomes, a woman'
The Second Sex, 1949

Born Simone-Ernestine-Lucie-Marie Bertrand de Beauvoir, she was a pre-eminent French existentialist philosopher who wrote on ethics, feminism, fiction, autobiography and politics. A deeply religious child, de Beauvoir had a crisis of faith aged 14 and became a lifelong atheist. In 1929, aged 21, she was the youngest student ever to pass the *agrégation* examination in philosophy, and became the youngest philosophy teacher in France. That same year, Jean-Paul Sartre asked to be introduced to her, and in him she found a partner who was her equal in intellect. They remained together until his death in 1980.

De Beauvoir's most famous and influential philosophical work, *The Second Sex*, an impressive investigation into women's oppression and liberation, began the 'feminist revolution'. She wrote that while men and women may have different tendencies, each person is unique. Culture forces a uniform set of expectations of what is 'female', which is contrasted with what is 'male', 'male' being equated with what is 'human'. Women are born humans, but society and culture force them to adapt to the role of a woman, subservient to the male: *'Society, being codified by man, decrees that woman is inferior; she can do away with this inferiority only by destroying the male's superiority.'* De Beauvoir argued that women can free themselves from this cultural preconception, both through individual decisions and collective action. She also wrote: *'The most mediocre of males feels himself as a demigod as compared with women.'* In 1954 her novel *The Mandarins* received the prestigious Prix Goncourt.

GEORGE BERNARD SHAW
1856–1950

'I wish all Americans were as blind as you'

Spoken to Helen Keller, quoted in *Bernard Shaw*, Hesketh Pearson, 1975

Shaw immensely admired Helen Keller (1880–1968), who had been deaf and blind from the age of 19 months. All her life Keller fought to overcome her disabilities, lecturing, writing and working for the cause of people with disabilities. She had been expected to die but recovered to become an extremely difficult young child. She could never speak properly as her vocal cords had not developed correctly, but a formerly blind teacher, Anne Sullivan, taught her to communicate. Keller's first book, *The Story of My Life*, was published in 1903, and in 1904 she graduated, becoming the first deaf-blind person to earn a Bachelor of Arts degree. She began lecture tours to raise money for the American Foundation for the Blind, and campaigned tirelessly to alleviate the living and working conditions of blind people, who at that time were usually badly educated and living in asylums. She said: '*The public must learn that the blind man is neither genius nor a freak nor an idiot. He has a mind that can be educated, a hand which can be trained, ambitions which it is right for him to strive to realize, and it is the duty of the public to help him make the best of himself so that he can win light through work.*'

In 1953 a documentary film, *The Unconquered*, was made about Keller's life, and it went on to win an Oscar as the best feature-length documentary. In 1962 the film *The Miracle Worker* was released, and the actresses playing Anne Sullivan and Helen Keller both received Oscars. Keller also wrote: '*Life is a grand adventure – or it is nothing*' and '*Keep your face to the sunshine and you can never see the shadow*'. She is buried next to Anne Sullivan.

LAUREN BACALL
1924 –

'You look like a God-damned rat pack'

Frank Sinatra's group of hard-drinking, womanizing friends such as Dean Martin, Sammy Davis Jr, Joey Bishop and Peter Lawford was known as the Rat Pack. Sinatra was one of the friends of Humphrey Bogart (1899–1957) who called themselves the Homby Hills Rat Pack, after the area of Hollywood where Bogart lived. One morning, Bogart's wife, Lauren Bacall, had come downstairs where the bedraggled Bogart and his friends were still smoking and drinking, made the above remark, and the name stuck. Bogart once said: *'People who don't drink are afraid of revealing themselves.'* On 'Bogie's' death in 1957, Frank Sinatra became the 'chairman' of his own Rat Pack.

Lauren Bacall was born Betty Joan Perske in New York City in 1924. Her cousin was Shimon Peres, the former Israeli Prime Minister (also born Perske). She became an usherette and part-time model, appeared on the cover of *Harper's Bazaar*, was spotted by the wife of producer Howard Hawks and took a screen test. (Bacall added an extra 'l' to her mother's maiden name of Bacal for her screen name.) As a result of a faultless audition, she appeared opposite Humphrey Bogart in *To Have and Have Not*, in 1944. They married a year later (Bogart was now 45) and they appeared in several Bogie-Bacall films. Bacall was surprised at her becoming a star – *'I was this flat-chested, big-footed, lanky thing'*, and also commented *'Stardom isn't a profession; it's an accident'*. A fashion icon from the 1940s onwards, Bacall starred in many films and on stage, and was devastated when Bogart died of throat cancer in 1957. After a relationship with Frank Sinatra, she married the actor Jason Robards in 1961, but divorced because of his alcoholism in 1969. She commented *'In Hollywood, an equitable divorce settlement means each party getting fifty percent of publicity'*.

SENATOR JOSEPH R. McCARTHY
1908–1957

'I have here in my hand a list of 205... a list of names'

'... This indicates the swiftness of the tempo of Communist victories and American defeats in the Cold War. As one of our outstanding historical figures once said, "When a great democracy is destroyed, it will not be from enemies from without, but rather because of enemies from within."... This is glaringly true in the State Department. There the bright young men who are born with silver spoons in their mouths are the ones who have been most traitorous... I have here in my hand a list of 205... a list of names that were made known to the Secretary of State as being members of the Communist Party and who nevertheless are still working and shaping policy in the State Department...'

Speech made at Wheeling, West Virginia, 9 February 1950

McCarthy, a Wisconsin Republican, first won election to the Senate in 1946 during a campaign marked by anti-Communist rhetoric. Partially in response to Republican Party victories, the Democratic President Harry S. Truman set up a 'loyalty programme' for federal employees. McCarthy's speech was an attack on Truman's foreign policy agenda, charging that the State Department and its Secretary, Dean Acheson, harboured 'traitorous' Communists. Both in a letter he wrote to President Truman the next day, and in an 'official' transcript of the speech that he submitted to the *Congressional Record* 10 days later, McCarthy changed the number from 205 to 57. Although he displayed this list of names both in Wheeling and then later on the Senate floor, McCarthy never made the list public. On 30 March 1950, at a news conference in Key West, Florida, President Truman stated: 'I think the greatest asset that the Kremlin has is Senator McCarthy... I don't need to elaborate on that.'

JEROME DAVID SALINGER
1919–

'I'd just be the catcher in the rye'

The Catcher in the Rye, 1951

In chapter 22 of the novel, Holden Caulfield asks Phoebe, '*You know that song, "If a body catch a body comin' through the rye?"*'. Phoebe answers, 'It's "*If a body meet a body coming through the rye!... It's a poem. By Robert Burns.*"' Holden then says that when children are playing in a field of rye near a cliff, he wants to catch them and stop them falling off the cliff.

The Catcher in the Rye still sells 250,000 copies every year with worldwide sales approaching 70 million. It is Salinger's first and only known novel, taking him ten years to write, and as the novel's popularity grew, Salinger became more and more reclusive. Salinger lives in Cornish, a small town in New Hampshire, and has not published an original work since 1965. Refusing interviews since 1980, he has explained his desire for privacy, saying '*It's all in the book*'. In a statement to the New York Times, Salinger defended his right to silence: '*There is a marvellous peace in not publishing. ... It's peaceful. Still. Publishing is a terrible invasion of my privacy. I like to write. I live to write. But I write just for myself and my own pleasure. ... I don't necessarily intend to publish posthumously, but I do like to write for myself. ... I pay for this kind of attitude. I'm known as a strange, aloof kind of man. But all I'm doing is trying to protect myself and my work.*'

The main character, 16-year-old Holden Caulfield, personifies teenage angst and is unpredictable in his likes and dislikes of people and things. In 1953, Salinger admitted that the novel was 'sort of' autobiographical, explaining that, '*My boyhood was very much the same as that of the boy in the book ... it was a great relief telling people about it.*' The book still appeals to 'outsiders'. The psychopath John Hinckley Jr. tried to assassinate Ronald Reagan in 1981 and a copy of the book was found in his hotel room. Mark Chapman notoriously said: '*The reason I killed John Lennon was to promote the reading of J. D. Salinger's The Catcher in the Rye.*'

EVA PERÓN
1919–1952

'I will return. And I will be millions'

Inscription on her tomb in Buenos Aires

Maria Eva Duarte de Perón was the second wife of Argentine President Juan Domingo Perón and the First Lady of Argentina from 1946 until her death. Born out of wedlock and living in poverty, aged 16 she travelled to Buenos Aires and worked at a radio station. She became the mistress of the Secretary of Labour, Juan Perón, and her charisma helped him to win popular support. In 1945 they were married, and she actively campaigned for his presidency. She directly appealed to the worst-off groups in Argentina, claiming to understand their plight. She kept her promises to the working classes and took such an interest that, in everything but name, she became the Secretary of Labour, supporting higher wages and greater social welfare benefits. Her view was *'Charity separates the rich from the poor; aid raises the needy and sets him on the same level with the rich'*.

Perón also took an active interest in health policy, supervising programmes to eradicate diseases such as tuberculosis, malaria and leprosy. In 1947 she set up the Perón Welfare Foundation, which distributed money, food and medicines to those most in need. She angered the ruling elite with her active campaign for female suffrage. Perón died from cancer on 26 July 1952, aged just 32. She had said: *'Time is my greatest enemy.'* Public grief was intense, and unprecedented in Argentina. When Juan Perón was overthrown in 1955, the new government had her body removed from the Ministry of Labour, hiding it in various places, then shipping it to Italy. Her body was exhumed in 1971 and returned to her husband. The musical *Evita* celebrates her life.

DYLAN MARLAIS THOMAS
1914–1953

'I've had eighteen straight whiskies. I think that's the record... After thirty-nine years, this is all I've done.'

His attributed last words

Dylan Thomas, a Welsh poet, short-story writer and dramatist, lived a bohemian lifestyle. His first book, *Eighteen Poems*, received great acclaim when he was just 20. His poems featured intense lyricism, and made him popular on reading tours of the USA. He was argumentative in public, drank to excess, was flamboyantly theatrical and read his work aloud with tremendous depth of feeling. Almost a legend in his own lifetime, he died in 1953 after a particularly long drinking bout in New York City, possibly from undiagnosed diabetes. He had once said: *'An alcoholic is someone you don't like who drinks as much as you do.'*

Thomas' freewheeling poems inspired Bob Zimmerman to become Bob Dylan, and among his best stories are *The Portrait of the Artist as a Young Dog* (1940), *A Child's Christmas in Wales* (1954) and the wonderful play *Under Milk Wood* (1954), which was broadcast on radio that same year. Its opening lines clearly show Thomas' style: *'To begin at the beginning: It is Spring, moonless night in the small town, starless and bible-black, the cobblestreets silent and the hunched, courters'- and- rabbits' wood limping invisible down to the sloeblack, slow, black, crowblack, fishingboat-bobbing sea.'* The first lines of his poem to his dying father are also remarkable:

> 'Do not go gentle into that good night,
> Old age should burn and rave at close of day;
> Rage, rage against the dying of the light.'

ENRICO FERMI
1901–1954

'There are two possible outcomes: If the result confirms the hypothesis, then you've made a measurement. If the result is contrary to the hypothesis, then you've made a discovery.'

Quoted in *Nuclear Principles in Engineering*, Tatjana Jevremovic, 2005

Fermi is remembered by some as the 'Father of the Atomic Bomb', and helped develop quantum theory. From 1934, at the University of Rome, he began bombarding various elements with neutrons. He found that this was effective in producing radioactive atoms, but did not realize that he had split the atom, believing that he had discovered elements beyond uranium. He won the Nobel Prize for Nuclear Physics in 1938, the same year that two German physicists performed a similar experiment when they split a uranium atom.

Fermi settled in the USA in 1938, and continued his work in nuclear fission. His team confirmed the potential for a self-sustaining nuclear chain reaction producing tremendous energy, and Fermi was placed in charge of the Manhattan Project, which developed the first atomic pile and produced the first nuclear chain reaction. His team moved to New Mexico and on 16 July 1945, the first atomic bomb was detonated there. Fermium, the 100th element in the periodic table, is named after him.

ALDOUS HUXLEY
1894–1963

‘To see ourselves as others see us is a most
salutary gift. Hardly less important is the
capacity to see others as they see themselves.’

The Doors of Perception, 1954

Aldous Huxley was an English novelist and
critic, who published travel books, histories, poems
and plays, and essays on philosophy, arts, sociology,
religion and morals. Aged 16, Huxley became
temporarily blind, and being unable to follow his
chosen career as a scientist, turned to writing. His first
novel, *Crome Yellow* (1921), is a witty criticism of
society, and in the next eight years he published 12
books, including *Point Counter Point*. He moved to
France, where in just four months he wrote his best-known novel, *Brave New
World* (1932), a classic work of science fiction. Other works of his include
The Devils of Loudon and the utopian novel *Island*. Moving to California, Huxley
wrote two books about mind-altering drugs, becoming a kind of guru to the hippy
movement. *The Doors of Perception* (1954), quoted above, was written to show
consciousness expansion via his use of LSD and mescaline.

Huxley was perhaps the greatest literary intellectual of his day, and the following
makes clear his contempt of politicians and religious demagogues: ‘*At least
two thirds of our miseries spring from human stupidity, human malice and those
great motivators and justifiers of malice and stupidity, idealism, dogmatism and
proselytizing zeal on behalf of religious or political idols.*’

ED MURROW
1908–1965

'We can deny our heritage and our history, but we cannot escape responsibility for the result'

'The line between investigating and persecuting is a very fine one and the junior Senator from Wisconsin has stepped over it repeatedly... This is no time for men who oppose Senator McCarthy's methods to keep silent. We can deny our heritage and our history, but we cannot escape responsibility for the result.'

CBS TV closing commentary in his documentary *See It Now*, 9 March 1954

At the end of Murrow's programme, Don Hollenbeck, CBS' regular 11 p.m. newscaster, said: '*I want to associate myself with every word just spoken by Ed Murrow.*' This sparked a smear campaign in the press, particularly in the papers owned by William Randolph Hearst, which led to Hollenbeck's suicide. A climate of terror existed in America, the flames fanned by McCarthy. Murrow's firm condemnation of his campaign, however, was the beginning of the end for McCarthy and his supporters. (McCarthy died of acute hepatitis three years later, discredited and hated by many Americans.)

Born Egbert Roscoe Murrow, Ed Murrow was a pioneer in TV news journalism, but had also been a noted war correspondent and broadcaster, based in London during World War II. He developed a distinct opening to all his reports, emphasizing '*This*', when saying '*This... is London*'. He also developed a standard ending to all his reports of '*Goodnight... and good luck*'. He flew on bombing raids, recording over the drone of the engines for later broadcasting of the vivid scenes of battle. He also reported from Buchenwald concentration camp, refusing to apologize to his listeners for the brutal scenes he described – '*I pray you to believe what I have said about Buchenwald. I have reported what I saw and heard, but only part of it. For most of it I have no words... If I've offended you by this rather mild account of Buchenwald, I'm not in the least sorry.*'

WILLIAM FAULKNER
1897–1962

'The aim of every artist is to arrest motion'

'The aim of every artist is to arrest motion, which is life, by artificial means and hold it fixed so that a hundred years later, when a stranger looks at it, it moves again since it is life.'

Interview in *Paris Review*, spring 1956

Born William Cuthbert Faulkner in New Albany, Mississippi, he joined the Canadian and later the British Royal Air Force during World War I. Faulkner never graduated from high school, and lived all his life in a small town in the poorest state of America, looking after a growing family of dependants and perpetually facing financial ruin. However, during the Great Depression, he somehow wrote a series of superb novels all set in the same small Southern county, including *The Sound and the Fury* (1929), *Sanctuary* (1931), *Light in August* (1932) and *Absalom, Absalom!* (1936). He created absorbing sagas of families living through the growth and fall of the South.

In 1940, Faulkner published the first volume of the Snopes trilogy, *The Hamlet*, to be followed by two further volumes, *The Town* (1957) and *The Mansion* (1959). *The Reivers* was his last work, published in 1962. Faulkner is regarded as one of the 20th century's greatest writers of novels and short stories. He has left us an enduring legacy of life in the Deep South and its racial tensions via an amazingly prolific output. In his 1949 Nobel Prize acceptance speech, he said: '*I believe that man will not merely endure; he will prevail. He is immortal, not because he alone among creatures has an inexhaustible voice, but because he has a soul, a spirit capable of compassion and sacrifice and endurance.*'

JACK KEROUAC
1922–1969

'The only people for me are the mad ones, the ones who are mad to live, mad to talk, mad to be saved'

On the Road, 1957

Jean-Louis Lebris Kerouac dropped out of Columbia University, was discharged on psychiatric grounds from the navy in World War II and joined the Merchant Marines. His autobiographical novel, *On the Road*, was published after seven years of being rejected by publishers. This first 'Beat novel' was based on Kerouac's drug-fuelled travels across America with his friend Neal Cassady. He wrote the book at his kitchen table over a period of just 20 days, on a single roll of telegraph paper, reinventing what was known as 'automatic writing', which appealed to songwriters, poets and novelists across the world. Bob Dylan wrote of the book: '*It changed my life like it changed everyone else's*' and Ray Manzarek, the Doors' keyboard player, said: '*If he hadn't wrote* On the Road, *the Doors would have never existed.*' Kerouac died of the effects of long-term Benzedrine addiction and alcoholism. He died of a brain haemorrhage caused by cirrhosis, itself the result of a lifelong addiction to alcohol.

ROBERT TRAILL SPENCE LOWELL
1917–1977

'I cowered in terror. I wasn't a child at all'

'My Last Afternoon with Uncle Devereux Winslow', *Life Studies*, 1959

Born into one of Boston's oldest and most prominent families, Lowell has been called the 'Father of the confessional poets' and his poetry grew out of his own unhappiness and disturbed life. Married three times, he was a heavy drinker and from 1949 was diagnosed with severe bipolar disorder. His depression meant that he spent periods in mental hospitals. Lowell's first and second books, *Land of Unlikeness* (1944) and *Lord Weary's Castle* (which won a Pulitzer Prize in 1947) were influenced by his conversion to Catholicism. He became a conscientious objector during World War II because of Allied fire-bombing of civilians, and was imprisoned as a result. Lowell also protested against the war in Vietnam, and his personal life was full of marital and psychological disturbances. Partly in response to his frequent breakdowns, Lowell began to write more directly from personal experience, and moved away from traditional metre and form. The result was his brilliant collection, *Life Studies* (1959), which changed the work of many subsequent poets. In 'The Drinker' (1964), he writes: '*The man is killing time – there's nothing else*', which sums up the bleakness Lowell felt. In his final year, he wrote: '*If we see the light at the end of the tunnel it is the light of an oncoming train.*'

BORIS LEONIDOVICH PASTERNAK
1890–1960

'Of what crime do I stand condemned?'

'Nobel Prize', 1959

By 1923, Boris Pasternak was accepted as a leading poet among his Russian contemporaries. After World War II, he began writing his only novel, *Doctor Zhivago*. The book is full of powerful metaphors, lyrically accentuating the beauty of life amidst the bitter tragedy of the Russian Revolution and Civil War that followed. It combines lyrical-descriptive and epic-dramatic styles, and was published in an Italian translation in 1957 after being smuggled out of the Soviet Union.

Pasternak was awarded the Nobel Prize for Literature in 1958, which he initially accepted, but was forced by the Russian government to rescind his acceptance. Bitterly disappointed, Pasternak secretly wrote the poem ' Nobel Prize' to show his disenchantment with the regime. He lived a life of fear and insecurity, especially after the worldwide fame of his novel – Russian intellectuals published their symphonies and poems dreading that a hint of disloyalty to the state might bring imprisonment or death. *'Of course I am prepared for anything. Why should it happen to everyone else and not to me?'* wrote Pasternak in one letter. Thousands braved official disapproval to attend Pasternak's funeral at the Peredelkino writers' settlement near Moscow. *Doctor Zhivago* was not published in Russia until 1988. Pasternak secretly wrote this poem after his official condemnation, living as someone reviled by the state and its acolytes.

WILLIAM ROBERTSON DAVIES
1913–1995

'The world is full of people whose notion of a satisfactory future is, in fact, a return to an idealized past'

A Voice from the Attic, 1960

One of the great figures in Canadian literature, Davies, a Welsh-Canadian, is best known for the *Deptford Trilogy* – *Fifth Business* (1970), *The Manticore* (1972) and *World of Wonders* (1975). After studying at Toronto and Oxford, he spent 20 years as a journalist in Oxford, and moved on to writing plays and novels. His *Salterton Trilogy* comprised his first novel, *Tempest-Tost* (1951), *Leaven of Malice* (1954) and *A Mixture of Frailties* (1958). From 1960 to 1981 he was a Professor of English at the University of Toronto, and his fame as a novelist grew throughout his life. His novels, often humorous, explore mysticism, the isolation of the human spirit, the passage from innocence to experience and quietly satirize bourgeois provincialism.

Davies wrote over 30 novels, as well as plays, essays and criticism, and was greatly honoured in the years before his death. In the essay collection *A Voice from the Attic*, he remarks: '*As a general rule, people marry most happily with their own kind. The trouble lies in the fact that people usually marry at an age where they do not really know what their own kind is*' and '*Our age has robbed millions of the simplicity of ignorance, and has so far failed to lift them to simplicity of wisdom*'. Davies also tells us, '*A truly great book should be read in youth, again in maturity and once more in old age, as a fine building should be seen by morning light, at noon and by moonlight.*'

JOHN FITZGERALD KENNEDY
1917–1963

'Ask not what your country can do for you'

'And so, my fellow Americans: ask not what your country can do for you – ask what you can do for your country. My fellow citizens of the world: ask not what America will do for you, but what together we can do for the freedom of man'

Inaugural Presidential Address, 20 January 1961, repeating the motto of Juvenal

After graduating from Harvard in 1940, Kennedy was in command of PT boat 109 which was rammed and sunk by a Japanese destroyer. Badly injured, he became a war hero for his actions in rescuing survivors. He became a Democratic Congressman, then a Senator from 1953, in the same year marrying Jacqueline Bouvier. After a back operation in 1955 he wrote *Profiles in Courage*, which earned him a Pulitzer Prize, and in 1960 he narrowly beat Richard Nixon to become President of the USA. He had pledged to make America great, and his economic programmes launched the country on its longest sustained expansion since World War II. Kennedy also took vigorous action in the cause of equal rights, calling for new civil rights legislation.

During Kennedy's presidency, the Berlin Wall was built and the Cuban Missile Crisis occurred. Kennedy went to Berlin and said, '*Ich bin ein Berliner*' – '*I am a Berliner*'. Of Cuba, he stated: '*I call upon Chairman Khrushchev to halt and eliminate this clandestine, reckless, and provocative threat to world peace... He has an opportunity now to move the world back from the abyss of destruction.*' His work towards the Test Ban Treaty of 1963 helped in the move away from the Cold War and towards world peace between the Great Powers. This treaty banned nuclear tests in outer space, in the atmosphere and under water, helping to slow the nuclear weapons race and better protect the environment. The USA, USSR and UK all signed the treaty, leaving it open for developing nuclear powers to sign it also. Hardly past his first 1,000 days in office, this charismatic president was gunned down in Dallas. He had been the youngest man to be elected president, and was the youngest president to die in office.

NIELS BOHR
1885–1962

'The opposite of a correct statement is a false statement. But the opposite of a profound truth may well be another profound truth.'

Quoted by his son Hans Bohr in 'My Father', published in
Neils Bohr: His Life and Work (1967)

Bohr, an eminent physicist, was born in Copenhagen, and made many contributions to our understanding of the structure of properties of atoms. In 1913, he published a theory about the structure of the atom based on an earlier theory of Ernest Rutherford. Rutherford had shown that the atom consisted of a positively charged nucleus, with negatively charged electrons in orbit around it. Bohr expanded upon this theory by proposing that electrons travel only in certain successively larger orbits. He suggested that the outer orbits could hold more electrons than the inner ones, and that these outer orbits determine the atom's chemical properties. In 1922 Bohr won the Nobel Prize for Physics, mainly for his work on atomic structure. He tells us: *'The very nature of the quantum theory... forces us to regard the space-time coordination and the claim of causality, the union of which characterizes the classical theories, as complementary but exclusive features of the description, symbolizing the idealization of observation and description, respectively'.* Fortunately, he also informs us that *'Anyone who is not shocked by quantum theory has not understood a single word'.*

Bohr also described the way atoms emit radiation by suggesting that when an electron jumps from an outer orbit to an inner one, it emits light. Later other physicists expanded his theory into quantum mechanics. During World War II, Bohr fled Copenhagen to escape the Nazis. At Los Alamos, New Mexico, he advised scientists developing the first atomic bomb. Returning to Copenhagen after the war, he promoted the peaceful use of atomic energy. Two of his more acute comments are: *'An expert is a person who has made all the mistakes that can be made in a very narrow field'* and *'Prediction is very difficult, especially about the future'.*

CHARLES DE GAULLE
1890–1970

'How can you govern a country which has two hundred and forty-six varieties of cheese?'

Speech made in 1951, quoted in *Les Mots du Général*, Ernest Mignon, 1962

De Gaulle was leader of the Free French during World War II, proclaiming over BBC Radio that *'France has lost a battle, but France has not lost the war'*, and was the architect of the Fifth Republic. He had served with distinction in World War I, and had strongly criticized French reliance on the Maginot Line for defence against Germany. In June 1940, German forces easily overran France, but de Gaulle refused to accept the French government's truce with the Germans and escaped to London, where he announced the formation of a French government in exile. In August 1944, de Gaulle was given a hero's welcome back in Paris, becoming President of the provisional government. However, as his desires for a strong presidency were ignored, he resigned and in 1953 he withdrew into retirement.

In 1958, a revolt in French-held Algeria helped bring down the Fourth Republic. De Gaulle returned to lead France once more, a new constitution was approved and de Gaulle voted in as President of the Fifth Republic. Strongly nationalistic, de Gaulle sought to strengthen his country, sanctioning the development of nuclear weapons, withdrawing France from NATO and vetoing the entry of Britain into the Common Market. He granted independence to Algeria in the faceof strong opposition. In 1967, on the balcony of Montreal City Hall, he shouted, *'Vive le Québec libre!'* (*'Long live free Quebec!'*), causing a diplomatic crisis. His political ideology, 'Gaullism', has been a major influence in French politics.

DR MARTIN LUTHER KING JR
1929–1968

'I have a dream'

'I have a dream that one day every valley shall be exalted, every hill and mountain shall be made low, the rough places will be made plain, and the crooked places will be made straight, and the glory of the Lord shall be revealed, and all flesh shall see it together.'

Excerpt from his speech made in Washington DC, 28 August 1963

King gave this wonderful speech from the steps beneath the Lincoln Memorial to the 250,000 people who had gathered for the 'March on Washington for Jobs and Freedom'. Arrested over 20 times for preaching racial equality, King was the youngest man to receive the Nobel Peace Prize. He gave all the award money to further the Civil Rights movement.

Michael Luther King Jr later had his name changed to Martin, and like his father and grandfather was pastor of the Ebenezer Baptist Church in Atlanta. He attended segregated public schools in Georgia, and took a BA in 1948 from Morehouse College, a black college in Atlanta from which both his father and grandfather had graduated. He received a doctorate from Boston University in 1955, by which time he was a pastor in Montgomery, Alabama and a member of the executive committee of the National Association for the Advancement of Colored People. In that year, he led the first great non-violent demonstration of black people in modern times. The bus boycott lasted 385 days, until the Supreme Court banned segregation on buses. His home was bombed and he was arrested, but he now travelled over six million miles preaching for civil rights. On the evening of 4 April 1968, he was standing on the balcony of his motel room in Memphis, Tennessee, where he was to lead a protest march for its striking garbage workers, when he was assassinated.

MUHAMMAD ALI
1942–

'I am the greatest! I'm the greatest thing that ever lived'

'I knew I had him in the first round. Almighty God was with
me. I want everyone to bear witness, I am the greatest! I'm the
greatest thing that ever lived. I don't have a mark on my face,
and I upset Sonny Liston, and I just turned twenty-two years
old. I must be the greatest. I showed the world. I talk to God
everyday. I shook up the world, I'm the king of the world. You
must listen to me. I am the greatest! I can't be beat!'

Cassius Clay (Muhammad Ali) after beating Sonny Liston for the first time,
25 February 1964

Born Cassius Marcellus Clay in Louisville, Kentucky, Ali changed his
name in 1964 and later converted to Sunni Islam and then Sufism. Winner of an
Olympic gold medal, as a professional boxer Ali was the only man at the time to
win three world heavyweight championships. *Sports Illustrated* and the BBC
awarded him the title 'Sportsman of the Century' in 1999.

Ali described his fast, athletic boxing style as *'Float like a
butterfly, sting like a bee'*. Under trainer Angelo Dundee, he
built his reputation by predicting in which round he would
win. He unexpectedly beat Sonny Liston in the world
championship in 1964, but was later stripped of his title
for becoming a conscientious objector and refusing to fight
in the Vietnam War. He was sentenced to five years in
prison but the sentence was suspended on an appeal to the
Supreme Court.

After more fights, in 1971 Ali took part in what was called 'the Fight of the
Century' against the undefeated new world champion, 'Smokin' Joe Frazier.
Frazier won on points, and in the same year Ali had his conviction reversed.
He then fought George Foreman in 'the rumble in the jungle' in Zaire, and won
even though his chances were thought minimal. In 1975, he defeated Joe Frazier
for the second time in 'the thrilla in Manila'. He lost the title to Leon Spinks
in 1978 but regained it. Now suffering from Parkinson's Disease, Ali is probably
one of the best-loved individuals in the world.

NELSON MANDELA
1918–

'An ideal for which I am prepared to die'

'Above all, my lord, we want equal political rights, because without them our disabilities will be permanent. I know this sounds revolutionary to the whites in this country, because the majority of voters will be Africans. This makes the white man fear democracy. But this fear cannot be allowed to stand in the way of the only solution which will guarantee racial harmony and freedom for all... The ANC has spent half a century fighting against racialism. When it triumphs, as it certainly must, it will not change that policy. This then is what the ANC is fighting. Our struggle is a truly national one. It is a struggle of the African people, inspired by our own suffering and our own experience. It is a struggle for the right to live. During my lifetime I have dedicated my life to this struggle of the African people. I have fought against white domination, and I have fought against black domination. I have cherished the ideal of a democratic and free society in which all persons live together in harmony with equal opportunities. It is an ideal which I hope to live for, and to see realized. But my lord, if needs be, it is an ideal for which I am prepared to die.'

His concluding words at his trial, Johannesburg, 20 April 1964

Mandela's trial opened on 9 October 1963, where he was named as Accused Number One and faced the death penalty. He and his colleagues were charged under the Suppression of Communism Act. Mandela denied he was a Communist and described himself as an African patriot who admired the Magna Carta and the Bill of Rights. His concluding words during this trial inspired support throughout the world. On 11 June 1964, Mandela and his seven co-defendants were sentenced to life imprisonment. He was sent to Robben Island, where he was placed in a stone cell measuring 7 feet square, lit at all times by a 40-watt bulb, and was set to hard labour in a quarry. He spent 27 years in prison.

BRENDAN BEHAN
1923–1964

'Bless you, Sister. May all your sons be bishops.'

Spoken to a nursing nun on his deathbed as she was taking his pulse

Brendan Behan's father had been imprisoned as a Republican, and in his early teens Behan joined the youth organization of the IRA. He was trained to use explosives but was arrested when he arrived in Liverpool and after detention at Walton Prison spent 1941 and 1942 in borstal (a type of youth prison). He wrote: *'There were few Catholics in this part of the world and the priest had a forlorn sort of a job but Walton had cured me of any idea that religion of any description had anything to do with mercy or pity or love.'* Returning to Dublin, Behan fired at two detectives during an IRA parade and was sentenced to 14 years. He was released in 1946 as part of a general amnesty and returned to painting and writing, but would serve other prison terms. After some time in Paris, he retuned to Dublin in 1950 and acquired a reputation as a hard-drinking rebel-rouser.

In 1954, his play *The Quare Fellow* was produced, and brought him permanent media attention when it was shown in London in 1956. The titular 'quare fellow', never seen on stage, is a condemned man in prison, and the play is in part a protest against capital punishment. Behan's second play, *An Giall* (1958), was translated into English, and Joan Littlewood's production of *The Hostage* (1958) led to further success for Behan in London and New York. One of its lines is: *'When I came back to Dublin, I was court-martialled in my absence and sentenced to death in my absence, so I said they could shoot me in my absence.'* Behan's autobiographical book *Borstal Boy* also appeared in 1958, but alcoholism and diabetes were affecting his health and writing. When he died in Dublin on 20 March 1964, an IRA guard of honour escorted his coffin in one of the biggest funerals Ireland has seen.

SIR LAWRENCE BRAGG
1890–1971

'The important thing in science is not so much to obtain new facts as to discover new ways of thinking about them'

Speech made at the inaugural Nobel Guest Lecture in 1965,
50 years after receiving his Nobel Prize

William Lawrence Bragg was the youngest ever recipient of the Nobel Prize, aged 25, when he was awarded it jointly with his father, Sir William Henry Bragg. Bragg was born in Adelaide where his father was Professor of Mathematics and Physics at its university. Lawrence studied there, gaining a first-class honours degree in mathematics aged only 19. In 1912, Max von Laue had performed groundbreaking work on the diffraction of x-rays by crystals, and Lawrence Bragg was the first to hypothesize that x-rays had a dual wave/particle nature, which became one of the most significant concepts in 20th-century physics. In 1915, he and his father were awarded the Nobel Prize for Physics for their joint work on x-ray crystallography. By mathematically analysing the way that x-rays were affected when aimed at certain substances, the Braggs were able to deduce their crystal structure (understanding the crystal structure of a substance is necessary to predict how that substance will behave under different circumstances). For example, they found that salt (sodium chloride) did not exist as individual single molecules, but in a regular lattice (crystal) structure, with alternating atoms of sodium and chlorine.

Many years later, James Watson worked for Bragg's x-ray research team at the Cavendish Laboratory in Cambridge when linking with Francis Crick to help reveal the structure of DNA. Lawrence Bragg was knighted in 1941, worked at the University of Manchester and became director of the Royal Institution.

WALT DISNEY
1901–1966

'All our dreams can come true,
if we have the courage to pursue them'

Walt Disney, quoted in Pat Williams *How to Be Like Walt: Capturing the Magic Every Day of Your Life*

Walt Disney attempted to enlist for World War I but was too young, so joined the Red Cross and drove an ambulance in France. After the war, he started a company, Laugh-O-Grams in Kansas City, which failed, and headed for Hollywood, becoming successful with his *Alice Comedies* in the 1920s. They featured a young live-action girl named Alice and a cartoon cat named Julius. Of his previous failure, he noted: '*You may not realize it when it happens, but a kick in the teeth may be the best thing in the world for you.*' He later said of his success with Mickey Mouse: '*If you can dream it, you can do it. Always remember that this whole thing was started with a dream and a mouse... The way to get started is to quit talking and begin doing.*' In 1932 his studio's first colour cartoon, *Flowers and Trees*, won the first of its Academy Awards. After more innovations, in 1937 he released the wonderful *Snow White and the Seven Dwarfs*, the first full-length animated musical feature. The film cost a mammoth $1,499,000 during the depths of the Depression.

During the next five years, Walt Disney Studios released animated classics such as *Pinocchio, Fantasia, Dumbo* and *Bambi*. Disney's dream venture of Disneyland Park opened in 1955. He said: '*We believed in our idea – a family park where parents and children could have fun – together... We did it Disneyland, in the knowledge that most of the people I talked to thought it would be a financial disaster – closed and forgotten within the first year.*' Disney began television production in 1954, and was among the first to present full-colour programming in 1961.

DOROTHY PARKER
1893–1967

'The first thing I do in the morning is brush my teeth and sharpen my tongue'
Attributed

Dorothy Parker was an American humorist, author, poet, critic and social activist, but is best known for her caustic wit. She had a prolific writing career with the *New Yorker*, *Vogue* and *Vanity Fair* and became famous for her short, viciously humorous poems. She also wrote the screenplay for the 1937 film, *A Star Is Born*.

She became a civil rights activist and a critic of those in authority – on hearing of President Coolidge's death, she remarked: *'How could they tell?'* Parker criticized Katharine Hepburn's performance in a Broadway play: *'She ran the whole gamut of emotions from A to B'*. Her refusal to give testimony to the House Committee on Un-American Activities in the early 1950s gained her a place on the 'Hollywood blacklist'. The National Association for the Advancement of Colored People created a memorial garden in her honour. Her one-liners, along the lines of those of Mae West, are legendary, and include:

'One more drink and I'll be under the host'

'Men seldom make passes – at girls who wear glasses'

'Ducking for apples – change one letter and it's the story of my life'

'Brevity is the soul of lingerie'

'If all the girls attending it [the Yale Prom] were laid end to end, I wouldn't be surprised'

'I shall stay the way I am because I do not give a damn'

'I discovered to my amazement that average men and women were delighted by the prospect of war'

'I discovered to my amazement that average men and women were delighted by the prospect of war. I had fondly imagined what most pacifists contended, that most wars were forced upon a reluctant population by despotic and Machiavellian governments.'

The Autobiography of Bertrand Russell, 1967–69

The 20th-century's greatest liberal thinker has unaccountably been omitted from *Time's* 100 most influential people of that century. He is also one of its two or three greatest philosophers, and arguably its greatest mathematician. By the time of his death, Russell had become one of the world's most influential critics of nuclear weapons and the American war in Vietnam. He had been a progressive all his life, advocating social democracy, women's rights and peace. Orphaned at the age of four, he was brought up by his grandparents. However, his grandfather, Prime Minister Lord John Russell, who in 1832 had forced through the Great Reform Bill and greater democracy, died when Bertrand was six. His grandmother was a dominating woman who tried to bend him towards politics.

At Cambridge University, Russell blossomed as a philosopher and mathematician, publishing *Principia Mathematica* with Alfred Whitehead between 1910 and 1913. He fought for women's suffrage, being dismissed from his post at Cambridge for arguing for a negotiated peace in World War I, and imprisoned for five months. He later visited Russia and was appalled by the system, as well as by the growing Fascism in Germany and Italy. He only turned away from non-violent pacifism following Hitler's invasion of Poland. After the war, he was among the first to warn of Russia's nuclear capabilities, and was the figurehead for the Campaign for Nuclear Disarmament (CND), hoping that Britain's unilateral disarmament could set an example to the world. By the late 1960s, he was campaigning against American involvement in Vietnam, wishing to set up a War Crimes Tribunal in Sweden for President Johnson's policy-makers. He once responded to a criticism: '*I am as drunk as a lord, but then, I am one, so what does it matter?*' In the last years before his death, Russell composed his autobiography, which ran to three volumes.

TALLULAH BANKHEAD
1902–1968

'Hello, Dahling'

Her trademark introduction, now adopted throughout the theatre world

At the age of 16, Tallulah Bankhead won a beauty contest in Alabama and moved to New York City to try her hand on Broadway. After five meagre years, she moved to London in 1923 and became the most popular actress in London's West End. She gained the attention of Paramount and returned to the US, but the roles they offered her did not suit her talent, so she made her success on Broadway. The parties she held would last for days. She chain-smoked 100 cigarettes a day and enjoyed Kentucky bourbon, making a habit of getting undressed and chatting in the nude. Another actress asked her, *'Tallulah, dear, why are you always taking your clothes off? You have such lovely frocks.'* Bankhead is widely remembered for her repartee, especially pertaining to vices:

> *'Cocaine, habit-forming? Of course not. I ought to know. I've been using it for years'*

> *'I'll come and make love to you at five o'clock. If I'm late, start without me'*

> *'If I had to live my life again, I'd make the same mistakes, only sooner'*

> *'Nobody can be exactly me. Sometimes even I have trouble doing it'*

And on seeing a former lover for the first time in years, she told him: *'I thought I told you to wait in the car'*.

R. BUCKMINSTER FULLER
1895–1993

'The Things to do are: the things that need doing, that you see need to be done, and that no one else seems to see need to be done'

Letter to Micheal, February 16, 1970

'Micheal' was a ten-year-old boy who had written to Fuller to ask whether he was a 'doer' or a 'thinker'. Known to his friends as 'Bucky', Fuller was a key innovator of the 20th century, known as a philosopher, cosmologist, thinker, visionary, inventor, architect, engineer, mathematician, poet and especially as a futurist. A global thinker, he coined the term 'Spaceship Earth', and his work has inspired many inventors. Fuller himself was the inventor of the Geodesic Dome, and a pioneer in utilizing basic geometrical shapes in design. He developed the 'Dymaxion Map of the World' as the first world projection to show the continents on a flat surface without visible distortion. The map shows the Earth as being one island in one ocean.

Much of Fuller's work was about exploring and creating synergy, which he found to be a basic principle of all interactive systems. He developed a subject called Synergetics, the 'Geometry of Thinking'. His key goal was the development of 'Comprehensive Anticipatory Design Science', the attempt to anticipate and solve humanity's major problems by providing *'more and more life support for everybody, with less and less resources'*. A utopian thinker, he was always looking for the means by which humans could survive long-term on this planet. He was fairly scornful of politicians, declaring: *'War is the ultimate tool of politics'*. His name was given to the family of complex carbon molecules called buckminsterfullerene (also known as 'Bucky Balls'), so named for their resemblance to his geodesic spheres.

DR ERNEST KLEIN
1900–1983

'Dedicated to the Sacred Memory of the Best Parents'

'Dedicated to the Sacred Memory of the Best Parents
My Dear Mother
Who after a Life of Self-sacrifice Died in Szatmar in 1940
And My Dear Father,
The World-Renowned Rabbi and Scholar,
Rabbi Ignaz (Isaac) Klein of Szatmar,
Who Died a Martyr of His Faith in Auschwitz in 1944;
And to the Sacred Memory of My Wife
And of my Only Child Joseph (Hayyim Israel)
Who Also Fell Victims to Nazism in Auschwitz in 1944'

Dedication in Klein's *Comprehensive Etymological
Dictionary of the English Language*, 1971

In the preface to Klein's book, we also read: '*I am what my MOTHER and my FATHER made of me.*' Ernest Klein was brought up in Szatmar in Hungary. He was awarded his PhD at the University of Vienna in 1925, and from 1931 to 1944 he was the Rabbi of the Jewish Congregation in Nové Zámky in Czechoslovakia. Then he was deported to Dachau concentration camp. On his return home he found that his father, wife, child and two of his three sisters had died at Auschwitz.

Klein moved to Toronto in 1951 to serve as a rabbi and to work for 11 hours a day, six days a week for 20 years on his dictionary, which was the result of a lifetime of study of all the Western languages. He was conversant with more than 40 languages ranging from Ancient Greek and Roman to modern languages, and believed that in tracing words to their origin, we are simultaneously tracing civilisation and culture to their real roots. He said: '*To know the origin of words is to know the cultural history of mankind.*' Prior to his death at the age of 83, Klein was working on a dictionary on medical terminology, which included biographies of 3,000 scientists, but it was never completed.

JACK BENNY
1894–1974

'I don't deserve this award, but I have arthritis and I don't deserve that either'

Attributed

Born Benjamin Kubelsky, Benny was an absolute master of comic timing. His act was best summed up by his friend the comedian George Burns in 1989: *'This was some great act this guy had; Jack Benny carried a violin he didn't play, a cigar he didn't smoke, and he was funniest when he said nothing.'* Benny left school to join vaudeville, and went on to a greater career on radio for *The Jack Benny Program*, which also became a successful television show. He billed himself as 'the Original Old Blue Eyes', and developed an image as a penny-pincher, inept at violin playing, and never admitted to being older than 39. On *The Jack Benny Show*, all the great stars of the day appeared – Humphrey Bogart, Liberace, Bob Hope and Raymond Burr (as Perry Mason). The following excerpt gives an indication of Benny's style when romancing Marilyn Monroe:

> Marilyn Monroe: *What about the difference in our ages?*
> Benny: *Oh, it's not that big a difference. You're 25 and I'm 39.*
> Marilyn Monroe: *I know, Jack. But what about 25 years from now when I'm 50 and you're 39?*
> Benny: *Gee, I never thought of that.*

Other bons mots of his include:

> *'Give me golf clubs, fresh air and a beautiful woman – and you can keep the golf clubs and fresh air'*
>
> *'I don't want to tell you how much insurance I carry with the Prudential, but all I can say is: when I go, they go too'*
>
> *'Modesty is my best quality'*
>
> *'My wife Mary and I have been married for forty-seven years and not once have we had an argument serious enough to consider divorce; murder, yes, but divorce, never.'*

MAE WEST
1893–1980

'Is that a gun in your pocket, or are you just glad to see me?'

Quoted in *Peel Me a Grape*, Joseph Weintraub, 1975
(usually quoted as 'Is that a pistol...')

Mary Jane (Mae) West was a playwright, actress, screenwriter and sex symbol who had problems with censorship. Beginning in vaudeville, her career took her into the film industry. A shapely, glamorous, non-smoking teetotaller, her comic asides and double-entendres made her name. West wrote a play, *Sex*, in which she starred on Broadway and for which she was arrested on morals charges in 1927 and sentenced to 10 days in prison for public obscenity. Her other plays included *Diamond Lil* (1928), which became a massive Broadway hit. She was 38 when she was offered her first movie contract, a small role in *Night After Night*. She was allowed to rewrite all her scenes, and George Raft commented on her appearance in the film: '*She stole everything but the cameras*'. A hat-check girl commented, '*Goodness, what beautiful diamonds!*' to which West retorted, '*Goodness had nothing to do with it.*'

West rapidly became the biggest box-office draw in the USA, and the second highest paid person after William Randolph Hearst. Increasing censorship of her screenplays led to her increased usage of double-entendres. Some of her better-known lines include:

'*Marriage is a great institution. I'm not ready for an institution*'

'*A hard man is good to find*'

'*I used to be Snow White... but I drifted*'

'*Give a man a free hand and he'll try to put it all over you*'

'*It's not the men in my life that count, it's the life in my men*'

'*Why don't you come up sometime, and see me?*'

ALEXANDER ISAYEVICH SOLZHENITSYN
1918–2008

'The next war... may well bury Western civilization forever'

Commencement speech for the incoming freshman class at
Harvard University, 1978

Solzhenitsyn fought on the front lines until virtually the end of World War II, when he was arrested for critical remarks in letters about *'the moustachioed one'* – Stalin. He was convicted of anti-Soviet behaviour and sentenced to eight years in a Kazakhstan labour camp. He underwent surgery for cancer in 1952 in the camp hospital, leading him to write *Cancer Ward*, published in the West in 1968. On completing his sentence in 1953, he was condemned to exile 'in perpetuity' and was sent to a desolate village in Kazakhstan. He wrote: *'I can say without affectation that I belong to the Russian convict world no less than I do to Russian literature. I got my education there, and it will last forever.'*

Under Khrushchev, in 1961 Solzhenitsyn used a pseudonym to have published *A Day in the Life of Ivan Denisovich*, based on his experiences in the labour camps. The regime blocked his efforts to have his other works published, but in 1970 he was awarded the Nobel Prize for Literature. *The Gulag Archipelago* was smuggled out of Russia on microfilm and published in Paris in 1973. Solzhenitsyn was arrested in 1974 and deported, settling in Vermont in the USA, where he wrote *August 1914*. He despaired of his country's transition to Capitalism: *'It would have been difficult to design a path out of communism worse than the one that has been followed... The name of "reform" simply covers what is latently a process of the theft of the national heritage.'* He also wrote: *'Our envy of others devours us most of all.'*

Solzhenitsyn's 1978 speech at Harvard, quoted above, painted a bleak future for Western civilization. The *'next war'* is that which would follow the two World Wars, which he felt were *'by far not on a world scale, not yet'*.

MOTHER TERESA OF CALCUTTA
1910–1997

'The poor people are very great people. They can teach us so many beautiful things'

Nobel Lecture, 11 December 1979

Agnes Gonxha Bojaxhiu was an Albanian Roman Catholic nun, born in Skopje (now in the Republic of Macedonia). She left home aged 18 to join the Sisters of Loreto as a missionary and never returned home. She first went to Loreto Abbey in Ireland to learn English before travelling to India in 1929, taking her first vows as a nun in 1931. She chose Teresa as her name after the patron saint of missionaries. For more than 45 years she ministered to the sick, orphaned, poor and dying in Calcutta. She said: '*By blood and origin I am Albanian. My citizenship is Indian. I am a Catholic nun. As to my calling, I belong to the whole world. As to my heart, I belong entirely to the heart of Jesus.*'

Mother Teresa founded the Missionaries of Charity, which expanded into other countries helped by her efforts in publicity and fundraising, and was awarded the Nobel Peace Prize for her humanitarianism in 1979. Six years after her death she was beatified by Pope John Paul II and given the title Blessed Teresa of Calcutta. Her sayings include:

'Love is doing small things with great love'

'The dying, the cripple, the mental, the unwanted, the unloved – they are Jesus in disguise'

'Let us not be satisfied with just giving money. Money is not enough, money can be got, but they need your hearts to love them. So, spread your love everywhere you go'

'If you judge people, you have no time to love them'

GEORGE BURNS
1896–1996

'Too bad all the people who know how to run this country are busy running taxicabs or cutting hair'

Life Magazine, December 1979

Born Nathan Birnbaum, the comedian's trademark was his ever-present cigar. He said: '*I smoke ten to fifteen cigars a day. At my age I have to hold on to something.*' He was the straight man to his wife Gracie Allen in *The Burns & Allen Show* from 1934 to 1950, but after her death in 1964 he created a new image as an amiable old comedian. He was 80 when he won the 1976 Oscar for Best Supporting Actor for *The Sunshine Boys*. He quipped '*Acting is all about honesty. If you can fake that, you've got it made*'. The best friend of comedian Jack Benny, Burns was meant to give Benny's funeral oration, but he was too overcome. He worked almost to his death, but was in too fragile health to attend his 100th birthday celebration. Many of his best jokes were about his age:

'First you forget names, then you forget faces. Next you forget to pull your zipper up and finally, you forget to pull it down'

'Everything that goes up must come down. But there comes a time when not everything that's down can come up'

'I can remember when the air was clean and sex was dirty'

'Sex at age 90 is like trying to shoot pool with a rope'

'When I was a boy the Dead Sea was only sick'

'It's good to be here. At 98, it's good to be anywhere'

'If you live to be one hundred, you've got it made. Very few people die past that age'

INDIRA GANDHI
1917–1984

'I don't mind if my life goes in the service of the nation. If I die today every drop of my blood will invigorate the nation.'

Last public speech at Orissa, 30 October 1984

Indira Priyadarshini Nehru was the daughter of Jawaharlal Nehru, independent India's first prime minister (from 1947 to 1964) and she spent her life in politics, being elected to Parliament in 1964. She was married to Feroze Gandhi (1912–1960) and had two sons, one of whom, Sanjay Gandhi (1946–1980), was a controversial figure in her government before he was killed in an aeroplane crash, and the other, Rajiv Gandhi (1944–1991), succeeded her as India's prime minister in 1984 but was killed in a bombing.

Gandhi became India's first female prime minister from 1966 to 1977, winning four successive elections. The successful execution of the Indo-Pakistan War (1971) under her guidance led to the creation of Bangladesh. She was again prime minister from 1980 to 1984, and in 1984 she used the military to suppress Sikh rebels and ordered an attack on a Sikh Golden Temple shrine in Amritsar. Over 1,000 Sikhs died, despite her maxim '*You cannot shake hands with a clenched fist*'. A few months later, the day after she made this remark at a rally in Orissa, Gandhi was assassinated by Sikh conspirators. She also said: '*If I die a violent death, as some fear and a few are plotting, I know that the violence will be in the thought and the action of the assassins, not in my dying*' and '*Martyrdom does not end something, it is only a beginning*'.

'My doctor told me to stop having intimate dinners for four. Unless there are three other people.'

Attributed

Welles suffered from weight problems, his average dinner consisting of two rare steaks and a pint of scotch. In 1938 he produced a radio broadcast version of *The War of the Worlds* (intended as a Halloween prank) and there was a nationwide panic, with many listeners convinced that the Earth was being invaded by Mars. The next day, Welles publicly apologized. The incident is mentioned in textbook accounts of mass hysteria and the delusions of crowds.

The first of Welles' films to be seen by the public was *Citizen Kane* (1941), a commercial failure which lost RKO $150,000, but is regarded by many as the best film ever made. Welles' performance as Charles Foster Kane was based upon the media tycoon William Randolph Hearst. Many of his next films, such as the brilliant *The Magnificent Ambersons*, were commercial failures and he exiled himself to Europe in 1948. His performance as Harry Lime in *The Third Man* (1949) was highly rated, but he then directed *A Touch of Evil*, which again failed in the US but won a prize at the 1958 Brussels World's Fair. In 1975, in spite of all his box-office failures, Welles received the American Film Institute's Lifetime Achievement Award, and in 1984 the Directors Guild of America awarded him its highest honour, the D.W. Griffith Award. Welles' reputation as a filmmaker has climbed steadily since his death.

RONALD REAGAN
1911–2004

'Tear down this wall!'

'General Secretary Gorbachev, if you seek peace, if you seek prosperity for the Soviet Union and Eastern Europe, if you seek liberalization: Come here to this gate! Mr Gorbachev, open this gate! Mr Gorbachev, tear down this wall!'

Speech made at the Brandenburg Gate to the people of West Berlin, 12 June 1987

Ronald Wilson Reagan was born in Tampico, Illinois, becoming a radio sports announcer. A 1937 screen test won him a Hollywood contract, and over the next 20 years he made 53 films. His first marriage was to the actress Jane Wyman, and in 1952 he married the actress Nancy Davis. As president of the Screen Actors Guild, his political views shifted from liberal to conservative, and in 1966 he was elected Governor of California, being re-elected in 1970. He had a landslide victory against President Carter in 1980 and in January 1981, Reagan took office. Only 69 days later, he was shot by a would-be assassin, but recovered. Reagan obtained legislation to stimulate economic growth, curb inflation, increase employment and strengthen national defence, whilst cutting taxes and government expenditures. Although incurring a huge deficit, the renewal of national self-confidence helped him easily win a second term as President. At the end of his second administration, the nation was enjoying its longest recorded period of peacetime prosperity without recession or depression.

In foreign policy, he tried to seek *'peace through strength'* but also attempted better relations with the Soviet Union. In meetings with Mikhail Gorbachev, he negotiated a treaty to eliminate intermediate-range nuclear missiles. The Reagan Presidency saw the thawing of Russo-American relations. The Berlin Wall was dismantled two years after his historic speech there, and 28 years since it had divided Berlin. President Bush gave a eulogy at Reagan's funeral service – *'Sure, our 40th President wore his title lightly, and it fit like a white Stetson. In the end, through his belief in our country and his love for our country, he became an enduring symbol of our country. We think of his steady stride, that tilt of a head and snap of a salute, the big-screen smile, and the glint in his Irish eyes when a story came to mind.'*

'We understand it still that there is no easy road to freedom'

'We dedicate this day to all the heroes and heroines in this country and the rest of the world who sacrificed in many ways and surrendered their lives so that we could be free.

Their dreams have become reality. Freedom is their reward.

We are both humbled and elevated by the honour and privilege that you, the people of South Africa, have bestowed on us, as the first President of a united, democratic, non-racial and non-sexist South Africa, to lead our country out of the valley of darkness.

We understand it still that there is no easy road to freedom.

We know it well that none of us acting alone can achieve success.

We must therefore act together as a united people, for national reconciliation, for nation building, for the birth of a new world.

Let there be justice for all.

Let there be peace for all.

Let there be work, bread, water and salt for all.

Let each know that for each the body, the mind and the soul have been freed to fulfil themselves.'

Speech made at his inauguration as the first democratically elected
State President of South Africa, 10 May 1994

In 1952, with Oliver Tambo, Mandela had opened the first black legal firm in South Africa. In November 1962 he was convicted for incitement to strike and jailed for five years. Whilst serving his sentence, he was charged with sabotage and sentenced to life imprisonment on Robben Island. Shortly after his release in 1990, he and his delegation agreed to the suspension of armed struggle. Nelson Mandela retired from public life in June 1999.

CHARLES EDWARD MAURICE SPENCER, 9TH EARL SPENCER
1964–

'Today is our chance to say thank you for the way you brightened our lives, even though God granted you but half a life'

'I stand before you today the representative of a family in grief, in a country in mourning, before a world in shock... Today is our chance to say thank you for the way you brightened our lives, even though God granted you but half a life. We will all feel cheated always that you were taken from us so young and yet we must learn to be grateful that you came along at all... Your joy for life transmitted wherever you took your smile and the sparkle in those unforgettable eyes. Your boundless energy which you could barely contain... But your greatest gift was your intuition, and it was a gift you used wisely... Without your God-given sensitivity we would be immersed in greater ignorance at the anguish of AIDS and HIV sufferers, the plight of the homeless, the isolation of lepers, the random destruction of landmines... For all the status, the glamour, the applause, Diana remained throughout a very insecure person at heart, almost childlike in her desire to do good for others so she could release herself from deep feelings of unworthiness of which her eating disorders were merely a symptom... It is a point to remember that of all the ironies about Diana, perhaps the greatest was this – a girl given the name of the ancient goddess of hunting was, in the end, the most hunted person of the modern age.'

Funeral speech for his sister Diana, Princess of Wales, Westminster Abbey, 1997

Princess Diana died in Paris, and her brother's remarkable eulogy, abbreviated above, was watched by over 100 million people around the world.

THOMAS EDWARD BURNETT JR
1963–2001

'I know we're all going to die... there's just three of us who are going to do something about it. I love you, honey.'

His last words to his wife, Deena

Burnett was the Vice-President and Chief Operating Officer of a medical devices company travelling on United Airlines Flight 93 from Newark to San Francisco on 11 September 2001. He called his wife four times to tell her that terrorists had taken over the plane. He and other passengers had been informed by mobile phones that the World Trade Center in New York had been hit by hijacked aeroplanes, so he and some of the crew and other passengers decided to fight the terrorists hand to hand. The hijackers planned to crash the plane into the Camp David presidential retreat or Capitol Hill, but in the end it impacted near a strip mine in Shanksville, Pennsylvania – the only one of four hijacked aircraft not to hit a US landmark. The plane had been redirected towards Washington DC.

The attacks, now usually referred to as 9/11, were a series of suicide attacks by terrorists from the organization al-Qaeda. Two aeroplanes crashed into the Twin Towers of the World Trade Center, causing them both to collapse within two hours and destroying nearby buildings. A third airliner crashed into the Pentagon. The terrorists used box-cutter knives to kill crew and passengers, and tear gas or pepper spray to keep passengers away from the first-class accommodation whilst they took over the flight cabins. There were 2,973 deaths in New York, Pennsylvania and Washington.

GEORGE W. BUSH

1946–

'A great people has been moved to defend a great nation'

'Good evening. Today, our fellow citizens, our way of life, our very freedom came under attack in a series of deliberate and deadly terrorist acts. The victims were in airplanes, or in their offices; secretaries, businessmen and women, military and federal workers; moms and dads, friends and neighbours. Thousands of lives were suddenly ended by evil, despicable acts of terror.

The pictures of airplanes flying into buildings, fires burning, huge structures collapsing, have filled us with disbelief, terrible sadness, and a quiet, unyielding anger. These acts of mass murder were intended to frighten our nation into chaos and retreat. But they have failed; our country is strong.

A great people has been moved to defend a great nation. Terrorist attacks can shake the foundations of our biggest buildings, but they cannot touch the foundation of America. These acts shattered steel, but they cannot dent the steel of American resolve.

America was targeted for attack because we're the brightest beacon for freedom and opportunity in the world. And no one will keep that light from shining.

Today, our nation saw evil, the very worst of human nature. And we responded with the best of America – with the daring of our rescue workers, with the caring for strangers and neighbours who came to give blood and help in any way they could...

This is a day when all Americans from every walk of life unite in our resolve for justice and peace. America has stood down enemies before, and we will do so this time. None of us will ever forget this day. Yet, we go forward to defend freedom and all that is good and just in our world.

Thank you. Good night, and God bless America.'

Speech made from the Oval Office following the 9/11 attacks on the World Trade Center's Twin Towers, 8.30 p.m., 11 September 2001.

COLONEL TIM COLLINS
1960–

'We go to liberate, not to conquer.'

Impromptu speech made to men of the Royal Irish Regiment
during the Iraq War, 2003

'We go to liberate, not to conquer. We will not fly our flags in
their country. We are entering Iraq to free a people and the only
flag which will be flown in that ancient land is their own. Show
respect for them. There are some who are alive at this moment
who will not be alive shortly. Those who do not wish to go on that
journey, we will not send. As for the others, I expect you to rock
their world. Wipe them out if that is what they choose. But if you
are ferocious in battle remember to be magnanimous in victory.'

This is the beginning of an inspirational address to the
600 men of the 1st Battalion of the Royal Irish Regiment,
when he urged his troops to wrap their fallen comrades in a
sleeping bag, fight on and grieve for them after the heat of
battle. The speech only survives because a reporter took it
down in short-hand. The oration won praise in a personal
letter from Prince Charles, while President George W. Bush is
understood to have requested a copy for the wall of the Oval
Office. Born in Belfast, Collins read economics at Queen's
University Belfast, and took a commission in 1981. In 1988 he passed selection
for the SAS and served two tours of duty with them. He next served in
operational duties in Northern Ireland and the Falklands with the RIR, was
promoted to Lieutenant Colonel aged 38, and assumed command of the 1st
Battallion RIR in 2001. He led the Battalion in East Tyrone (being awarded the
Queen's Commendation for Valuable Service) and in Iraq during the Second Gulf
War. Despite heavy fighting around Basra, no men of his battalion were lost.
He was awarded the OBE in 2004, and promoted to Colonel, leaving the Army
in that year. He was known as 'Nails', to his men, a reflection of his strong
character and unflinching determination. Collins resigned his commission
because of under-funding for troops leaving them vulnerable and
under-equipped, bureaucratic and ineffective management, and lack of support
when he was accused of mistreating Iraqi civilians. He was cleared of all charges
and won libel damages against various media.

JIMMY CARTER
1924–

'Mattie was an angel of God, a messenger of God'

'The most extraordinary person whom I have ever known in my life is Mattie Stepanek... we exchanged greetings and formed, I would say, an instantaneous bond of love... [One of his poems was] 'I Could... If They Would':

"If they would find a cure when I'm a kid...
I could ride a bike and sail on rollerblades, and
I could go on really long nature hikes.
If they would find a cure when I'm a teenager...
I could earn my license and drive a car, and
I could dance every dance at my senior prom.
If they would find a cure when I'm a young adult...
I could travel around the world and teach peace, and
I could marry and have children of my own.
If they would find a cure when I'm grown old...
I could visit exotic places and appreciate culture, and
I could proudly share pictures of my grandchildren.
If they would find a cure when I'm alive...
I could live each day without pain and machines, and
I could celebrate the biggest thank you of life ever.
If they would find a cure when I'm buried into Heaven...
I could still celebrate with my brothers and sister there, and
I could still be happy knowing that I was part of the effort"

Really, in the New Testament language, angel and messenger are the same, and there's no doubt that Mattie was an angel of God, a messenger of God.'

Eulogy given for Mattie Stepanek, 2004

Matthew Stepanek suffered from Dysautonomic Mitochondrial Myopathy and outlived his expected lifespan, writing poems of love and peace from the age of six and inspiring millions with his bravery. He died in 2004, aged 14. Former US president Jimmy Carter had met him in 2001 and kept firmly in touch.

DAW AUNG SAN SUU KYI
1945-

'My life is the cause for democracy and I am linked to everybody else in that cause. I cannot just think of me.'

Words reported by Glenys Kinnock, *New Statesman*, 14 August 2006

Suu Kyi is one of the world's greatest advocates of non-violence, being the figurehead of the struggle for democracy in Burma (Myanmar) since 1988. Her father was Burma's independence hero, Aung San, who was assassinated when Suu Kyi was just two years old. In 1988 she left London to nurse her dying mother in Burma. There was a national uprising against the undemocratic 'Regime of the Generals', and she joined the new political party, the National League for Democracy. She gave many speeches calling for freedom, but the generals shot and killed up to 10,000 unarmed demonstrators, including women, children and students. Despite this, the regime was forced to call for a general election in 1990.

Suu Kyi began to campaign for the NLD, but she and many others were detained by the regime. Although she was under house arrest, the NLD went on to win 82 per cent of the seats in Parliament, but the results were ignored by the generals and controls tightened upon the people. Suu Kyi was held from 1989 to 1995, and again from 2000 to 2002. She was imprisoned once more in May 2003 after the Depayin Massacre, when around 100 of her supporters were beaten to death by the generals' forces. She was moved from prison back into house arrest in late 2003, and has been there ever since. She was refused the right to see her children and was denied the chance to see her husband, Michael, before he died of cancer. The regime has put constant pressure on her to join her family in exile abroad, but she knows that would be an admission of failure for the democratic cause. Suu Kyi won the Nobel Peace Prize in 1991, the Sakharov Prize from the European Parliament, the United States Presidential Medal of Freedom, and the Jawaharlal Nehru Award from India. She has called on people around the world to join the struggle for freedom in Burma, repeating the message: '*Please use your liberty to promote ours.*'

BARACK HUSSEIN OBAMA II
1961–

___

'Yes, we can'

'Hello, Chicago. If there is anyone out there who still doubts that America is a place where all things are possible, who still wonders if the dream of our founders is alive in our time, who still questions the power of our democracy, tonight is your answer

... It's the answer spoken by young and old, rich and poor, Democrat and Republican, black, white, Hispanic, Asian, Native American, gay, straight, disabled and not disabled, Americans who sent a message to the world that we have never been just a collection of individuals or a collection of red states and blue states. We are, and always will be, the United States of America... It's been a long time coming, but tonight, because of what we did on this date in this election at this defining moment, change has come to America...

The road ahead will be long. Our climb will be steep. We may not get there in one year or even in one term. But, America, I have never been more hopeful than I am tonight that we will get there. I promise you, we as a people will get there. This is our time, to put our people back to work and open doors of opportunity for our kids; to restore prosperity and promote the cause of peace; to reclaim the American dream and reaffirm that fundamental truth, that, out of many, we are one; that while we breathe, we hope. And where we are met with cynicism and doubts and those who tell us that we can't, we will respond with that timeless creed that sums up the spirit of a people: Yes, we can. Thank you. God bless you. And may God bless the United States of America.'

Excerpts from his presidential acceptance speech, 5 November 2008

Barack Obama's presidential campaign always stressed change, hope and the can-do attitude which has always prevailed in America. Obama was the Junior Senator for Illinois when he announced his candidacy for President of the United States on 10 February 2007. He became the Democratic nominee on 3 June 2008 after defeating Hillary Clinton in a 17-month primary campaign. Obama became President-elect after defeating John McCain on 4 November 2008 to become the 44th president on 20 January 2009. He was only the fifth African-American senator in US history, and is the first African-American President.

Index

Browning, Robert (1812-1889)
'God's in His heaven – All's right with the world!' 188

Buddha (c.563-c.483 BCE)
'Doubt everything. Find your own light' 13

Bunyan, John (1628-1688)
'Hanging is too good for him, said Mr Cruelty' 118
'Who would true Valour see' 119

Burnett, Thomas Edward (1963-2001)
'I know we're all going to die... there's just three of us who are going to do something about it. I love you, honey' 370

Burns, George (1896-1996)
'Too bad all the people who know how to run this country are busy running taxicabs or cutting hair' 364

Burns, Robert (Rabbie) (1759-1796)
'My luve is like a red, red rose' 160

Burton, Robert (1577-1640)
'See one and you've seen them all' 95

Bush, George W. (1946-)
'A great people has been moved to defend a great nation' 371

Butler, Samuel (1835-1902)
''Tis better to have loved and lost than never to have loved at all' 229

Byron, Lord (1788-1824)
''Tis strange, but true; for truth is always strange; Stranger than fiction' 179

C

Caesar, Julius (100-44 BCE)
'Et tu, Brute?' (You too, Brutus?) 38
'Veni, vidi, vici' (I came, I saw, I conquered) 36

Camões, Luís vaz de (1525-1580)
'He who, solely to oppress, Employs or martial force, or pow'r, achieves No victory; but a true victory Is gain'd when justice triumphs and prevails' 83

Capone, Al (1899-1947)
'They cannot collect legal taxes from illegal money' 290

Carlyle, Thomas (1795-1881)
'The greatest scene in Modern European history' 189
'Work is the grand cure of all the maladies and miseries that ever beset mankind' 221

Carnegie, Dale (1888-1955)
'Any fool can criticize, condemn, and complain – and most fools do' 307

Carter, Jimmy (1924-)
'Mattie was an angel of God, a messenger of God' 373

Cavell, Edith Louisa (1865-1915)
'Patriotism is not enough. I must have no hatred or bitterness for anyone' 267

Cervantes (c.1547-1616)
'There are only two families in the world, my old grandmother used to say, The Haves and Have-Nots' 91

Charles V, Emperor (1500-1558)
'To God I speak Spanish, to women Italian, to men French, and to my horse – German' 82

Chartres, Francis (1675-1732)
'HERE continueth to rot The Body of FRANCIS CHARTRES' 132

Chekhov, Anton (1860-1904)
'In all the universe nothing remains permanent and unchanged but the spirit' 245

Chesterfield, Earl of (1694-1773)
'Old Mr Lowndes, the famous Secretary of the Treasury, used to say "Take care of the pence, and the pounds will take care of themselves."' 138

Childers, Robert Erskine (1870-1922)
'Take a step forward, lads. It will be easier that way' 282

Christie, Agatha (1890-1976)
'He tapped his forehead. "These little grey cells. It is up to them."' 277

Churchill, Winston (1874-1965)
'I have nothing to offer but blood, toil, tears, and sweat' 313
'Never in the field of human conflict was so much owed by so many to so few' 316
'This was their finest hour' 315
'We shall fight on the beaches' 314

Collins, Colonel Tim (1960-)
'We go to liberate, not to conquer' 372

Collins, Michael (1890-1922)
'Early this morning I signed my own death warrant' 278

Confucius (551-479 BCE)
'A man should practise what he preaches, but a man should also preach what he practises' 14

Congreve, William (1670-1729)
'Music has charms to soothe the savage breast' 122

Conrad, Joseph (1857-1924)
'The terrorist and the policeman both come from the same basket' 255

Copernicus, Nicolaus (1473-1543)
'Face the facts' 79

Cowper, William (1731-1800)
'God moves in a mysterious way His wonders to perform' 149

Cromwell, Oliver (1599-1658)
'Warts and all' 106

Curie, Marie (1867-1934)
'You cannot hope to build a better world without improving the individuals' 297

D

Dante (1265-1321)
'Abandon hope, all ye who enter here' 68

Darwin, Charles (1809-1892)
'For my own part I would as soon be descended from that heroic little monkey' 227

Davies, W.H. (1871-1940)
'What is this life if, full of care, We have no time to stand and stare?' 259

Davies, William Robertson (1913-1995)
'The world is full of people whose notion of a satisfactory future is, in fact, a return to an idealized past' 345

Da Vinci, Leonardo (1452-1519)
'Iron rusts from disuse; stagnant water loses its purity and in cold weather becomes frozen; even so does inaction sap the vigour of the mind' 77

de Beauvoir, Simone (1908-1986)
'One is not born, but rather becomes, a woman' 331

de Gaulle, Charles (1890-1970)
'How can you govern a country which has two hundred and forty-six varieties of cheese?' 348

De la Mare, Walter (1873-1956)
'"Is anybody there?" said the Traveller, Knocking on the moonlit door' 263
'Look thy last on all things lovely, Every hour' 271

de Tocqueville, Alexis (1805-1859)
'Democracy and socialism have nothing in common but one word: equality' 187

Defoe, Daniel (1660-1731)
'The best of men cannot suspend their fate: The good die early, and the bad die late' 123

DeMolay, Jacques (c.1245-1314)
'Let evil swiftly befall those who have wrongly condemned us – God will avenge us' 67

Demosthenes (384-322 BCE)
'The man who runs away may fight again' 33

Descartes, René (1596-1650)
'Ego cogito, ergo sum' (I think, therefore I am) 100

Dickens, Charles (1812-1870)
'Annual income £20, annual expenditure £19-19s-6d, result happiness. Annual income £20, annual expenditure £20-0s-6d, result misery' 198

Dickinson, Emily (1830-1886)
'"Hope" is the thing with feathers' 211

Diderot, Denis (1713-1784)
'There are three principal means of acquiring knowledge available to us' 139

Diogenes of Sinope, 'The Cynic' (c.412-323 BCE)
'I am a citizen of the world' 32

Disney, Walt (1901-1966)
'All our dreams can come true, if we have the courage to pursue them' 355

Disraeli, Benjamin (1808-1881)
'There are three kinds of lies: lies, damned lies and statistics' 234

Donne, John (1572-1631)
'No man is an island' 96

Dostoevsky, Fyodor (1821-1881)
'If the devil doesn't exist, but man has created him, he has created him in his own image and likeness' 233

Douglass, Frederick (1818-1895)
'What, to the American slave, is your Fourth of July?' 201

Drouet, Juliette (1806-1883)
'I recognize you in all the beauty that surrounds me' 180

E

Edison, Thomas Alva (1847-1931)
'Genius is 1 per cent inspiration and 99 per cent perspiration' 252

Einstein, Albert (1879-1955)
'Imagination is more important than knowledge' 289

Eliot, George (1819-1880)
'A woman dictates before marriage in order that she may have a habit for submission afterwards' 228

Eliot, T.S. (1888-1965)
'Human kind cannot bear very much reality' 305

Elizabeth I, Queen (1533-1603)
'I know I have but the body of a weak and feeble woman, but I have the heart and stomach of a king' 84

Emerson, Ralph Waldo (1803-1882)
'A foolish consistency is the hobgoblin of little minds' 190
'The shot heard round the world' 185

Empedocles (490-430 BCE)
'The nature of God is a circle of which the centre is everywhere and the circumference is nowhere' 19

Erasmus, Desiderius (1466/1469-1536)
'In the country of the blind, the one-eyed man is king' 74

Euripides (480-406 BCE)
'Events will take their course, it is no good of being angry at them; he is happiest who wisely turns them to the best account' 23

Everett, Edward (1794-1865)
'If this boy passes the examinations he will be admitted and if the white students choose to withdraw, all the income of the college will be devoted to his education' 193

F

Farouk I, King of Egypt (1921-1965)
'The whole world is in revolt. Soon there will be only five Kings left – the King of England, the King of Spades, the King of Clubs, the King of Hearts and the King of Diamonds' 329

Faulkner, William (1897-1962)
'The aim of every artist is to arrest motion' 341

Fawkes, Guy (1570-1606)
'A desperate disease requires a desperate remedy' 90

Fermi, Enrico (1901-1954)
'There are two possible outcomes: If the result confirms the hypothesis, then you've made a measurement. If the result is contrary to the hypothesis, then you've made a discovery' 338

Fielding, Henry (1707-1754)
'His designs were strictly honourable' 136

Fields, W.C. (1880-1946)
'I was in love with a beautiful blonde once, dear. She drove me to drink. It's the one thing I am indebted to her for' 322

Fitzgerald, F. Scott (1896-1940)
'In the real dark night of the soul it is always three o'clock in the morning, day after day' 301

Flaubert, Gustave (1821-1880)
'You can calculate the worth of a man by the number of his enemies, and the importance of a work of art by the harm that is spoken of it' 205

Fletcher, John (1579-1625)
'Man is his own star' 102

Ford, Henry (1863-1947)
'Any customer can have a car painted any colour that he wants so long as it is black' 284

Francis, St (1182-1226)
'Where there is hatred, let me sow love; where there is injury, pardon; where there is doubt, faith' 65

Franco, General Francisco (1892-1975)
'Our war is not a civil war... but a Crusade' 309

Frank, Anneliese Marie (1929-1945)
'Perhaps through Jewish suffering the world will learn good' 326

Franklin, Benjamin (1706-1790)
'The body of Benjamin Franklin, printer (like the cover of an old book, its contents worn out, and stript of its lettering and gilding) Lies here, food for worms' 154

Freud, Sigmund (1856-1939)
'What progress we are making. In the Middle Ages they would have burned me. Now they are content with burning my books' 294

Friedman, Pavel (1921-1944)
'I never saw another butterfly' 323

Frost, Robert (1874-1963)
'But I have promises to keep, And miles to go before I sleep' 287
'The land was ours before we were the land's' 324
'Two roads diverged in a wood, and I – I took the one less travelled by, And that has made all the difference' 269

Fuller, R. Buckminster (1895-1993)
'The Things to do are: the things that need doing, that you see need to be done, and that no one else seems to see need to be done' 358

G

Galileo (1564-1642)
'I do not feel obliged to believe that same God who endowed us with sense, reason, and intellect had intended for us to forgo their use' 98

Galois, Evariste (1811-1832)
'Don't cry, I need all my courage to die at twenty' 181

Gandhi, Indira (1917-1984)
'I don't mind if my life goes in the service of the nation. If I die today every drop of my blood will invigorate the nation' 365

Gandhi, Mahatma (1869-1948)
'I am a man of peace. I believe in peace. But I do not want peace at any price' 279

George IV, King (1762-1830)
'Harris, I am not well. Get me a brandy' 192

Geronimo (1829-1909)
'Once I moved like the wind. Now I surrender to you, and that is all' 239

Gildas Badonicus (c.498-c.570 or 583 CE)
'Death has entered through the windows of their pride' 60

Gladstone, William Ewart (1809-1898)
'You cannot fight against the future. Time is on our side' 220

Goering, Hermann (1893-1946)
'A total solution of the Jewish question' 320

Goethe, Johann Wolfgang von (1749-1832)
'Omniscient I am not, but well-informed' 169
'Words are mere sound and smoke, dimming the heavenly light' 168

Goldsmith, Oliver (1730-1774)
'Ask me no questions and I'll tell you no lies' 143

Grahame, Kenneth (1859-1952)
'There is nothing – absolutely nothing – half so much worth doing as simply messing about in boats' 256

Gray, Thomas (1716-1771)
'The curfew tolls the knell of parting day' 137

H

Hardy, Thomas (1840-1928)
'I leant upon a coppice gate when Frost was spectre-grey' 250

Harlow, Jean (1911-1937)
'Would you be shocked if I changed into something more comfortable?' 292

Harvey, William (1578-1657)
'[The heart] is the household divinity which, discharging its function, nourishes, cherishes, quickens the whole body, and is indeed the foundation of life, the source of all action' 97

Hawthorne, Nathaniel (1804-1864)
'Caresses, expressions of one sort or another, are necessary to the life of the affections, as leaves are to the life of trees' 204
'Our souls went far away among the sunset clouds' 186

Heloise (1098-1164)
'Of all the wretched women I am the most wretched and amongst the unhappy I am the unhappiest' 63

Heraclitus (c.535-c.475 BCE)
'Nothing endures but change' 15

Herbert, George (1593-1633)
'Let all the world in every corner sing, My God and King!' 99

Herodotus (c.485-c.425 BCE)
'The most hateful torment for men is to have knowledge of everything but power over nothing' 21

Hippocrates (460-377 BCE)
'As to diseases, make a habit of two things – to help, or at least, to do no harm' 28
'Whenever I go into a house, I will go to help the sick' 29

Hitler, Adolf (1889-1945)
'The German people are not a warlike nation' 303

Hobbes, Thomas (1588-1679)
'No arts, no letters, no society, and which is worst of all, continual fear and danger of violent death, and the life of man solitary, poor, nasty, brutish, and short' 104

Hood, Thomas (1799-1845)
'With fingers weary and worn, With eyelids heavy and red' 191

Hopkins, Gerard Manley (1844-1889)
'Look at the stars! look, look up at the skies!' 232

Horace (65-8 BCE)
'Carpe diem' (Seize the day) 40
'Nil desperandum' (Never despair) 39

Housman, A.E. (1859-1936)
'What are those blue remembered hills, What spires, what farms are those?' 246

Hughes, James Langston (1902-1967)
'My soul has grown deep like the rivers' 281

Hugo, Victor (1802-1885)
'There is always more misery among the lower classes than there is humanity in the higher' 215
'We must never forget those terrible, but so sweet, hours when you were close to me' 200

Hume, David (1711-1776)
'Never literary attempt was more unfortunate than my Treatise of Human Nature' 133

Huxley, Aldous (1894-1963)
'To see ourselves as others see us is a most salutary gift. Hardly less important is the capacity to see others as they see themselves' 339

J

Jacobs, Harriet Ann (c.1813-1897)
'Cruelty is contagious in uncivilized communities' 212

Jefferson, Thomas (1743-1826)
'All men shall be free to profess, and by argument to maintain, their opinions in matters of religion' 152
'We hold these truths to be self-evident: that all men are created equal; that they are endowed by their Creator with (inherent and) inalienable rights; that among these are life, liberty, and the pursuit of happiness' 145

Jerome, Jerome K. (1859-1927)
'I like work: it fascinates me. I can sit and look at it for hours' 243

Jesus (7-2 BCE-26-36 CE)
'Blessed are the meek: for they shall inherit the earth' 45

Joan of Arc (c.1412-1431)
'Hold the cross high so I may see it through the flames!' 72

Johnson, Samuel (1709-1784)
'Resolve not to be poor: whatever you have, spend less' 150

Jones, David Michael (1895-1974)
'This all depriving darkness split now by crazy flashing' 308

Jonson, Ben (c.1573-1637)
'Drink to me, only, with thine eyes' 93

Joyce, James Augustine Aloysius
(1882-1941)
'Stately, plump Buck Mulligan came
from the Stairhead' 283

Juvenal (c.65-c.128 CE)
'Quis custodiet ipsos custodes?' (Who
will guard the guards themselves?) 54

K

Keats, John (1795-1821)
'A thing of beauty is a joy for ever' 175
'Here lies One Whose Name was writ in
Water' 177
'Season of mists and mellow fruitfulness'
176

Kempis, Thomas á (c.1379-1471)
'O quam cito transit gloria mundi'
(O how quickly passes away the glory
of the earth) 71

Kennedy, John Fitzgerald (1917-1963)
'Ask not what your country can do for
you' 346

Kepler, Johannes (1571-1630)
'Nature uses as little as possible of
anything' 94

Kerouac, Jack (1922-1969)
'The only people for me are the mad ones,
the ones who are mad to live, mad to
talk, mad to be saved' 342

Keynes, John Maynard (1883-1946)
'This long run is a misleading guide to
current affairs. In the long run we are
all dead' 285

Khayyám, Omar (1048-1122 CE)
'The moving finger writes' 62

King, Martin Luther (1929-1968)
'I have a dream' 349

Kingsley, Charles (1819-1875)
'Young blood must have its course, lad,
and every dog its day' 217

Kipling, Rudyard (1865-1936)
'If you can keep your head when all
about you Are losing theirs' 257
'The female of the species is more deadly
than the male' 258

Klein, Dr Ernest (1900-1983)
'Dedicated to the Sacred Memory of the
Best Parents' 359

L

La Bruyère, Jean de (1645-1696)
'There are but three events in a man's life:
birth, life and death. He is not
conscious of being born, he dies in
pain, and he forgets to live' 120

La Fontaine, Jean de (1621-1695)
'Beware, as long as you live, of judging
people by appearances' 112

La Rochefoucauld, François Le Duc de
(1613-1680)
'Absence diminishes small loves and
increases great ones, as the wind
blows out the candle and fans the
bonfire' 110

**Laclos, Pierre Ambroise François
Choderlos de** (1741-1803)
'A man enjoys the happiness he feels, a
woman the happiness she gives' 151

Lao-Tzu (c.600 BCE)
'Give a man a fish and you feed him for
a day. Teach him how to fish and you
feed him for a lifetime' 7

Lawrence, Thomas Edward
(1888-1935)
'All men dream: but not equally' 288

Lazarus, Emma (1849-1887)
'Give me your tired, your poor, Your
huddled masses yearning to breathe
free' 237

Leacock, Stephen Butler (1869-1944)
'Personally, I would sooner have
written Alice in Wonderland
than the whole Encyclopaedia
Britannica' 262

Lenin, Vladimir Ilyich (1870-1924)
'The substitution of the proletarian for
the bourgeois state is impossible
without a violent revolution' 273

Lincoln, Abraham (1809-1865)
'The world will little note nor long
remember what we say here' 216

Livingstone, David (1813-1873)
'Who will help heal this open sore of the
world' 230

Livy (59 BCE-18 CE)
'It is worthwhile for those persons who
despise all things human in
comparison with riches' 44

Lloyd George, David (1863-1945)
'The world is becoming like a lunatic
asylum run by lunatics' 295

Locke, John (1632-1704)
'Though the familiar use of the Things
about us, takes off our Wonder; yet it
cures not our Ignorance' 121

Lovelace, Richard (1618-1657)
'Stone walls do not a prison make, Nor
iron bars a cage' 103

Lowell, Robert Traill Spence
(1917-1977)
'I cowered in terror. I wasn't a child at all'
343

Lucretius Carus, Titus (c.99-c.55 BCE)
'Nothing can be created out of nothing' 35

M

Macaulay, Thomas Babington
(1800-1859)
'No man who is correctly informed as to
the past, will be disposed to take a
morose or desponding view of the
present' 197

McAuliffe, Commander Anthony
(1898-1975)
'NUTS!' 327

McCarthy, Senator Joseph R.
(1908-1957)
'I have here in my hand a list of 205...
a list of names' 334

McGonagall, William Topaz
(1830-1902)
'Beautiful Railway Bridge of the Silv'ry
Tay!' 244

Machiavelli, Niccolò (1469-1527)
'There is nothing more difficult to take in
hand, more perilous to conduct, or
more uncertain in its success, than to
take the lead in the introduction of a
new order of things' 76

Magee, John Gillespie (1922-1941)
'Put out my hand, and touched the face
of God' 318

Malory, Sir Thomas (c.1405-1471)
'Whoso pulleth out this sword of this
stone and anvil, is rightwise King
born of all England' 73

Malthus, Thomas (1766-1834)
'Population, when unchecked, increases
in a geometric ratio. Subsistence only
increases in a mathematical ratio' 161

Mandela, Nelson (1918-)
'An ideal for which I am prepared to die'
351
'We understand it still that there is no
easy road to freedom' 368

Mao Zedong (1893-1976)
'Every Communist must grasp the truth:
"Political power grows out of the
barrel of a gun"' 310

Marcus Aurelius, Emperor (121-180 CE)
'Nowhere can man find a quieter or more
untroubled retreat than in his own
soul' 57

Marie Antoinette (1755-1793)
'I am calm, as one is when one's conscience reproaches one with nothing' 156

Marlowe, Christopher (1564-1593)
'Was this the face that launch'd a thousand ships And burnt the topless towers of Ilium?' 89

Marvell, Andrew (1621-1678)
'But at my back I always hear Time's winged Chariot hurrying near' 105

Marx, Groucho (1890-1977)
'Remember, men, we're fighting for this woman's honour, which is possibly more than she ever did' 293

Marx, Karl (1818-1883)
'Go on, get out. Last words are for fools who haven't said enough' 236

Melville, Herman (1819-1891)
'A whale ship was my college and my Harvard' 199

Meredith, George (1828-1909)
'Golden lie the meadows: golden run the streams' 209

Michelangelo (1475-1564)
'I've finished that chapel I was painting. The Pope is quite satisfied' 75

Mill, John Stuart (1806-1873)
'The legal subordination of one sex to another – is wrong in itself' 224

Milton, John (1608-1674)
'Eyeless in Gaza at the Mill with slaves' 114
'They also serve who only stand and wait' 115

Mitchell, Margaret (1900-1949)
'Here in north Georgia, a lack of the niceties of classical education carried no shame, provided a man was smart in the things that mattered' 302

Molière (1622-1673)
'We must eat to live, not live to eat' 111

Montagu, Lady Mary Wortley (1689-1762)
epitaph of 153

Montesquieu, Charles-Louis (1689-1755)
'Liberty is the right to do everything which the laws allow' 135

Moses (1393-1273 BCE)
'Thou shalt have no other gods before me' 6

Mother Teresa of Calcutta (1910-1997)
'The poor people are very great people. They can teach us so many beautiful things' 363

Murrow, Ed (1908-1965)
'We can deny our heritage and our history, but we cannot escape responsibility for the result' 340

Mussolini, Benito (1883-1945)
'This Berlin-Rome connection is not so much a diaphragm as an axis, around which can resolve all those states of Europe with a will towards collaboration and peace' 304

N

Nárvaez, Ramón María (1800-1868)
'I do not have to forgive my enemies, I have had them all shot' 223

Nelson, Horatio (1758-1805)
'Kiss me, Hardy' 167

Newbolt, Sir Henry (1862-1933)
'Play up! and play the game!' 247

Newton, Isaac (1642-1727)
'Nature and Nature's laws lay hid in night' 130
'The great ocean of truth lay all undiscovered before me' 131

Nietzsche, Friedrich (1844-1900)
'Woman was God's second mistake' 242

Nostradamus (1503-1566)
'The blood of the just will be demanded of London burnt by fire in three times twenty plus six' 81

O

Oates, Captain Lawrence Edward Grace (1880-1912)
'I am just going outside and may be some time' 260

Obama, Barack Hussein (1961-)
'Yes, we can' 375

Oppenheimer, Julius Robert (1904-1967)
'If the radiance of a thousand suns were to burst at once into the sky, that would be like the splendour of the mighty one... Now I am Death the destroyer of worlds' 328

Orwell, George (1903-1950)
'Big Brother is watching you' 330

Ovid (43 BCE-c.18 CE)
'Time the devourer of everything' 42

Owen, Robert (1771-1858)
'Women will be no longer made the slaves of, or dependent upon men... They will be equal in education, rights, privileges and personal liberty' 173

Owen, Wilfred (1893-1918)
'The old Lie: Dulce et decorum est Pro patria mori' 270

P

Paine, Thomas (1737-1809)
'The most formidable weapon against errors of every kind is reason' 158

Parker, Dorothy (1893-1967)
'The first thing I do in the morning is brush my teeth and sharpen my tongue' 355

Pascal, Blaise (1623-1662)
'"God is or He is not." But to which side shall we incline?' 113

Pasternak, Boris Leonidovich (1890-1960)
'Of what crime do I stand condemned?' 344

Patrick, St (Padrig) (c.389/390-c.461)
'Christ in the heart of everyone who thinks of me' 59

Patton, General George S. (1885-1945)
'America loves a winner' 325

Pepys, Samuel (1633-1703)
'And so to bed' 112

Perón, Eva (1919-1952)
'I will return. And I will be millions' 336

Petronius (d.66 CE)
'One good turn deserves another' 47

Pheidippides (c.530-490 BCE)
'We have won!' 12

Pindar (518-438 BCE)
'A dream of a shadow is our mortal being' 18

Plato (427-347 BCE)
'No evil can happen to a good man, either in life or after death' 31

Pliny the Elder (23-79 CE)
'In these matters the only certainty is that nothing is certain' 48

Pliny the Younger (63-c.113 CE)
'Augustus, the child of fortune, lived to perfect what Julius [Caesar] had only designed' 50

Plutarch (c.46-c.120 CE)
'I am writing biography, not history' 52

Polo, Marco (1254-1324)
'I have not told half of what I saw' 69

Pope, Alexander (1688-1744)
'For fools rush in where angels fear to tread' 125

Protagoras (*c.*481-420 BCE)
'Man is the measure of all things: of things which are, that they are so, and of things which are not, that they are not' 23

Proust, Marcel (1871-1922)
'Everything great in the world is done by neurotics: they alone founded our religions and created our masterpieces' 280

Publilius Syrus (*fl.*46 BCE)
'Judex damnatur ubi nocens absolvitur' (The judge is condemned when the guilty is acquitted) 37

Pythagoras (582-500 BCE)
'Declining from the public ways, walk in unfrequented paths' 11

R

Rabelais, François (*c.*1494-*c.*1553)
'Je n'ai rien vaillant; je dois beaucoup; je donne le reste aux pauvres' (I have nothing, owe a great deal, and the rest I leave to the poor) 80

Reagan, Ronald (1911-2004)
'Tear down this wall!' 367

Rogers, Will (1879-1935)
'My ancestors didn't come over on the Mayflower, but they met at the boat' 299

Roosevelt, Franklin Delano (1882-1945)
'A date which will live in infamy' 321
'In the future days, which we seek to make secure, we look forward to a world founded upon four essential human freedoms' 319
'The only thing we have to fear is fear itself' 296

Roosevelt, Theodore (Teddy) (1858-1919)
'There is a homely adage which runs "Speak softly and carry a big stick, you will go far"' 251

Rossetti, Dante Gabriel (1828-1882)
'Eat thou and drink; to-morrow thou shalt die' 235

Rousseau, Jean-Jacques (1712-1778)
'Man was born free, and everywhere he is in chains' 141

Routleigh, George (1745-1802)
'Here lies in the horizontal position' 162

Russell, Lord Bertrand (1872-1970)
'I discovered to my amazement that average men and women were delighted by the prospect of war' 356

Rutherford, Ernest (1871-1937)
'In science, there is only physics: all the rest is stamp collecting' 306

S

Salinger, Jerome David (1919-)
'I'd just be the catcher in the rye' 335

Santayana, George (1863-1952)
'Those who cannot remember the past are condemned to repeat it' 254

Schweitzer, Albert (1875-1965)
'Here, at whatever hour you come, you will find light and help and human kindness' 264

Scott, Sir Walter (1771-1832)
'No, this right hand shall work it off' 219

Sedgewick, Major-General John (1813-1864)
'They couldn't hit an elephant at this distance' 218

Seneca, the Younger (4-65 CE)
'It is quality rather than quantity that matters' 46

Shakespeare, William (1564-1616)
'Good Friend for Jesus Sake Forbeare To Dig the Dust Encloased Heare' 92
'Once more unto the breach, dear friends, once more' 87
'To be, or not to be: that is the question' 88

Shaw, George Bernard (1856-1950)
'I wish all Americans were as blind as you' 332
'The golden rule is that there are no golden rules' 253

Shelley, Percy Bysshe (1792-1822)
'Hail to thee, blithe Spirit!' 178

Sheridan, Richard Brinsley (1751-1816)
'A man may surely be allowed to take a glass of wine by his own fireside' 170

Simonides of Kea (*c.*556-468 BCE)
'Go tell the Spartans, thou who passest by, That here, obedient to their laws, we lie' 17

Smith, Adam (1723-1790)
'With the great part of rich people, the chief enjoyment of riches consists in the parade of riches' 147

Smith, Frederick Edwin (1872-1930)
'"You are extremely offensive, young man." – Judge Willis "As a matter of fact, we both are, and the only difference between us is that I am trying to be, and you can't help it." – F.E. Smith' 291

Smith, Sydney (1771-1845)
'Macaulay is like a book in breeches... He has occasional flashes of silence... that make his conversation perfectly delightful' 207

Socrates (469-399 BCE)
'The life which is unexamined is not worth living' 26

Solzhenitsyn, Alexander Isayevich (1918-2008)
'The next war... may well bury Western civilization forever' 362

Sophocles (495-405 BCE)
'One word frees us of all the weight and pain of life: That word is love' 24

Spencer, Charles Edward Maurice, 9th Earl (1964-)
'Today is our chance to say thank you for the way you brightened our lives, even though God granted you but half a life' 369

Spenser, Edmund (1552-1599)
'The noblest mind the best contentment has' 85

Spinoza, Baruch (1632-1677)
'Man is a social animal' 117

Stalin, Josef (1879-1953)
'Our hand will not tremble' 272

Stanton, Elizabeth Cady (1815-1902)
'The Bible and the Church have been the greatest stumbling blocks in the way of woman's emancipation' 238

Steele, Sir Richard (1672-1729)
'Reading is to the mind what exercise is to the body' 124

Steinbeck, John Ernst (1902-1968)
'In the souls of the people the grapes of wrath are filling and growing heavy, growing heavy for the vintage' 312

Sterne, Laurence (1713-1768)
'Of all the cants which are canted in this canting world, though the cant of hypocrites may be the worst, the cant of criticism is the most tormenting!' 142

Stevenson, Robert Louis (1850-1894)
'Home is the sailor, home from the sea, And the hunter home from the hill' 241

Stilwell, General Joseph W. (1883-1946)
'Don't let the bastards grind you down' 311

Stowe, Harriet Beecher (1811-1896)
'I did not write it. God wrote it. I merely did His dictation' 203

Suetonius Tranquillus, Gaius (c.69-c.122 CE)
'The Ides of March have come' 53

Sun Tzu, General (c.500 BCE)
'All Warfare is based on deception' 10

Suu Kyi, Daw Aung San (1945-)
'My life is the cause for democracy and I am linked to everybody else in that cause. I cannot just think of me' 374

T

Tacitus, Publius Cornelius (c.56-c.120 CE)
'They make it a wilderness and call it peace' 51

Talleyrand, Charles-Maurice de (1754-1838)
'This is the beginning of the end' 226

Tennyson, Alfred, Lord (1809-1892)
'Cannon to right of them, Cannon to left of them, Cannon in front of them' 206

Tertullian, Quintus Septimius Florens (155/160-222/230 CE)
'Out of the frying pan into the fire' 57

Tesla, Nikola (1856-1943)
'The scientists from Franklin to Morse were clear thinkers and did not produce erroneous theories. The scientists of today think deeply instead of clearly. One must be sane to think clearly, but one can think deeply and be quite insane' 298

Thales (c.635/620-c.546/543 BCE)
'(The most difficult thing in life is to) Know Thyself' 9

Thomas, Dylan Marlais (1914-1953)
'I've had eighteen straight whiskies. I think that's the record... After thirty-nine years, this is all I've done' 337

Thoreau, Henry David (1817-1862)
'One world at a time' 213

Thucydides (c.460/455-c.400/395 BCE)
'The strength of an Army lies in strict discipline and undeviating obedience to its officers' 25

Tolstoy, Count (1828-1910)
'Can it be that there is not room for all men on this beautiful earth under these immeasurable starry heavens?' 202

Torricelli, Evangelista (1608-1647)
'Is it a surprise that into the vessel, in which the mercury has no inclination and no repugnance, not even the slightest, to being there, it should enter and should rise in a column high enough to make equilibrium with the weight of the external air which forces it up?' 101

Toussaint L'Ouverture (1743/1746-1803)
'In overthrowing me, you have cut down in Saint Dominique only the trunk of the tree of liberty. It will spring up by the roots for they are numerous and deep' 164

Traherne, Thomas (c.1637-1674)
'You never enjoy the world aright, till the Sea itself floweth in your veins' 116

Twain, Mark (1835-1910)
'The report of my death was an exaggeration' 248

U

Utter, Colorado Charlie, C.H. (1838-1912)
'Wild Bill, J.B. Hickok, killed by the assassin Jack McCall in Deadwood, Black Hills, August 2, 1876. Pard, we will meet again in the happy hunting ground to part no more. Good bye, Colorado Charlie, C.H. Utter' 231

V

Vaughan, Henry (1622-1696)
'I saw Eternity the other night' 107

Verne, Jules (1828-1905)
'The sea is everything' 225

Vespasian, Emperor (9-79 CE)
'Dear me, I believe I am becoming a God' 49

Virgil (70-19 BCE)
'Do not trust the horse, Trojans. Whatever it is, I fear the Greeks even when they bring gifts' 41

Voltaire (François Marie Arouet) (1694-1778)
'Pour encourager les autres' (To encourage the others) 140
'This is no time to make new enemies' 148

von Clausewitz, General Karl (1780-1831)
'War is nothing but the continuation of politics with the admixture of other means' 184

W

Wallace, William (c.1270-1305)
'I have brought you to the ring, now dance if you can' 66

Watts, Dr Isaac (1674-1748)
'Our God, our help in ages past' 127

Welles, George Orson (1915-1985)
'My doctor told me to stop having intimate dinners for four. Unless there are three other people' 366

Wells, Herbert George (1866-1946)
'Human history becomes more and more a race between education and catastrophe' 276

West, Mae (1893-1980)
'Is that a gun in your pocket, or are you just glad to see me?' 361

Whitman, Walt (1819-1892)
'O Captain! My Captain! our fearful trip is done' 222
'What I tell I tell for precisely what it is' 208

Wilberforce, William (1759-1833)
'They charge me with fanaticism. If to be feelingly alive to the sufferings of my fellow-creatures is to be a fanatic, I am one of the most incurable fanatics ever permitted to be at large' 174

Wilde, Oscar (1854-1900)
'Each man kills the thing he loves' 249

Wollstonecraft, Mary (1759-1797)
'You know not how much tenderness for you may escape in a voluptuous sigh' 159

Wordsworth, William (1770-1850)
'My heart leaps up when I behold A rainbow in the sky' 165

Wren, Sir Christopher (1632-1723)
'Lector, si monumentum requiris circumspice' (Reader, if you seek his monument look around you) 129

X

Xenophon (431-c.355 BCE)
'Thalassa! Thalassa! (The sea! The sea!)' 30

Y

Yeats, William Butler (1865-1939)
'Things fall apart; the centre cannot hold' 275

Young, Edward (1683-1765)
'Procrastination is the thief of time' 134

Quercus Publishing Plc
21 Bloomsbury Square
London
WC1A 2NS

First published in 2009

A catalogue record of this book is available from the British Library

ISBN: 978 1 84866 004 5

All pictures in this book © Topfoto
Text by Terry Breverton
Typeset by Lapiz Digital, India
Index by Patricia Hymans

Printed and bound in China

10 9 8 7 6 5 4